Strategic Leadership and Management in Nonprofit Organizations
Theory and Practice

Martha Golensky
Grand Valley State University

LYCEUM
BOOKS, INC.

Chicago, Illinois

© 2011 by Lyceum Books, Inc.

Published by

LYCEUM BOOKS, INC.
5758 S. Blackstone Avenue
Chicago, Illinois 60637
773-643-1903 fax
773-643-1902 phone
lyceum@lyceumbooks.com
www.lyceumbooks.com

6 5 4 3 2 1   11 12 13 14

ISBN 978-1-933478-68-5

Printed in Canada.

Library of Congress Cataloging-in-Publication Data

Golensky, Martha.
  Strategic leadership and management in nonprofit organizations : theory and practice / Martha Golensky.
     p. cm.
  Includes bibliographical references and index.
  ISBN 978-1-933478-68-5 (pbk. : alk. paper)
  1. Nonprofit organizations—Management. 2. Nonprofit organizations. 3. Strategic planning. I. Title.
  HD62.6.G64   2010
  658.4′092—dc22

                                                              2010007062

In loving memory of my mother and father,
Pauline and Nathan Golensky

Contents

Preface

Survival is a basic concern for virtually all organizations, whether public, for-profit, or not-for-profit. However, the current climate for many nonprofits, both large and small, is especially difficult due to the decline in government support, increased competition for the private dollar, heightened interest by funders and the general public in accountability, and the advent of managed care, which is now dictating many internal management decisions. This means leaders and managers must be more strategic than ever in securing material and human resources to maintain mission integrity, which is defined here as serving present and future clients or consumers in the most effective, efficient, and ethical manner.

This book reflects the knowledge and experience I have gained through fifteen years as a nonprofit executive followed by twelve years as a full-time academic, teaching non-profit management courses, conducting research on leadership and decision-making, and providing consultation to local organizations on management issues. Although the book incorporates the work of many scholars in the field of nonprofit studies, it is fundamentally practical in its orientation, taking as its departure point the smorgasbord of challenges facing real-life decision-makers in today's world—challenges around service delivery, staff performance, financial stability, the board of directors, strategic planning, program effectiveness, the uses of technology, and so on.

Freire's concept of problem-posing education (1993), which encourages individuals to perceive the world as an ever-changing reality and provides the necessary tools to deal constructively with it, influenced both the content and approach of this work. The principal audience for the book is students and professionals who are about to or have recently entered the workplace, be it as interns or employees, in direct practice or a supervisory role, to help them understand how their agencies function and to better appreciate the conflicting demands on top management. However, more experienced staff, especially those engaged in the daunting task of effecting organizational change, may also find the book a useful resource. As essential as it is to have the technical competency to do the job, it is equally important to be able to navigate skillfully through the intricacies of the work environment.

The most distinctive feature of the book is the use of an extended case study to illustrate different leadership and management issues. The case, which I wrote and classroom-tested, depicts a human service organization with which I am personally familiar. Unlike most case studies, this one tells the organizational story from two viewpoints, those of the executive director and the board president, who disagree on the best strategy for the agency's future. Thus, the case mimics real life, where critical decisions are seldom simple. As the next-best thing to direct participation, "cases provide a bridge between professional education and practice in that they permit students to vicariously experience problems faced by practitioners" (Weaver, Kowalski, & Pfaller, 1994, p. 174). By addressing a range of significant organizational issues as seen through the eyes of the key decision-makers, the case featured here should stimulate both personal reflection and lively discussion about basic concepts and processes and their consequences.

In addition to the case study, the book includes many examples of the issues non-profit leaders and senior managers must face, some of which are relatively new concerns, such as how to incorporate individuals who wish to volunteer only now and then (episodic volunteering), and some of which, like promoting the effectiveness of the board of directors, have a long tradition. Although most of these examples are drawn from the human services, the arena I know best, they depict situations common to a variety of settings. With regard to source material, I have used both recent and traditional references, to recognize the contributions of those scholars and practitioners who paved the way for the considerable body of knowledge that now exists on nonprofits. In several instances, the seminal work was done decades ago but remains timely.

ORGANIZATION

The book is organized into four sections. The introduction to each section summarizes the contents and lists key themes. Portions of the case study, addressing many of these same themes, appear in the introductions for sections 2 to 4. The last part of the case, with the resolution of the conflict between the two main characters, appears only in the accompanying teacher's manual, so readers can reach their own conclusions about the issues in the case. All of the sections end with discussion questions and selected references pertaining to the material just presented.

Section 1 provides the context for the rest of the book. Here the focus is on the characteristics of a nonprofit organization, with an explanation of the specific attributes of both charitable and member-serving nonprofits; the historical development of the nonprofit sector as a whole and of the human services subsector; and a general review of the political and economic climate in which nonprofits must operate.

In section 2, the concept of leadership is examined from several perspectives, starting with general theories of leadership and the particular structure of leadership in a nonprofit. Next, the multiple roles of the nonprofit professional leader are delineated, to recognize that, particularly in small and midsized organizations, the same person may serve as manager and administrator, motivated by different priorities when functioning in each capacity. Ethical issues are also considered. The last two chapters in this section are concerned with the theoretical and practical aspects of decision-making, and the relationship between organizational culture and organizational change, a critical element of present-day leadership and management in nonprofits.

Sections 3 and 4 address the specific skills of the nonprofit leader involved in securing material resources and managing human resources, respectively. In section 3, strategic planning, program planning and evaluation, resource generation, organizational performance indicators, and technology and communication are the areas of emphasis.

Section 4 includes chapters dealing with leadership to create and protect a culture of integrity, human resources matters, the practical aspects of board governance, and the role of volunteers at the service delivery level.

A comprehensive bibliography at the end of the book is organized by the chapter themes, for those who wish to pursue a given topic in more depth. Lastly, a teacher's manual has been prepared to accompany the text. It contains suggestions on ways to present the information covered in each of the book chapters as well as exercises and assignments suitable for applying what has been learned to everyday practice. With a few exceptions, this is original material that I developed over the years and tested thoroughly in the classroom. Also included is my version of a management audit, which I found to be an effective final course project.

REFERENCES

Freire, P. (1993). *Pedagogy of the oppressed* (Rev. ed.). New York: Continuum.

Weaver, R. A., Kowalski, T. J., & Pfaller, J. E. (1994). Case-method teaching. In K. W. Prichard & R. M. Sawyer (Eds.), *Handbook of college teaching: Theory and applications* (pp. 171–178). Westport, CT: Greenwood Press.

Acknowledgments

On some level, all of the staff and board members with whom I was associated during my practitioner years have contributed to this book. As they played out their different roles, sometimes positively and sometimes negatively, they illustrated the organizational dynamics delineated in the book.

In a more direct fashion, the students at Grand Valley State University whom I taught first in the School of Public and Nonprofit Administration and then in the School of Social Work afforded me the opportunity to test out my views on how nonprofits operate and to refine my perceptions through our interactions inside and outside the classroom.

A third group of individuals who must be acknowledged are the nonprofit executives and board members who participated in my various research projects. Their generosity in sharing their triumphs and their disappointments helped me stay current with developments in the field; their reflections on the challenges they faced on a daily basis provided a necessary grounding in reality.

Finally, I want to offer special thanks to my academic and practitioner colleagues who read chapters of the book in draft form and provided helpful suggestions for improving the work: Carol Barbeito, Stephen Block, Patricia Evans, Robyn Gibboney, Naomi Kappel, Nancy Macduff, John McClusky, Ellen Netting, Lois Smith Owens, Donna Panton, Peter Schwartz, Steven Smith, and Stephen Wernet. I am particularly indebted to Ann Breihan, who not only read two chapters but also kept me relatively sane and focused throughout the long writing process.

Understanding the Nonprofit Sector

The first part of this book is designed to introduce a number of basic concepts regarding the nonprofit sector in the United States, although some of the material may be applicable to not-for-profits in other countries as well. The intent is to establish the context for the rest of the book by providing useful definitions and background information about the sector.

Chapter 1 attempts to identify the different types of nonprofit organizations, including those classified as public charities under section 501(c)(3) of the Internal Revenue Code as well as those considered member-serving or mutual benefit organizations.

Chapter 2 offers an overview of the historical development of nonprofits. It also provides specific background information on human service organizations (HSOs), for several reasons: they represent the largest and most diverse subgroup of charitable nonprofits, they are arguably the nonprofits most recognized by the general public, and the case study that is used throughout the book deals with situations occurring in an HSO.

Chapter 3 explores the external political and economic climate in which nonprofits must operate and the ramifications of this environment on internal decision-making by top leaders. It also explores the interrelationships among the three sectors of society.

KEY THEMES

Chapters 1 to 3 address these topics and concerns.

- The distinguishing characteristics of a nonprofit organization: What makes a nonprofit a nonprofit, and why does it matter?
- The role of nonprofits in American society from colonial days to the present: What historical circumstances must be considered to understand the nonprofit sector?
- The evolution of the human services subsector: What sets an HSO apart from other types of nonprofits?
- The impact of the external political-economic climate on internal operations and strategic decision-making: Why is political-economy theory so applicable to nonprofit organizations today?

- The dynamic relationship between nonprofits and government: What are the driving forces that have shaped their interactions over time?
- The multifaceted dimensions of the relationship between nonprofits and the business sector: Is the commercialization of the nonprofit sector a positive or negative development?

1

Definition of a Nonprofit Organization

Harvard College, founded in 1636, holds the distinction of being the first charitable corporation founded in the American colonies, although it lacked many of the characteristics now associated with such organizations. By the middle of the eighteenth century, a variety of voluntary entities had been formed, but it is only since the latter part of the twentieth century that nonprofits began to occupy a place of major importance in American society. Today, there are over 1.5 million nonprofits, each contributing in its own way to the richness of our culture. This chapter establishes the parameters of the not-for-profit world, with attention to organizations qualifying as public charities as well as those primarily serving their own members.

WHAT'S IN A NAME?

Generally speaking, we can identify three major sectors of society: government, also known as the *public sector*; business, often called the *corporate sector*; and voluntary organizations, usually referred to as the *nonprofit sector*. If the average citizen were asked to describe the purpose of the first two of these, he or she would most likely respond that governments exist to protect and promote the interests of the general public, and businesses exist to turn a profit (O'Neill, 2002).

However, this little exercise is not so simple when we turn to nonprofits, which come in many shapes and sizes. If that same average citizen were asked for examples of nonprofits, the expected response might be the American Red Cross, the YMCA, or the Girl Scouts—large organizations with high visibility. A more savvy individual might be able to identify the homeless shelter, a health clinic, a soup kitchen, and so on—locally familiar names recognized for their good works and service to the community. Yet this ignores the many nonprofits that have a much narrower purpose, to benefit their members. In fact, it is possible to divide the nonprofit sector into two very broad categories, *public-serving* and *member-serving* organizations. The National Taxonomy of Exempt Entities (NTEE), a project of the Urban Institute's National Center for Charitable Statistics (NCCS), is a well-recognized classification system that provides detailed information on the scope of the nonprofit sector. Table 1.1 presents an overview of the organizational categories.

Table 1.1 Overview of the nonprofit sector, 2006

Types of organizations	Number of organizations	Percentage of all organizations
501(c)(3) public charities	904,313	61.2
501(c)(3) private foundations	109,852	7.4
Other 501(c) nonprofits	464,029	31.4
All nonprofits	1,478,194	100.0

Source: National Center for Charitable Statistics (2008), Urban Institute, with modifications of the IRS Business Master File 01/2007 (Retrieved March 16, 2008, from http://nccsdataweb.urban.org/PubApps/ Profile1.php?state=US).
Note: The figures exclude foreign and governmental organizations.

Because of the difficulty in pinpointing the mission of a nonprofit, over the years observers have used a variety of terms to capture this sector, such as *not-for-profit, voluntary, philanthropic,* and even *third* (Grobman, 2004; O'Neill, 2002; Wolf, 1999). Outside of the United States, the term *nongovernmental organization* (NGO) is frequently used. In 1980 a national organization based in Washington, DC, called Independent Sector, was launched to act as a kind of common space for the diverse institutions making up the nonprofit world to share their concerns and plan joint action.

According to Hall (1992), the distinguishing feature of American NGOs, what makes them so important in the grand scheme of things, is their institutional culture developed over time, which incorporates "values, resources, organizational technologies, legal infrastructure, and styles of leadership" (p. 2). Nonprofits, by their very nature, perform certain basic roles in society that other institutions cannot. For example, they are often the first to react to a growing societal problem. Without the constraints imposed on both the public and private, for-profit sectors, voluntary organizations are freer to experiment with new ideas and processes. Once these innovative approaches have been developed and proven effective in addressing the problem, government and even business may then step in to support and expand on this work. The AIDS crisis is a case in point. At the same time, nonprofits, such as museums and historical societies, preserve our traditions. Nonprofits also reflect the diversity of American society by supporting minority and local interests as well as a broad range of political views. Some nonprofits function as watchdogs, monitoring and overseeing both government and the marketplace. Others fulfill less weighty but no less important social and recreational needs (O'Neill, 2002). And these are but a few examples of the richness of the not-for-profit sector.

TURNING A NEGATIVE INTO A POSITIVE

The most accurate way to describe a nonprofit may be to note what it isn't, that it is not a part of government and does not have a profit motive, but this seems to beg the question of a full definition. One way to address the matter is from a legal perspective. A nonprofit is created essentially as a matter of state law, although a few have been chartered by the U.S. Congress. The first decision in the process is to determine the type of organization, with most contemporary nonprofits choosing to become a corporation (Greenfield, 1999). The next step is to develop the articles of incorporation, a document that establishes the organization's purpose as well as its goals and objectives and is signed by those responsible for forming the nonprofit, known as the *incorporators*. Once this document has been filed and approved by the designated state agency, technically the incorporators have fulfilled their duty, but many elect to play other roles on behalf of the organization, including fund-raising, recruiting staff, and even purchasing property.

Part of the necessary legal structure for a nonprofit is a voluntary board of directors who accept responsibility that the organization will carry out its defined mission and will use its funds solely to achieve that end. The board is selected at the first formal organizational meeting, which the incorporators are expected to attend. It often happens that some if not all of the incorporators are elected as members of the initial board. Moreover, an organization may decide to have members, who are granted legal power to vote on the affairs of the corporation, as a mechanism to ensure that the board does not have sole authority to govern.

A second key document, the bylaws, sets forth rules for how the organization will be operated, including details on the composition and responsibilities of the board and its officers, the committee structure, the fiscal year, when and how meetings will be conducted, protections against losses or damages, a provision for amending the bylaws, and other procedural matters as warranted. These bylaws should be formally adopted at an organizational meeting and this action noted in the minutes, the official record of all that transpired. In addition, the minutes should reflect the election of directors and officers, a decision on the use of one or more financial institutions, and authorization given to someone to seek tax exemption and take any other actions required by law (Greenfield, 1999; Grobman, 2004).

As just noted, once incorporated, one of the most important actions for a nonprofit is to acquire tax-exempt status under section 501(c) of the Internal Revenue Code by completing Form 1023 for public charities and Form 1024 for other types of nonprofits, both of which can be downloaded from the Internal Revenue Service (IRS) Web site. Many that receive this special qualification will also be exempt from certain state taxes, such as sales, use, and real property.

Public Charities

Of the total number of nonprofits, public charities constitute the lion's share, having passed the one-million mark as of the most recent count by the IRS. NCCS (2008) values the 2006 total revenue for public charities at over $1 trillion and total assets at more than $2 trillion. Within this group, some organizations are classified as sectarian or faith-based, meaning they operate under the auspices of or with the financial backing of a specific religious denomination. The largest subsectors by number of organizations are those set up for religious or spiritual purposes, educational institutions, arts and culture groups, and those providing human services.

To be considered a public charity, an organization must meet the requirements set forth in section 501(c)(3) of the IRS code. Before applying for exempt status, the organization needs to obtain an employer identification number (EIN), even if there are no employees. As part of the submission process, the organization must attach copies of its articles of incorporation, showing certification of filing by the appropriate state office, and its bylaws, if they have already been adopted. Obtaining IRS recognition of 501(c)(3) exempt status conveys a certain level of legitimacy. It also brings many concrete benefits. Besides the most obvious one, exemption from virtually all federal and many state taxes, these nonprofits are eligible to receive tax-deductible contributions from both individuals and institutional funders such as foundations and United Way, thus providing a great incentive to prospective donors.

The burden of proof is on the organization to demonstrate it meets the code's requirements for recognition of exemption. Except for churches and most public charities with annual gross receipts under $5,000, organizations that wish to be considered under section 501(c)(3) must apply for recognition of this status, generally within twenty-seven months from the date of formation. Exempt purposes include

> Charitable, religious, educational, scientific, literary, testing for public safety, fostering national or international amateur sports competition, and preventing cruelty to children and animals. The term *charitable* is used in its generally accepted legal sense and includes relief of the poor, the distressed, or the underprivileged; advancement of religion; advancement of education or science; erecting or maintaining public buildings, monuments or works; lessening the burdens of government; lessening neighborhood tensions; eliminating prejudice or discrimination; defending human and civil rights secured by law; and combating community deterioration and juvenile delinquency. (IRS, 2009)

Strangely enough, although this language is quite inclusive, as O'Neill (2002) notes, it fails to specify health care, which accounts for a substantial amount of the expenditures and staff of the whole nonprofit sector.

Beyond establishing its charitable purpose, the organization has to satisfy two conditions. First, it must affirm that "none of its earnings . . . inure to any private shareholder or individual" (IRS, 2009). In other words, any monies that a charitable nonprofit realizes must be used to support its mission. However, this does not mean a public charity cannot suitably compensate its employees, commensurate with salaries in other organizations within its field and in accordance with community standards. Another misconception is that these organizations cannot turn a profit. In truth, a well-run organization should aspire to end the fiscal year with revenues in excess of expenses, which can then be applied to enhance programs and services.

The second restriction is that public charities may not engage in attempting to influence legislation, commonly known as lobbying, as a substantial part of their activities, or risk the loss of tax-exempt status. In practice, the organization cannot contact members or employees of a legislative body or urge the public to do so to propose, support, or oppose legislation. As to involvement in a political campaign, it is absolutely prohibited for public charities to participate directly or indirectly in a campaign on behalf of or in opposition to a candidate for elective public office, nor may the organization contribute funds or make public statements, whether verbal or written, in this regard.

Despite these strong statements on disallowed advocacy-related activities by 501(c)(3)s, the law provides considerable leeway as to what an organization may do. The operative word here is "substantial," which is determined by the level of human and material resources dedicated to such endeavors. For example, an exempt organization may attempt to educate the public on issues of public policy by holding meetings and by preparing and distributing materials that lay out the facts of the matter. It may also engage in voter-education programs, including the publication of voter guides and the holding of public forums, as long as this is done in a nonpartisan way; encourage voter registration; and conduct get-out-the-vote drives, again without favoring one candidate or party over another (IRS, 2009).

Furthermore, it is permissible to communicate with members of the organization to discuss legislation as long as you do not urge them to take action, and in doing a nonpartisan analysis of a legislative issue, the report need not be neutral or objective as long as all the facts are presented in a full and fair manner. In addition, the organization may respond to written requests from a legislative body for technical advice on pending legislation, lobby legislators regarding matters that might affect the organization's own existence or status, and discuss broad issues whose resolution might necessitate some legislative action without reference to specific legislation (Smucker, 1999). Yet many nonprofits continue to refrain from any lobbying, either due to the erroneous belief that it is illegal or out of a concern for potentially negative public and constituent perceptions of their actions. When in doubt about the appropriateness of such activities, it may be advisable to seek legal counsel.

Once the IRS determines an organization qualifies for exemption under section 501(c)(3), one final hurdle must be jumped. Under the federal tax law, charitable organizations are assumed to be private foundations unless they can prove they are public charities by meeting one or more of these requirements.

- [They] are churches, hospitals, qualified medical research organizations affiliated with hospitals, schools, colleges and universities,
- have an active program of fundraising and receive contributions from many sources, including the general public, governmental agencies, corporations, private foundations or other public charities,
- receive income from the conduct of activities in furtherance of the organization's exempt purposes, or
- actively function in a supporting relationship to one or more existing public charities (IRS, 2009).

If the application process is successful, the organization will receive a "determination letter" from the IRS, classifying the entity as a public charity in regard to both tax exemption and tax deductibility. Annually, the organization must file a return with the IRS. For most it is Form 990, although nonprofits with gross receipts under $500,000 and with assets less than $1,250,000 may use the much shorter Form 990-EZ, and those with gross receipts under $25,000 may use the electronic Form 990-N (e-Postcard). Here, all of the financial support received during the year is listed as well as all disbursements, categorized by function as program services, management and general, or fund-raising (IRS, 2009; see www.guidestar.org for further information). A charitable organization also must make available for public inspection its three most recent returns and provide copies of these documents upon request for no charge other than a reasonable fee to cover reproduction costs (Greenfield, 1999).

Member-Serving Organizations

Although some observers may question whether public charities really deserve the "public" label because, unlike government agencies, they do not necessarily serve everyone who might be eligible for their services (Wolf, 1999), those nonprofits set up as member-serving make no such claims about equity, proudly identifying their respective constituencies, who frequently pay dues to receive programs and services. Another way to categorize these organizations is to say they are "of mutual benefit," a legal term used in many states. As shown in table 1.1, the IRS has recognized well over 400,000 mutual benefit organizations, which take many forms and directions; some of the more prominent types are discussed below. NCCS estimates 2006 revenue for mutual benefit organizations in excess of $3.5 billion and total assets at just over $900 billion.

These member-serving organizations have been divided into more than thirty sections by the IRS. Some have just a handful of eligible organizations, such as the nine exempt nonprofits classified as trusts for prepaid group legal services under section 501(c)(20), while the largest in size, social welfare organizations, which fall under section 501(c)(4), had 116,539 member groups in 2006, according to NCCS. Other sizable sections in 2006 were fraternal societies, with 84,049, some of which are categorized under section 501(c)(8) and others under section 501(c)(10); business leagues, chambers of commerce, and boards of trade, with 72,549 under section 501(c)(6); social and recreational clubs, with 56,778 under section 501(c)(7); labor and agricultural organizations, with 56,460 under section 501(c)(5); and veterans' organizations, with 35,164 under section 501(c)(19). Collectively, these sections accounted for over 90 percent of all mutual benefit organizations in 2006. Financial support for these organizations may come from member dues, contributions by individuals and groups, fees for service, and fund-raising activities, such as benefits, walk-a-thons, direct mail campaigns, and so on.

Although many of the same requirements for exemption apply to both public charities and member-serving nonprofits, each non-501(c)(3) section has its own special provisions. One of the main distinguishing features between the two broad types of nonprofits is that, with a few exceptions, contributions to mutual benefit organizations are not tax deductible. The primary difference between the two is that mutual benefit organizations do not serve the needs of the general society, at least not by direct intent, but with some of these groups, such as those working to better the lives of ethnic minorities or to improve labor laws, at times this distinction can seem a bit contrived (O'Neill, 2002). However, when it comes to fraternal groups or political parties, which also fall into this category of nonprofit organization, the difference in purpose is very clear.

According to the IRS (2009), to receive tax exemption under section 501(c)(4) as a social welfare organization, the stated intent must be "to further the common good and general welfare of the people of the community, such as by bringing about civic better-ment and social improvements." These groups may seek legislation directly pertinent to their programs, and so engaging in lobbying as the primary activity will not affect their exempt status. Depending on the extent of the lobbying, it may be necessary to notify members of the percentage of dues applied to these activities or to pay a special proxy tax to the government. Like public charities, social welfare organizations cannot directly or indirectly participate in a political campaign for or in opposition to a specific candidate for public office, but they may engage in certain political activities as long as this is not their principal function, keeping in mind that expenditures here may be taxable.

To qualify for exemption as a fraternal society, the organization must have a pur-pose derived from a common tie or the pursuit of a common goal, and engage in a wide range of fraternal activities. Many operate under the lodge system, which requires mini-mally a parent organization and a subordinate, often called a lodge, branch, or the like, chartered by the parent and mainly self-governing. An organization falling under section 501(c)(8) is designated as a beneficiary society, order, or association; one of the require-ments is to provide for the payment of life, sick, accident, and other benefits for its mem-bers or their dependents. In contrast, an organization considered a domestic fraternal society, order, or association, under section 501(c)(10), cannot provide for the payment of benefits to its members, although it can arrange coverage with insurance companies without affecting its exempt status.

Organizations exempt under section 501(c)(6) include business leagues, chambers of commerce, real estate boards, boards of trade, and even professional football leagues. According to the IRS, the definition of this kind of nonprofit is "an association of per-sons having some common business interest, the purpose of which is to promote such common interest and not to engage in a regular business . . . for profit." Trade and pro-fessional associations qualify as business leagues under this definition. Activities must be carried on to further the interests of an entire industry or all elements of an industry within a given geographic area, but not to benefit any individual. Even though chambers of commerce and boards of trade fall into this category, they differ in that their purpose is to promote the common economic interests of all commercial enterprises in a partic-ular community or trade.

A social club, to be exempt under section 501(c)(7), must be organized for pleasure, recreation, and other similar purposes and direct its activities to these ends. There are strict prohibitions against discrimination toward any person based on race, color, or reli-gion, with the exception of a club that "in good faith" is set up to promote the teachings of a specific religion and, accordingly, restricts its membership to those within that denomination. The IRS states that "an essential earmark of an exempt club is personal contact, commingling, and face-to-face fellowship" among members. Membership must also be limited and facilities generally used only for members, their dependents, and guests. Furthermore, it is expected that for the most part, a club will be supported by dues, membership fees, and assessments, but it may receive up to 35 percent of its gross receipts from sources outside of its membership, with certain limitations.

With regard to labor and agricultural organizations, section 501(c)(5) of the code reiterates the basic inurement principle prohibiting the use of net earnings to benefit members. More important, its objectives "must be the betterment of conditions of those engaged in the pursuit of labor, agriculture, and horticulture" as well as to improve the quality of their products and develop greater efficiency in the three identified areas. Like social welfare organizations, these groups may engage in lobbying in order to promote legislation germane to their basic programs and remain exempt, but members may need to be informed about the percentage of dues used. Alternatively, the organization might be required to pay a proxy tax to the government. In addition, engaging in certain political activities is permitted as long as this does not extend to overt support for or opposition to an individual running for public office.

For exemption under section 501(c)(19), the organization, also known as a post, must serve the interests of veterans directly or through a trust or foundation. At least 75 percent of its members must be past or present members of the U.S. Armed Forces (USAF), and at least 97.5 percent must be present or former members of the USAF, cadets in one of the armed services academies or an ROTC program, or "spouses, widows, widowers, ancestors, or lineal descendents" of those referred to in the previous two provisions. Many of the allowable purposes for these organizations are obvious, such as sponsoring patriotic activities or assisting disabled and needy war veterans and their dependents, but others seem more in keeping with the requirements noted for other subsections, and indeed some posts are recognized instead as social welfare organizations, social clubs, or fraternal organizations.

To maintain their tax exemption, all member-serving nonprofits must file either Form 990 or Form 990-EZ with the IRS each year.

FINAL THOUGHTS

When the Frenchman Alexis de Tocqueville visited the United States in 1831 and subsequently wrote his seminal work *Democracy in America* in 1835, he immortalized the principle of collectivity he observed in the numerous voluntary associations encountered during his travels. To Tocqueville (1983), these organizations, in their very diversity, represented the essence of democracy and reflected the true spirit of this new country. Today, with new charitable and member-serving organizations emerging each year, we continue to celebrate the importance and vitality of the nonprofit sector.

Historical Development of Nonprofit Organizations

As a people, we Americans consider ourselves to be generous with both money and time in support of worthy causes, and the facts back up this claim. According to estimates provided by the Giving USA Foundation (2009) in its annual survey, despite the poor state of the economy, individuals provided over $229 billion in charitable contributions in 2008, or 75 percent of total donations. With respect to volunteering, in a report issued by the U.S. Bureau of Labor Statistics (2008), approximately 60.8 million people gave of their time without compensation between September 2006 and September 2007, representing 26.2 percent of the population. Moreover, there is a clear link between volunteering and philanthropy; in 2008 over 78 percent of adult volunteers contributed at least $25 to a charitable cause compared to just 39 percent of nonvolunteers ("Volunteering in America," 2009).

On the other hand, the "can do" spirit of self-help is very much a part of the American culture. We are especially taken with individuals who have succeeded in rising above life's obstacles through their own efforts, and thus we become very disheartened when someone whom we have lauded for such accomplishments proves ultimately not to have deserved our accolades. Case in point: In 2008 a highly publicized memoir written by a woman who claimed to have grown up in the most difficult of circumstances as part of California's gang culture but had managed to find a new life in Oregon and earn a college degree, and had now started a foundation to help those with backgrounds similar to hers, turned out to be a fraud. The author was revealed to have been raised in an intact family in an affluent neighborhood; any knowledge of gangs was tangential at best. The book was withdrawn by the publisher amid a flood of negative and condemnatory news stories.

This chapter explores the influences dating back to ancient times that have shaped the modern face of American philanthropy, tracing the development of the nonprofit sector from colonial days to the present. The growth of the human services subsector is also discussed in an attempt to clarify why this particular group of nonprofits has drawn so much attention within the national debate over the best ways to care for the less fortunate members of society.

TRACING THE EVOLUTION OF THE U.S. NONPROFIT SECTOR

The nonprofit sector as we know it today began to take shape in the years following the Civil War, when the role of voluntary organizations in American society became more clearly realized. However, it was not until the 1970s that an actual "sector" could be said to exist, that is, as a somewhat cohesive, united body of organizations; over 90 percent of the nonprofits now in existence were formed after the Second World War (Hall, 1994). Perhaps one sign of the increased importance of these organizations in modern times is the growing use of the term *civil society* to represent the sector, to highlight its size and diversity not only in the United States but worldwide, and to acknowledge it as differentiated from but deeply connected to both the public and private for-profit sectors. As Boris (1999, p. 2) notes, "[Nonprofit] organizations produce 'social capital,' the norms of trust and cooperation that permit societies to function."

The Origins of Philanthropy in the New World

In tracing philanthropy's roots back to ancient times, it is possible to see the origins of two somewhat contradictory approaches, the impulse toward individual service to help those in need in a selfless manner and the push toward social reform through collective action, which Benjamin Franklin demonstrated was just a different way of manifesting self-help principles. The first thread can be traced back to the Judeo-Christian belief system of love, justice, and mercy while the second is derived from the Greek and Roman experience, albeit somewhat limited and often motivated by the efforts of a few of the more enlightened thinkers of the day, of enacting legislation to alleviate some of the suffering of the poor. Indeed, the idea of social reform, such as it was, all but disappeared with the decline of the Roman Empire. During the Middle Ages and up to the time of the Protestant Reformation, charity was administered by religious groups. The increasing involvement of government in addressing social problems really dates from the Reformation to the present (Cass & Manser, 1983).

Life in the Colonies

Within the American colonies, the English influence was strongest in shaping policies and practices. Accordingly, many of the same patterns for dealing with the poor, the aged, and so on were imported by the settlers, with modifications to fit local sensibilities. Yet it would be a mistake to believe that true philanthropy as we understand it existed in the colonies in the seventeenth and eighteenth centuries. For instance, antipathy toward those who seemed able-bodied or might have brought misfortune on themselves was very strong (Cass & Manser, 1983). In general, church and state were the dominant institutions. The family was viewed as a "public institution" and was legally required, unless lacking the necessary resources, to assume responsibility "for economic production, education, and social welfare" (Hall, 1994, p. 5). Harvard College, founded in 1636 and considered the oldest charitable corporation in the colonies, was actually a public entity under the laws of the time; it was not until 1865 that its status changed to that of a private institution in the modern sense.

Benjamin Franklin was something of an anomaly for his times because even though he believed in the idea of self-regulation, he became a champion of collective action within the community, initially to spread the concept of self-reform through mutual benefit societies but then expanding his efforts to help found a number of public-serving associations in Philadelphia by the middle of the eighteenth century. In terms of anything resembling a nonprofit sector, however, the American Revolution represents a real turning point, although the voluntary associations that came into existence in the latter part of the century were still not private entities but rather took their authority through restricted forms of public delegation. In addition, these quasi-private corporations, while widespread throughout the new nation, varied greatly in purpose and powers from state to state, establishing a pattern of nonuniform regulation that continues to this day. Differing views over public and private power even contributed to the rise of the first political parties (Hall, 1994; Hammack, 2001).

Growing Pains in the Nineteenth Century

The nineteenth century was a time of enormous social and political change in America, with the end of slavery, the wrenching effects of the Civil War, the movement toward a more industrialized society, and the creation of labor unions, to name some of the key developments. This was also a time of great change for voluntary associations as they shifted from being public to private corporations, with a concomitant growth and diversification in types of services and programs "as a reaction to the admittedly inadequate governmental care of the poor, desire to aid special groups in the population, the effective propagandizing of the social reformers, and the desire of many religious groups to provide for the needs of their own" (Cass & Manser, 1983, p. 19).

Two landmark Supreme Court cases set the precedent for the privatization of nonprofits. The first case reached the Court in 1818. It involved the efforts of the State of New Hampshire to take over Dartmouth College, with Daniel Webster acting on behalf of the college. The Court upheld Webster's argument that even though the institution had been chartered by the state, individuals had made gifts and bequests to Dartmouth's trustees and, in so doing, established a private contract with obligations protected under the Constitution. The net effect of this decision was to alter the nature of the corporation from public to private by expanding the protection of private action provided through the Bill of Rights to collective action. The second case, *Vidal v. Girard's Executors*, which was heard in 1844, reversed an earlier, unfavorable decision by the Court. In this instance, the Justices supported the position taken by the attorneys for the Girard estate, affirming the right under federal law of individuals to create charitable trusts that corporations were then allowed to administer and thus giving charities a much needed level of legal security, despite the fact that individual states could choose to limit this activity (Hall, 1994; Hammack, 2001).

As mentioned in chapter 1, the French statesman and philosopher Alexis de Tocqueville made a historic visit to America in 1831. In his subsequent book detailing his observations, Tocqueville marveled at the diversity of the nonprofits he encountered in his travels: "I met with several kinds of associations in America of which I confess I had no previous notion; and I have often admired the extreme skill with which the inhabitants of the United States succeed in proposing a common object for the exertions of a great many men and in inducing them voluntarily to pursue it" (1983, p. 54). There is no doubt the writings of foreign visitors such as Tocqueville brought a much broader recognition of the role of nonprofit organizations in the early days of this new country, but, as Hall (1994) points out, it is important to temper this enthusiasm with the reality that only in the Northeast did voluntary associations play such a central role during the first half of the nineteenth century. Public institutions remained the preferred organizational form in both the West and the South.

As in the aftermath of the American Revolution, the years following the Civil War ushered in another period of growth for the nonprofit sector. In 1865 Harvard College, with a shift in the composition of its board of overseers from clergymen to lawyers and businessmen and with the influx of individual gifts and bequests assuming more significance than government funding, became a private institution for all intents and purposes. A key event occurred in 1874 when Harvard's president persuasively defended the institution's tax exemption to the Massachusetts General Court by presenting a clear case for the economic benefits to the public from private charities. The state legislature subsequently increased the ceiling on tax exemption for charitable property and the range of charitable organizations qualifying for tax exemption; this law became the model for others seeking to broaden the role of private institutions, but with more success in the Northeast than in other sections of the country (Hall, 1994).

An alliance of sorts between the corporate world and wealthy individuals resulted in an increasing reliance on private nonprofit organizations, including universities, libraries, hospitals, museums, social agencies, professional groups, and private clubs, during the last decades of the nineteenth century. With the support of the middle class and blue-collar workers, the variety and number of mutual benefit organizations, such as labor unions and fraternal groups, increased significantly, while a growing awareness of the effects of poverty in America's cities on the part of the middle and upper classes led to creating many different kinds of nonprofits to serve the sick, the poor, and the disabled (Hall, 1994). One example of an innovative approach to meeting social problems was the settlement house, which became the focal point for local residents in many urban areas to obtain information and concrete services, especially newly arrived immigrants, who needed help in adjusting to the American way of life (Jansson, 2005).

The principle of tax exemption for public charities as part of the U.S. tax code was established with the earliest version of this legislation, the Wilson-Gorman Tariff Act of 1894. The act called for a flat 2 percent tax on corporate income, but stated that the tax should not apply to organizations established solely for charitable, religious, or educational purposes, including fraternal groups. Even though this law was declared unconstitutional by the Supreme Court the following year, the basic concept of exemption was set. The language of the 1894 act in reference to privileged tax treatment for nonprofits was reflected in the Revenue Act of 1909, which also introduced the prohibition against private inurement for charities; deductibility for individual charitable donations and bequests was added in the Revenue Acts of 1917 and 1918 (Arnsberger, Ludlum, Riley, & Stanton, 2008).

New Directions for a New Century

In the last years of the nineteenth century and continuing into the new century, some observers began to be concerned about the effects of industrialization on society. Business leaders like Andrew Carnegie and John D. Rockefeller signaled a somewhat new direction for philanthropy by wealthy individuals, a more personal approach that was derived from the Progressive movement that took hold in America. These concerns were perhaps best articulated by Carnegie in his essay "The Gospel of Wealth," which put forth the idea of equality of opportunity to replace the equality of condition now that the latter had become more difficult, if not impossible, due to the concentration of wealth in the hands of just a few (Hall, 1994).

Carnegie advocated that the man of wealth, after ensuring that the legitimate needs of his heirs have been attended to, should "consider all surplus revenues which come to him simply as trust funds, which he is called upon to administer . . . in the manner . . . best calculated to produce the most beneficial results for the community" (1983, p. 104). Ultimately, it was determined that the best way to carry out these ideas was through a new charitable form, the foundation, that would have the staff and resources to investigate the most advantageous uses of wealth. The first modern foundation was set up by the widow of businessman Russell Sage in New York City in 1907, for the purpose of "the improvement of social and living conditions in the United States." The Carnegie Corporation of New York followed in 1911, and the Rockefeller Foundation, created "to promote the well-being of mankind throughout the world," in 1913. In addition, the first community chest, today better known in most communities as United Way, was formed in Cleveland in 1913. The next year Cleveland also became the site of America's first community foundation, a philanthropic entity that centralizes the management of many charitable trusts for the purpose of meeting local needs (Hall, 1994).

Through the first half of the twentieth century, there was a proliferation of all types of voluntary organizations, locally, regionally, and nationally. Starting with World War I, the concept of public-private partnerships began to take hold, but in the years immediately following the war, under the leadership of Herbert Hoover, government's role was more that of cheerleader, encouraging and coordinating the efforts of the various charities and the businesses supporting them, than an active participant. This perspective continued to dominate during the early years of Roosevelt's New Deal, but the Great Depression of the early 1930s forced a major shift in policy, when it became evident that private agencies, even with the assistance of local and state governments, were unable to cope with the full range of issues affecting the poor, the unemployed, the aged, and the chronically ill. It was essential that the federal government become directly involved in addressing this crisis. Initially, the response was in the form of emergency measures; the first permanent Social Security legislation was enacted in 1935 (Cass & Manser, 1983; Hall, 1994). However, there was still a place for the private sector. The legislation that increased the tax burden on corporations and wealthy individuals also provided incentives for major giving, with the introduction of the corporate tax deduction for charitable contributions in the Revenue Act of 1936 (Arnsberger et al., 2008).

Yet, prior to 1960, it would be a mistake to overstate the general importance of non-profits outside of the Northeast and the Great Lakes states, other than to meet the needs of wealthy and well-established men. For the poor, people of color, and women, especially when attempting to organize outside the framework of major religious traditions, it was a different story, with state policies often thwarting their efforts. After 1960 the impact of the nonprofit sector expanded greatly both socially and economically, thanks in large measure to the growing affluence of the American people, the Great Society programs of the Johnson Administration, and the civil rights movement. Greater affluence meant more demand for services, including those offered by voluntary organizations. At the same time government spending for health, education, and social services increased, becoming a substantial income source for many nonprofits that continues to the present. Finally, in recognition of the ongoing resistance toward people of color by local governments, Great Society programs covered the costs of services provided by both public and private agencies (Hammack, 2001).

Even though Presidents Nixon, Ford, and Carter were relatively conservative in their views on social reform, spending for social programs increased dramatically through the 1970s. Indeed, the modern welfare state really began to take shape during this period, with the passage of legislation making the Food Stamp Program mandatory and establishing the Supplementary Security Income (SSI) Program, to name just two important initiatives that extended the policies of the Great Society. Other notable achievements included the Family Planning and Population Research Act and the Occupational Safety and Health Act (OSHA), which gave the federal government authority to oversee industrial safety standards (Jansson, 2005).

Changes in the Political and Economic Landscape

Despite these positive steps, beginning in the early 1950s the nonprofit world was coming under increased scrutiny by some members of Congress, who had become concerned about perceived tax loopholes for charitable deductions as well as the liberal-leaning policies of certain large foundations, such as Ford, Carnegie, and Rockefeller. One House committee formed in April 1952 was charged with determining whether these exempt organizations were using their resources in ways that were counter to the best interests of the United States; its report, issued in January 1953, exonerated foundations and reaffirmed their loyalty. However, this did not satisfy all the critics, and thus a second committee was authorized in April 1954 to take a broader look at the role of foundations, concluding that they were not supporters of Communism but raising questions about their sheer numbers and the lack of government oversight and regulation of their essentially private activities (Hall, 1994).

In the succeeding years the challenges to the growth and power of foundations continued. Ongoing questions about the current tax system added to the controversy, which led to congressional hearings on tax-exempt organizations and subsequent passage of the 1969 Tax Reform Act. Although this legislation was less severe than some had feared, one of the clear messages was the absence of adequate information about the nonprofit sector, opening the door to many misconceptions about its function in society. Recognizing that this hostility toward foundations and other exempt organizations was not going away, John D. Rockefeller III took the initiative to underwrite special commissions to begin gathering the necessary data that might satisfy the critics. An important contribution of the Peterson Commission, which published its findings in 1970, was to make a case for philanthropy going beyond foundations to include a broad range of voluntary groups supported by both public and private funds. A second blue-ribbon panel was formed in 1973 to develop an empirical database on private philanthropy and its relationship to government. Formally known as the Commission on Private Philanthropy and Public Needs but more commonly called the Filer Commission, after its chairman, this group drew on the expertise of economists, sociologists, tax attorneys, and others knowledgeable about NGOs to produce a comprehensive report establishing the existence of and need for a separate, voluntary sector, to complement and counterbalance public sector activities (Hall, 1994).

Yet, even with data that delineated the size and importance of the nonprofit sector in the United States, some myths persisted. Perhaps the most damaging misconception was that voluntary organizations relied primarily on individual and corporate giving; in reality, government support had become the major source of revenue for many of these organizations. The Reagan administration reestablished conservatism as the dominant political paradigm, and this meant significant changes for nonprofits. For example, contrary to all evidence showing certain social problems as being national in scope, a principle that had become well established after the Great Depression, it was now believed that voluntary organizations, with the support of state and local governments, could reassume much of the responsibility for addressing these very same problems (Cass & Manser, 1983). "In the conservative equivalent of Roosevelt's first 100 days in office, Reagan during his first eight months secured major budget cuts, tax cuts, the elimination of many regulations, reductions in the federal government's policy roles, and massive increases in military spending" (Jansson, 2005, p. 312).

Although Reagan was not as successful in pushing through his policies during the latter part of his first term, and his second term can best be described as a stalemate, his belief in a smaller federal government and greater expectations of the private sector has persisted in succeeding administrations. However, the impact on nonprofit organizations has not been uniform. The expansion of corporate giving in response to governmental pressures has benefited arts and culture groups as well as education. Federal policies have led to massive changes in the health care arena, with some hospitals becoming for-profit companies and those remaining as nonprofits having to operate in a more businesslike manner, leading to cuts in services to the needy (Hall, 1994). For human service agencies, we have seen a variety of strategies adopted to help these groups survive and thrive, such as greater diversification of funding streams and even mergers, which will be discussed in some detail in the next section of this chapter.

The jury is still out in regard to the opportunities and threats that lie ahead for the nonprofit sector, charities as well as member-serving organizations, in today's global economy. One trend that does seem clear is that public confidence in the purity of organizational motives has been somewhat eroded in the wake of several very public scandals involving top executives using funds meant for programs and services for their personal gain, in United Way of America, the Smithsonian Institution, the American Parkinson Disease Association, and others. Over the last several years, the American Red Cross has experienced a high degree of leadership turnover as questions have been raised about the allocation of contributions earmarked for disaster relief. As a result, even local nonprofits find themselves under greater scrutiny. On the other hand, charitable giving in the United States exceeded $300 billion in 2008, for the second year in a row (*Giving USA*, 2009).

Table 2.1 provides an overview of historical milestones in the development of the American nonprofit sector. As Hall (1994) notes, even though history is a rather imperfect guide to the future, it does show that the challenges voluntary organizations are fac-

Table 2.1 Historical milestones in the development of the U.S. nonprofit sector

Time period	Events
1636	Harvard College established as first "charitable" entity.
Mid-eighteenth century	Benjamin Franklin and friends introduce mutual-benefit and public-serving voluntary associations in Philadelphia.
Post–American Revolution	Wide variety of nonprofit corporations are chartered throughout the new nation.
First half of nineteenth century	Two landmark Supreme Court cases set legal precedents for private nonprofits.
	Tocqueville (and others) brings broader recognition to the sector.
Second half of nineteenth century	Congress includes exemption for charities in first federal income tax code.
	Numbers and types of nonprofits increase significantly.
First half of twentieth century	New charitable entities (e.g., foundations, community chests) are created.
	Federal government steps in to address effects of Great Depression.
Second half of twentieth century	Modern welfare state takes shape in 1960s and 1970s.
	Filer Commission provides hard data to support value of the sector to society.
	Reagan administration policies change government-nonprofit relationship.
The present	Nonprofits are coping with numerous changes in the external environment.

ing at present are nothing new. Perhaps the individuals now responsible for guiding these organizations can take some comfort in that knowledge.

THE HUMAN SERVICES SUBSECTOR

For many Americans the organizations falling within the human services subsector are what come to mind when they think about the nonprofit world, whether they have availed themselves of these services or not. Just consider the sheer diversity of the work: food pantries, homeless shelters, child care programs, adoption and foster care programs, mental health clinics, residential care, senior centers, substance abuse programs, educational and training facilities, employment counseling and placement services, family and youth services, and so on—something for every age and income group. In addition, when we contemplate the values upon which this nation was built, meeting the needs of the less fortunate would certainly rank close to the top of the list. Yet through the decades, eligibility for benefits, the types of services provided, the manner in which they are implemented, and the resources dedicated to these kinds of efforts have often caused controversy in response to shifting perspectives and priorities.

Social Welfare in the Eighteenth Century

During the period from 1750 to 1800, a new society began to evolve in America that discarded many of the ideas about class distinctions brought with the settlers from Europe. As the colonists obtained land, they came to see themselves as stakeholders in a new culture, with their future tied to their own initiative. In keeping with this emphasis on individualism, after the American Revolution the framers of the Constitution established an elaborate system of checks and balances to ensure a limited federal government, one consequence being that social policy became the responsibility of state and local government, with the exception of enacting laws to further the "general welfare," a vague term at best. The net result of these decisions was that the federal government did not play a strong role in social welfare until almost 150 years after the founding of the republic (Jansson, 2005).

As noted earlier, local government in the colonies provided assistance to the sick, the disabled, and the aged poor. However, those considered able-bodied were expected to fend for themselves; a prevailing view was that poverty represented a moral failing or at least a failure of will and that poor families negatively affected the economy. At the same time, private charitable agencies were developed, generally under religious auspices, with many sponsoring educational self-help programs that reflected the value placed on economic opportunity for all (O'Neill, 2002).

Social Welfare in the Nineteenth Century

The Founding Fathers believed they had created a utopian society in which major social problems would not arise. Unfortunately, this belief served to blind the colonists and even later generations to the reality of the needs springing up right before their eyes: "Even in the 19th century, when the nation began to develop an urban society and other social needs became relatively widespread, the persistent notion of the American utopia perpetuated a kind of collective denial" (Jansson, 2005, p. 59).

Many of the urban ills we see today, such as large numbers of unskilled and semi-skilled workers who fall into poverty, existed as well in the early small cities of America. The situation was exacerbated in the first half of the nineteenth century when waves of poor immigrants began arriving in the cities, and at the same time, many Americans migrated west and from the countryside to the city, contributing to a number of social problems, including alcoholism, prostitution, criminal acts, and youth unrest. One reaction to the latter issue was to build orphanages for youth under age sixteen who had left home or whose parents voluntarily committed them due to insufficient resources. The broader response was to launch a moral crusade implemented through local governments and private, usually sectarian agencies (Jansson, 2005).

Gradually, in the middle and late nineteenth century, attitudes toward those suffering social ills began to change as theorists advanced the idea that society was the cause of these problems, rather than personal weakness. Local and state governments expanded their efforts to serve the poor and even developed new programs. Wealthy individuals with a reformist mentality contributed resources and leadership to found nonprofit social service agencies, including the American Red Cross, the YMCA and YWCA, settlement houses, charity organization societies, and asylums for the blind and deaf (O'Neill, 2002). Nevertheless, the role of the federal government in social welfare remained largely unchanged even in the period following the Civil War and in the beginning stages of the Industrial Revolution in America.

Social Welfare in the Twentieth Century and Beyond

An earlier section of this chapter detailed the major shift in public policy in the 1930s due to the Great Depression, resulting in the federal government's assumption of responsibility for addressing social problems across the nation. The way the nonprofit sector has evolved in the United States, that is, its prominent place in the provision of social services but also the peculiar blending of public and private actions, can be seen as one effect of these policy changes having come much later than in most other industrialized countries (Salamon, 1999).

The three principal social welfare programs under the New Deal consisted of old age pensions (the Social Security program), unemployment insurance, and cash assistance through categorical programs such as Aid to Families with Dependent Children (AFDC). In the face of political opposition to these programs, the new social welfare system was a step in the right direction but retained many of the flaws of the past: uneven coverage for different segments of the population, fairly limited funding of services, and the continuation of state and local governments' dominance since education, traditionally overseen at the state and local level, absorbed a large portion of social welfare spending. Starting with the Great Society programs of the 1960s and through the 1970s, many of the New Deal reforms were completed and even expanded to include a national health insurance plan for the elderly (Medicare), a federal-state program of health care for the poor (Medicaid), the creation of a network of community action agencies and preschool programs in low-income neighborhoods (Head Start, for one), and more aid to the disadvantaged in employment and training, social services, and housing (Salamon, 1999). One of the notable developments in the period from the mid-1960s to 1980 was the increase in federal government spending on social welfare; from 1965 to 1975, most of this growth came in the form of actual program expansion (Salamon, 1999).

However, although a number of the Great Society programs have endured, these efforts were not an unqualified success. Critics suggest President Johnson focused too much on enacting new legislation and not enough on the implementation of the resulting programs. The substantial dollars now flowing to these programs brought a resurgence of opposition to the federal government's role in effecting social reforms as well as renewed antipathy toward the poor and people of color. The Vietnam War only exacerbated the situation, since those for and against the conflict tended to have the same polarized views of the welfare state (Jansson, 2005). Thus, the stage was set for the cutbacks in social welfare spending by the federal government during the Reagan years.

Perhaps the more lasting legacy of the manner in which the American welfare state has evolved is the partnership between government and the nonprofit sector that endures to this day. Even at the height of the Great Depression, private organizations continued to provide social services. Yet, this relationship has changed over time, and some would say the character of the sector has changed as well. For one thing, since the 1980s federal government support has been uneven, benefiting education and health organizations at the expense of the human services. In response, nonprofits have attempted to diversify their funding sources, especially through earned-income strategies such as increasing their reliance on fees for service and engaging in other kinds of commercial ventures (Gronbjerg, 2001; Salamon, 1999). For-profits now vie with voluntary organizations for the performance-based contracts that have become a favored funding mechanism of government agencies as they have moved from direct providers to procurers of social services. Tapping into Medicaid dollars has become a primary source of financial support for many types of social service programs (for example, child welfare and substance abuse) as older forms of support like block grants have been curtailed. Moreover, government has adopted managed care principles, which emphasize efficiency sometimes at the expense of quality of service, to guide financial decision-making, further increasing uncertainty about the constancy of revenues for provider agencies (Gronbjerg, 2001).

Another major policy shift occurred at the end of the first term of the Clinton administration, when AFDC, an entitlement, was replaced by a new welfare program, the Temporary Assistance for Needy Families block grant (TANF), which gave each state the latitude to set eligibility requirements and determine how benefits would be provided, without imposing any uniform standards for measuring the results (Jansson, 2005). One aspect of the new welfare reform legislation, frequently referred to as the "charitable choice" provision, allowed faith-based organizations to continue receiving federal funds for offering social services, as they had long been able to do, but also permitted them to openly display religious artifacts, a significant departure from past practices. Subsequent legislation in the period from 1996 to 2000 gave further legitimacy to these ideas. President George W. Bush then acted to make charitable choice a key feature of his domestic program by signing three executive orders in an attempt to implement this initiative. In the end, Congress did not approve some of the major components of the program because of concerns that, despite restrictions prohibiting a faith-based organization from proselytizing or withholding services from individuals not of that particular faith, it would be very difficult to monitor whether these standards were being upheld (Grobman, 2004; Jansson, 2005). In February 2009 President Obama issued an executive order creating the White House Office of Faith-Based and Neighborhood Partnerships, reaffirming the separation of church and state but also the enduring value of faith-based organizations to help people in need in their communities (Obama Announces, 2009).

FINAL THOUGHTS

What does the future hold for human service organizations and the people they serve? Predictably, the impact of TANF has varied dramatically from state to state, with some localities much more generous with both time and resources than others. Accordingly, "success" in this arena is open to a variety of different interpretations, but certainly poverty and inequality are still very much a part of American life. In this environment, the need for a healthy, viable nonprofit sector is not likely to diminish.

Political and Economic Considerations **3**

Today, as perhaps never before, nonprofit organizations must operate in a complex and ever-changing environment full of a wide range of political and economic concerns that in turn affect internal decision-making. We are living in an extended period of government cutbacks and increased competition for the private dollar, of privatization and managed care policies and practices, of greater and sometimes conflicting demands from a variety of stakeholders for both fiscal and programmatic accountability. In light of these challenges, organizational leaders must determine the most effective and appropriate ways to ensure a continuing flow of the resources necessary to provide the programs and services consistent with the organizational mission without compromising its integrity.

In the typical nonprofit, the heaviest responsibility for addressing these challenges falls on the chief executive officer, who must therefore be skilled in the art of boundary spanning, which might encompass such diverse activities as securing financial and in-kind resources, establishing and maintaining the organization's legitimacy, negotiating formal and informal agreements with other organizations, participating in advocacy coalitions, and positioning the organization to take advantage of new opportunities (Edwards & Yankey, 2006).

This chapter focuses on the boundary-spanning role of the nonprofit professional leader by examining the theoretical and practical dimensions of navigating through the murky waters of present-day organizational life, shaped in large measure by a highly politicized and multifaceted marketplace.

A THEORETICAL MODEL

Change is not something that comes easily to most individuals; most of us would prefer to stay within the comfort zone of the known rather than leaping into unfamiliar territory even when all objective signs point to the latter as the better course of action. Groups and organizations share the same propensity. In a subsequent chapter of this book, we will look at strategies to effect change, but here our interest is in understanding the nature of change from a more philosophical vantage point. It is also important to clarify that the kind of change under discussion is not simply cosmetic but is at a

much more fundamental level of transformation, resulting in a different way to concep-
tualize and/or manage the operations of the organization.

Wernet (1994) suggests that from the theoretical perspective of economic deter-
minism, change occurs in reaction to the constraints imposed on the organization, causing it to adapt to its environment within its particular service niche; in contrast, from the
perspective of strategic choice, the organization acts in a more proactive, anticipatory
manner to secure essential resources and ensure survival. A theory that encompasses
both of these viewpoints is political economy, which takes into account organizational
goals and structure in its emphasis on the interrelationships between political and economic forces within and external to the organization. Furthermore, this theory acknowledges the effects of organizational culture on leaders' decision-making, meaning that
choices may be dictated by ingrained patterns of behavior as well as by more objective
considerations (Wernet, 1994; Zald, 1970). Put another way, political-economy theory is
concerned with the internal actors who have the formal authority over how decisions are
made by the organization as well as those who influence the decision process, and with
the external political and economic factors that shape critical decisions on resources the
organization needs.

The main implications of this theory are that as levels of supply and demand in the
marketplace for an organization's "products"—its programs and services, which may
include both tangible and intangible goods—fluctuate, so does the organizational
response. When competition for resources is low, the organization does not feel threatened, but when competition is high, the impetus for change, to restore that sense of stability, is much stronger. At the same time, the linkages the organization has forged with
various constituencies in the external political environment can play a mediating role in
regard to the external economic environment (Wernet, 1994). For nonprofits, groups
with the most obvious relevance would include supporters, such as funders and direct
beneficiaries of services, and those with legislated control over the organization, such as
regulatory agencies. However, even actual or potential competitors must be taken into
consideration; a full understanding of market conditions may dictate forging agreements
that turn competitors into collaborators. In short, "this approach postulates that economic and political forces, structures, pressures, and constraints (1) are among the most
significant motivators of change and (2) are the key factors shaping directions of change"
(Zald, 1970, p. 256).

THE EXAMPLE OF MANAGED CARE

For nonprofits operating in the physical and behavioral health arenas, managed care
policies and practices offer a pertinent application of political-economy theory. As noted
in chapter 2, during the Johnson administration two major health-care programs were
instituted: Medicare, to address the health needs of the elderly, and Medicaid, for the disabled and poor. As a result, by the 1970s the federal government had become a major
funder of the U.S. health-care system, and its response to rising costs was to tighten stan-

dards and monitoring procedures through diagnosis-related groups in hospitals and other provider settings. Despite these efforts, medical expenses continued to increase through the 1980s and into the 1990s. With the development of more sophisticated technology, it became possible to implement more widespread monitoring, using what we now know as managed care procedures, with the goal of integrating health-care services and expenditures. Managed care organizations, such as health maintenance organizations (HMOs) and employee assistance programs (EAPs), evolved out of the desire to not only control costs but also increase effectiveness as reflected in the quality of services (National Association of Social Workers, 2006).

Mental health and substance use disorders first received recognition as medically based illnesses requiring professional interventions in the late 1950s, but it was not until the passage of the Health Maintenance Organization Act of 1973 (PL 93-222) that HMOs began to offer even minimal coverage for these disorders. Deinstitutionalization of patients from state mental hospitals along with the community health movement of the 1960s and 1970s, funded initially by the federal government, were also factors in establishing insurance coverage for mental health treatment (NASW, 2006). In 1982 the Tax Equity and Fiscal Responsibility Act (PL 97-248) was enacted, providing additional financial incentives for prepaid programs, which were seen as a way to counter the high costs and utilization of health services under Medicare and Medicaid (Gibelman, 2001–2002).

In principle it is hard to dispute the stated intentions of managed care policy to improve efficiency and effectiveness. Unfortunately, in practice, it has often proven difficult to reach both of these desired ends. For example, to contain costs, managed care organizations, which act as an intermediary between the funding source and those seeking assistance, have imposed strict requirements on eligibility for service, limited the choice of providers, and mandated the allowable treatment options. In addition, these programs tend to use a medical model focusing on the elimination or treatment of symptoms rather than a social health model, whose emphasis is much broader, with the result that the consumer may not receive the full range of services necessary to address either the immediate or the underlying problems that motivated the individual to request help in the first place (NASW, 2006).

Today the primary responsibility for community mental health services has devolved to the states, with federal assistance as established under the State Comprehensive Mental Health Services Plan Act of 1986 (PL 99-660). Although block grants continue to be a part of the financial support package, Medicaid is now the dominant source of funding for treatment and support services for children and adults coping with severe mental illness. A typical arrangement is for a local community mental health center (CMHC) to obtain funding from a state government agency and then contract with private community-based providers to deliver the services. In many cases, referrals are channeled through a CMHC-operated agency, acting as a gatekeeper, once consumers have demonstrated that they meet the stringent eligibility requirements involving residency, income, and the presenting problem(s).

This system is imperfect on many levels. While individual and family needs for assistance keep increasing, the CMHC often does not receive a commensurate increase in its level of support, which in turn restricts the number of providers under contract and the dollars allocated to them. As a result, eligible people can be denied help because the provider agencies are already at capacity and cannot accommodate them; a person's only recourse may be to pay higher fees for services through non-CMHC providers. Other market forces also come into play. Most managed care contracts reimburse on a per-person basis to a predetermined group of consumers, thus shifting the burden for cost containment to the provider. Whereas the original intent of these contracts was to motivate providers to be more efficient in using resources, the actual effect has been to increase uncertainty about revenues (Gronbjerg & Smith, 1999). In an attempt to cope with this uncertainty, some providers have resorted to unethical practices such as misrepresenting benefits, screening out consumers with more serious problems, and limiting or even withholding appropriate treatment, because of its cost. Others have responded by reducing staff levels through layoffs or attrition, thus placing a greater burden on the remaining practitioners and middle managers to continue services and handle the excessive paperwork associated with heightened accountability demands under managed care (Gibelman, 2001–2002).

THE TIES THAT BIND

This discussion on managed care highlights an important dimension of nonprofit life, the multiple stakeholders with which these organizations interact on a regular basis. We will explore this issue in more detail with reference to just one type of nonprofit, the human service organization (HSO). As shown in figure 3.1, internally the primary stakeholders include clients, staff, and the board of directors, and externally, funders, regulatory agencies, and other nonprofits in the community, which may be allies or competitors.

Of the various perspectives advanced to shed light on interorganizational behavior, stakeholder theory can serve as a unifying megaframework. Grounded in feminist theory, this conceptualization emphasizes empowerment of a broad range of constituencies. The principal value orientation becomes trying to satisfy the individual preferences of all these groups, something that in practice can be more difficult to achieve because the interests of some stakeholders may be at odds with those of others. The sum total of the interactions with different stakeholder groups represents multiple bilateral relationships (Abzug & Webb, 1999).

From an economic standpoint, we might think of these interactions as exchanges with incomplete contracts, that is, agreements in which certain aspects cannot be enforced retroactively because not all conditions can be anticipated and thus stipulated in the contract. For instance, in hiring a new staff member, there may be clarity about work hours and the tasks associated with the position, but it is virtually impossible to specify how much energy the new employee must exercise in doing the job. Moreover, even if it were possible to anticipate likely behaviors, it is not necessarily cost effective to

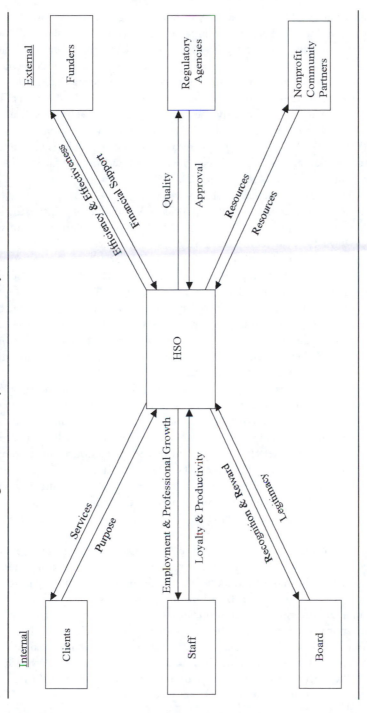

Figure 3.1 Relationships between HSO and key stakeholders

try to determine what should be done in every instance. It may also be the case that the goods or services involved in the exchange cannot be precisely measured (Bowles, 2004). Consider a charge issued to a board committee spelling out the members' duties. Should someone miss meetings or otherwise fail to live up to the charge, there is little recourse beyond removing the person from the committee, which may lead to an undesirable outcome if the individual then resigns from the board. Peer pressure may be the most effective way to keep the marginal employee or the less productive trustee in line. Thus, in regard to nonprofits, where contracts are often incomplete, the laws, informal rules, and conventions "that have evolved to cope with the resulting incentive problems favor interactions that are personal, strategic, durable and in which both norms and the exercise of power play important roles" (Bowles, 2004, pp. 257–258).

Figure 3.1 illustrates that the relationship between each stakeholder group and the organization involves expectations of mutual gratification. The arrows pointing toward the organization represent what is contributed to it; the arrows pointing toward the stakeholders show what is expected in return. Arguably, clients are the most important stakeholders for a social agency, as the reason for its existence, but many HSOs seem to ignore client needs in service delivery, resulting in a system that is overly bureaucratic and inflexible rather than holistic and accessible (Cohen, 2002). Due to a fairly recent trend in the nonprofit world toward viewing clients as customers or consumers, such a cavalier attitude may no longer be tenable. From this standpoint, quality becomes a higher priority, necessitating a basic change in the way staff members relate to those who use the organization's products and services to create a better fit between customer expectations and perceptions about services (Selber & Streeter, 2000).

A key to improving service quality is enhancing staff commitment to the organizational mission and goals. To achieve this, the CEO must develop and nurture a sense of shared values within an organizational culture that is supportive of them (Packard, 2001). Taken a step further, acceptance by staff of proposed changes, such as in service delivery, is tied to employees' identification with the leader's vision for the organization and his or her actions in furthering that vision (Jaskyte, 2004). In addition, it is important to recognize the impact on staff members of the turmoil in today's human service environment, and to find a way to meet the diverse needs of the contemporary workforce while encouraging the desired levels of productivity, efficiency, and effectiveness (Perlmutter, Bailey, & Netting, 2001).

The third critical internal stakeholder group for HSOs is the board of directors. Since the board will be dealt with in much greater depth in subsequent chapters, here it is sufficient to note that the motivations for board service are complex, ranging from the altruistic to more self-serving reasons. Board members, as representatives of the community, legitimize the organizational mission; in return they receive recognition and praise for their service, which are nonmonetary rewards but nonetheless have their own value. Even though the leadership responsibilities in nonprofits are shared in some kind of partnership between the board and the CEO, both research and practical experience suggest that it is the executive who bears the main burden for ensuring that the trustees fulfill their governance function (Herman & Heimovics, 1991).

Moving to external stakeholders, HSOs depend heavily on government but also foundations and corporations for financial support, with these sources representing as much as 75 percent of total income for many organizations (Young & Steinberg, 1995). Because nonprofits tend to rely on multiple funders, organizational leaders must learn how to manage the sometimes conflicting expectations of these diverse supporters for effective, efficient performance. More and more, government contracting has become a factor in the funding mix, bringing increased challenges that influence decision-making and sometimes negatively affect internal relationships (Smith & Lipsky, 1993). In recent years, another complication has been the growing competition for these same dollars from for-profit companies, which will be addressed in the next section of this chapter.

For this type of nonprofit there are two primary types of regulatory groups, those that give legal approval to programs and services and those that provide validation of the fulfillment of designated standards. For the most part, issues pertaining to health and safety as well as social welfare are state responsibilities, administered through a variety of government agencies either locally or statewide. States also license professions such as social work. Accreditation, on the other hand, is generally a voluntary action taken by the board and staff to ensure internal quality as measured against independently determined best practices for like organizations (Ginsberg, 2001).

Relationships with other nonprofits, the last external group, are complex, for these organizations may be allies and even collaborators, or, as just noted, competitors. In figure 3.1 the focus is on the partnership potential of these relationships, ideally with an expectation of a complementary exchange of resources. Management attitudes toward collaboration—the degree to which it is viewed as beneficial or disadvantageous to the organization—can affect the desire to engage in such practices as well as the extent of the resources committed to making these efforts successful (Foster & Meinhard, 2002). While funders and regulatory bodies may encourage collaboration as a means toward greater efficiency and effectiveness, these agreements tend to arise under specific environmental conditions; thus difficulty in adapting successfully to changing conditions may affect their long-term viability (Takahashi & Smutny, 2002).

Within the context of political-economy theory, all of these stakeholder groups have some degree of influence over organizational decision-making. We can view the board of directors as having positional power, regulatory agencies as having oversight authority, and funders, of course, as having the power of the checkbook. Staff can also exercise power by reflecting positively or negatively on the organization through their delivery of services; if unionized, staff can affect the economics of the organization by bargaining for higher salaries and more benefits. As for clients, those who have the wherewithal to pay for services certainly make a statement in their choice of a provider, but even those whose fees are covered through contracts or under insurance plans play an important role in how the organization is viewed within the community. Finally, the nature of the resources controlled by potential collaborators as well as the strength of their connections in the external political environment may determine whether they function as a full partner or in a lesser capacity in any joint ventures.

In this section, the emphasis has been on HSOs, but every not-for-profit must deal with the same basic constellation of stakeholders, although there may be some variations from one subsector to another from an economic and political perspective. For example, vendors are apt to be more of a factor in settings like hospitals in which technology is so critical to high-quality care. In many HSOs, volunteers help realize significant personnel cost savings, especially in times of financial uncertainty. In museums and other arts and culture organizations, members of auxiliaries have a long history of performing vital services, such as staffing the gift shop and reception desk, leading tours of the facility, and organizing fund-raisers. Additionally, they support the sponsoring organization via dues and direct monetary gifts. In return these insiders may get advance notice of new exhibits and free tickets to events along with public recognition of their contributions.

Bottom line: A careful assessment of the different groups with which an organization interfaces, keeping in mind the bilateral nature of stakeholder relationships, is the first step toward the development of a set of strategies that maximize the benefits and minimize any negative aspects of these interactions.

THE PERMEABILITY OF SECTOR BOUNDARIES

As discussed in chapter 1, we can identify three major sectors of society: government, for-profit, and nonprofit. It was also indicated that whereas the basic functions of government and businesses are fairly clear, to protect and promote the interests of the general public, and to return a profit to shareholders respectively, the role of nonprofits seems to be more difficult to categorize.

Part of the reason nonprofits fail to fit easily into a specific niche is the diversity of types of organizations and the activities they undertake, but another explanation lies in the complicated relationships that exist with the other two sectors. Sometimes nonprofits act as partners with government to realize social goals, but they can also become adversaries when their goals do not mesh. Similarly, nonprofits and for-profits function as both collaborators and competitors. One example of collaboration is the contributions nonprofit educational and research institutions have made to business through scientific breakthroughs that lead to new commercial products. Yet businesses now engage in head-to-head competition with voluntary organizations in service areas that, in the past, might have been seen as the purview of nonprofits, and vice versa—with hospitals and day-care provision examples of the former and state-of-the art fitness centers in YMCAs an example of the latter.

One of the more intriguing developments has been the movement of some corporations into the human services, in partnership with public sector agencies. An active player in this field is Affiliated Computer Services, Inc. (ACS), once a division of Lockheed Martin, the weapons manufacturer, and now part of Xerox. The company Web site delivers a seductive message:

> Many eligibility systems are antiquated and program managers want to know how to replace them without breaking the bank. And in many states, each health and human services program has its own eligibility system and processes, creating inef-

ficiencies. So states are looking to streamline processes and integrate programs to share information. ACS works with states to understand their stakeholders' needs. . . .We help states move away from a program-centered model to a client-centered model that focuses on desired social outcomes and creates a service delivery model that complements rather than competes with program goals toward self-sufficiency. (Retrieved April 26, 2010, http:/www-acs.inc.com/humanservices.aspx)

The not-so-subtle promise is that ACS can use its experience and know-how in business to realize the same kind of economic efficiencies for its government partners. ACS has been successful in obtaining contracts for welfare and workforce programs, with Texas and Florida its largest markets. Of course, this begs the question of whether efficiency should be the highest value when the lives of vulnerable people are at stake.

Interactions between Nonprofits and Government

Young's approach (2000) to categorizing the relationship between nonprofits and government in the United States is linked to economic theory. His analysis suggests three different lenses for viewing this relationship—supplementary, complementary, and adversarial—noting that each has seemed dominant in different historical periods but all three continue to be relevant. Table 3.1 presents the essence of his thesis.

The Supplementary Lens
From the supplementary perspective, nonprofits step in voluntarily as service providers when government has not been able to fulfill the demand because citizens vary so widely regarding the levels, qualities, and types of public goods they want and how much they are prepared to pay for them. This is the basic premise of the theory of government failure. In consideration of political norms, governments tend to be most responsive to a dominant group or to use the preferences of the average voter as a guide to a uniform

Table 3.1 Models of nonprofit-government relations in a political-economy context

Model	Economic theory	Dominant eras
Supplementary	Government failure	Late 19th century/early 20th century 1980s and 1990s 2000s?
Complementary	Public goods and transactions-costs	1960s and 1970s 1980s and 1990s 2000s?
Adversarial	Government failure and contract failure	Early 19th century 1950s–1970s 1990s 2000s?

Source: Adapted from Young, 2000.

provision of public goods, which means that citizens whose preferences differ from those of the average voter or who are not part of the dominant group will remain unsatisfied. Even though other potential solutions to this problem exist, for example, purchasing private-market goods, none is a perfect answer, leaving room for nonprofits to help fill the need. Young (2000) also points out that the involvement of private nonprofits likely will differ from one subsector to another. Where people's tastes vary widely, such as in the arts, nonprofit provision will tend to be high; in an area like public safety, citizen preferences may be more homogeneous, and thus nonprofits will be less active; and in the social services, provision of goods by nonprofits is apt to vary over time with the changes in what people want.

Table 3.1 illustrates that in different periods in the history of the United States, one or another of the three lenses has been a stronger factor (see chapter 2 of this book for a more detailed discussion of historical developments from colonial days to the present). In the late nineteenth century, when government care of the poor was widely considered inadequate, the number and types of voluntary organizations grew substantially. The supplementary view was again dominant in the early twentieth century, a time of relative passivity on the part of government, and once more during the 1980s and 1990s, in response to the policies initiated in the Reagan administration that favor a smaller federal government and place a greater burden on the private sector, with the steepest cutbacks in social welfare spending. As for the present, the belief that the private nonprofit sector can function effectively even with limited government support still seems to prevail.

The Complementary Lens

From the complementary perspective, nonprofits and government interact cooperatively in the provision of public services. According to Salamon (1995), who sees this arrangement as a logical, viable response to powerful political forces, "the . . . pattern of government-nonprofit partnership has much to recommend it, combining as it does the capacity to generate resources and set priorities through a democratic political process and the ability to deliver services through smaller, locally oriented, private nonprofit groups" (p. 198). Young (2000) offers both public goods and transactions-costs theory, the latter part of the larger economic theory of organizations, to explain the rationale behind the complementary lens. Under the first rubric, it is important to understand the phenomenon of "free riding." When there is an attempt to provide collective goods voluntarily, if the amount of the particular good is not finite and is available to all, there is no incentive for people to contribute to its provision or to pay for its consumption. One possible solution to this problem is to use peer pressure to make people feel guilty for their behavior, but another is coercion, as in the power of the state to tax. From this second option comes the idea of government financing public goods but not necessarily being directly involved in service delivery.

Transactions-costs theory helps explain why it may be more cost-effective for government to contract out services to private organizations, especially in light of the general perception that large bureaucracies are inefficient. The reality is that there will be costs associated with internal growth, even when justified, and it may actually be cheaper to increase service provision through an external source in the private sector with lower labor and production costs.

This same theory suggests two plausible reasons why government might prefer to deal with a private nonprofit rather than a business. First, to meet the preferences of its citizens, government may find nonprofits more advantageous because they are generally knowledgeable about the communities in which they are based and thus in a better position to offer services, within the limits of the contract, to fit local needs. Second, given that voluntary organizations do not operate from a profit motive as do businesses, they are much less likely to cut corners inappropriately. As a result, government may find it less expensive to monitor their performance and ensure that the agreed-upon services are being provided at the specified level and quality.

The complementary relationship between government and nonprofits seems to be more prevalent in industries such as the social services, where the problem of free riding is significant, where it would require a large bureaucracy to oversee direct public production, and "differences in local preferences favor some differentiation of services to alternative locales and consumer groups" (Young, 2000, p. 155). Young's observation seems on the mark when we note the historical periods identified in table 3.1 as strongly affected by this lens, the 1960s and 1970s, and the 1980s and 1990s. As the American welfare state began to take shape in the mid-twentieth century, the number of charitable nonprofits proliferated, to deliver not only human services but also cultural, educational, and health services, with government financing. In the 1980s and 1990s, privatization of public services was the dominant paradigm, even with the efforts of the federal government to control spending through cutbacks and managed care practices. Today, contracting continues to be a major income stream for many nonprofits.

The Adversarial Lens

The interactions between nonprofits and government from an adversarial perspective are reciprocal, in the sense that each party functions in different ways to influence the other's behavior. For example, nonprofits may advocate for changes in public policy or for more funding to provide services in response to an emerging need, and government can use its authority to place restrictions on advocacy efforts or increase its regulatory control over service delivery.

Young (2000) again presents two economic theories to clarify the adversarial relationship. Government failure theory is useful to understand how diverse racial and ethnic groups are able to make their voices heard and gain attention for their demands through collective action and savvy politicking despite the apparent lack of incentive on the part of government to entertain their concerns. Similarly, actions by nonprofits can spur government involvement in service areas that previously generated little or no interest. Demonstration projects funded through foundation grants can establish the viability of a particular approach to a problem and, when coupled with a well-designed campaign to increase public awareness and support, can put pressure on government to step in. The HIV/AIDS epidemic is a case in point. In the early 1980s, when this disease first emerged in a significant way, it was perceived as a problem primarily affecting the socially marginal (i.e., gays and minorities, especially those with limited resources). The direct response to the issue came from the nonprofit sector through the formation of new organizations, underwritten for the most part by individual contributions and foundation grants. However, by the early- to mid-1990s, the longer-term, broader impact of the epidemic, affecting the middle class, including women and children, as well as the original groups, was clearly recognized, leading to greater involvement by the federal government in funding and shaping services (Chambre & Fatt, 2002).

The theory of contract failure helps account for the other side of the adversarial equation, government efforts to oversee and regulate the behavior of nonprofits and even press for change. According to this theory, nonprofits become the provider of choice when consumers are unable to adequately evaluate the quality or quantity of a service, a condition known as *information asymmetry*. There are three distinct situations in which consumers are likely to be less well informed than sellers: (1) when a good or service is especially complex or technical, such as with health care, where one must rely on the expertise and judgment of the medical provider; (2) when a donor supports a worthy cause and must depend on the integrity of the recipient group to deliver the promised service; and (3) when someone purchases services on behalf of another, such as a mother seeking day care for a young child or an adult choosing a nursing home for an elderly, frail parent. For this last scenario, it may be difficult for the purchaser to determine whether the client, the child or the aged parent, is receiving the level of care negotiated with the provider (Young & Steinberg, 1995).

In such situations, whereas for-profits might be tempted to exploit consumers to their own advantage, voluntary organizations are considered less susceptible to contract failure and therefore more efficient because of the prohibition against individuals, staff or board members, profiting from any excess revenues (the nondistribution constraint). In addition, the nature of their internal governance structure, built on a model of shared leadership and an explicit commitment to a higher purpose, makes them more trustworthy since there is little incentive or opportunity to cheat consumers. Yet, government must still act to protect the interests of the general public, and this necessitates policing the behavior of providers, even nonprofits, to ensure they comply with all the conditions required of tax-exempt entities and do not violate the trust placed in them (Young, 2000).

Table 3.1 identifies three historical periods when the adversarial lens has seemed to dominate. In the early ninteenth century, although voluntary associations played a key role in the Northeast, public institutions were preferred in the West and South. Beginning in the 1950s and into the early 1970s, certain legislators took exception to the tax-exempt status of nonprofits, especially foundations. These efforts were effectively countered by the nonprofit sector through privately funded commissions. The 1960s and 1970s also were a time of protest against government policies by African Americans, women, and other groups experiencing discrimination. During the 1990s, antagonism toward nonprofits by some members of Congress was manifested through attempts to restrict advocacy. Now and into the future, we can expect nonprofits and government to engage in some form of adversarial behavior "for the simple reason that these parties independently pursue objects whose impacts are felt differently by the two parties" (Young, 2000, p. 157).

The Political Significance of Contracting

Contracting between government and nonprofits has been discussed in economic terms, but it is also important to consider the political ramifications of this so-called partnership, especially for human service organizations, which rely so heavily on public funding. From the perspective of some observers, this is not a relationship between equals; because government controls the purse strings, there is a power differential that can place nonprofit providers at a considerable disadvantage in terms of maintaining their autonomy. However, this perceived imbalance is often tempered in practice by market forces of supply and demand. In urban areas, where there may be a number of viable providers of, say, treatment for mental disorders, government is in a stronger position to dictate the conditions of the partnership than in more rural communities, where there may be only a single provider of the desired services.

In their seminal work on this topic, *Nonprofits for Hire*, Smith and Lipsky (1993) address the downside to contracting. For example, one prerogative of a private agency has been the freedom to determine who will be served and what services will be offered within the parameters of the organizational mission. Under the terms of a contract, since government operates from the principle of equity, the provider may be forced to accept all clients falling within a targeted group rather than those most compatible with its mission. Similarly, the nonprofit may be pressured to offer services of a certain kind and at a prescribed level rather than having the leeway to make a determination based on individual need. Funder expectations may also include demands for upgraded facilities and a larger, more professionalized staff, without offering the concomitant dollars to effect these changes. Moreover, contracting may alter the board-executive relationship by shifting authority to the latter as the primary link to the government agency, thereby diminishing the board's traditional oversight role. For clients, perhaps the biggest change is perceptual. Smith and Lipsky (1993) use the term *street-level bureaucrats* for the workers in the private agency, who become, from the consumer's viewpoint, the embodiment of the state. As a result, accountability is shifted away from government to the provider in the event of any dissatisfaction with the services received.

On the positive side, contracting can be the mechanism for a nonprofit to expand its services and client base, and although the continuity of government support can never be taken for granted, it is often the case that once having secured a contract, assuming no major problems with performance and an ongoing need for the organization's expertise, the provider can be reasonably assured of renewal from year to year, with the understanding that contract terms may well change over time. Brown and Troutt (2004) suggest it is possible to establish a long-term cooperative relationship between a nonprofit and a government funder when the contract is based on trust. This requires "a choice of attitude in which each contracting party acts according to the assumption that the parties share common goals, which makes supporting each other mutually beneficial" (p. 8).

Maintaining professional standards, reducing or eliminating transactions costs associated with both contract management and service delivery, establishing clear lines of communication and accountability, and focusing on a mission shared by all players are essential ingredients to achieving a successful partnership.

Interactions between Nonprofits and Business

As with government, the relationship between nonprofit organizations and for-profits can be adversarial, in the sense that there may be direct competition to provide various kinds of goods and services, but it can also be complementary, as when a corporation underwrites the costs for research conducted by an educational institution that leads to new product development, or supplementary, as when voluntary associations step in to provide certain collective goods, such as day care or transfused blood, to make up for inefficiencies in the private marketplace in the allocation of resources (Young & Steinberg, 1995). This last point is an illustration of market failure theory, the counterpart to government failure theory discussed in the previous section.

Abzug and Webb (1999) offer an analysis of the possible range of nonprofit/for-profit interactions by identifying seven stakeholder roles that nonprofits might fill. These include the *community watchdog group* that mobilizes around a particular interest, such as polluting the environment, in opposition to corporate policies perceived to be counterproductive; the *competitor*, whose tax-exempt status may allow for lower fees for the same product or service offered through a for-profit; the *customer*, acting as an educated consumer, individually or as part of a consortium, to secure the best price for desired commodities; *employees or managers*, organized through unions or professional associations to gain bargaining advantages; the *government contractor* that acts as an intermediary between a corporation and government, such as when a medical supply company deals with a nonprofit hospital or HMO regarding Medicare; *stockholders*, exercising their ownership rights on behalf of pension funds or endowment trusts; and *suppliers*, providing medical or educational services, for example, through contracting and other arrangements.

The Commercialization of Nonprofits

A persistent myth about nonprofit organizations is that private donations, from individuals, foundations, and corporations, represent the largest source of revenue. In fact, most nonprofit organizations have begun to rely on fees for service, product sales, property rentals, and other money-making activities as a significant part of their financial planning. Some observers have decried these practices, often referred to as the commercialization of the field, especially within human service agencies, as detracting from the intended purpose of voluntary organizations: "The nonprofit sector has swung far away from its voluntary base. . . . It has swung too far away from support by contributions and too far toward fees for service. It has swung too far away from principle and toward expediency" (Mason, 1996, p. 12).

Even though it may be understandable why people wax nostalgic about a time that, in large measure, is long gone, today's nonprofit leader must be prepared to address current realities in regard to obtaining needed resources. I learned this lesson many years ago on becoming executive director of a large Girl Scout council and discovering that the organization annually netted $1 million from its cookie sales, which was its primary revenue source and paid for the majority of troop activities as well as covering management expenses at headquarters. The evidence that this was big business came from the formal cookie tastings, organized by each bakery approved by our parent body, which determined who would receive the highly coveted contract to provide our product. Imagine a group of women sitting around a conference table solemnly munching on six different varieties of cookie and then cleansing their palates in order to repeat the process for the other two contenders. Whatever initial amusement value the ritual had was quickly replaced by an appreciation of the importance of this income stream to the organization's financial security. Pressure on nonprofits to be more businesslike in their operations now comes from both internal and external stakeholders.

Until quite recently there was only a vague sense of what it meant to behave in a businesslike way in a nonprofit setting. With an in-depth qualitative study of a Canadian nonprofit, Dart (2004) developed a typology to give more clarity to the term and increase understanding of the impact of this approach on a human service organization. There are four distinct elements that can be associated with nonprofit businesslike behavior: (1) program goals congruent with pro-social values but framed in the context of revenue generation, profit, or financial surplus; (2) service delivery structured in ways consistent with commonly recognized ideas of businesses and business planning, such as focusing the provision of services on core competencies to increase volume; (3) a strong entrepreneurial approach to running the organization, as evidenced by decentralizing overall responsibility for programs to the individual managers; and (4) the generalized use of business terminology even in contexts not directly connected to business-related matters. This research suggests that behaving in a businesslike manner need not be incompatible with broadly recognized nonprofit mandates to serve the public, as long as the strategies adopted remain consistent with the organizational mission.

The issue of nonprofits competing with for-profits has been controversial, perhaps due to a lack of understanding of the nature of the competition. The heart of the matter is "whether they compete head-on by providing the same kinds of services to the same kinds of clients or occupy a different niche within a given industry" (Young & Steinberg, 1995, p. 26). For the most part, the commercial activities engaged in by nonprofits are closely related to their missions and involve activities that would be of little interest to businesses because they are unprofitable; legal services for the poor is a good example. In mixed industries, meaning that both sectors are active, sometimes nonprofits and for-profits occupy different niches. With regard to day-care centers, for instance, information asymmetry may lead consumers experiencing difficulty in assessing the quality of the services to choose a nonprofit, while the better informed, choose a for-profit provider. This arrangement is efficient from an economist's perspective. In other industries, like hospitals, the two appear to compete head-to-head for the same customers. Despite evidence suggesting nonprofits offer slightly different services than for-profits in such cases, competition may make it more difficult for a nonprofit to offer the level of public benefit (care for the uninsured and so on) it might otherwise provide (Young & Steinberg, 1995).

However, when nonprofits engage in activities an outsider might view as somewhat peripheral to their missions, it can raise concerns in the community, especially from the smaller businesses with which they complete directly, that the tax advantage they enjoy is unfair (Gibelman, 2003; Young & Steinberg, 1995). To some readers, it may come as a surprise that something as well established as Girl Scout cookie sales has been legally challenged by certain state attorneys-general on this basis, with the intent to apply the federal Unrelated Business Income Tax (UBIT), which is similar to the corporate income tax, to the dollars raised. Thus far, the Girl Scouts have prevailed by demonstrating that this program teaches participants responsibility and leadership skills and is therefore directly related to the organizational purpose. On the other hand, certain nonprofits, especially larger organizations, consciously decide to engage in commercial endeavors unrelated to their missions, knowing the profits from these ventures will be subject to UBIT. An example here would be a human service organization that owns a piece of land and turns it into a parking lot with spaces rented at the going market rate. Nonprofits may also create for-profit subsidiaries to finance their charitable work, and a few even elect to give up their tax-exempt status to become for-profits, due to economic incentives or because they feel they will be more able to accomplish their missions.

Collaboration between Nonprofits and For-Profits

To balance the ledger, it is important to note the many instances of collaboration between nonprofits and businesses. Two illustrations mentioned earlier in this chapter are research undertaken by educational institutions funded by corporations that leads to the development of new products, and services supplied by nonprofits to for-profits on a contractual basis, such as operating the employee assistance program. By the same token, nonprofits buy goods and services from for-profits, which may be of particular benefit to smaller, local businesses. Moreover, a nonprofit with a government contract may choose to subcontract part of the work to a for-profit.

Operating from the perspective of social responsibility and sometimes enlightened self-interest, corporations provide financial support to not-for-profit organizations through grants, in-kind contributions, and matching-gifts programs, a topic that will be explored in much greater detail in a later chapter. On a more personal level, for-profits may loan staff to nonprofits on a temporary basis to provide assistance in technical areas such as upgrading the computer system or improving financial management procedures. For example, it is common in many communities for one or more loaned executives to assist the local United Way during its annual workplace campaign. Additionally, mid- and upper-level managers and executives often agree to serve as board members of nonprofit organizations, bringing expertise in many vital areas as well as useful connections to human and material resources. Finally, representatives of both for-profits and nonprofits may be invited to participate in a joint effort convened by a government agency or an elected official to address a pressing social problem at the local, regional, state, or even national level.

FINAL THOUGHTS

Since the downturn in the economy that began in 2008, resulting in major losses by some of the most well-regarded corporations in America, such as General Electric and General Motors, it remains to be seen whether this will silence those pushing for nonprofits to emulate the for-profit sector. One possible outcome may be that the blurring of the boundaries between the sectors will become even greater, with more businesses exploring the opportunities to be realized from moving into service areas generally associated with charitable organizations. Perhaps the tables will be turned, and for-profits will seek to learn from the most successful nonprofits how to implement what Mason (1996) calls expressive-assisted instrumentality (p. 286), which refers to the process of enabling organizational members to live their values to achieve a desired end. Or it may be the right moment for some modern-day equivalent to John D. Rockefeller III to underwrite a special commission to explore ways to better society as a whole, this time involving representatives from all three sectors working together toward this common goal by making the most of their respective talents and strengths.

Discussion Questions for Section 1

Chapter 1

1. All charitable organizations are nonprofits, but not all nonprofits are charities. What is the significance of this statement to our understanding of the nonprofit sector?

Chapter 2

2. If you could interview any historical figure who contributed to the development of the U.S. nonprofit sector, who would you choose, and why? What three questions would you most like to ask him or her?

3. How do you account for the varying perceptions of the human service subsector from colonial days to the present?

Chapter 3

4. Wernet (1994) maintains that "resources are . . . the crucial link for operation and survival. . . . Organizations change only when there is a significant shift in resources." (p. 95). Do you agree or disagree with his statement as it pertains to nonprofit organizations? Support your position.

5. The Filer Commission's recommendation in the late 1970s to establish within the Treasury Department a permanent agency on charitable nonprofits was not implemented. If you could create such an agency now, what would be its most important responsibilities and constituencies? On what basis did you formulate these conclusions?

6. A social agency based in a midwestern city that provides rehabilitation services to the mentally ill has an annual budget of $80 million, mostly through fulfilling government contracts. Is an organization of this magnitude an aberration or a sign of progress for the nonprofit sector? Justify your opinion.

SELECTED READINGS FOR SECTION 1

Chapter 1

Greenfield, J. M. (1999). *Fund raising: Evaluating and managing the fund development process* (2nd ed.). New York: Wiley.

Grobman, G. M. (2004). *An introduction to the nonprofit sector: A practical approach for the twenty-first century.* Harrisburg, PA: White Hat Communications.

Internal Revenue Service. (2009). *Tax information for charities and other non-profits.* Retrieved May 6, 2010, from http://www.irs.gov/charities

O'Neill, M. (2002). *Nonprofit nation: A new look at the third America.* San Francisco: Jossey-Bass.

Chapter 2

Cass, R. H., & Manser, G. (1983). Roots of voluntarism [Excerpt from *Voluntarism at the crossroads*]. In B. O'Connell (Ed.), *America's voluntary spirit* (pp. 11–22). New York: Foundation Center.

Gronbjerg, K. A. (2001). The U.S. nonprofit human service sector: A creeping revolution. *Nonprofit and Voluntary Sector Quarterly, 30,* 276–297.

Hall, P. D. (1994). Historical perspectives on nonprofit organizations. In R. D. Herman (Ed.), *The Jossey-Bass handbook of nonprofit leadership and management* (pp. 3–43). San Francisco: Jossey-Bass.

Hammack, D. C. (2001). Introduction: Growth, transformation and quiet revolution in the nonprofit sector over two centuries. *Nonprofit and Voluntary Sector Quarterly, 30,* 157–173.

Jansson, B. S. (2005). *The reluctant welfare state: American social welfare policies; Past, present and future* (5th ed.). Belmont, CA: Brooks/Cole.

Salamon, L. M. (1999). *America's nonprofit sector: A primer* (2nd ed.). New York: Foundation Center.

Chapter 3

Abzug, R., & Webb, N. J. (1999). Relationships between nonprofit and for-profit organizations: A stakeholder's perspective. *Nonprofit and Voluntary Sector Quarterly, 28,* 416–431.

Dart, R. (2004). Being "business-like" in a nonprofit organization: A grounded and inductive typology. *Nonprofit and Voluntary Sector Quarterly, 33,* 290–310.

National Association of Social Workers. (2006). Managed care. In *Social work speaks: National Association of Social Workers Policy Statements, 2006–2009* (7th ed., pp. 260–265). Washington, DC: NASW Press.

Salamon, L. M. (1995). *Partners in public service.* Baltimore: Johns Hopkins University Press.

Smith, S. R., & Lipsky, M. (1993). *Nonprofits for hire: The welfare state in the age of contracting.* Cambridge, MA: Harvard University Press.

Wernet, S. P. (1994). A case study of adaptation in a nonprofit human service organization. *Journal of Community Practice, 1*(3), 93–112.

Young, D. R. (2000). Alternative models of government-nonprofit relations: Theoretical and international perspectives. *Nonprofit and Voluntary Sector Quarterly, 29,* 149–172.

Young, D. R., & Steinberg, R. (1995). *Economics for nonprofit managers.* New York: Foundation Center.

SECTION 2
Leading in Turbulent Times

Building on the background material presented in section 1, this section explores the concepts associated with leadership as well as its manifestation in the typical nonprofit organization operating in today's challenging environment. The case study featured throughout this book begins here. The first part of the case will serve as a reference point for the theoretical and practical matters addressed in chapters 4 to 7.

Chapter 4 identifies the different theories developed over the years to explain leadership and discusses their practical implications. It also introduces the model of shared leadership, between a paid chief professional officer and a voluntary board of directors, that is common in a great many nonprofits, along with some variations. Within this framework, the relationship between the top professional and the board is delineated.

Chapter 5 puts professional leadership in context by presenting in some detail the concept of organizational culture, which both shapes and is shaped by the organizational leader. This discussion leads logically to an examination of the multidimensional nature of the CEO position and its diverse responsibilities.

Chapter 6 focuses on what many view as the quintessential responsibility of a leader, decision-making, with a detailed account of the different considerations and approaches to the decision process. I introduce a versatile tool for both group and individual decision-making and illustrate its use.

Chapter 7 acknowledges the reality that organizational change is now a constant factor in nonprofit organizational life and that the process of change is influenced by the organizational culture, the quality of leadership, and the demands of the external environment. I identify and evaluate strategies for effecting change.

KEY THEMES

Chapters 4 to 7 address these topics and concerns.

- The construct and reality of leadership: What are the chief attributes and indicators of an effective leader?
- The joint responsibility for nonprofit governance: What factors contribute to a successful board-executive relationship?

- The link between organizational culture and organizational actions: How is overt organizational behavior shaped by deep-seated assumptions and practices, especially those espoused by top leaders?
- The complexity of the CEO position in nonprofit organizations: Can we identify explicit circumstances under which a CEO would choose to function as a leader, a manager, or an administrator?
- The challenges in making the "right" decisions: How can the often competing expectations of organizational stakeholders best be addressed?
- The mechanisms of organizational change: How do effective nonprofit leaders cope with environmental uncertainty?

Conflicting Agendas for the Future of a Youth Agency, Part 1

Having avoided self-scrutiny for most of its sixty-year history, a youth agency is forced to take a hard look at its future when finances begin to decline. The executive director and the board president hold differing views on the appropriate course of action, and the reader is asked to decide which position is in the best interests of the organization.

It was the night before the September meeting of the board of directors of the Youth Services Network (YSN), a midsized social agency providing educational and recreational programs to youth in a major metropolitan area. Margaret Stover, YSN's executive director, was trying to fall asleep with little success. Thoughts of the next day's meeting kept intruding. How would the board react to the strategic planning committee's report? How would the latest financial report, which projected a substantial deficit for the fiscal year unless the reserves were tapped, affect the discussion? While she was already on record as being in favor of the committee's recommendations, should she adopt an active or a passive role in the debate?

The situation had become more complicated after the phone call she received earlier in the day from Sal de Marco, the board president. Stover had been disappointed when de Marco had declined to serve on the strategic planning committee due to his business obligations, but she had accepted his explanation at face value and had made every effort to keep him informed about the deliberations. During the last several months as the committee was meeting, de Marco had been noncommittal about YSN's future, which was surprising in view of his long association with the organization. Whenever Stover had pressed him for some kind of reaction to the minutes of the committee meetings or to the preliminary findings that had been distributed prior to the June board meeting, his only response was "Let's let the process proceed." Today, however, de Marco had informed her that he did not feel he could support the committee's recommendations and was preparing a statement to present to the board. Judging by the cool tone of his voice, Stover deduced that de Marco's statement would not only find fault with the report but also be less than complimentary of her.

How had their relationship, which had seemed so strong when she was hired, deteriorated to the point that they were this far apart on such a critical issue?

History of YSN

YSN is a nonsectarian, not-for-profit organization providing camping, educational, social, recreational, and cultural programs and services to young people ages six to twenty-four in a major northeastern metropolitan area. As articulated in its mission statement, "the purpose of the organization is to improve and further the well-being and happiness of boys and girls who participate in its activities by helping them develop needed skills, a system of personal values, and a sense of self-worth in order to meet the challenges of the present and future, and to become productive, constructive members of society."

YSN was founded in 1946 by Trevor Clinton, who envisioned an organization that would use recreation as an incentive for engaging boys in positive activities to help prevent juvenile delinquency. At first, programs were provided at several storefront recreation centers scattered around the city. A few years later, an overnight camping program was started at a nearby state park. In the mid-1970s YSN entered into an agreement with the local housing authority to operate community centers in housing projects. Early on, the organization began to organize citywide tournaments for various sports, notably track and field and boxing, which generated considerable publicity and attracted the attention and support of major sports figures. Although girls participated in certain activities almost from the beginning, they were not fully incorporated into YSN's programs until the late 1980s.

YSN's founder was something of a visionary in securing financial support for the organization. Drawing on his connections in the sports world, Clinton put together one of the first direct mail campaigns on behalf of a nonprofit and, interestingly enough, sent solicitations playing on the theme of preventing juvenile delinquency to a national mailing list rather than confining the effort to the immediate area. This approach proved to be very successful; it generated virtually all of the organization's operating money for most of its history and also yielded numerous bequests over the years, allowing YSN to develop a modest portfolio of investments.

For close to fifty years—first as executive director and then as a member of the board—Clinton dominated the organization. For the initial board of directors he selected friends and acquaintances, who were expected to rubber-stamp his decisions, and maintained further control by not having rotational terms. The rare vacancies were filled by personal friends or business acquaintances of the current members, with all selections subject to Clinton's final approval. In recent years the board has included second-generation family members of the original trustees and a few former program participants. Election of the first woman board member occurred in the mid-1980s.

When Clinton retired as executive, he named his associate director as the second CEO. No other candidates were considered. The new executive's main attributes were his loyalty to the founder and the personal relationships he had developed with certain board members. Clinton also installed his son as YSN's director of development and director of camping and arranged that his son would report directly to the board, of which the founder was now a member. This unusual supervisory arrangement continued even after Clinton's death in 1994.

In 2000 the second executive director was forced to resign due to illness. As the third executive director the board selected an individual whose athleticism seemed to

Table C.1 Board profile ($N = 18$)

Gender		Occupation	
Male	14	Accountant	2
Female	4	Banker	2
Ethnicity		Corporate executive	2
Caucasian	15	Financial consultant	4
African American	3	Government employee	2
Age		Insurance executive	2
41–50	4	Nonprofit manager	1
51–60	9	Small business owner	2
Over 60	5	Travel writer	1
Years of service			
1–5	4		
6–10	3		
11–19	5		
Over 20	6		

embody the very essence of the organization's mission. Although the new executive had limited senior management experience, the search committee believed his knowledge of fiscal monitoring, gained during his previous work at United Way, would be a major advantage.

The new CEO soon noticed serious irregularities in the way the direct mail campaign was being managed. In fact, the evidence showed that the founder's son had been defrauding YSN for several years for his personal gain. Faced with this information, the board had no choice but to ask the founder's son to resign, and, on the advice of legal counsel, initiated a lawsuit against him. As a group, board members felt a certain amount of discomfort in having to assume a more traditional governing role. But for a number of longtime members whose fondness for the late founder still ran deep, the legal action was very painful indeed. Even though these members understood the necessity for the lawsuit, both to restore YSN's good name and to demonstrate their own fiduciary responsibility as trustees, they were unable to separate the "message" from the "messenger" and consequently never forgave the executive director for forcing them into such a difficult position.

In the second year of his tenure, the executive director inadvertently offended a powerful trustee, a former board president who had had a particularly close relationship with the previous CEO and was now serving as chair of the finance committee. When this individual returned to active service following major surgery, he accused the executive of withholding important negative financial information from other members of the finance committee during his absence. After two more years, the third executive resigned, worn down by the finance chair's constant sniping, continuing fallout from the direct mail scandal, and YSN's deteriorating fiscal position.

Toward the end of 2004, a search committee was formed, chaired by Sal de Marco. A relatively new board member, he was the nephew of a former YSN senior staff member and had himself been a program participant. Initially, a male candidate proposed by the second CEO through his remaining friends on the board appeared to be the front runner. However, the final choice was Margaret Stover, who had extensive prior experience as a nonprofit executive. In announcing the board's decision, de Marco said, "We selected the best person for the job, one whose proven skills in organizational development, long-range planning, and fiscal management, along with a background in community center work and camping, offer the right combination to provide the kind of leadership YSN needs to move steadily forward."

Leadership was exactly what YSN needed, especially since the third executive director, drawn into crisis management, had had little opportunity to address long-term issues. The new competitive environment for nonprofits demanded careful planning and informed decisions by both the CEO and the board. Stover faced the challenge of dealing with an organization that had been rudderless for some time.

The Nature of Leadership

Leadership is one of those terms many people have attempted to define, each putting a slightly different spin on the matter. Most of us believe we know a good leader when we see one, and can often provide concrete examples of behavior to support our judgment. Yet, one person's admirable boss may be another's epitome of a tyrant. This subjectivity in determining who is worthy of following is an important component of any discussion on leadership, for leaders, in practice, cannot exist without followers. It is also important to consider the past as well as the current political and economic conditions, both internally and externally, of an organization, or a nation, to understand why a particular leadership style may prevail or fall out of favor at a certain point in time.

Leadership in a nonprofit is typically a responsibility shared by a paid professional, with the title of executive director, president, CEO, or some other variant, and a board of directors, a group of community volunteers of a size, composition, and expertise as specified in the organizational bylaws. Some observers of the relationship between the two halves of the *leadership core* (my term) have characterized it as a partnership, although not necessarily between equals. Others believe that either the executive or the board does or should dominate. There is also disagreement on the particulars. Carver (1990), for instance, maintains that a board of more than seven people is counterproductive and that it should use standing committees sparingly if at all, and then only to help create policy. However, in a study of four boards, the most effective, efficient one had forty-four members and twelve working committees meeting on a regular basis and assuming a broad range of responsibilities, some of which, such as reviewing case files, would be strictly staff functions in other settings (Golensky, 1994).

This chapter, in addressing questions of leadership both in a general sense and in the way a nonprofit is led, will help the reader begin to understand why leaders make certain decisions and take particular actions, and the impact of the setting on these deliberations.

THE MEANING OF LEADERSHIP

To define the term *leadership*, one obvious starting point would be a standard dictionary. The eleventh edition of *Merriam-Webster's Collegiate Dictionary* (2003), for example, tells us this is the capacity to lead and that a *leader* can be a guide or conductor, someone who "has commanding authority or influence." In turn, the verb *to lead* offers several useful descriptors: (1) "to direct the operations, activity, or performance" of an entity; (2) "to have charge of" something; (3) "to go at the head"; (4) "to be first in or among"; and (5) "to guide someone or something along a way."

The definition of leadership also seems to vary, at least in emphasis, by the type of organization. In a business setting, a leader may be seen as someone who is able to bring higher levels of performance out of others, beyond what these individuals would normally achieve on their own (Anderson, 1984). For a social agency, as one might expect, a higher purpose may be articulated: "A leader helps communities of people take risks and envision a better future for themselves, encourages commitment, and helps people move ahead along a path to accomplish their goals" (Brueggemann, 1996, p. 73). Here, instead of focusing primarily on productivity, the leader assumes more of an enabling role in order to help those reporting to her or him attain goals that are implied to be mutually desirable. However, as Gummer reminds us in his classic 1980 piece on organization theory, self-interest is a strong motivating force in every work setting. The central thesis of what he calls the power-politics model is that concerns over resources, especially their availability and distribution, and about securing one's place in the organizational hierarchy dictate individual actions and interactions. The implications of these observations for how one leads will be explored more fully in the next chapter.

Power, Authority, and Influence

The various definitions of leadership all seem to include some common elements. One of these is power, which in and of itself offers little by way of a clear or precise explanation of social interactions but does point us toward a better understanding of interpersonal relationships through its primary manifestations, authority and influence. Authority is virtually synonymous with legitimacy and flows downward. Influence, on the other hand, is more dynamic, can vary in degree, and is multidirectional (Bacharach & Lawler, 1980). In other words, when we talk about power as a social phenomenon, it has a latent quality. Thus we tend to recognize power when it is applied through persuasion, to convince others to accept certain ideas, beliefs, or decisions, or through the formal use of one's position or title to make decisions then conveyed to others as expected actions.

This perspective is reflected in French and Raven's typology of the bases of social power (1959): "We define power in terms of influence, and influence in terms of psychological change" (p. 150). Noting that it is not so much a question of how much influence one party (the CEO perhaps) may exercise to obtain a desired result from another (such as a subordinate) but of how much could be exerted (the maximum potential), the authors identify five specific bases of power (Anderson, 1984, p. 225).

1. *Reward power.* The ability to give valued rewards (money, praise, promotion) to subordinates.

2. *Coercive power.* The ability to give punishments (demotions, reprimands, pay cuts) to subordinates.

3. *Legitimate power.* The "right" to demand compliance because of position or title.

4. *Expert power.* The use of superior knowledge, expertise, or skills to achieve compliance.

5. *Referent power.* Personal identification with the "agent of influence" and the desire to gain this person's approval (cited in Anderson, 1984, p. 225).

Some additional sources of power that seem especially pertinent for a leader in a modern organization include the ability to cope successfully with uncertainty, expertise in the use of technology, control over knowledge and information, effective management of workforce diversity, and control of scarce resources (Morgan, 1986).

Theories of Leadership

Over the years, many theories of leadership have been advanced, which can be classified into three approaches. *Trait* theories emphasize the physical and psychological characteristics of the individual. *Behavioral* theories focus on the actions that set a leader apart from other organizational members. Finally, *situational* or *contingency* theories attempt to capture the specific characteristics of the situation, including those pertaining to the followers or subordinates as well as the context in which the situation occurs, that enable one person to be effective when another would not be (Anderson, 1984; Brueggemann, 1996). Table 4.1 identifies some of the major research efforts in each of the three categories.

Table 4.1 Theories of leadership

Approach	*Research directions*
Trait	Hereditary factors
	Personal factors
	Personality and performance
Behavioral	Performance and attitudes
	Task- vs. person-centered
	Theories X, Y, and Z
Situational or contingency	Continuum of leadership behavior
	Contingency theory
	Life-cycle theory
	Path-goal theory
	Leadership-participation theory

Sources: Adapted from Anderson, 1984; Brueggemann, 1996; Hollander, 1978; Van Fleet & Yukl, 1989.
Note: The areas of research listed in this table reflect the major schools of thought regarding leadership, rather than specific studies. However, some of the items are identifiable as the work of individual researchers, as noted in the text.

The Trait Approach

The first studies, beginning just before and continuing into the early years of the twentieth century, saw leadership as relatively constant, something that could be traced to innate traits such as height, weight, intelligence, and appearance, in what we might call the "leader is born not made" school of thought. As Anderson (1984) notes, the simplicity of this approach has considerable appeal, for if it were possible to isolate the traits of a leader, say, if it could be proved that these individuals are consistently brighter than others or are more likely to have blue eyes, then leadership selection would be very straightforward. Most of the earliest research supported the general belief that leadership could be traced to hereditary factors (Hollander, 1978), which made sense at a time when the majority of people in such positions were white males from wealthy families and social norms existed as to what a leader looked like (tall, square-jawed, and so on). Although this viewpoint has been largely discredited, having a surname such as Rockefeller, Kennedy, or Bush still seems to confer certain advantages.

As efforts continued to relate physical and personal factors to both becoming and being a successful leader, the only measure seemingly with some merit was intelligence. For instance, a 1959 review by Mann of 125 studies of the relationship between personality and leadership, representing over 700 findings, showed that in 46 percent of the cases, intelligence was positively associated with leader status. More significantly, from all of these published reports, it became clear that other variables, especially the situation and group members' expectations, had to be considered as well to determine successful leadership performance (as discussed in Hollander, 1978).

Today we continue to use traits historically associated with leadership as a way to gauge the personal strengths and weaknesses of prospective executives and other senior managers, albeit with a focus on somewhat more sophisticated behaviors, like the capacity to organize data in meaningful ways or the ability to interact effectively with peers (Anderson, 1984). Yet even with better techniques, this approach can have mixed results, as shown in a study of a social agency's process to select a new CEO (Golensky, 2008). As a first step, the board developed a profile of the desired attributes, knowledge, and skills for the position, resulting in a list of sixty qualities then used to formulate the questions for applicants. Although it was suggested the candidates also be asked to articulate how they would resolve typical situations they might encounter on the job, this was not done. On paper, the person chosen seemed to be a wonderful fit for the organization, but subsequently she revealed herself to be highly controlling and has systematically altered the composition of the board to tilt the balance of power strongly in her favor. While there is no evidence thus far to suggest the organization has become less effective, it has lost one of its most valuable resources as independent-minded trustees have been replaced by individuals all too willing to follow the executive's lead.

The Behavioral Approach

When it became clear that traits alone were insufficient indicators of leadership ability, researchers began to study the actual behaviors exhibited in work settings. As shown in table 4.1, these studies tended to classify the leader's actions according to an emphasis either on the task or on individual needs, based on the recognition that every effective group requires someone to fulfill both instrumental and expressive roles (Anderson, 1984). The first major research program, conducted in the late 1930s at the University of Iowa, investigated leadership styles. The conclusions were that group performance and attitudes were least positive under the laissez-faire or permissive style, attitudes were best with the democratic or participatory leader, and performance was highest with the autocratic or directive leader. However, the researchers also found that when the leader left the room, there was no real change under the laissez-faire and democratic leaders, but under the autocratic leader, performance deteriorated significantly, suggesting that using majority-rule decision-making and similar methods produced a more desirable outcome over time (Van Fleet & Yukl, 1989).

The second important effort, called the Ohio State studies, divided behavior affecting motivation and performance into two categories, initiating structure and consideration. Planning, coordinating, and directing were some of the managerial behaviors in the first category; friendliness, recognizing others' contributions, being thoughtful, and so on demonstrated consideration. The general findings supported the hypothesis on the need for the two types of behavior but also showed considerable style variations from leader to leader, with most exhibiting mixed task/relationship behaviors (Brueggemann, 1996). About the same time, another group of researchers was studying similar phenomena at the University of Michigan, under the direction of Rensis Likert. They found being sensitive to employees' personal concerns and setting high group performance standards were the keys to effective leadership (Van Fleet & Yukl, 1989). Building on these research outcomes, in 1964 Robert R. Blake and Jane S. Mouton created the Managerial Grid (now known as the Leadership Grid), labeling the horizontal axis "Concern for Production" and the vertical axis "Concern for People," to chart behaviors. For example, the 5.5 leader, at the midpoint of the scale on both dimensions, would probably achieve satisfactory results. Training instruments still used today were developed from the model. Although under the right conditions, any of the orientations might be acceptable, 9.9, the high-relationship/high-task-orientation style, is viewed as the best combination (Anderson, 1984; Brueggemann, 1996).

Before concluding the discussion on the behavioral approach to leadership, we need to consider the work of Douglas McGregor, who in *The Human Side of Enterprise*, written in 1960, proposed his Theory X and Theory Y. The first, focusing on the task and taking a very negative, closed perspective, assumes workers must be coerced, controlled, or threatened to be productive. On the other hand, Theory Y is optimistic and open about employees, postulating that they are eager to work and to accept responsibility. Here people are seen as having the capacity for self-direction, so rewarding them for their achievements brings greater commitment. While McGregor stated that the two theories were not polar opposites, this is often how they have been perceived, and many observers have drawn the conclusion that adopting Theory Y can be equated with good leadership. More recently, Japanese management practices, which emphasize group decision-making and a holistic concern for workers, have received considerable attention in the United States and elsewhere, because they appear to lead to high productivity and dedication to the organization. This approach has been labeled Theory Z, and is viewed as a middle ground of sorts between Theories X and Y (Anderson, 1984; Brueggemann, 1996).

Situational or Contingency Theories

A problem associated with both trait and behavioral research has been the difficulty in applying the findings satisfactorily to different leadership situations. Fred Fiedler, for one, struggled from 1951 to 1966 to verify the relationship between the people and task orientations before concluding the two are not constants applying to all groups. The situation was seen as the missing variable accounting for why one style might work well with certain groups but be dysfunctional with others. His contingency theory posits that "leadership . . . should vary depending on nonleadership variables, such as needs of the group and its climate" (Brueggemann, 1996, p. 79). However, because Fiedler believed both leadership style and the group situation were static, he maintained it would be easier to find situations that fit the leader's style rather than expecting him or her to adapt. Unfortunately, he was not able to demonstrate which groups would best match a specific leadership style (Brueggemann, 1996).

The earliest work in this area was produced by Robert Tannenbaum and Warren Schmidt in 1958. They developed a model defining a continuum of leadership behavior to reflect different combinations of control and freedom regarding decisions by group members, ranging from the situation in which a manager makes a decision and simply announces it to the group to the other extreme, where a considerable amount of latitude is given to subordinates to participate in the decision process. The choice of which leadership style to select depends on the individual's personality and values as well as the subordinates' psychological needs and abilities and the organization's values, traditions, and culture. Most important, what the leader wants to accomplish will inform this decision. For example, if the goal is to improve teamwork, a participative style would be warranted, whereas in a crisis when a quick decision must be made, a more directive approach would be appropriate (Anderson, 1984).

In 1969 Paul Hersey and Kenneth H. Blanchard put forth the life cycle leadership model, which agreed with Fiedler that the leader's behavior is based on that of the followers but differed by assuming that leadership is not fixed. The leader makes adjustments according to the followers' readiness or maturity level in performing specific tasks. As maturity increases, the leader should decrease task-oriented behaviors and increase relationship-oriented behaviors until a moderate work level is achieved, at which point both types of behavior taper off to allow for more self-direction (Anderson, 1984; Brueggemann, 1996). Around the same time, Robert House proposed the path-goal theory. With this approach, the leader motivates subordinates by increasing the rewards for good performance and providing the means for staff to fulfill their work goals. In other words, a kind of exchange occurs between the leader and followers: If subordinates see a link between high productivity and their personal goals (financial payoffs, job satisfaction, and so on) and the leader is making the "path" to these goals clearer and easier to attain, they are more likely to be higher producers. The two key variables are the personal characteristics of group members and the work environment (Anderson, 1984; Van Fleet & Yukl, 1989).

The last research to be discussed builds on the work of Tannenbaum, Schmidt, and others on the democratic or participative leadership style. Frank A. Heller, first with Gary Yukl and then independently, developed a descriptive approach to this topic, concluding that (1) leaders perceive that subordinates require more time to learn how to make decisions than leaders do; (2) when leaders believe there is a large difference between their skills and those of subordinates, they are more likely to be autocratic; and (3) the amount of participation used is influenced by the manager's organizational level. Going one step farther, Victor Vroom and Phillip Yetton took a normative perspective on the most appropriate degree of participation. Their model starts with a decision tree that poses a series of questions about different situations the leader might face in a given setting. The responses to these questions yield an analysis of the situational elements, so that the feasibility of using less or more participation can be determined. For the final step, the choice is between short-term pressures such as the need to meet a deadline and longer-term considerations (staff development, for one). In the first instance, the leader is more apt to adopt an autocratic style, but the second case would favor participative decision-making. An important factor throughout this process is decision effectiveness, based on both the quality of the decision and its acceptance by the followers (Van Fleet & Yukl, 1989).

A SHARED LEADERSHIP MODEL

As noted at the beginning of the chapter, in most nonprofit organizations, leadership is a responsibility shared by a chief professional officer, however titled, and a board of directors made up of community volunteers, with *community* defined by the organizational jurisdiction as a local, regional, state, national, or international entity. In the business world, one finds what may seem to be a similar model, but there is a critical difference: a corporate CEO is also a board member, very often serves as board chair, and generally has a great deal of overt influence on the selection of the remaining board members. In recent times, with the greater focus on accountability, some corporations have elected to appoint a nonexecutive board chair, but this is the exception rather than the rule. For nonprofits it is much rarer to allow the executive director to vote on policy matters, although some larger organizations do list the executive as a board officer. In the public sector many agencies and bureaus have governing boards as well; however, covering their similarities to and differences from boards in the private, voluntary sector is beyond the scope of this book.

We now take a closer look at the roles and responsibilities of the nonprofit board as stated in the prescriptive literature, while addressing how actual performance seems to diverge from these norms. The next section delineates the structural and interpersonal relationship between the two halves of the leadership core. In chapter 15 the nuts and bolts of forming and maintaining a high-functioning board will be the focus, but here the intent is to establish a basic level of understanding about governance as it is exercised in the nonprofit world.

Defining Governance

Houle (1989) views the term *governing* as multifaceted, encompassing authority, control, responsibility, and, in many settings, prestige. The definition of the verb *to govern* in *Merriam-Webster's Collegiate Dictionary* (2003) has a similar emphasis but adds that this authority is especially for the purpose of directing the making and administration of policy, which, as we will see, is a particularly important distinction in clarifying the role of a nonprofit board. To encompass all of the aspects of what a nonprofit board is authorized to do, Miriam Wood (1996) has put forth one of the most comprehensive definitions: "Governance . . . consists of decisions and actions linked to defining an organization's mission, to establishing its policies, and to determining the control mechanisms it will use to allocate power, establish decision-making processes, and set up procedures for performing specific tasks" (p. 3).

Preferring to describe the modern nonprofit as a tripartite system, in which the staff represents the third party that complements the work of the board and executive, Houle (1989) traces the existence of groups similar to boards back to ancient times. He identifies the earliest recorded use of the tripartite system in the United States as occurring in 1636 at Harvard, when the board fired the first full-time president. According to Wood (1996), present-day conceptualizations of governance find their antecedents in higher education in the 1960s, when the idea of accountability to multiple stakeholders took root. This suggests a political model of decision-making in which the organizational leader(s) must find a way to articulate a common purpose forcefully enough to bring together competing interests vying for increasingly scarce resources.

The Role and Responsibilities of a Nonprofit Board

For the most part, the nonprofit literature has been stingy in proffering a pure definition of governance (Stone & Ostrower, 2007). Instead, there is a tendency to move directly into a discussion of the expectations for the board, often from a normative perspective, assuming perhaps that everyone already knows what a board is, which professional experience and research suggest may be misguided. The failure to provide board members with a clear sense of what it means to be a board prior to asking these individuals to perform as a board is one of the main reasons for ineffective governance.

Legal and Fiduciary Duties
First, the board must fulfill certain legal and fiduciary responsibilities: (1) the *duty of obedience* requires the board to act solely within the scope of its corporate powers as determined by state and federal laws and by the organization's charter and/or articles of incorporation and its bylaws; (2) the *duty of loyalty* specifies that board officers and members act in good faith and not allow self-interest to take precedence over organizational inter-

ests; and (3) the *duty of care* asks that the board act diligently and prudently in managing the organization's affairs (Nonprofits' Insurance Alliance of California [NIAC], 2001). These principles reflect the landmark 1974 ruling in the so-called Sibley Hospital case by Judge Gerhard Gesell, in which he found the hospital trustees not guilty of the charges of self-interested decision-making that had been brought against them. In issuing his ruling, the judge noted the lack of legislation on trustee liability at that time and then addressed the circumstances under which board members might be at risk, with some advice on how to avoid future problematic situations (Houle, 1989).

Almost every state has now enacted some kind of legislation to provide minimal protection to volunteers for personal liability when carrying out their assignments on behalf of a nonprofit, but none of these laws protect against willful acts or alleged breaches of federal and state laws such as those prohibiting discrimination. Moreover, in most states there is no legal protection for board members unless the organization has a directors-and-officers (D & O) liability insurance policy that applies to the claim, and with the exception of New Jersey and Virginia, state laws do not offer even minimal protection for the organization. The federal Volunteer Protection Act of 1997 is very similar to the existing state laws in its provisions. Regrettably, no legislation prevents lawsuits, even the most frivolous. Over 90 percent of the claims against nonprofit boards are employment-related, typically for sexual harassment, discrimination, or wrongful termination, with the remainder associated with an alleged breach of fiduciary duty such as self-dealing, mismanagement, and acting outside of the scope of the organization's charter, bylaws, and policies (NIAC, 2001).

To minimize the likelihood of legal action in any of these areas, a board can take simple precautions to demonstrate good faith. To guard against employment claims, a lawyer should review the organization's personnel policies regularly to ensure the language complies with current law and does not contain any language that could provide the basis for a suit; the organization should then follow the policies to the letter and document all related actions. To protect themselves against possible fiscal liability, trustees should be familiar with what is specified in the organizational charter and bylaws, attend board and committee meetings regularly, read informational material sent prior to meetings about impending actions, make sure that minutes are kept of all meetings and stored in a secure place, hold top management accountable for complying with all legal and technical requirements, and pay especially close attention to the monies flowing into and out of the organization. Adding a conflict-of-interest policy statement to the bylaws (see exhibit 4.1 for sample language) and requiring that each trustee annually sign a declaration affirming the policy are proactive steps to be taken, along with participating in permissible advocacy in support of clearer and more favorable legislation on board liability.

Functional Responsibilities

In an attempt to clarify the difference between governance and management, various authors have compiled a list of responsibilities the board is expected to fulfill. Howe (1995), for example, believes there are just seven responsibilities of a nonprofit trustee, regardless of setting: attendance at board meetings and participation on committees;

Exhibit 4.1 Conflict-of-Interest Policy

A. No part of the Childcare League's funds, other property, and/or income thereof shall personally benefit any board member.

B. Each board member shall exercise utmost good faith in all transactions while performing his/her duties to the organization. Board members shall be held to a strict standard of honest and fair dealing between themselves and the League. They shall not use their positions, or any knowledge gained as a result, in such a way that a conflict might arise between the interests of the League and those of the individual.

C. Board members shall not accept any gift, favor, or hospitality that may influence, or appears to influence, decisions or actions affecting the League.

D. Any possible conflict of interest on the part of a board member must be disclosed promptly to the board as a whole and made a matter of record through an annual review procedure and in situations in which the conflict could affect board actions or decisions.

E. Any board member who has a possible conflict of interest shall not vote or exercise his/her personal influence in the disposition of the matter. The minutes of the meeting must reflect the disclosure and his/her abstention from participation.

F. The chairperson shall distribute annually to all board members, and to new trustees joining the board, a Conflict-of-Interest Statement that must be completed and signed by each one. These shall be kept on file for the duration of each board member's term(s).

CONFLICT-OF-INTEREST STATEMENT

1. Please disclose any business or nonprofit interest in which you or any member of your immediate family (spouse, parents, children) may have the potential for conflict with the interests of the League.

2. Please disclose any relationship that you deem to be within the spirit, if not the letter, of the conflict-of-interest policy, keeping in mind that protection from real or apparent conflict of interest is intended to help avoid even the appearance of impropriety.

_____   _____
Signature   Date

Note: The organizational name listed in this exhibit is a pseudonym, but the language of the document is an accurate reflection of the organization's existing policy. The policy extends to the organization's staff and volunteers, each of whom is required to sign a similar statement annually.

determination of the mission and participation in periodic strategic planning; financial management; selection, support, and evaluation of the executive; program oversight and support; participation in fund-raising; and assurance of board effectiveness. As part of program oversight and support, he includes being an advocate in the community to advance the organization's image.

Yet, the hard evidence continues to show a divide between what boards are expected to do and what they actually do. For instance, in a study comparing what boards understand their responsibilities to be versus their performance of these tasks, Green and Griesinger (1996) found both the trustees and the CEOs surveyed agreed that the tasks enumerated in the nonprofit literature are important, but the data also revealed current performance was considerably below the desired level in virtually every category. Formally evaluating the CEO, involvement in fund-raising, community interaction, and board self-assessment were some of the categories with the widest gaps. More recent research in 2002–3 comparing human service organizations in California, Michigan, and North Carolina resulted in similar findings. In interviews with selected CEOs, when it came to the level of trustee involvement, the main concern that emerged was the board's lack of understanding of its core responsibilities. Somewhat surprisingly, the board members interviewed did not disagree. When asked whether his colleagues adhered to what he had just described as their principal duties, one board president summed up the general sentiment: "I think they all believe it. I think they all understand it. I don't think they all practice it" (Golensky, 2005).

THE BOARD-EXECUTIVE RELATIONSHIP

Arguably, the most important relationship within a not-for-profit is that between the board of directors and the CEO. Despite the typical characterization of the association as a partnership, which may be fairly accurate from a legal perspective, this label fails to fully capture the emotional and personal connection that often develops from participating together in an enterprise whose aim is to make a positive contribution to the betterment of society. In the best of circumstances, the initial goodwill the board feels toward the newly hired executive deepens over time; in addition, individual trustees may form a bond with the CEO more akin to friendship than business.

When the two halves of the leadership core share a clear understanding of respective responsibilities as well as a mutuality of interests and intents, appreciation, and respect, an organization tends to operate smoothly and cope effectively with issues as they arise. However, for a variety of reasons, the board-executive link is often difficult and complex. The very structure of a typical organization is a primary cause for tension. As discussed above, the board carries the legal responsibility for the programmatic and financial integrity of the organization, but it is the top professional who is usually perceived as its public face, the embodiment of its mission, goals, and values. When used creatively, this inherent tension can bring about a healthy give-and-take in policy discussions and decision-making, but if resentments build up due to inadvertent miscues, perceived slights, or unmet expectations that may never have been clearly verbalized, the departure of the executive may be the unfortunate outcome.

Whatever the length of the CEO's tenure, staff turnover at the highest level has serious implications for the organization. Staff may express their sense of loss through behavior ranging from increased absenteeism to the reduction of services to clients. Programs initiated by the executive may deteriorate without the support from the top. Funding bodies may view the executive's leaving as a sign of internal instability. And the board itself may be thrown into confusion when deprived of the professional guidance on which it has depended. The causes for the break play a role in determining the severity of the impact. If the executive dies or retires, there may be a strong emotional reaction, but this is not likely to impede the organization's ability to function. Although the voluntary departure of the CEO, even under the most amicable of circumstances, may produce some of the difficulties just enumerated, generally the organization will return rather quickly to its normal state. The most serious and lasting consequences are apt to follow when the departure is forced, except in cases of clear malfeasance.

Power Dynamics

Ralph Kramer has been one of the leading voices disputing the idea of the board-executive relationship as a standard partnership. Instead, he suggests that interactions within the leadership core are politically motivated and constantly shifting in response to internal and external conditions, bringing a range of possible behaviors from collaboration to profound disagreement. To fully comprehend the dynamic nature of the board-executive relationship, one must take into account at any given time the structure, size, age, type, and fiscal system of the organization; the personal attributes and resources each side of the leadership core can draw upon; and the specifics of the situation the organization is confronting (Kramer, 1985). In fact, boards and CEOs do not always react alike to the same concerns. In one research project, when asked about the most important governance challenges facing nonprofits today, the board members and executives identified the same six categories but not in the same priority order. What was ranked number one by the trustees, funding, was only fourth on the CEOs' list; conversely, the executives' first priority was clarification of the board role and responsibilities, which stood at number three for the board members (Golensky, 2000).

When considering the respective sources of power for the board and the CEO, obviously both enjoy the legitimacy conferred by position in the organization, the board's derived from its corporate, legal authority and the executive's from professional status and title. Kramer (1985) prefers the term "resources for influence" to identify what each person contributes to the mix. Individual board members may offer access to funds, connections within the community, knowledge and skill, time and energy, and strong commitment to the organizational mission. The CEO may draw on some of the same resources, such as knowledge and skill, but also has the advantage of controlling the flow of information going out to the board and of being a full-time employee rather than a volunteer. With longevity, executives often increase their influence on internal decision-making through informal relationships developed with the trustees as well as with key community stakeholders.

The size and nature of the organization and the issues it is facing also can affect the way the board and CEO interact. For instance, in larger settings, communication and accountability become more complicated, tipping the balance of power in favor of the executive, whereas in smaller organizations, the CEO may find it harder to keep the board from becoming involved in operations, thus overstepping its policy-making role. The more technical or clinical the services provided by the organization, the greater the likelihood the board will defer to the executive on programmatic concerns, but it may be a very different story when finances or personnel practices are under discussion, especially if the matter is viewed as precedent setting or where the reputation of the organization is at stake. A final factor is whether the organization is dealing with routine business, which will generally be left to the executive, or is in crisis mode, when the board is probably more dominant (Golensky, 1993; Kramer, 1985).

Houle (1989) has identified four particularly problematic scenarios with regard to the board-executive relationship: (1) the executive who dominates to the point the board feels almost superfluous; (2) the dominant board that reduces the executive to the equivalent of a clerk; (3) a board sharply divided over a policy or procedural matter, a situation exacerbated when the executive or the board chair joins one of the factions, or worse, when they take opposing positions; and (4) a relationship marred either by cronyism or antagonism between the executive and one or more board members. He also describes a fifth situation that has the potential to create problems, when there are dual executives reporting to the board. Many cultural organizations, for instance, have both an artistic director and a general manager. Similarly, a hospital may have a medical director as well as an administrator. If it is not possible to clarify the role, sphere of influence, and lines of accountability for all parties to everyone's satisfaction, then an accommodation must be reached to allow the organization to function effectively. Imaginative, flexible leadership from the executive and the board chair, preferably acting together, assuming they are not part of the problem, may be the best way to resolve these situations, but, as Houle (1989) notes, preventing them from arising in the first place is a far better strategy.

The Organizational Life Cycle

Organizations are not static but tend to evolve and change over time. It stands to reason then that since the board and executive are so interdependent, their relationship may also fluctuate with the stage of organizational development. Some nonprofits come into existence through the vision of one individual, who sees a societal problem and takes the initiative to mobilize family, friends, and associates to fill the board role, to address the perceived need; this was the pattern followed by Youth Services Network (YSN), the organization in our featured case study. In other cases, an organization results from the collective action of a group of concerned citizens. Initially, the group assumes the management responsibilities of raising funds, implementing programs and services, and so on as volunteers, but at the point this arrangement no longer is practical, they may name one of the group members or decide to hire a professional staff person to take over the lead role in handling day-to-day administrative duties.

During the formative stage, everyone tends to be so busy getting the organization up and running that interpersonal conflict is not much of an issue. However, problems can develop at a time of transition. It then becomes clearer whether we are dealing with a following or a leading board (see Houle's scenarios 1 and 2). In the first instance, by choice or necessity, the board is dominated by a strong CEO, perhaps the founder, who consciously or not reserves most of the power and authority for him- or herself. Such a board may never learn to function properly and therefore may be unable to assume the role and responsibilities expected of it by society at large and, more particularly, within the laws that govern nonprofit corporations. When the individual responsible for establishing an organization becomes so controlling and overbearing that the differing but legitimate views of others, especially those of the board, are discounted, we have the phenomenon known as *founder's syndrome*. An individual operating in this manner has essentially lost sight of what it means to be a leader. Carried to an extreme, these behaviors can destroy organizational stability and initiative (Block, 2004; Mathiasen, 1983).

At the opposite end of the spectrum is the leading board, which is proactive, sometimes in the extreme, and tends to control the operations of the organization. This may occur because the board founded the organization, there is a gap between CEOs, or there is an organizational crisis. Whatever the original reason, a leading board may find it difficult to share power and authority with the executive director. Often, a smaller group of trustees, perhaps the executive committee, steps into the leadership vacuum created by the overt or covert dissension between the full board and the CEO to become the primary decision-maker, breeding resentment among those not part of the "in-group" and creating the third scenario of factionalism discussed earlier. Such divisions can negatively affect staff morale, thus potentially compromising organizational performance, as well as cause board turnover (Mathiasen, 1983).

Often the board appears to go through the same kind of life cycle as the organization. Mathiasen (1990) identifies three distinct stages in this process, the organizing board, the governing board, and the institutional board. The first stage is characterized by the two board types, following and leading, just described. In the second stage, committees are formed, there is greater reliance on the professional staff, and frequently new trustees with different skills are recruited to augment or replace older members. These changes may bring about a leadership style of shared power between the board and CEO. As the organization progresses to the third stage, the board may increase in size, rely even more on committees to do its work, and identify fund-raising as its primary activity. Similarly, Wood (1989, 1992) describes a cyclical model in which the board moves from a strong commitment to the agency's mission in its early stages to a goal-achievement focus as the organization becomes more bureaucratic, that is, with substantive committees, a managerially oriented executive, more diversity in funding, and so forth. She also maintains the board will adopt a participatory (independent and hands-on), corporate (active partnership), or ratifying (rubber-stamp) operating style depending on whether it feels compelled to demonstrate ownership of the organization or, conversely, has confidence in the leadership of the top professional. In a crisis she predicts a rapid shift from the ratifying style back to the participatory style and then a gradual move into the corporate style as the crisis subsides.

Governance Models

Despite some evidence of congruence between the organizational and the board life cycles, progressing along the evolutionary continuum is not inevitable for all nonprofits, and the trajectories of the two cycles may not remain in sync. Some boards, and some organizations, reach a particular point and see no need to, choose not to, or are unable to make further changes (Mathiasen, 1990). This was certainly the case with the Coalition (a pseudonym), an organization featured in an intensive research study of governance discussed more fully below. Even after nearly twenty years of serving the community, the organization had retained its original grassroots quality, with a small staff, plain offices, and minimal use of technology. It evidenced the characteristics noted by Wood (1989, 1992) for groups in the early stages of development; the board seemed content to leave most of the decision-making to the CEO, a situation that for the most part suited the executive as well. Although a few board members recognized it was not healthy for the organization to rely so disproportionately on their top professional, there appeared to be little impetus to alter the status quo.

The good news is there are several well-defined models of governance from which an organization may choose if and when the leadership core wishes to make a change. Ideally, the organization will reevaluate its current model periodically as a regular part of strategic planning, rather than waiting for a crisis to trigger a review. Table 4.2 provides a comparison of the major features of some of the most common models.

The Classic or Traditional Model

The classic model is probably the most common board type in nonprofit organizations, the one generally adopted in the formative stage and most closely adhering to the role and responsibilities for a board described in the prescriptive literature: "The organization is expected to serve the public benefit and its board is expected to function as . . . steward to safeguard the public interest" (Axelrod, 1994, p. 120). Board size varies, but since most of its work is accomplished through committees supplemented as needed by ad hoc task groups, especially as the organization matures, there must be a sufficient number of trustees with a mix of skills to fulfill this duty. The basic job of the board is oversight and monitoring, with the primary goal being to maintain standards. Board meetings tend to adhere closely to a preset agenda covering both current issues and those recognized as potentially of concern in the future.

Officially, a classic board subscribes to the idea that it sets the policies and the CEO implements them, after providing the necessary information on matters under consideration, and then reports back on organizational performance. However, in practice the executive may exercise considerable influence over decisions, especially with longevity. For example, from the point of hire, the CEO has both legitimate and expert power and

Table 4.2 Comparison of board types by key features

Type of board	Governance	Work mode	Configuration	Expectations of staff
Classic or traditional: Follows prescriptive literature re role, responsibilities	Oversight & monitoring	Multiple committees & task forces	Size varies; skill-based	Provide information, implement policies, report back to board
Corporate: Subscribes to strict separation between policymaking (board) & operations (management)	Professionalism & efficiency	3 standing committees	18–24 members, ideally	CEO part of board, given leeway to be creative and productive
Policy governance: Driven by values and guiding principles	External focus on "moral ownership"	Act as whole to set policies (ends, means, board-staff relations, board process)	Small; few or no standing committees	CEO accountable for organizational performance, adhering to means policies
Executive leadership: Variation on classic model but repudiates "heroic" board	CEO central to governance	See classic model above	See classic model above	CEO as doer, decision-maker, board nurturer, entrepreneur
Contingency: Variation on classic model	Power differentials recognized	See classic model above	See classic model above	Responsibilities may vary and be negotiated over life cycle

increases referent power as his or her tenure grows. The executive also has access to reward and coercive power through knowledge of opportunities for personal and professional growth that can be passed along to or withheld from individual board members and by making recommendations to the nominating committee on board officers and committee chairs.

The Corporate Model

As the name implies, the corporate model is somewhat akin to the governance structure of a for-profit, at least philosophically. Cost effectiveness and professionalism are highly valued as guiding principles, explaining the heavy emphasis on the separation of policy-making and operations, which "calls for a new working environment and for new relationships and communication styles from the top to the bottom rung of the organization" (Fram & Brown, 1988, x). A board size of eighteen to twenty-four members is considered manageable and therefore ideal. Only three standing committees are recommended, meeting as necessary so as to use board time as efficiently as possible: The executive committee, comprising the CEO, board officers, and one member at-large, sets board agendas, reviews all materials, and presents its findings and recommendations to the full board. The planning/resources committee assists the CEO with planning and monitors the activities of any ad hoc committees. The assessment committee, with the executive, develops the organizational goals, which are subject to the executive committee's review and ratification by the entire board, and is responsible for monitoring goal attainment and the CEO's performance.

The executive, charged with directing long-range planning and developing the organization's future vision, is considered part of the board and may have voting power, if permitted under state law. The board is expected to provide the CEO with sufficient leeway to be creative and productive and to respect the executive's authority over staff.

The Policy Governance Model

The policy governance model is known familiarly as the "Carver model," after the individual who developed it. The board is viewed as the key vehicle for governing the organization, guided by values and core principles and responsible to those stakeholders considered to have "moral ownership" of the organization (Carver, 1990). The board should be small and have few if any standing committees, to encourage the idea of acting with one voice. Governance is achieved through generating written policies in four areas: (1) ends, to determine what needs to meet, for which beneficiaries, and at what cost; (2) means, to determine how to achieve goals prudently and ethically by setting limits on the CEO's authority; (3) board-executive relationship, to clarify the board's approach to delegation and assessing the CEO's performance; and (4) board process, to address how governance and leadership will be exercised.

The board has but one employee, the CEO, dealing with other staff only to gather specific information for developing or monitoring policies. In setting Executive Limitations, policies are written as to what is unacceptable behavior (for example, staff may not be treated with disrespect), which implies that anything not specifically limited is open to the CEO's discretion. Because of this provision, before adopting the Carver model, it is essential to establish that the executive believes in a democratic ideology and will exercise the values of open sharing, truthfulness, loyalty, and fairness in regard to the board (Kramer, 1985), for a less ethical individual can easily subvert the policies to gain control over the organization, keeping the board engaged in meaningless busywork.

The Executive Leadership Model

In outward appearance, the executive leadership model is very close to the classic model in its approach, but it explicitly repudiates the "heroic" ideal of board leadership embodied in the prescriptive literature on governance, as being impractical and essentially unachievable by a group of volunteers whose primary interests lie elsewhere (Herman & Heimovics, 1991). Here the board's legal role is maintained, but the model acknowledges the reality that it is the executive who most often functions at the center of organizational leadership. A key element of this kind of leadership is helping the board members carry out their duties and gain satisfaction from their service to the agency.

For this model to work effectively, decision-making should be viewed as a responsibility shared by the two halves of the leadership core, and the focus must be on doing the work rather than spending time uselessly on attempts to separate policy from administration when in fact such distinctions vary as circumstances change. Among the CEO's main responsibilities is securing the resources necessary to achieve the organizational mission; thus it is the executive who is the principal boundary spanner, bringing the board into the mix as warranted (Herman & Heimovics, 1991). However, because most of the burden for success or failure rests on the executive, a potential drawback of the model is whether the CEO will have sufficient time to nurture the board while also addressing all of the other internal and external tasks that go with the position.

The Contingency Model

Like the previous option, the contingency model is essentially a variation on the classic model. The main distinction is the clear recognition of power differentials in the board-staff relationship and the impact of change over time on how business is conducted. Accordingly, there is a continual need to negotiate the ways in which the board and CEO interact as opposed to the assumption that this association remains static as environmental conditions ebb and flow. Harris (1993) has suggested that even the division of labor between the board and senior staff ought to be subjected to periodic review. Using a process called total activities analysis (TAA), the board's standard responsibilities are considered within the context of all the essential organizational tasks, allowing for a frank discussion about perceptions of who is or should be doing the various functions—staff, board, or the two acting together—to determine whether to reposition assignments to maximize relative strengths at that time.

Additional support for the contingency model comes from a study of four human service organizations conducted in 1991–92, where the intent was to identify the factors contributing to a positive board-staff relationship, one that endured, promoted mission accomplishment, and was beneficial for all parties. Three key elements emerged as materially influencing this type of relationship: (1) executive assets, the sum total of the CEO's personal attributes and professional qualifications, similar to Kramer's "resources for influence" (1985); (2) board-executive congruence, the level of agreement between the two on management philosophy and leadership style; and (3) agency context, the composition of the organization's internal and external environment. The conclusion was that stability within the leadership core is most likely to occur when there is high congruence between the board and CEO coupled with the board's perception of the executive as having the requisite assets to take advantage of positive environmental forces and to overcome any negative forces that might threaten the organization's resources. Subsequent studies have confirmed these findings (Golensky, 1994, 2005).

FINAL THOUGHTS

To bring this discussion to a close, consider these wise words: "Both the governing board and the executive . . . are critical components of the . . . leadership system of the [not-for-profit] organization in these turbulent times. Failure to accept and institutionalize this premise is a major contributing factor to, if not the cause of, the 'distressed situation' in which many organizations find themselves today" (Kirk, 1986, p. 17).

The Practice of Leadership

In the previous chapter we reviewed the meaning of leadership in terms of its component parts and the different conceptualizations that have been advanced since just before the start of the twentieth century up to the present. We then discussed the leadership structure typically used in nonprofits, in which power and authority is shared, in some fashion, between the board of directors and the executive, ending with a detailed consideration of this all-important relationship. Now, taking into account all of these theories, the spotlight in this chapter will be squarely on the professional side of the equation as we explore leadership in practice.

However, as we know, organizational leadership does not exist in a vacuum but is exercised in a specific setting, the dynamics of which both shape and are shaped by the actions of the CEO. The term used most often to capture this phenomenon is *organizational culture*, defined by Hofstede and Hofstede (2005) as "the collective programming of the mind that distinguishes the members of one organization from another" (pp. 282–283). The first section of this chapter will address this concept in some detail, to provide a context for the practical aspects of leadership.

Being a nonprofit CEO can be very rewarding. Knowing that, through the decisions you make and the resources your organization has at its disposal, you are in a position to help alleviate a social problem such as homelessness or to enable inner-city children to become more successful in school and therefore in life can be enormously satisfying, both professionally and personally. At the same time, no one disputes that running a nonprofit can be frustrating, for stakeholder expectations remain high even when unrealistic. Furthermore, it is a demanding job that encompasses many diverse and often competing tasks, some of which can and should be delegated to others, although knowing what and when to delegate is something of an art. Yet, no matter how skillful the delegation, the ultimate responsibility for organizational performance rests with the executive. As Harry Truman famously said, the buck stops here!

You might wonder at this point why anyone would aspire to such a difficult-sounding career. By the end of the chapter, a fuller picture should emerge of what the job of top professional in a not-for-profit setting entails, with all of its possibilities and challenges. After examining the concept of organizational culture, the next sections address the reality that to perform effectively at the highest organizational level means fulfilling multiple roles, moving from one to another as needs and circumstances dictate.

ORGANIZATIONAL CULTURE

Let's assume you have just moved to the community. In order to get to know your new home, you have decided to spend part of the day at the local public museum and the rest at the botanical and sculpture gardens. Walking into the museum for the first time, you find the building very modern in design, with a rather sterile glass exterior and a rounded entry. The information desk is along the wall farthest from the doors, and once you make your way to it, the volunteers continue their personal conversation for several minutes before turning their attention to you. That afternoon, as you approach the doors into the main building of the gardens, you enjoy the spectacular plants that line both sides of the path as well as the colorful small sculptures dotted here and there. It seems as though the minute you walk in, someone notices you, greets you with a smile, and directs you to the information desk, where there are several volunteers at the ready.

What you have just experienced are the *observable artifacts* (Schein, 1990) of these two organizations, that is, things you can see, feel, and even smell that provide some insights into a given setting, albeit on a fairly superficial level. From your first impressions you might reasonably have concluded that customer service is not one of the museum's highest priorities but might have a totally opposite view of the botanical gardens. In this example nothing much was at stake personally, but would you take the matter as lightly if you were coming to each arts organization for your first job interview? Other kinds of artifacts include everything from the dress code, the manner in which people interact with colleagues and outsiders, and the emotional intensity of the place to annual reports, statements of philosophy, and similar tangible "products."

Many meanings have been offered for the word *culture* within organizations, such as norms, philosophy, climate, rules, regular forms of behavior, and so on. For Schein (1985), these meanings may reflect culture but fail to capture its essence. To get to the broadest sense of the term, he offers the following definition: "A pattern of basic assumptions—invented, discovered, or developed by a given group as it learns to cope with its problems of external adaptation and internal integration—that has worked well enough to be considered valid and, therefore, to be taught to new members as the way to perceive, think, and feel in relation to those problems" (p. 9).

To understand an organization's culture, it is necessary to burrow more deeply beyond the observable artifacts, which while informative do not help us perceive why they have been developed or what they mean to organizational members. At the next level are *values*, the espoused ideologies or principles often articulated initially by someone in a leadership position regarding expected behavior in some aspect of the organizational work. For instance, the CEO of a behavioral health organization may say, "Talk therapy is the cornerstone of our services" because of a conviction that this is the most effective approach for the agency's consumers. If this methodology proves to be effective

Table 5.1 Levels of organizational culture

Level	Description
1. Observable artifacts	Created physical and social "products" characteristic of the setting (e.g., physical layout, dress code, annual report, overt member behavior)
2. Espoused values	Expressions of personal convictions to explain or justify expected behavior (e.g., CEO states, "We believe in promoting the self-worth of every staff member.")
3. Deep-seated assumptions	Guides to actual behavior that have become so ingrained as not to require conscious thought (e.g., CEO really subscribes to the belief that staff are untrustworthy; employees therefore must fill out detailed time sheets on a daily basis.)

Source: Adapted from Schein, 1985.

in practice, not just once but over a period of time, it comes to be accepted as a given, no longer to be questioned, and to be followed without much if any conscious thought. You know you have reached the third and deepest level of *basic assumptions* when you ask a colleague why she handled a situation in a particular manner, and the response is "That's how we always do it." Even assumptions that are not testable can become part of the fabric of organizational life through social validation, by group members embracing the beliefs that seem consistently to reduce uncertainty and anxiety (Schein, 1985, 1990). Table 5.1 summarizes the three levels of organizational culture.

In sum, organizational culture is historically derived, socially constructed, and often resistant to change, and it is maintained not only by its group members but also by the other stakeholders interacting with the organization, such as consumers, funders, and regulatory agencies (Hofstede & Hofstede, 2005). For nonprofits with strong and highly identifiable cultures, this can be a big advantage. The March of Dimes, for instance, was able to rely on its loyal donor base and long-standing reputation to shift its mission from defeating polio to preventing premature births, birth defects, and infant mortality after its original purpose was accomplished with the development of the Salk and Sabin vaccines, and so remain in operation rather than disbanding.

Acculturation

For organizational members below the top management level, learning the culture begins with the hiring process. The next step in becoming socialized to the organization occurs on the first day of work with an orientation provided by more experienced staff, which may include distributing documents such as a personnel manual that lists rules and procedures, and continues throughout the probationary period and beyond with regular supervision. Most work settings also have an informal organization, which does not appear on the organizational chart but can be a powerful force in enforcing behavioral norms. The informal organization consists of individuals who generally hold no formal position of authority but are viewed by others as significant figures due to their expertise, control over vital information, relationships with powerful group members, and so on. In many organizations, the secretary to the CEO, by performing a gatekeeper function, is one such person. Other examples will easily come to mind from personal experiences in different settings.

Furthermore, culture exists at multiple levels within an organization (Schein, 1985). Each unit or professional group is likely to have its own artifacts, values, and assumptions; as a result, new staff may actually go through two or more layers of socialization. For example, in a nonprofit whose mission is to move homeless individuals toward becoming more economically self-sufficient, the counseling department might see its basic function as helping clients overcome their emotional and psychological issues to achieve a more positive self-image, while the training and placement department is likely to focus on assisting the clients in developing concrete work-related skills that will enable them to obtain and keep a job. The staff makeup for the first unit may be social workers, and for the second, individuals with an education or business background. If these two departments view themselves as having conflicting instead of complementary interests, their views could cause difficulties for the entire organization, depending on where group members place their primary loyalty.

For a newly hired CEO, the orientation process will differ from that for other, less visible new employees, with the initial contact more likely to be a welcoming reception, but it is almost a guarantee that everyone will be watching and listening during the first days and months for cues about leadership style and expectations. To learn the culture will require reading documents for insights into how the organization has addressed the demands of "external adaptation and internal integration," to use Schein's words, and listening closely in order to glean the historical nuances in the stories told by longtime group members, in particular, as well as in the most casual remarks exchanged by staff. In truth, "many organizational events and processes are important more for what they express than for what they produce: they are secular myths, rituals, ceremonies, and sagas that help people find meaning and order" (Bolman & Deal, 1991, p. 244). A retirement party for an employee leaving after twenty years of service illustrates this point. In a time of uncertainty and ambiguity, which characterizes much of the landscape for nonprofits at present and in the foreseeable future, viewing an organization through a symbolic frame meshes with the reality of experience.

The Individual in the Group

Although the emphasis in most discussions of organizational culture is on the group, it is important to keep in mind that every group is a collection of individuals who each have personal values, needs, and goals. Yet, a cross-organizational study confirmed that employees' values seemed to differ more by gender, age, education, and nationality than by organizational membership (Hofstede & Hofstede, 2005), which confirms the strength of the socialization process just discussed. On the other hand, in a nation such as the United States, where individualism has been a perceived norm since its founding, it would be imprudent for top management to ignore the element of self-interest as a motivating factor for group members in organizational life. Leaders therefore must engage in a kind of balancing act between individualist and collectivist tendencies.

New executives are generally accorded a "honeymoon period" to gain their footing, but once having become established in the leadership position, these individuals must face the fact that they now embody their followers' aspirations and represent the collective voice of the entire organization to the external world (Gardner, 1990). In time, as noted earlier, many of the values of the top professional become group members' practices, so it is the organizational leader who has the most to do with creating and managing the organizational culture, and as we will see in chapter 7, recreating it if circumstances dictate. In fact, one way to judge the quality of someone's leadership is by how that individual deals with culture. Just think about the founder of YSN in our featured case study and the influence he had on the way that nonprofit has conducted itself both internally and externally. Its successes and failures can be traced directly to this individual's espoused values that became the closely held beliefs for the entire organization, for better or for worse. Thus, "culture and leadership . . . are two sides of the same coin, and neither can really be understood by itself" (Schein, 1985, p. 2).

LEADERSHIP VERSUS MANAGEMENT

Some observers of organizational behavior see a rather sharp demarcation between the functions of management and leadership. Moreover, these individuals consider management and administration synonymous. Bennis (1999), for one, perceives managers (and administrators) as people who do things in the right way, whereas leaders do the right thing. In other words, managers and administrators are primarily concerned with the efficient operation of the organization, but for leaders, even though they have an awareness of current operations, effectiveness is foremost as they articulate strategies and direction for the future (Wallis & Dollery, 2003).

However, as catchy as Bennis's words are, they do not reflect the fact that in the majority of small and midsized nonprofits, the top manager or administrator and the leader are one. Thus, it is probably not very useful to expend much energy on semantics: "Management functions such as planning, organizing, and controlling cannot be separated from the influence process necessary in leadership. The real issue is whether a group of people can achieve [their] common goal" (Rosenbach & Taylor, 1989, p. 2). Accordingly, the emphasis should be placed on getting the job done, effectively, efficiently, and ethically, that is, on the process and the end results. The position taken in this book is "that one cannot be a successful nonprofit manager without being a good leader" (Edwards & Austin, 2006, p. 16). This means that when I talk about setting vision and overall direction for an organization, the person filling that role will generally be referred to as the *leader*; when it is more a nuts-and-bolts matter, then *manager* will be the term of choice; and when the issue encompasses both dimensions, the terms *leader* and *top manager* will be used interchangeably.

Table 5.2 Characteristics of transformational and transactional leadership

Dimension	Transformational leadership	Transactional leadership
Organizational climate	Unstable, crisis-mode	Stable, routine
Sense of identity	Self-determined	Purposive
Bases of power	Positional, referent	Positional, reward
Sources of influence	Moral purpose, intellectual stimulation	Tangible & intangible exchanges
Strengths	Visionary, motivational	Manages uncertainty, effective in goal attainment
Values	Empowerment, justice, integrity	Trust, fairness, respect

TRANSFORMATIONAL AND TRANSACTIONAL LEADERS

Before more closely examining the different functions that must be performed in the typical nonprofit as it strives to carry out its designated purpose, we will consider one further way of looking at the role and responsibilities of the top professional, the concepts of transformational and transactional leadership (see table 5.2).

Transformational Leadership

The word *transformation*, according to Webster's dictionary, describes the act of causing a major change in the form, nature, or function of something or someone. This type of leader tends to emerge during times of instability and crisis within an organization, which creates a climate that may be more receptive to a push for bold action and even a radical departure from the norm. An individual using this leadership style is often depicted as having charisma, or personal magnetism, a term originally coined by the eminent sociologist Max Weber (1947), and therefore charismatic leadership is essentially a synonym for transformational leadership.

This leadership style can be defined in three distinct ways: (1) by its effects on followers, (2) by the behavior of the leader that encourages transformative actions, and (3) by attributions of charisma that followers and observers accord to the leader (Howell, 1997). From the first perspective, a transformational leader's strong self-confidence and belief in pursuing a certain course of action motivates and inspires followers to embrace the proposed change (Kuhnert & Lewis, 1989). Using the second definition, the leader not only articulates a compelling vision for the future but also sets a personal example for followers to emulate and demonstrates confidence in the proposed new direction through frequent communications and interactions with other group members. From the attributional viewpoint, observers believe the leader has special talents to command loyalty from followers and inspire them to align their needs, values, and goals with his or hers to the point of their being willing to make personal sacrifices to realize the new organizational vision (Howell, 1997). In short, transformational leaders rely on both referent and positional power; they are perceived by their followers as inspirational, supportive, and intellectually stimulating, moving them to reach their fullest potential and to work effectively for the greater good of the organization (Howell, 1997; Mary, 2005).

Nonetheless, charismatic or transformational leadership may have a dark side. Although some of these leaders clearly act through legitimate channels of authority to reach collective goals and are genuinely concerned about the well-being of followers, others seem to be almost intolerant of stability and may exaggerate organizational deficiencies or even manufacture crises to keep up the level of excitement on which they thrive. Such individuals exhibit a high degree of narcissism, emphasize goals that originate from self-interest, and foster unquestioning obedience and dependence in followers (Howell, 1997). On a very practical level, they may neglect important managerial and administrative tasks and thus fail to build a solid infrastructure to sustain the organization over time (Mason, 1996).

Transactional Leadership

The transactional leader operates through a system of exchanges, as the word *transaction* implies, and is more apt to appear under stable and routine conditions. The relationship between leader and followers is one of reciprocal influence and mutual benefit, that is, the leader provides followers with something they value and receives value in return. Two levels of exchange have been noted. In lower-order transactions, "leaders clarify the role followers must play and the task requirements followers must complete to reach their personal goals while fulfilling the mission of the organization" (Kuhnert & Lewis, 1989, p. 194). Higher-order exchanges, in contrast, involve non-concrete rewards derived from an interpersonal bond between the leader and followers based on mutual respect and trust (Kuhnert & Lewis, 1989). When senior staff in a nonprofit concealed the effects of cancer on their longtime CEO by quietly assuming many of her duties until her death, they were engaged in a higher-order exchange.

Hollander (1978) emphasizes the dynamic nature of the relationship between leader and followers, as influenced by the situation in which they function. The situation encompasses organizational tasks, resources, history, social structure and rules, size, and so on. The leader and followers are joined in a "psychological contract" (p. 73); they and the situation, taken together, represent a kind of closed system of interaction, although the external environment can and frequently does affect aspects of the system (for example, the acquisition and use of resources). The followers expect the leader to set group standards and values, treat them fairly, and reduce situational uncertainty, to the extent possible. As long as these expectations are met, the followers carry out their part of the exchange by providing loyalty and productivity, with self-motivation an equally important determining factor. Day-to-day organizational life is mostly about pursuing defined goals, which meshes with the profile of the quiet, dependable transactional leader who knows how to get the work done (Hollander, 1978; Howell, 1997).

Comparing the Two Leadership Styles

Similar to the debate over the separation between leadership and management, there have been differences of opinion as to whether transformational leadership is more desirable than transactional leadership or just represents a refinement of it. Those holding that transformational leadership is superior maintain that the bond between followers and the transactional leader is more tenuous than that between followers and the transformational leader, especially when lower-order exchanges are in effect. For instance, if pay raises are set by the board rather than by the CEO, the latter's bargaining power is lessened (Kuhnert & Lewis, 1989). Moreover, because the transactional leader relies on reward and positional power, discontent and competition may arise among followers if the distribution of rewards, both tangible and intangible, is not perceived to be equitable (Manning, 2003).

As illustrated in table 5.2, these two leadership styles can be compared along several dimensions, some of which have been noted in the previous sections, such as the type of leadership most likely to emerge in unstable versus stable organizations, their different bases of power, and the sources of influence used most often in each case. The remaining three dimensions—sense of identity, strengths, and values—are perhaps the most critical ones to consider since they speak to the personal side of leadership. When these characteristics are viewed side by side, the ideal leader would be one who possesses all of them. Thus, the most tenable position seems to be that both styles are necessary, that transformational leadership augments the effectiveness of, but does not replace, transactional leadership (Bass & Steidlmeier, 1998).

PERFORMING MULTIPLE ROLES

To carry out organizational business, the CEO, along with senior staff and the board, must be prepared to take on three separate but overlapping roles, as leader, manager, and administrator. As Werther, Berman, and Echols (2005) note, "Each of the three roles offers a mindset that suggests a different priority. Success comes from knowing which perspective to apply when" (p. 22). For these three authors, the main responsibility of the leader, which they view as a shared role between the executive and the board president (also titled *board chair* in some settings), is to set a vision for what the organization is seeking to become, capturing the main elements of the mission. A vision statement provides more clarity about the desired direction and is often inspirational in identifying specific goals and objectives even if they are not fully attainable. Thus, a medical research facility might have "Eradicate cancer in our lifetime" as its mission, and then its vision statement would expand on the importance of this cause, including the gains made to date and what remains to be done. Working within the mission and vision statements, the manager must direct how organizational resources are to be allocated to reach the designated goals and objectives. It is then up to the administrator to strike a good balance between the frequently conflicting needs of the various internal and external stakeholders.

Role Uncertainty

Although the responsibilities of each of the three roles seem relatively clear and distinct conceptually, in practice there is a certain ambiguity as to which role one should play at any given time. Unfortunately, no magic formula exists to simplify the process other than remaining flexible enough to shift roles as necessary, but there can be consequences for allowing uncertainty to prevent the manager from donning the leader's hat or vice versa even when the situation dictates making this switch. On one hand, the individual who avoids the leader role can cause a loss of organizational focus; on the other hand, focusing too much on being a leader when a manager is what is needed can result in organizational stagnation. And ignoring the administrator role may mire an organization in conflict. The main error to avoid is falling back on more comfortable role patterns that worked in the past but are inappropriate or ineffective in meeting the demands of the present (Werther et al., 2005).

The board of directors of a human service organization providing rehabilitative services learned this lesson the hard way when the founder and longtime CEO notified the board chair of a serious financial problem, a deficit of approximately $1.25 million. Two years prior to this crisis, the organization had adopted a new management and service delivery system, involving a complicated fee-for-service structure with its affiliates. The executive had been so caught up in his leadership role that he had failed to provide the necessary managerial oversight for those responsible for generating regular financial reports. As a result, he did not recognize staff were struggling to fulfill their duties within the new system and was himself taken by surprise when told of the shortfall. The board stepped in and took control, establishing procedures to restore fiscal stability and improve affiliate relationships. The CEO, who had earlier announced plans to retire at the end of the year, was allowed to finish out his days at the organization but with severely restricted, nonoperational responsibilities (Golensky & Walker, 2003).

Expectations and Performance

In view of the complexity of the contemporary world, it is helpful to put nonprofit leadership and management in perspective by considering roles and responsibilities through an analytical lens. One such framework is Quinn's "competing values model," which looks at effectiveness and leadership on two dimensions, flexibility versus control and internal versus external (as cited in Edwards & Austin, 2006). As shown in table 5.3, the result is four separate quadrants, each with its specific goals and task requirements of the top professional to achieve these ends.

External Flexibility

In the external-flexibility quadrant, the desired outcomes for the organization are to protect its legitimacy and enhance resource acquisition, necessitating the use of boundary-spanning skills on the part of the CEO (see chapter 3). Most of the activities undertaken will involve individuals and entities external to the focal organization and therefore not

TABLE 5.3 Organizational goals and leadership tasks

Quadrant	Goals	Tasks
External flexibility	Protect legitimacy Enhance resource acquisition	Raise funds Advance reputation Negotiate agreements Lobby legislators Interact with regulators Market programs
Internal flexibility	Build cohesive workforce Motivate staff to achieve high productivity	Mentor staff Facilitate group interaction Maintain good communication Administer fair personnel policies
Internal control	Maintain organizational structure Facilitate steady work flow	Establish fiscal controls Coordinate budget planning Monitor execution of policies and procedures Collect and process information Administer quality standards
External control	Establish clear organizational direction Determine desired output levels	Oversee short- and long-term planning Set organizational goals and objectives Monitor productivity Direct staff activities Stay abreast of environmental trends

Source: Adapted from Quinn's competing values model (as cited in Edwards & Austin, 2006).
Note: Model dimensions are internal-external on the horizontal axis and flexibility-control on the vertical axis.

under its direct control. Accordingly, to be successful in this role, the executive must be open to new ideas and adaptable enough to take advantage of opportunities as they are presented, whether it is a matter of raising funds, protecting the organization's reputation, negotiating formal and informal agreements, lobbying legislators, interacting with regulators, or modifying programs and services to fit current demands (Edwards & Austin, 2006).

As a manifestation of the situational approach to leadership, this quadrant tests the professional's political acumen and personal relationships both outside of and within the organization, for power dynamics are likely to come into play when the executive must evaluate a new set of circumstances and then reaches a decision to commit resources already earmarked for one purpose to something else less clearly defined under long-term planning but with the potential for a bigger payoff. Even if acting quickly seems justified by the information available and existing conditions, the CEO's ability to change direction independently may be constrained depending on the board's perception of its role in boundary-spanning consistent with the governance model in place.

Internal Flexibility

In the second quadrant, internal flexibility, the emphasis is on building a cohesive workforce and motivating staff to achieve a high level of productivity. The kinds of programs and services delivered by nonprofits are generally considered "labor-intensive" because they involve a high degree of interpersonal activity. Hence, the human relations side of the equation is very important (Edwards & Austin, 2006). Some executives clearly relish having close contact with staff and maintain an open-door policy so that employees can bring concerns directly to their attention; others may want to delegate much of the day-to-day responsibility here to others on the management team. This decision may be influenced by organizational size, time constraints, or an honest appraisal of whose skills best match the tasks of mentoring and group facilitation. However, delegation does not absolve the CEO from creating a positive work environment through regular communication with staff and establishing personnel policies that are fairly and consistently implemented.

The duality between achieving the work and recognizing individual needs—knowing how to strike a good balance between the two—reflects the behavioral approach to leadership discussed in the last chapter. As you will recall, the most effective leader is the one who is judged by followers as strong in both areas.

Internal Control

The primary goal in the internal-control quadrant is to maintain the organizational structure and a steady work flow, which requires technical competence to oversee "budgeting and fiscal controls, scheduling procedures, information and communication systems, personnel administration systems, technical training programs, reporting systems, evaluation and quality control measures, and management of technical equipment and physical facilities" (Edwards & Austin, 2006, p. 12). In larger organizations, this work is likely to be carried out under the direction of a senior manager with a title such as chief operating officer (COO) but delegated to other members of the management team, for example, the budgeting aspects to a chief financial officer or controller, personnel matters to a human resources officer, evaluation to a quality-control officer, and so on. Smaller nonprofits that have a more compressed staff structure will have to consolidate the monitoring and coordinating responsibilities in some fashion, with even the top professional assuming some of the tasks; outside contractors may also be used for the more specialized work.

Obviously the use of computers is particularly important in this quadrant to ensure that resources are allocated in the most efficient and effective manner. Being able to generate consistent, accurate data on service usage for both internal and external audiences is absolutely essential in this age of accountability. In fact, because technology now impacts virtually every area of organizational life, it merits its own chapter in the next section of this book.

External Control

In the external-control quadrant, establishing a clear organizational direction, accomplished through short-term and strategic planning, and ensuring that the level of organizational output is consistent with this direction are the principal goals, with maintaining mission integrity always in the forefront of all decision-making activities (Edwards & Austin, 2006). Whereas the attributes associated with the transformational leader are necessary to achieve the desired outcomes in the human relations or internal flexibility quadrant, here the qualities of the transactional leader are more apt to be called upon (see table 5.2). In other words, motivation must now be translated into productivity. One of the responsibilities of the top professional is to stay abreast of trends in the external environment that might affect the kinds of programs the organization offers as well as its consumer base and then use this knowledge to inform planning and decision-making. Therefore, some of the boundary-spanning skills discussed earlier appear to be equally valid in carrying out the tasks in this quadrant, although with a different organizational purpose in mind.

Factoring in Trait Theories of Leadership

As noted in chapter 4, trait theories still come into play when making hiring decisions. In considering the various tasks in the four quadrants of the competing values model, we can formulate a picture of the ideal nonprofit CEO: creative, politically astute, inspiring, empathetic, technically adept, dependable, systematic, generative, and task oriented. Rarely do we find all of these traits embodied equally in a single person, which reinforces the importance of surrounding the top professional with a team of competent individuals to complement his or her strengths and offset any weaknesses.

Some traits are innate; other qualities can be learned. Falling into the latter category is the ability to manage time effectively, which crosses all of the quadrants. Given the overwhelming number of issues that confront a nonprofit executive on a daily basis, it is helpful to have some kind of organizing principle to draw on in order to make the best use of the hours in the day. One such tool is a two-by-two matrix that prioritizes activities according to their importance and their urgency. Important and urgent matters such as crises, serious problems, and projects with tight deadlines rate top consideration. Next are important matters that are not urgent, which would include long-term planning, staff development, relationship building, and professional development. Taking care of one's health and mental well-being also falls into this group. Returning telephone calls, attending meetings and dealing with drop-in visitors are examples of activities that are urgent but not important, while busywork and sorting through junk mail belong in the category of neither important nor urgent and are simply time wasters. With discipline, it may be possible to reorient priorities to spend time where it is most needed (DiPadrova & Faerman, 1998).

Patterns of Leadership

Drawing on different aspects of some of the most well-known leadership theories, Schmid (2006) has developed an analytical model to link the choice of a leader exhibiting particular characteristics with certain kinds of human and community service organizations. From the behavioral approach, he has labeled the vertical axis as task-oriented versus people-oriented, and similar to the competing values model, he has used internal orientation versus external orientation for the horizontal axis, to create four separate quadrants (see table 5.4). Many of the tasks discussed within the competing-values model are also found here but in a less codified way. For instance, human relations activities are addressed in all four quadrants since one expressed purpose of this model is to demonstrate how a specific leadership style meshes with group members' levels of professionalism as well as with the requirements dictated by organizational structure.

Internal Task Orientation

The internal task orientation features organizations like residential facilities for disadvantaged children and institutions serving people with retardation, which tend to be very rule-bound, hierarchical settings where the professional staff determine most of the details of daily life for those in care. The authority vested in the CEO is highly centralized, with virtually no input by lower-level organizational members into the decision-making process, and there is little tolerance for ambiguity. Since the emphasis is on goal attainment and maintenance of the organizational structure, planning, budgeting, top-down communication, and coordination are the important tasks. For such nonprofits,

Table 5.4 Patterns of leadership

Quadrant	Leadership behaviors	Leadership style
Internal task orientation	Planning, budgeting, coordinating services Enforcing rules and regulations	Transactional
External task orientation	Achieving goals and legitimation Obtaining resources and establishing organizational domain	Authoritarian
Internal people orientation	Selecting, developing, motivating staff Establishing procedures for problem solving and conflict resolution	Transactional and transformational mix
External people orientation	Developing staff capabilities/team building Securing resources, building alliances, and engaging in political activities	Transformational

Source: Adapted from Schmid, 2006.
Note: Model dimensions are internal-external on the horizontal axis and task orientation–people orientation on the vertical axis.

Schmid (2006) believes a transactional leader, here defined as the one "who sets goals, clarifies desired outcomes, provides feedback, and exchanges rewards for accomplishment" (p. 182), would represent the best fit. Settings like this would be characterized as controlling and directive toward organizational members.

External Task Orientation

The management pattern described for external task orientation is very similar to that of organizations with a strong internal task orientation. Thus, we are again looking at more or less closed systems, with home care organizations serving the elderly being a good example. The reason for placing these nonprofits toward the external end of the axis is that, with the entrance of for-profits into fields previously dominated by voluntary agencies, there is now greater competition for financial support and market share, necessitating more boundary-spanning activities on the part of the top professional to secure vital resources. The leadership pattern one might expect to find in these organizations would be authoritarian, with a strong focus on the task, perhaps to the exclusion of any concern for the human factor other than as a means to an end, and a strong reliance on positional authority to control decision-making and problem-solving processes (Schmid, 2006).

Internal People Orientation

Community service organizations and agencies providing services to at-risk children and youth in the early stages of life-cycle development would appear to fit the management pattern for the internal people orientation. In both cases, staff tend to be granted a good deal of autonomy in delivering services. Like YSN in our case study, often these would be nonprofits dominated by the individual whose vision led to the establishment of the agency. However, in Schmid's model (2006), the leader's main focus is on selecting, developing, and motivating the staff as an important first step in attempting to more clearly differentiate program activities and the division of labor. Interestingly, the leadership type described for this quadrant represents a mixture of the transformational and transactional styles: The top professional must be concerned with helping employees achieve self-fulfillment in their work. At the same time, the leader must establish processes and mechanisms for problem solving and conflict resolution, as well as keep control over decision-making.

External People Orientation

As the same two types of organizations associated with the previous quadrant begin to move into the later stages of development, Schmid (2006) suggests they would then more closely fit the pattern of an external and people-focused orientation. Although the leader would continue to emphasize staff development and training, the intent here is to prepare the followers to cope more effectively with external uncertainties and constraints. Boundary-spanning skills such as creating alliances and taking advantage of opportunities that might reduce the organization's heavy reliance on stakeholders outside of the organization would come into play now as in external task orientation. Ideally, the leader would have the ability to adjust to changing circumstances and adopt a democratic or participative style in order to use staff talents and knowledge to the maximum. If the leader cannot make these adjustments, the organization may suffer the effects of founder's syndrome (see chapter 4).

FINAL THOUGHTS

Both of the analytical models just described offer a picture of nonprofit organizations as moving along an external-internal continuum. This view of organizations reflects the concepts of open and closed systems: "*Open-system* perspectives are concerned with how organizations are influenced by interactions with their environments, whereas *closed-system* approaches are more concerned with internal structures and processes" (Netting, Kettner, & McMurtry, 2004, p. 214). Of particular interest in turbulent times, open systems tend to be more able to adapt quickly to external changes and so increase their chances for survival, which would seem to lend further support to the importance of the leader's possessing excellent boundary-spanning skills to acquire the resources necessary for producing and then marketing the organization's products or services. What we are talking about is really a series of exchanges of inputs for outputs, suggesting that the transactional leader may be more in tune with today's world.

Yet without the willing and even enthusiastic support of other group members, the top professional will find it very difficult to position the organization for maximum effectiveness. Indeed, one of the biggest challenges facing nonprofit CEOs is gaining and retaining the trust of followers so that the whole is greater than the sum of its parts. In this regard, the transformational leader would offer obvious advantages, leading to a different way to consider the use of power in organizations, by directionality. Although *power over*, reflecting the leader's explicit or implicit dominance of others, is probably the most familiar form, we also find *power from*, representing the ability to resist unwanted demands, and *power to*, as another way of expressing empowerment of followers (Hollander & Offermann, 1990).

In the end, the most effective CEO would be the individual most capable of moving fluidly from the role of leader to that of manager or administrator and back, and seeing no inconsistency between inspiring group members to reach their fullest potential and being more directive with respect to daily operations to meet stakeholder expectations, as the situation demands.

Decision-Making

The need to solve a problem is frequently the impetus that initiates a decision-making process, but problem solving is just one of the possible outcomes of this kind of process. Picking a restaurant for Sunday dinner involves a decision but not a problem. Problem solving is thus more limited than decision-making even though the terms are often treated in practice as synonymous. Solving a problem tends to be essentially a cerebral activity, whereas decision-making is much more personal, requiring a conceptualization of the situation but also drawing on one's emotions and values. Furthermore, decision-making implies taking action to implement the resulting ideas, solutions, and plans (Kaye, 1992).

Arguably, making decisions on critical matters is the quintessential responsibility of a leader. The success or failure of any nonprofit may literally hinge on the quality of the decisions the top professional makes, independently or in concert with the board, on issues believed to be of long-term consequence, which leads logically to the conclusion that not all decisions need to be or should be reached at the highest organizational level. In fact, a rule of thumb is, whenever possible, to delegate this responsibility to the lowest possible level. One nonprofit implemented this principle by creating a graph to show its zones of decision-making: individual, day-to-day decisions fell to the operational staff; small-group, time-limited decisions, such as developing the annual budget, to interdependent staff teams; agencywide operational decisions, such as creating a management information system, to multidisciplinary staff teams; broad management decisions affecting the entire organization, to the leadership team; and policy decisions, to the board of directors (Golensky & DeRuiter, 1999, p. 146).

In addition to consequentiality, which takes into account the seriousness of the matter and the degree to which a decision departs from the norm, might affect operations across the board, and could have long-lasting effects, other factors that distinguish strategic decisions from run-of-the-mill decisions include their rarity, whether the conclusions reached might set a precedent, and the sheer complexity of the issue. When something arises that is new to the organization, it is unlikely the CEO and the board will have previous examples to show the way, and so handling the matter becomes more problematic. Similarly, a decision, such as whether to merge with another organization, that is likely to place constraints on the subsequent allocation of resources would by necessity fall to the top leadership to address. In short, the extent to which these factors are present or absent will determine in large measure how the decision process unfolds (Hickson, Butler, Cray, Mallory, & Wilson, 1986).

This chapter examines decision-making from all of these perspectives, first from a conceptual point of view and then with regard to practical considerations of who should be included, what information is needed, and how the process should be carried out. It also describes a specific model of decision-making that has proven useful for both groups and individuals.

DECISION-MAKING STRATEGIES

Just like the theories on leadership delineated in chapter 4, over the years there have been different ideas proposed to explain the process of making decisions. This section will set forth some of the more well-known approaches as well as some useful ideas about the process that have received less attention, especially as they might apply to the nonprofit sector.

Optimizing

The optimizing strategy takes as its primary goal to select the course of action with the greatest payoff, which means considering the relative value of every viable alternative through a thorough analysis of its costs and benefits. At its most normative, this theory assumes a kind of ideal situation in which the decision-maker is fully informed and rational and able to weigh the various alternatives with mathematical precision. However, common sense tells us that people do not typically behave in optimal ways, and collecting and processing the huge amounts of information required to undertake pure optimization would be very expensive in time, effort, and money. Moreover, it is difficult not to be influenced by less rational considerations, including personal values and relationships with other group members. As a result, the end product is often a suboptimizing solution in which some of the hoped-for benefits are realized but others are lost (Janis & Mann, 1977). For example, a caseworker may accept a promotion to a management position with higher pay and prestige only to realize she misses the satisfaction of helping individual clients improve the quality of their lives.

For many behavioral scientists the optimizing strategy is more of a prescriptive model with a set of standards that organizations should strive to reach when making decisions in order "to avoid miscalculations, wishful thinking, and vulnerability to subsequent disillusionment" (Janis & Mann, 1977, p. 25).

Satisficing

The work of Herbert Simon has taken the reality of optimizing into account by focusing on the individuals within organizations. With March (1958), he recognized the uncertainty resulting from not having perfect knowledge of all the variables that might influence the decision process nor all the likely consequences of the decision as well as the effects of group identification. This phenomenon is known as *bounded rationality*. Since all decision-making carries some degree of risk, it may be more practical to aim for reducing the uncertainty, to the extent possible, such as by following practices preset by the organization to handle routine matters. Arriving at an acceptable if not optimal outcome that would meet a minimal set of standards is called *satisficing*: "Sometimes more than one criterion is used, but always it is a question of whether the given choice will yield a 'good enough' outcome" (Janis & Mann, 1977, pp. 25–26).

Although this view of human limitations may seem a bit cynical, it does fit with the play-it-safe mentality that is predominant in many organizations in both the for-profit and nonprofit sectors. For a new CEO or even one of longer tenure who feels on somewhat shaky ground with the board, there is little incentive to propose a bold move when all that is expected is that the recommended course of action be an improvement over the status quo.

Incrementalism

Despite some of its shortcomings, satisficing can result ultimately in reaching the optimal goal, albeit very slowly. Another way of considering this strategy is as a series of incremental steps, which may be successful in moving an organization forward without causing undue resistance from other group members, since the change comes about so gradually. Charles Lindblom (1959, 1979) is perhaps the person most closely associated with this approach, based on his discussion of "the science of muddling through" in the context of formulating government policy. However, because his work contrasts how decisions should be made with how they are actually made, it has universal applicability to all types of organizations.

As noted earlier, the ideal method for making decisions would be to consider the possible alternatives and then use a process of rational deduction to arrive at the best one. Instead, the decision-maker uses a strategy of "disjointed incrementalism" (Lindblom, 1979, p. 523) by considering only a restricted number of choices in contemplating marginal change as the desired end. Remote possibilities, even if important, are discarded so as not to complicate the process and prevent the other key players from accepting the proposed course of action, which is rarely seen as a solution to a problem but, rather, as a way to alleviate it. Thus, one might come back to a situation time and time again, in the hope of making small improvements with each attempt. Here ends are adjusted to means instead of the other way around, with practicality as the highest value.

The Garbage Can Model

The garbage can strategy is about choice, or perhaps the lack of it in the conventional sense, for it takes as its premise that organizations are guided by a variety of inconsistent and ill-defined preferences. In the absence of a cohesive structure, group members use the procedures available to them to interpret what was done in the past and what they are currently doing as they are taking action. From this perspective we might view an organization as "a collection of choices looking for problems, issues and feelings looking for decision situations in which they might be aired, [and] solutions looking for issues to which they might be the answer" (Cohen, March, & Olsen, 1980, p. 145).

Unlike the purely rational organization imagined in the optimizing approach, here the organization is seen as endlessly adapting and responding to diverse internal and external constraints in reaching decisions (Cyert & March, 1963). A situation calling for a decision is likened to a garbage can into which group members, whose participation may vary over time, drop their interpretations of the problem and possible solutions as they are generated. Each of these elements, although independent, becomes a factor in decision-making as they become mixed together. Making a decision, then, is not an orderly process progressing from point A to point B; action becomes possible when the right combination of problems, solutions, and participants comes together in a timely manner. While not ideal, this approach does allow the organization to move forward (Cohen et al., 1980).

Mixed Scanning

As a synthesis of optimizing and extreme incrementalism, mixed scanning, as developed by Etzioni (1967), accommodates the stringent requirements of the one and the sometimes overly casual but practical considerations of the other to provide another method of decision-making. With this approach, an organization would employ some of the features of optimizing, such as the systematic collection of pertinent information, along with a sequential review of relevant alternatives to narrow down the possibilities in order to make fundamental policy decisions, but an incremental process based on simple forms of satisficing would be used to deal with any subsequent issues arising from the strategic decision, which may lead to gradual revisions of the action plan and perhaps pave the way for a new major decision (Janis & Mann, 1977).

Organizational leaders must therefore first take into account the seriousness of each dilemma that is presented to determine the level of resources—time, energy, personnel, and money—to commit to the decision-making process. Intended by Etzioni as a normative or prescriptive model, mixed scanning "has the virtue of adaptive flexibility at different stages of decision making" (Janis & Mann, 1977, p. 38); as such, it lends itself to work-related decisions at all levels of an organization, such as for time management, and could even be used by individuals on personal matters.

The Four-Force Model

Less well-known perhaps than the other approaches just discussed, the four-force model may be even more in tune with today's turbulent environment. It equates organizational effectiveness with "potential capacity," which "refers to the optimal match of individual decision styles, task demands and organizational climate" (Driver & Rowe, 1979, p. 141). According to these authors, making a decision is not simply a reaction to a given stimulus that leads to a particular conclusion; it also involves a politically influenced exchange process that is much more complex than simply choosing among alternatives.

The decision process here begins with an external stimulus and then proceeds through a series of steps until the parties identify a new direction, one consistent with organizational objectives but also addressing individual interests. In any given situation, environmental demands from without as well as the internal climate, peer-group pressure, the task at hand, and individual needs and styles influence the way decisions are made. Each of these four factors may differentially affect the final disposition of the matter, but especially by knowing the leader's thinking habits, perceptions, needs, motives, aspirations, and fears, we can better understand why certain decisions are made and how they are implemented. Adopting a more person-centered focus may result in more effective decision-making, thereby ensuring beneficial outcomes for the organization (Driver & Rowe, 1979).

Consensus

Consensus decision-making is a process that is used by many grassroots associations, feminist collectives, and other small, essentially volunteer-run groups because of its egalitarian, inclusive, and participatory philosophy that is consistent with their democratic ideals. It is similar to satisficing in that the goal is to come to a reasonable, not necessarily optimal outcome that all members of the group can accept, but the way in which that end is achieved is quite different. Although there is generally a facilitator whose role is to help move the process along, to the extent possible, everyone's input is actively solicited and considered of equal value.

Depending on the ground rules the group has established, even a single person can block acceptance of a decision. Thus, strategies such as compromise and trade-offs are used in an effort to bring a dissenter to the point of being comfortable with the proposed resolution of the issue at hand. The proposal may then be rephrased in order to reach an agreement. One of the potential drawbacks to this approach is that it can be very time consuming, but on the positive side, individual group members may have a greater commitment to a decision achieved through consensus (Wikipedia, 2008).

A Final Word

Table 6.1 summarizes these decision-making models, making it easy to compare their key features. In the end, as with so many of the dimensions of organizational life, taking a contingency approach, with the ability to draw on whichever model best suits the situation of the moment, may present the optimum course of action for the leader.

Table 6.1 Approaches to decision-making

Strategy	Assumption	Comment
Optimizing	Assumes a rational process based on full information and careful weighing of alternatives to achieve the greatest payoff.	This prescriptive model is often difficult to attain.
Satisficing	Assumes a bounded rationality, i.e., limited or constrained by personal qualities and group identification.	The goal is to reach an acceptable if not optimal solution based on a minimal set of standards.
Incrementalism ("muddling through")	Assumes a slow, gradual approach to a desired end by considering a restricted number of choices to achieve a minimal change acceptable to others.	Practicality is the highest value, with ends adjusted to means.
Garbage-can model	Assumes the organization lacks a cohesive structure and so is endlessly adapting and responding to internal and external constraints.	The process is not orderly, but it does allow for choice and problem resolution.
Mixed scanning	Assumes a process using features of both optimizing and incrementalism, the former for major decisions and the latter for subsequent issues that arise.	This normative model is flexible, lending itself to wide use.
Four-force model	Assumes a politically influenced exchange process initiated by an external stimulus.	Decisions are differentially affected by environmental factors, peers, the task, and individual needs and styles.
Consensus	Assumes an egalitarian, inclusive, and participatory process to reach a reasonable decision with which group members are comfortable.	Compromise and trade-offs may be used to enable dissenters to accept the proposal.

PRACTICAL CONSIDERATIONS

As previously noted, the decision process, particularly in regard to critical issues, is complex. Depending on the issue, the outcome of the deliberations may have a profound impact on the organization and its key stakeholders, extending well into the future. Accordingly, the pressure on the leadership core to make the "right" choice can be overwhelming—right being a subjective judgment depending on one's personal interest in the matter under review. Moreover, it is seldom the case that only one important concern is facing the organization at a given point in time, so there may be multiple problems to be addressed, each one with its own claim on organizational resources.

With major stakeholders placing so much emphasis on accountability, decision-makers in both the public and private nonprofit sectors often seek to protect themselves from criticism by using as much objective, relevant information as they can possibly obtain to lay claim to some degree of rationality, even when the actual decision process does not follow the optimizing model (Ben-Arieh, 2008).

Stages in the Decision Process

When circumstances permit, the decision process would include all of these steps.

1. Defining the situation or problem
2. Collecting and studying the facts pertaining to the issue
3. Formulating the possible choices
4. Anticipating the likely outcomes of these choices
5. Selecting the best available solution
6. Implementing the decision
7. Evaluating the results immediately after action has been taken and again at a later date to judge the full impact.

As the sequence unfolds, the leader should consider the feelings of all affected parties to the extent possible and maintain a flexible posture to allow for any alteration in the plans that seems warranted (Skidmore, 1995).

Rather than discussing this process in the abstract, let us consider the different steps within the context of an issue that a small charitable nonprofit might encounter, how to accommodate a different population within its traditional service mix. For this illustration, we will assume the organization's primary constituency has been African American youth living in a low-income neighborhood. It has been noted that a social condition becomes a problem only when someone judges it to be negative or harmful (Kettner, Moroney, & Martin, 2008). The triggering event in this scenario is a visit to the CEO by the councilman serving the district in which the organization is located, to make a strong case for including Hispanic youth, whose families have become an increasingly visible part of the community over the past year, in the agency's programs.

Since the politician has been a good friend to the agency, the CEO agrees to look into the matter. The first step is to gather relevant information, including demographics on the current makeup of the community as well as projections for the next five years. In addition to collecting technical data, the executive seeks out individuals with some expert knowledge of the issue, for example, a board member who as the pastor of a local black church would be attuned to the feelings of the more established African American residents toward the newcomers. From this initial step, the scope of the problem can be formulated. Next, possible alternatives are generated and reviewed; an important consideration is whether another nonprofit in the immediate area or nearby would be in a better position to serve the Hispanic young people, perhaps one that already has a Spanish-speaking staff member. As no other agency is a viable candidate, the CEO then weighs the effects of a service expansion on the available organizational resources.

Fortuitously, it turns out that one of the current counselors speaks some Spanish and would be willing to work on his language skills should the additional youth become clients. Since the possibility of having to hire a new person had been a potential roadblock, now the CEO feels comfortable making the case before the board to accede to the councilman's request. The proposed resolution is presented as a win-win situation: Not only will this action cement the positive feelings of a major stakeholder toward the organization, the service expansion should provide justification for requesting an increase in contract dollars from the agency's government funder. After the board approves the request, the CEO turns the practical details of implementation over to the program director. One month after the new clients have been incorporated into agency activities, the change is discussed positively at a staff meeting; a year later, the CEO remains pleased by the results of the decision.

Modes of Decision-Making

From their extensive research on strategic decisions, Hickson et al. (1986) have identified three different ways of making decisions that take into account the manner in which the process unfolds.

In *fluid* processes, things appear to move quite smoothly, with the main activity conducted at regularly scheduled meetings through set committees. As a result, there tend to be fewer delays and impediments. Fewer experts are called upon, but they are respected for their knowledge and opinions. Although this kind of decision is made at the highest organizational level and can be precedent setting, it is generally reached quite quickly, in a matter of months. Obtaining financial support for a new program would be a good example. In larger organizations the development director might initiate the process, while in smaller settings it would probably be the CEO. In either case the main deliberations would take place at meetings of the board's fund-raising committee, with staff supplying information as needed. If a grant or contract is sought, the funder's established deadline for submitting a proposal would place time parameters on the process.

In *sporadic* processes, many delays are common due to a variety of obstacles, from outright resistance to the matter at hand, which is often highly consequential and potentially controversial, to having to wait for certain reports to be generated. A number of people, both within and outside the organization, are likely to participate in the process, each bringing different levels of expertise and influence as well as personal interests. As a result, deliberations tend to be prolonged and move in fits and starts until a decision is reached by the top leaders. The actual case of a public museum's conversion to nonprofit status falls into this category. As the oldest museum in the state and with three boards involved (its formal, city-appointed board; a membership-based volunteer support group; and a foundation established to solicit funds and build an endowment), it is not surprising that it took nearly ten years to bring the matter to a final resolution.

In *constricted* processes, there tends to be less scope for negotiation about the issue of concern, and the decision is made high up in the organizational hierarchy but often below the top level, or at least by the CEO alone without board input. Because the matter is perceived to have limited consequences and relevant information is readily available, discussions generally take place through regular staff channels, with perhaps help from selected external experts. The decision may be reached in just months. An illustration of this kind of process would be upgrading the organization's management information system with computers donated by a local corporation. Although program staff would be asked to propose ideas for new data elements to be added to the system, the actual changes would be implemented by the MIS director and her staff, assisted by a tech person working for the donor. The CEO would simply announce the change to the board.

Hickson et al. (1986) then added one further element to explain the decision process, as shown in table 6.2, upon discovering that the politicality of the issue, referring to the degree to which influence is exercised by both internal and external actors to affect the outcome of the process, along with its complexity, significantly affected how the process unfolded. This resulted in three distinct "modes of decision-making" (p. 174): *tractable-fluid*, for unusual but noncontroversial matters; *vortex-sporadic*, for weighty and controversial matters; and *familiar-constricted*, for normal and recurrent matters.

Table 6.2 Modes of decision-making

Mode	*Characteristics*
Tractable-fluid	Unusual but noncontroversial subject
	Diffuse but not serious consequences
Example: Seeking funding for a new program	Limited participation
	Formally channeled process
	Precedent setting
	Evenly influenced
Vortex-sporadic	Weighty and controversial subject
	Serious consequences
Example: Changing corporate status	Diverse participation
	Prolonged, irregular discussion
	Not precedent setting
	Highly politicized by external interests
Familiar-constricted	Comparatively well-known subject
	Limited consequences
Example: Upgrading the MIS system	Limited participation
	Limited discussion
	Not precedent setting
	Internally determined

Source: Adapted from Hickson et al., 1986.

Group Decisions

Even though certain decisions could be made unilaterally by the CEO and some, such as during a crisis, may have to be made in this manner, given the nature of most nonprofits, the majority of decisions will be handled through a group process. This can be a complicating factor, but it undoubtedly ensures greater buy-in and legitimacy of the outcome. Other possible advantages of this type of decision-making are the ability to generate a greater number of alternatives and process more information, improvement in coordination, and enhanced communication. On the downside, however, group decisions tend to take longer and can be compromised or unduly dominated by a few key individuals. In addition, groups can have difficulty in coming to a decision, possibly due to *groupthink*, a phenomenon in which the desire to reach consensus is so strong that an independent and realistic appraisal of alternatives is ignored (Skidmore, 1995).

Scope and Authority

Depending on the organizational structure, some issues may fall within the purview of an established group, such as a board committee charged in the bylaws with overseeing investments or a staff task force composed of all department heads that meets annually with the CEO to help construct the operating budget. When setting up new groups that may be task and/or time limited, it is important for the organizational leader to determine in advance the scope of involvement and the extent of delegation for each situation and convey these parameters as clearly as possible to the individuals invited to take part in the endeavor. Otherwise, the process may have unintended consequences, for example, when staff believe their efforts will be more than just advisory, only to discover their views have little bearing on the final decision. Resentment and reluctance to accept the decision may result.

Nutt (1989) has identified four types of participation: (1) *comprehensive*, for a group involving all those likely to be affected by a decision and given the full authority to make the decision; (2) *complete*, for a fully representative group whose charge is only to make recommendations or comment on a proposed action; (3) *delegated*, for a group composed of selected stakeholders but with full decision-making authority; and (4) *token*, for a group with both limited representation and authority. Comprehensive participation is viewed as the most effective. Complete participation is hampered by the restrictions on authority. In delegated participation, buy-in tends to extend only to those directly involved, who must then try to persuade nonparticipants to accept their decision. Token participation, which uses its selected members strictly in an advisory capacity, is considered the least effective of all.

Managing the Group Process

The substance of the decision process as well as the type of participation selected will influence the composition of the group. For the most important decisions, the CEO is apt to involve those seen as the best critical thinkers, those with expertise essential to the issue, those perceived to be especially loyal to the organization and to the top leader, and those with influence over other group members, in some combination. Size is also a consideration. Small groups, with five the preferred number, are often better for evaluation and judging tasks and for addressing concrete problems because they encourage equal involvement, discourage the development of factions, and can act more quickly. Conversely, bigger groups seem to be more advantageous for developmental tasks and abstract problems where members benefit from hearing diverse viewpoints that can lead to innovative solutions, but the danger of factions forming is greater, increasing the difficulty of coming to a consensus on the matter at hand (Nutt, 1989).

Another factor is that the interactions within a small group move along an expressive-instrumental continuum. Included in the social-emotional area are members' positive or negative expressions of their personal feelings toward each other; on the instrumental side are the separate actions to achieve the defined purpose for the group, such as presenting facts, deliberating, stating opinions, and voting. The key point here is that, frequently, different people fulfill the roles of task leader and social leader (Mason, 1996). Thus, it may be the individual formally designated as committee chair who develops and distributes the meeting agenda, calls the meeting to order, keeps the discussion orderly and productive, sums up the actions taken, and announces the next steps while someone else emerges to attend to the overall mood of the group, stepping in with a word or a gesture to dispel tensions, make sure the quieter members feel their views are respected, and generally promote cohesion.

Finally, Tropman (2006) reminds us that decision-making comes down to making choices, often among competing sets of values, and with choices there will always be winners and losers. He prefers to call the process "decision-building" (p. 217) to recognize that it is really a question of putting together disparate elements to create a whole, combining knowledge of the steps in the process with skill in helping those involved move forward in a timely and beneficial manner, maximizing the gains of multiple stakeholders to the extent possible.

SIX THINKING HATS

The Six Thinking Hats method, developed by Edward de Bono (1999), is a practical tool to facilitate constructive decision-making by groups and individuals. Formally trained as both a physician and psychologist, de Bono is one of the world's foremost experts on the structure and functions of the brain. Over many years he has examined the manifestations of mental processes for evidence of underlying systems to make some sense of the different patterns within the brain's neural networks (de Bono, 1967).

These studies led to the conceptualization of *lateral thinking*, which in today's vernacular might be equated with "thinking outside the box," as compared to the more familiar *vertical thinking*, in which thoughts move in a logical, linear fashion, much like the workings of a computer. In contrast, "lateral thinking has to do with rearranging available information so that it is snapped out of the established pattern and forms a new and better pattern" (de Bono, 1969, p. 237). In practice, the two types of thinking are complementary. When one cannot find the solution to a problem using vertical thinking or when a new idea is required, lateral thinking should be used. We have all had moments in which a sudden insight enables us to solve a problem that had seemed very complex, and the answer then appears so obvious. By developing an ability to use lateral thinking, a person might be able to call upon insight at will. On the other hand, vertical thinking, as determined by past experience and the needs of the moment, is preferable in everyday living, for otherwise each action and sensation would have to be analyzed as it occurs, leading to an unbearable complexity. Furthermore, once lateral thinking has occurred, vertical thinking is applied to test its validity and to integrate the new idea or approach within one's memory bank so that it can be used again in similar situations (de Bono, 1967, 1969).

Always concerned about the practical applications of his work, de Bono (1999) subsequently introduced the concept of *parallel thinking*, better known as the Six Thinking Hats method, which stems from research demonstrating that thinking is a multifaceted process incorporating facts, feelings, values, logic, and creativity. His work has shown that when we attempt to think in more than one way simultaneously, the result is confusion because we are trying to do too much, thus taxing the brain's capacity. Argument has been the foundation of Western thought since the time of Socrates, Plato, and Aristotle. Logic and analysis are used, often in a confrontational or adversarial way, to convince others of the correctness of your viewpoint. In contrast, based on the teachings of Confucius, the focus of parallel thinking is on behavior rather than on personality or psychological makeup, in order to find a way to be constructive and move forward by having everyone involved look at a particular situation or issue in the same way at the same time. All ideas, even when contradictory, are accepted and considered valid; later on, either one idea is chosen or the final product is crafted to include the various positions.

To illustrate the differences between the Socratic method and parallel thinking, imagine that four people are each standing on one side of a large house and, using their cell phones to communicate, are trying to persuade each other that their perspective is the best one to describe the house. Using parallel thinking, however, all four would walk to the front, the back, and the two sides of the house together, so they can experience the same view at the same time and share their ideas face-to-face. In doing so, the final picture of the house that emerges is likely to be fuller and more accurate (de Bono, 1999).

Putting on the Hats

As summarized in table 6.3, the Six Thinking Hats method is essentially an extended role-play and, when used with groups, is presented as a game with set rules, which acts as a powerful social mechanism to promote cooperation. Each mode of thinking is represented by a different-colored hat as a symbol of the role being occupied at that time; yet wearing a specific hat is not descriptive but directional, meaning that a certain kind of thinking is going on (for example, the facilitator might say, "Before making a final choice, let's have some black hat thinking now"). The key point is that everyone's knowledge, experience, and intelligence can be brought to bear on a given matter by moving together in a prescribed direction (de Bono, 1994, 1999).

Table 6.3 Overview of six thinking hats method

Symbol	Cognitive mode	Application
White hat	Factual, informative	Lays out information, from opinion to checkable facts
Red hat	Emotional, intuitive	Legitimizes expression of feelings
Yellow hat	Constructive, positive	Identifies values and benefits
Black hat	Critical, cautionary	Assesses risks; "devil's advocate"
Green hat	Creative, provocative	Searches for and generates new ideas and possibilities
Blue hat	Organizing, managing	Orchestrates and structures thinking process

Source: Adapted from de Bono, 1999.

As shown, there is some logic in the choice of color in each case. White, for instance, is frequently associated with neutrality, and inasmuch as the expression "seeing red" is a common phrase for being angry, red seems appropriate for the emotional dimension. Although the white hat is used primarily for informational purposes, the red, yellow, and black hats are applicable to assessment as well. Lateral thinking is an important part of green-hat thinking, which is not just the purview of the "idea person" in the group but something to which everyone can contribute by deliberately setting out to think creatively. The blue hat is generally worn by the group facilitator or leader. It is a critical role, as the person wearing this hat determines the agenda (to which others may contribute), controls the flow of the discussion by naming the hat to be worn initially and then calling for a change from one hat to another, makes observations on the progress of the group, and brings the discussion to a close by summarizing what has been decided, articulating next steps, if warranted, and preparing a final report at the appropriate time (de Bono, 1999).

The hats may be used singly, to request a type of thinking, or in a sequence to either explore a topic or solve a problem. Moving sequentially from one hat to another at the facilitator's direction may simply evolve from the discussion or may be preset to fit a particular need. If, for example, the subject is one that might evoke strong feelings in the group members, it makes sense to schedule the red hat first to bring these feelings to the surface before going on to white- or black-hat thinking. The reality is that values and emotions do give relevance to our thinking; if not allowed to be a legitimate part of the process, they can emerge, unbidden, at inopportune times or even become the underlying cause for not embracing the group's decision or action. Similarly, in an assessment situation, the yellow hat is often used before the black hat to ensure that the benefits of the issue are articulated before focusing on possible obstacles. If done in the reverse, the group may become discouraged prematurely and never give an option its due. However, there is no set formula for sequencing; it is a skill developed over time, as is knowing how long to allow a discussion under one hat before switching (de Bono, 1994, 1999).

An Illustration

A midsized nonprofit providing direct services to families around issues of suspected child abuse is considering a merger with a small grassroots organization whose mission is advocacy on the same issue. The two CEOs, after meeting twice to explore the possibilities of joining forces and having identified enough compelling reasons for further deliberation, have now received approval from their respective boards to continue the conversation. A seven-person ad hoc committee has been formed, with three representatives from each agency, at different staff levels, and the vice president for programs from the local United Way, of which both nonprofits are members. The United Way executive, with training in the Six Thinking Hats method and being the most neutral on the merger, has agreed to be the facilitator.

At the first committee meeting, the facilitator, wearing the blue hat, has proposed that the agenda be to develop a formal statement of purpose for the merger, to bring back to the two boards as soon as possible and ultimately to share with all staff. To date, the staff, other than those sitting around the table, have been told some kind of collaboration is up for discussion but not the specific nature of the talks, so as not to raise unfounded concerns. However, since the word is likely to get out before long, it makes sense to ensure that whatever is communicated is based on fact. With everyone in agreement, the facilitator asks them to put on the red hat and gives each a minute or two to express personal feelings on the idea of a merger.

As might be expected, the resulting comments are mostly variants on "I fear we'll lose our organizational identity." The facilitator then requests some white-hat thinking, which includes hard data but also beliefs that can be checked. Thus, it is acceptable for a group member to say, "On the whole, merger has not been a familiar strategy in our community." Another comments that she'd recently read a journal article stating that mergers were becoming more common among nonprofits. A third person reminds the others that the two organizations have had a history of working together over the years on an informal basis. When this line of thinking has been pursued as far as it can go, the facilitator asks the group members to put on the yellow hat, to identify the potential benefits of a merger. It seems everyone has done some reading on the topic, and it does not take much time to make a list of the generally accepted incentives, from realizing economies of scale by purchasing in bulk to decreasing competition for limited resources. The CEO of the advocacy organization offers perhaps the most positive thought: "We would be stronger through linking with a larger nonprofit with more programs, and in the end, all of our clients would be better served by pooling our resources."

Putting on the black hat is the logical next step. As the opposite of the yellow hat, it is worn to engage in what we commonly call critical thinking to ensure all risks are assessed. The biggest drawbacks to a merger that emerge are a feared loss of autonomy, especially for the smaller agency; the possible loss of some management positions where there is duplication (for example, both now have bookkeepers on staff); the cost of having to change signage and stationery and to market the new entity; and most of all, the inherent difficulty in combining two quite different organizational cultures. At this point, the facilitator decides to shift to the green hat, which represents the full range of creativity and therefore is concerned with finding alternative solutions to previously recognized problems as well as ways of approaching a new issue. Using a tactic always available during a session, he first asks that each person do some individual thinking for two or three minutes to come up with ideas for moving the merger forward and then goes around the table person by person to hear the results.

To everyone's surprise, it is a female counselor from the larger organization, normally quiet in meetings and perceived as rather timid, who offers an unexpected thought to address the major impediments that have been identified: "What if we approach merger as a blender? Everyone seems to be assuming it's an all-or-nothing situation, but blenders have various settings, from low to high, including stir, chop, mix, beat, and so on." The other committee members quickly pick up on this metaphor, and before long, a gradual process of increasing levels of collaboration over two to three years, with a "cooling-off" period between levels to assess reactions internally and externally, begins to take shape. This would allow the two organizations to test out the idea of merger before making a final commitment, and even if the last step is never taken, some of the benefits, such as joint purchasing, could be realized nonetheless.

Since the facilitator believes the group has gone as far as it can for now, he summarizes the main points of the discussion. Everyone agrees the staff member who conceived of the blender metaphor should write a position paper on the proposed solution and circulate it to the others for comments and reactions. A second meeting is scheduled for the following week to finalize the details. At that time, the committee will also make plans for a combined board and staff meeting involving both agencies to lay out the concept. It is further agreed to keep the details of the committee's work confidential so the new idea can be presented in the most effective way.

Later that evening, in reflecting on the meeting, the facilitator noted that the benefits of the method presented as part of his training had indeed been realized: (1) By harnessing everyone's power and then working together in the same direction, the quality of the thinking process was enhanced. (2) By laying out all thoughts in parallel rather than responding to each point as it was raised, the work was completed in just two hours. (3) Ego, in the absence of confrontational and adversarial thinking, did not become an obstacle to productivity. (4) Results were optimized because establishing a specific time for each mode of thinking eliminated confusion (de Bono, 1999).

FINAL THOUGHTS

As noted at the beginning of this chapter, problems come in all sizes and shapes, not all of them requiring the attentions of the top professional. However, once an issue has reached the critical stage, organizational members tend to look for direction to the person or persons occupying the leadership role, who may even be volunteers, depending on the type of organization. Although it may be quite tempting to do nothing, failing to take action in the hope that the dilemma will somehow resolve itself is generally not wise; procrastination often complicates an already difficult situation. Given the potential pitfalls, decision-making can be an act of courage, especially if stakeholder opinions differ on the most desirable course to follow. Even when using the optimizing strategy, it is possible to be misled by faulty or incomplete information, to jump to a premature conclusion due to time constraints, or to realize too late one's normally sound judgment has been adversely affected by personal feelings or the flawed opinions of so-called experts.

When the realization hits that a recent decision may have been an error, there are likely to be conflicting emotions, depending on the perceived organizational and personal consequences of the actions that have been put in motion. After assessing the possible damage, the individual or group may elect to (1) admit the mistake and then undo the decision by moving in a different direction that seems more prudent, (2) look for a compromise solution by curtailing implementation of the decision without fully disowning it, or (3) go forward with the original decision in the belief that it is still the most desirable of the available alternatives (Janis & Mann, 1977). In all enterprises, the reality is mistakes will happen. Therefore, the true test of leadership may be in how missteps are acknowledged and then rectified.

Organizational Change

These are volatile times for all nonprofit organizations as the expectations and rewards emanating from the external environment are constantly shifting. The burden may be especially heavy for the human services subsector. Although called upon to deliver an ever-larger proportion of social services, these organizations "are facing reduced federal funding, a shift from grants to service contracts, multiple stakeholder demands, increased competition among service providers, pressure to demonstrate efficiency and effectiveness to sustain funding, and heavy competition for various sources of support" (Jaskyte & Dressler, 2005, p. 24).

It is no exaggeration to say that in light of such pressures, organizational survival may be in the balance if the leadership is not up to the task of finding ways to respond to these diverse challenges in an effective manner. In the words of the CEO of a human service organization headquartered in a midwestern city, "The not-for-profit world [today] is . . . a hard-nosed, cutthroat business." From a study of mortality patterns for nonprofits in a major U.S. metropolitan area, Bielefeld (1994) compared the use of three approaches representing possible responses to the uncertainties noted above—generating income through new revenue strategies, attempting to increase legitimation by funders through activities to enhance the prestige or reputation of the organization, and realizing cost savings through retrenchment—by organizations that ceased to operate and those that survived. Overall, he found the organizations that failed were younger and smaller, used fewer strategies, with a heavier reliance on retrenchment, and had less diversified funding than the survivors, but patterns also varied widely across and within industries, which speaks to the complexity of organizational change.

This chapter addresses organizational change in both conceptual and practical terms. The relevant theories can be divided into two major categories: *selection models* perceive the environment as the major source of change, with organizational survival predicated on the degree of fit with the external world, whereas *adaptation models* view top leaders as being able to initiate change to further the organizational mission (Galaskiewicz & Bielefeld, 1998). In applying these theories, we will explore the role of the organizational leader in managing change and the viability of different kinds of strategic responses to external threats and opportunities.

THE UBIQUITY OF CHANGE

As in the previous chapter on decision-making, here the focus will be on major shifts in the essential character of the organization rather than on routine changes that may be more cosmetic in nature (see table 7.1). We are talking about something that fundamentally alters the organization in one or more of these areas: legitimacy, sector, professionalism, technology, mission, structure, funding, leadership, and societal values—each to be analyzed within its own specific context before any action is taken (Perlmutter & Gummer, 1994). In other words, it is the distinction between a grassroots group realizing it has grown so much that it now must formalize the way it conducts business (major shift) and deciding to hold its weekly all-staff meeting on Monday rather than Friday morning (minor shift).

Leaders must determine how to respond appropriately to each situation, taking into account the implications of decisions on organizational efficiency, effectiveness, and productivity. Furthermore, these considerations need to be site-specific; what is of grave concern in one setting may be relatively trivial in another, and vice versa. For example, a nonprofit board was informed by its CEO that the camping director hired earlier in the year had been fired for poor performance due to his unsuccessful attempt to juggle two jobs, for he had never relinquished his similar position with another nonprofit. The board saw the matter as grounds to force out the executive director. However, the board at the other agency placed the full blame on the camping director's deception, and its CEO suffered no repercussions. Same issue but very different reactions.

Therefore, each organization has to weigh the pros and cons of individual strategies to determine potential costs, likely benefits, and its own level of risk tolerance. In the marketing and business management literature there is a classic typology of strategy selection. The Defender tends to stick to past practices and attempt to execute the strat-

Table 7.1 Major organizational transformations

Area of change	Nature of change
Legitimacy	Informal to formally sanctioned organization
Sector	Nonprofit to for-profit or public status (or vice versa)
Professionalism	Personnel shift from one professional group to another
Technology	Computerization of data Shift in treatment modalities
Mission	Revision of organizational purpose to maintain viability
Structure	Organizational redesign Redistribution of functions and authority
Funding	Shift in the resource mix
Leadership	Transition in role occupant and/or style
Societal Values	Internal adaptation to conform to external realities

Source: Adapted from Perlmutter & Gummer, 1994.

egy as well as or better than anyone else; the Prospector is an innovator, willing to take risks in providing new products and services and regularly experimenting with reactions to emerging trends; the Analyzer tries to be efficient but also competitive with the rest of the industry; and the Reactor will take action reluctantly, only when faced with strong threats (Miles & Snow, 1978). In the last analysis, the biggest challenge in effecting organizational change may be to remain flexible and receptive to new possibilities but also sensitive to the impact on key stakeholders.

Theoretical Considerations

From the different theoretical approaches that address relations between organizations and the environment, the following models, summarized in table 7.2, have been chosen because they offer useful insights into the process of change in nonprofit settings.

Selection Models

From the selection perspective, environmental effects on organizations are the primary sources of change. Organizations have a limited capacity to change themselves, and their core features tend to remain the same.

Under population ecology theory, the basic unit of analysis is a set of organizations with shared characteristics, such as size, age, and field of specialization. For instance, all nonprofits providing day care would be considered part of the same industry. In general, organizations compete for limited resources, such as membership or capital, against others with similar capacities and consumer profile in the same geographic space, meaning

Table 7.2 Theories of change

Selection model	Adaptation model
Source of change: environment	*Source of change*: organization
Population ecology theory: Shared organizational characteristics; organization seeks competitive position within its ecological niche.	*Contingency theory*: No single structure fits all organizations; tactical moves to align organization with environmental features.
Institutional theory: Impact of cultural patterns on organizational behavior to secure legitimacy; use of coercion, socialization, and normative mechanisms to promote conformity.	*Resource dependency theory*: Reliance on a limited number of external resources can constrain organization; strategic adaptations to change power balance.
	Political-economy theory: Interrelationship between internal and external political and economic forces; organization reacts to levels of marketplace supply and demand.

Sources: Adapted from Galaskiewicz & Bielefeld, 1998; Schmid, 2004.

they occupy a certain ecological niche. However, even though the organizations may resemble each other in structure and vulnerability to external constraints, those enjoying a closer fit with environmental conditions, whether political, economic, social, legal, or technological in nature, are better positioned to survive (Galaskiewicz & Bielefeld, 1998; Schmid, 2004). Consider that in times of high unemployment, community colleges tend to increase enrollment at the expense of liberal arts institutions because of their emphasis on training or retraining individuals to meet local business needs, and in only two years.

In contrast, institutional theory focuses more on the influence of cultural patterns in defining and enforcing appropriate organizational behavior. Political, economic, and social factors explain how legitimacy is conferred. Thus an organization may adopt standards mandated by a legal or regulatory body, become socialized to particular community values, or adjust to doing business in ways that become taken for granted. It also happens that some external institutional change, like the passage of new legislation, may suddenly confer legitimacy on a certain group of organizations. Accordingly, organizations may exercise rationality in choosing work procedures, but "more often conformity is less conscious" (Galaskiewicz & Bielefeld, 1998, p. 8).

The board's attitude toward the camping program at YSN, the agency in our case study, is a good illustration of this theory. Despite changes in the campers, with many now exhibiting severe behavioral problems, the trustees saw no need to train the counselors to deal with these new challenges, consistent with the long-held belief that two weeks in the country cured all ills.

Adaptation Models

Unlike the previous classification, the fundamental assumption of adaptation models is that organizations can and will make changes to ensure survival and goal attainment. In fact, top leaders are expected to initiate strategies to achieve these positive ends as they gain a better understanding of the organization's internal and external environments. The three main approaches here are contingency theory, resource dependency theory, and political-economy theory.

In line with contingency theory, no one structure is effective for all organizations. Instead, each organization must know its own environment; the closer the fit, the more likely the organization will keep uncertainty at a manageable level and maintain an adequate flow of resources. Tactical moves are based on what would be most advantageous under current conditions. For instance, agencies operating in highly competitive niches may be more apt to alter their programs or to use political know-how to get ahead. Similarly, a determination that the external environment is either turbulent or stable will result in different internal responses regarding staffing patterns, rules and regulations, and so forth (Galaskiewicz & Bielefeld, 1998; Schmid, 2004). An example is the decision of a mental health agency in a midwestern city to change its primary methodology to short-term, solution-focused therapy to be more in tune with managed care principles in order to beat out the competition for government contracts.

The main premise of resource dependency theory is that when organizations can exercise some control over the acquisition of resources, they are more able to shape their relationships with external funding sources and ensure survival. In contrast, those dependent on a limited number of outside resources will be more constrained and vulnerable to negative consequences (Bielefeld, 1994). Strategies here might include making programs and services especially cost effective and distinctive to increase market appeal and diversifying revenue to include a variety of sources, from foundation and corporate grants and individual gifts to fees for service, dues, product sales, and other similar endeavors. These kinds of efforts help reduce the power imbalance that otherwise may occur in the exchange process of obtaining essential resources. The CEO of a neighborhood health clinic in a California city summed up this approach: "Part of what I try to do is . . . focus on our core mission and see where we can get funded for what we want to do rather than doing what you can get funding for. . . . The game is to . . . [identify] a lot of things that work together."

Finally, even though political-economy theory is considered an adaptation model, in practice it encompasses some elements of both viewpoints in that the organization may sometimes be reactive to its environment and, at other times, much more proactive in order to secure necessary resources and survive. This theory suggests there is a close relationship between political and economic forces outside of and within the organization, and as the levels of supply and demand fluctuate in the marketplace for the organization's "products" (its programs and services), so does the organizational response (Wernet, 1994). For a more extensive discussion of this theory, see chapter 3.

Applying Theory

The Coalition, a nonprofit in a small East Coast city, is the only provider of prevention services to address child abuse and neglect within the surrounding county. As such, it is not in direct competition with other organizations for scarce resources (population ecology theory). Yet its growth has been stymied by adherence to practices consistent with the values of its founding group of social workers; it still operates in a grassroots style some thirty years later (institutional theory). In response to being informed by its major funder, United Way, of a significant cut in the allocation for the next fiscal year due to the poor outcome of the annual campaign, the organization has been forced to lay off staff and give up two rooms in its rented space (political-economy theory). The longer-term effect is that the Coalition must devise strategies to increase revenue from other sources, both old and new. The organization is now in negotiations with local law enforcement and social services personnel to create the first child advocacy center in the state (resource dependency and contingency theories).

Change versus the Status Quo

Strategic management is the descriptive term for the leader's efforts to establish a good fit between the organization and its environment so the former can realize its goals and objectives consistent with its mission and available resources while being responsive to the latter's demands. This necessitates building an organizational structure as well as selecting and developing personnel capable of bringing about a desired change. In contrast, *operations management* is more concerned with maintaining organizational equilibrium and fostering employees' loyalty and commitment to the already established rules and values. Although both types of management are needed within an organization, given their different purposes, there is the potential for conflict unless the leader can strike the right balance between the two (Wortman, 1981).

Putting all of this in perspective, Senge (2006, pp. xvi–xvii) maintains that organizations need to be aware of the interconnectedness of today's world but also recognize that everything seems to be in a state of flux: "On the one hand building enterprises capable of continually adapting to changing realities clearly demands new ways of thinking and operating. So do the sustainability challenges. . . . On the other hand, the dysfunctions of the traditional management system keep many organizations in perpetual firefighting mode, with little time or energy for innovation."

As to how organizational culture influences change, some observers argue that when group members share similar values, due to the high level of control over behaviors and beliefs, employees can be easily moved to embrace innovation. However, others perceive strong cultures as a mechanism for social control and therefore detrimental to innovation. In such settings, they say, the leadership is primarily concerned with promoting uniformity, loyalty, and commitment to the organization, which increases the difficulty of responding quickly to changes in the external environment and finding new ways to respond to emerging problems (Jaskyte & Dressler, 2005).

These opposing positions on fostering innovation are consistent with a perception of decision-making as either purposive or passive. In the first instance, the board and the chief professional officer anticipate opportunities in the environment and initiate action after weighing the available options, while in the second case, preserving the status quo is a priority, so that when action finally must be taken, it is reactive in nature (Wernet & Austin, 1991). The X factor seems to be the way in which the leader exercises the role of change agent, which is the focus of the next section.

MANAGING CHANGE

As indicated above, the external world exerts enormous political and economic pressures on nonprofit organizations. Therefore, with rare exceptions, it is no longer a question of whether but how organizational leaders will respond to these challenges. As one nonprofit CEO put it, "I sometimes miss the old days when we were small and everyone knew everyone else. But, given the environment in which we now work, . . . there is no turning back. . . . It's a matter of positioning ourselves further up the chain."

According to Webster's dictionary, the verb *to manage* means "to handle or direct with a degree of skill," which is further clarified as "to exercise executive, administrative, and supervisory direction," "to work upon or try to alter for a purpose," and "to succeed in accomplishing." All of these definitions will come into play as we consider the practicalities of bringing about change.

The Profile of an Effective Leader

In chapter 4 the term *executive assets* was introduced to refer to the sum total of personal qualities and professional attributes a leader can command. In selecting a new leader, the board weighs the assets of the various candidates for the position against the needs of the organization, and strives to find the best fit. Once hired, the CEO is continually judged, both formally and informally, on how these same qualities and attributes are applied on behalf of the organization. We will now consider what combination of assets seems most conducive to helping group members embrace a new organizational vision.

The "Ecology of Leadership"

In discussing selection models of change, the idea was presented that organizations occupy ecological niches, which are the arenas in which these entities operate day-to-day. Senge (2006, p. 319) uses the term "ecology of leadership" to refer to interrelationships of different kinds of leaders within a corporate setting: the local line leader, who is responsible for overseeing daily practices within each work group; the network leader, who helps connect work groups and line leaders to build greater organizational capacity; and the executive leader, whose efforts bring the whole enterprise together. The same could be said about a nonprofit, with some simple title substitutions (unit supervisor for local line leader, and so on).

The key message is that leadership is not the purview of a single person, especially when it is a matter of developing a climate for innovation; each type of leader needs the others to break down the potential systemic barriers to change. A learning organization then must be a setting in which staff, at all levels, perceive the realization of personal and organizational goals as mutually achievable and desirable and work together toward these ends. Senge (2006) envisions three fundamental leadership roles, as designer, teacher, and steward.

As a *designer*, the leader must appreciate the organization as a living system and be willing to experiment and take some risks before settling on one direction. Often this will require identifying different ways to communicate with both internal and external stakeholders not only to formulate new purpose and vision statements but also to engage key constituencies in the change process. In many respects, designing is an application of incrementalism, taking small steps over time to achieve a larger result, which means the designer may get little individual credit at the end of the day. Therefore, in fulfilling this role the leader must derive satisfaction from being part of accomplishing something meaningful to the entire group.

The leader as *teacher* begins by recognizing the absence of an important capacity within the organization. For example, the reward system may foster competition and stifle the free flow of ideas, an essential step in achieving change. Senge (2006, p. 329) believes "great teachers create space for learning and invite people into that space." A major challenge is to enable group members to see that reality can be rechanneled to achieve a new vision for the organization. One successful approach is applying systems thinking to problems, so that the larger patterns of how things have typically been done become clear; from that vantage point, it is easier to focus as a team on what the future might be. To fulfill the teacher role, the leader must demonstrate a personal desire to learn and grow.

Stewardship is embodied in the concept of servant-leadership developed in the mid-1960s by Robert Greenleaf. Here the desire to serve precedes the desire to lead (as discussed in Senge, 2006). This idea is both practical and idealistic, for in uncertain times, individuals are much more likely to follow someone they trust to have their best interests at heart and who seems guided by a higher purpose. However, Senge (2006) also points out the paradoxes of this role. The leader must seem to be pointing the organization in a positive direction but without closing off other possibilities. At the same time, it is necessary to balance the pursuit of what is new and emergent with the responsibility to conserve the essential nature of the organization. (For a fuller consideration of servant-leadership, see chapter 13.)

Creative Leadership

An organization may also be seen as a system of human energy, by replacing traditional ideas of effective leadership through controlling followers with the image of the leader as seeking to release the potential of group members and guide their energy toward mutually desirable goals. This is the fundamental principle of exercising *creative leadership* (Knowles, 1990, p. 183).

Knowles, a longtime expert on adult learning, has borrowed from the management and education literature regarding assumptions about human behavior (McGregor's Theory X and Theory Y and Rogers's views on experiential learning, respectively) to characterize the differences between the two types of leadership. Essentially, creative leaders believe that people desire to be challenged and to assume responsibility, while controlling leaders believe staff must be coerced into working hard. Under the first set of assumptions, people will be more productive when they feel that the locus of control resides within them and their individual potential is being tapped. These views lead to the following propositions characterizing creative leadership:

1. Operating on the principle that followers will be more committed to decisions they have participated in making, creative leaders, except perhaps in times of crisis, will involve staff in all aspects of the planning process—assessing needs, identifying goals, developing action steps, implementing the plan, and evaluating results.

2. Because creative leaders trust in the power of self-fulfilling prophesies, they openly express their faith in the ability of group members to do superior work and wait for staff to meet their high expectations.

3. Creative leaders strive to bring out the individual capabilities of their followers rather than asking them to conform to some preconceived stereotypes. Such individuals value a pluralistic work environment and a team approach, seeing their primary role as enabling all group members to reach their full potential.

4. To stimulate creativity within the organization, these leaders exhibit innovative behavior themselves, thus signaling to other group members that it is not only acceptable but desirable to be creative. In this kind of environment, mistakes are considered learning opportunities, and risk taking is applauded.

5. Creative leaders fully understand the ubiquity of continuous change and develop the necessary skills to manage it effectively. Their goal is to lead an innovative organization, that is, one with a flexible structure that values interdependency, multidirectional communication, and both "collaborative policy-making and policy-execution" (Knowles, 1990, p. 189).

6. In motivating followers, these leaders recognize that internal sources such as personal achievement and recognition, work that is fulfilling, and opportunities for advancement and growth are often more significant than salary, status, working conditions, and other external aspects of organizational life.

7. Creative leaders comprehend that individuals tend to move from a dependent state toward increasing independence as they mature. Because that transition is not easy or natural for everyone, however, leaders must be prepared to act as facilitators to help group members achieve a comfortable level of self-directed productivity.

As suggested in table 7.3, effecting organizational change requires some combination of the most desirable assets of both the transactional and the transformational leader.

Table 7.3 Two perspectives on leadership in promoting change

Dimensions	Characteristics	
	Ecological leadership	*Creative leadership*
Structure	Organization as a living system	Interdependent work environment
	Interactive on multiple levels	Flexible
Atmosphere	People-centered	People-centered
	Caring	Pluralistic team approach
	Trusting	Emphasis on internal motivators
Management philosophy and attitudes	Systems thinking	Shared power
	Risk tolerant	Risk tolerant
	Innovative	Innovative
	Interdependency	High expectations = high performance
	Designer, teacher (and learner), steward	Facilitator
Decision-making and policymaking	Interative, incremental	Collaborative
	Participative (all relevant parties)	Participative (all relevant parties)
Communication	Multidirectional	Multidirectional
	Open flow	Open flow

Sources: Adapted from Knowles, 1990; Senge, 2006.

The Relationship between the Organizational Life Cycle and Culture

Just like people, organizations go through a maturation process, moving through different stages of development that feature different cultural markers. This journey can be smooth or bumpy, depending on whether the organizational culture evolves in a way to provide stability to group members while also demonstrating the ability to respond well to external changes. For example, after going through the early stages of growth and becoming thoroughly established in its particular ecological niche, the organization may reach a point where it has matured and is still relevant or it has begun to stagnate. Under the former conditions, incremental adjustments may be all that is required, but in the case of stagnation, more drastic measures, even to the point of a total restructuring of the organization, may be called for (Schein, 1985).

Once again, the intervening variable that can make innovation more palatable as the internal reaction to an external stimulus is the nature and quality of the leadership: "An integrating and inspiring type of leadership is needed to give . . . structural and systems changes a meaning for the people involved. The outcome should be a new and coherent cultural pattern" (Hofstede & Hofstede, 2005, p. 309). However, because in each developmental phase an organization is likely to face different tasks—establishing its legitimacy and building an infrastructure in the early growth years, differentiating products and services along with ensuring a steady flow of resources in the middle stages, and, in the best-case scenario, maintaining its relevance and internal stability at the point of maturity—it stands to reason that leadership style may also have to vary across the organizational life cycle. In some instances, the same individual is capable of shifting leadership patterns in the transition from one stage to the next, but when this does not occur, the board may find itself in the uncomfortable position of having to force out its top professional, who may even be the founder, or else the organization will suffer the consequences of a poor fit between its needs and the leader's assets. In fact, whenever a leadership transition occurs, and for whatever reason, the issue of fit must always be an important consideration in the hiring process (Schmid, 2006).

The case study featured in this text clearly illustrates the points just made. The founder's authoritarian style never deviated over the years, even as external conditions changed, but the weak board he had installed was not able or willing to see the negative impact on the stability of YSN. By the time the founder died, the board's passivity had become so ingrained that it floundered badly in its attempts to find and support new leadership.

Leadership and Organizational Culture

Let us now take a closer look at the role of the leader in establishing and modifying the organizational culture. For the sake of this discussion, we will assume an evolution similar to that of YSN, to wit, an organization formed through the vision of a single person, who becomes its executive director. The founder then brings in others to create a core group that shares his or her vision. As this new enterprise develops, still more people are recruited or hired to carry out its defined mission, and an organizational history begins to take shape.

Normally, founders are individuals with a high level of self-confidence and determination who are motivated by a strong concern for a particular social issue that does not appear to be receiving enough or the right kind of attention. Because they had the original idea, they generally also have strong feelings about how the organization should go about its business in order to fulfill its purpose, and they readily convey their thoughts and preferences on all aspects of organizational life. As Schein (1985, p. 221) notes, "The things that solve a group's problems repeatedly and that reduce anxiety will survive and become a part of the culture, but only those solutions that are proposed or invented become candidates. . . . Cultures do not start from scratch. . . . Powerful members will try to impose their assumptions." For new organizations, no one is more powerful than the founder, who commands all of the resources for influence included in French and Raven's classic 1959 typology: reward power, coercive power, legitimate power, expert power, and referent power.

According to Schein (1985), there are five primary mechanisms the founder uses to create a culture. First, group members quickly become aware of the things to which the leader pays close attention, through both formal and casual remarks as well as by systematic measurement and control, and what is virtually ignored. The second clear signal is how the leader responds to a perceived crisis, whether it is the potential loss of a funding source or a subordinate's criticism. Savvy leaders also recognize that their own visible behavior conveys a strong message and often engage in deliberate role modeling, but for group members, informal messages are even more powerful, such as when the CEO is observed walking through the building and randomly stopping to talk with employees at all levels. The criteria used for allocating rewards and punishments represent another strong indicator of priorities, values, and assumptions—something anyone going through an annual performance review experiences firsthand. Last, and especially powerful, are the criteria governing hiring, promotion, and firing, for the consistent application of these standards ensures that like-minded individuals will be part of the team. When systems, procedures, physical space, and formal statements of organizational philosophy, along with more symbolic acts like telling stories about key events, mesh with these primary mechanisms, the basic assumptions are reinforced.

However, the very success of the founder and others in the original core group in developing a strong organizational culture can present serious roadblocks for a new leader, especially one brought in with a mandate to effect change. Even though newly hired executives are normally accorded respect by other group members owing to their formal position, it is essential to remember that leadership is a multilevel process of social exchange. Therefore, for a leader to reconfigure a culture to be more conducive to innovation, the followers must develop enough trust in the CEO to accept that what they will be gaining is far more important to the future of the organization than what they may have to give up.

The *idiosyncrasy credit model* (Hollander, 1978) sets forth what has to occur for the leader to become a successful change agent. Imagine a kind of bank account into which followers can deposit credits to recognize the leader's respect for group norms and competence in furthering the organizational mission. Credits can also be lost if the leader fails to meet expectations or is perceived to be acting out of self-interest. It is only when sufficient credits have been accumulated that the leader can propose and then implement change without incurring serious resistance. At that point, the leader can even deviate from group norms, but not from role expectancies. Unfortunately, sometimes circumstances work against the newcomer, as illustrated by what occurred in a large Girl Scout council.

When the longtime executive director of the council contracted cancer but decided not to resign, in the name of sisterhood, a strong cultural value, senior staff took over most of her tasks, without board knowledge or approval, for three years, until the CEO's death. This decision had major ramifications for the next executive director.

Routine business had been maintained, but from indicators such as declining membership, the board had rightly concluded the organization was stagnating and instructed the search committee to find someone for the top job who could be an immediate change agent. The new executive had strong managerial abilities and experience but no history within Girl Scouting, which proved to be problematic when she began to introduce changes in her first year, as mandated by the board. The senior staff, having become used to directing the organization, were reluctant to give up their power, especially to someone they viewed as an outsider. While they approved of the new CEO's plans for enhancing the volunteers' role, they undermined her attempts to revise staffing patterns to increase productivity. Not wishing to exacerbate the situation, the executive did not tell the board why she was unable to move the organization forward as quickly as they had wanted, causing many of the trustees to blame her for the slow progress. By her third year, the CEO had become more and more isolated and frustrated, and decided to resign.

Under the circumstances, it might have been better to hire someone whom the staff would perceive as more in sync with group norms, allowing the new CEO to begin collecting idiosyncrasy credits to help her implement changes, but she also erred by not obtaining a better sense of the organizational culture before accepting the job. Had the CEO been able to persuade the board to hold off on major changes, she would have had more opportunity to demonstrate her competency and further increase her support from group members. Thus, everyone bore some responsibility for the outcome.

STRATEGIES FOR CHANGE

Some organizational changes happen spontaneously due to forces in the environment that seem almost beyond anyone's control. However, given today's turbulent environment, very few nonprofits can afford to remain passive or reactive in their response to external pressures; instead, they must do their best to be proactive while protecting the organization's essential identity, an executive asset Schmid (2004, p. 106) calls "copeability." In this section, the focus will be on planned change.

Although some maintain that people consciously choose a single approach to solve a particular class of problems, Morris and Schunn (2004) suggest that many possible strategies are available and so the choice among them is made based on the match between the characteristics of the problem (task demands) and the decision-maker's knowledge and experience solving similar problems (processing demands). In other words, the degree to which a problem is familiar is likely to influence the use of a specific strategy; moreover, strategies that have worked in the past are more apt to be used in the future. Accordingly, strategy selection may well vary over time in response to problems, tasks, individuals, and different points of organizational development.

Earlier in this chapter, *strategic management* was defined broadly as referring to the leader's efforts to establish a good fit between the organization and its environment. Now we turn our attention to the steps in the process of implementing change, which is generally implied if not explicit whenever the emphasis is on strategy. As part of this discussion, the results of a study of the approaches selected by nonprofit leaders in their attempt to remain viable and competitive will be delineated.

The Change Process

Like the decision-making process covered in chapter 6, change often begins with diagnosing present conditions to identify the situation or problem necessitating a move in a different direction. Goals for change are then set, based on this analysis. Perhaps the most critical step is to define and manage the transition stage, the period between what was and what will be in terms of organizational tasks, the people responsible for the work, how they operate, and the structure supporting their efforts, since change is likely to affect any or all of these variables. After the transition, an evaluation should take place to determine whether the goals have been accomplished. Finally, the new direction must be stabilized and routines established, but the organization also needs to remain flexible enough to respond should further changes be warranted (Anderson, 1984).

Force-Field Analysis

During the diagnostic and goal-setting phases, one of the most useful tools is force-field analysis, developed by Brager and Holloway (1992), which is a way to identify the stakeholders who are internally and externally disposed to support change and those who are opposed. What is particularly interesting about this model is it can be applied by anyone in the organizational system who elects to be a change agent. Its basic concepts are derived from Kurt Lewin's field theory. Lewin maintained that each person lives in a particular psychological universe, with human behavior resulting from the totality of the interactions between the person and the environment. Even though equilibrium is the desired state, stability is in reality a dynamic condition brought about by elements that exert either a positive or negative force and are constantly moving in opposition to each other in the attempt to achieve homeostasis. Change occurs when the system's equilibrium is disrupted by a shift in these forces (Brager & Holloway, 1992; Hall & Lindzey, 1957). For example, a hungry individual tends to move toward food but, once his appetite has been satisfied, he is likely to reject additional servings.

Later in his career, Lewin applied his ideas in many practical directions, including group dynamics, and his work has had a major influence on organizational development studies. Force-field analysis assesses the strength of the opposing forces to determine whether a desired change within the organization is feasible and, if so, to provide an action plan for effecting the change. The first step is to consider the available options for addressing the problem of concern, choosing the one (or possibly more) that best supports agency values and can be accommodated within the available resources. Next, it is necessary to identify the group members with the power to adopt or reject the proposed change as well as those in a position to influence the decision-makers, called respectively *critical actors* and *facilitating actors* (Brager & Holloway, 1992, p. 18). The third step is to put together a balance sheet of sorts, showing the positive and negative forces, in as specific terms as possible, that the change agent must consider to move the organization toward the desired outcome (Brager & Holloway, 1992).

If merger were the goal, for instance, a positive (driving) force might be the close personal relationship between the CEOs of the likely merger partners, who would certainly be critical actors. A negative (restraining) force might be fear of job loss among the line staff in both agencies. Once having determined the strength of these forces, the change agent can begin to devise strategies to increase the positive forces and decrease or at least neutralize the negative ones. A strategy in this particular scenario might be to enlist the help of unit supervisors (facilitating actors) in allaying the fears of their staff about the merger's possible impact.

Lewin's Planned-Change Model

Lewin's work also included a three-step model of planned change that is applicable to the transition and stabilizing phases of an organizational shift. These steps consist of (1) unfreezing the behavior of group members by coming to terms with the underlying driving and restraining forces, (2) helping staff to learn the desirable behavior associated with moving in a new direction, and (3) refreezing by routinizing practices and procedures to reestablish stability within the organizational system (Medley & Akan, 2008; Schein, 1985). Returning to the merger example, an example of unfreezing would be to provide hard data showing a decline in financial support and increased competition for services, which would make a good case for considering an alliance. Once the merger is under way, organizational leaders might form task groups made up of staff from the two partner agencies to begin working through operational details such as how services will now be delivered, what new technologies might have to be adopted, and so on. Refreezing could involve issuing a new mission statement for the merged entity, installing new signage, and beginning to institutionalize desired behaviors, ultimately leading to the internalizing of the values and assumptions of the new organizational culture.

Results of a Three-State Study of Strategic Management

In 2002–3, a comparative study of social agencies in California, Michigan, and North Carolina providing direct client services was undertaken to identify the nature and scope of the management strategies adopted in response to the changing external environment (Golensky & Mulder, 2006). One hundred twelve CEOs agreed to participate. For the central survey question, they were asked to review a list of strategies, grouped under the headings Productivity Improvement, Retrenchment, New Revenue, and Transformational, and check all that applied. As a second step, the respondents were asked for their perceptions on the success of these efforts. The results are shown in tables 7.4 and 7.5.

One of the study hypotheses was that organizational leaders would use multiple strategies, and in fact, twenty-five distinct strategies were exhibited in the four categories. Although these behaviors were different, they were not necessarily unrelated. For example, using more volunteers often is a corollary of reducing paid staff, and introducing new services, may require changes in marketing techniques. Also, even though most respondents indicated the strategies used either met or exceeded expectations, there were clear preferences. Of the internal measures, improvements in productivity were implemented more widely than retrenchment, and externally, the CEOs were more inclined toward securing new revenue than transforming the organization.

Table 7.4 Internal strategies

Productivity improvement strategies used and perceived level of success

	N	Exceeded expectations	Met expectations	Below expectations	Unsuccessful
Upgraded computer systems	90	29	51	6	NA
Improved staff training	71	14	52	3	NA
Improved internal coordination among staff/departments	66	19	41	2	NA
Increased staff recognition	51	13	33	5	NA
Increased staff incentives	31	10	16	3	1

Retrenchment strategies used and perceived level of success

	N	Exceeded expectations	Met expectations	Below expectations	Unsuccessful
Increased staff workload	50	4	31	10	NA
Reduced staff	32	3	21	4	NA
Used more volunteers	35	8	20	6	NA
Consolidated program sites	15	4	10	NA	NA
Cut/reduced programs	19	1	14	1	1
Tightened eligibility	14	3	9	NA	NA
Restricted benefits	10	2	7	NA	NA

Source: Golensky, M. & Mulder, C. A. (2006). Coping in a constrained economy: Survival strategies of nonprofit human service organizations. *Administration in Social Work*, *30*(3), 17.
Note: In most cases, frequencies for success levels do not equal those for usage because not all respondents indicated level of success.

Table 7.5 External strategies

New revenue strategies and perceived level of success					
	N	*Exceeded expectations*	*Met expectations*	*Below expectations*	*Unsuccessful*
Started new services	76	20	43	11	NA
Approached new funders	83	18	41	14	6
Raised fees for services	34	4	18	9	2
Introduced new products	13	3	6	2	NA
Improved marketing & PR	70	18	35	14	NA
Increased referrals	30	11	15	2	NA
Increased lobbying efforts	25	8	10	5	2

Transformational strategies used and perceived level of success					
	N	*Exceeded expectations*	*Met expectations*	*Below expectations*	*Unsuccessful*
Formed collaboration	61	20	29	8	1
Merged	9	2	4	NA	NA
Considered closing	2	—	—	—	—
Franchised program(s)	7	4	2	1	NA
Restructured the board	25	5	16	2	NA
Revised the mission	24	3	19	1	NA

Source: Golensky, M. & Mulder, C.A. (2006). Coping in a constrained economy: Survival strategies of nonprofit human service organizations. *Administration in Social Work*, *30*(3), 18. Article copies available from the Haworth Document Delivery Service: 1-800-HAWORTH. E-mail address: docdelivery@haworthpress.com. *Note*: In most cases, frequencies for success levels do not equal those for usage because not all respondents indicated level of success.

Under productivity improvement, upgrading computer systems was used as a strategy almost three times as often as increasing staff incentives; in the retrenchment category, an organization was five times more likely to increase staff workload than to restrict client benefits; for the new revenue category, approaching new funders was selected over introducing new products by a ratio of six to one; and regarding transformational strategies, while 55 percent indicated they had formed some type of collaboration, just a handful had gone so far as to merge with another nonprofit. Yet it would be unfair to conclude these leaders were not risk takers, for over a fifth had restructured the board, usually by increasing the number of people with direct access to financial or other critical resources, and an equal number had undertaken the difficult step of revising their mission to clarify the organization's service niche.

The responses of the participants in this research study to the external pressures they were facing suggested that the desire to meet client needs was the primary driving force, but other organizational dimensions were also taken into consideration. One might conclude then, in line with the model proposed by Morris and Schunn (2004), that the decision to use multiple strategies rather than a single approach was based on prior knowledge or experience; the chances of success, perhaps derived from positive outcomes achieved by peers as ascertained through networking; and the potential costs, both real and psychic, attached to implementation. When considering Miles and Snow's 1978 typology, the respondents acted most like Analyzers, which are organizations functioning under both stable and variable conditions. "In their stable areas, these organizations operate routinely and efficiently through ... formalized structures and processes. In their more turbulent areas, top managers watch their competitors closely for new ideas, and then rapidly adopt those which appear to be the most promising" (p. 29). However, depending on the state of the economy and other equally pertinent factors, in the future nonprofit leaders may need to become Prospectors, open to even higher levels of innovation, to remain competitive.

Forging Strategic Alliances

As the results above show, nonprofits are choosing to engage in some form of alliance with like organizations more and more often to enhance capacity building or respond to regional and communitywide problems. Many funders have also encouraged applicants to consider this approach to reduce duplication of services and thus increase efficiency.

Strategic alliances represent "intentional, interorganizational relationships created to benefit the organizational partners and, ultimately, the organizations' consumers" (Bailey & Koney, 2000, p. 4). To help determine which kind of alliance might be most advantageous to pursue, it is possible to place the different types on a continuum from least to most formal and risky, taking into consideration the degree to which autonomy is maintained or reduced as well as the costs in money and time to effect the alliance (Arsenault, 1998; Kohm & La Piana, 2003; Reilly, 2001).

1. *Cooperation* is the most informal and least risky kind of interaction, usually characterized by a loose structure, total autonomy for each participant, and an emphasis on sharing nonmonetary resources, such as information. The arrangement may be referred to as an affiliation; mutual support is the goal. Examples are a referral network, and event cosponsorship.

2. *Temporary coordination* is somewhat more formal in structure, involving some planning to establish communication channels, identify common tasks, and divide up responsibilities. Examples are a task force of representatives from youth agencies convened by a local foundation to explore more efficient service delivery methods, and a coalition of health care organizations pursuing more favorable tax legislation at the state level.

3. *Long-term coordination* involves partnering with complementary organizations whereby members generally handle their own regular activities and maintain separate boards but cede some autonomy and may pay dues to a parent body that is responsible for common operational areas (for example, fund-raising, marketing, planning). Examples are associations and federations such as the Girl Scouts, YMCA, American Red Cross, and United Way.

4. *Collaboration* is a more formal and enduring relationship entered into by two or more organizations for mutual benefit to achieve common goals, involving a jointly developed structure, shared resources, and mutual authority and accountability for success. Within this category, again moving from a less to a more binding relationship, are four arrangements.

- Consortiums share a specific community or area of interest, and members combine resources to address issues each could not tackle alone. Typically, one agency acts as convener, and a core staff member oversees the joint activities. A formal agreement governs participation in the consortium, but members retain autonomy on matters outside the alliance's scope.
- A joint venture is undertaken to accomplish a specific purpose. It is often time-limited and narrowly defined, with the parties retaining a high level of autonomy under a contractual agreement. If the initial alliance is successful, the organizations may then form a legally recognized partnership for an indefinite period.
- Networks are often set up today in a formal way via contracts and other legal documents to deal with managed care pressures. This kind of alliance strives to improve service delivery to consumers. Members usually retain their independence regarding core functions.
- Management service organizations (MSOs) are created to achieve greater efficiency and effectiveness. They focus on administration rather than program and are especially useful in negotiating government contracts. One organization may provide management services to other nonprofits for a fee, or several organizations may form a partnership, limited to administrative functions.

Sometimes organizations determine that circumstances dictate an even more radical solution and decide to merge, which entails creating a new corporation, usually with a new name, structure, governance, and so forth. When one of the entities absorbs the other(s), the process may be called a consolidation, or in the for-profit world, an acquisition (Golensky & Walker, 2003).

Since power and authority are generally shared in an alliance, particularly in the less formal types, leadership tends to revolve around relationship building, participatory planning, and collective decision-making (Gil de Gibaja, 2001).

FINAL THOUGHTS

The vignette about the Girl Scout council presented earlier clearly illustrates that, while group members may be willing to make allowances for and work around questionable, contradictory behavior by the founder or other longtime leader, they are less likely to do so for someone relatively new to the leadership position. One conclusion to be drawn is that timing is everything when it comes to introducing innovations into established settings. Furthermore, it is much easier to change practices than values, so if it is deemed necessary to make some fundamental alterations, the leader will undoubtedly have to rely on unfreezing strategies, such as helping group members understand and accept that the current culture has become dysfunctional. It may also require the judicious use of incentives to retain those who will support the changes and encourage the departure of those who cannot, replacing them with people more capable of implementing the organization's new direction (Schein, 1985).

In the literature on conflict management, *rhetorical sensitivity* refers to the ability to change one's communication style in response to the demands of different situations; the higher the ability to adapt in this manner, the more effective the individual will be in working with a variety of audiences to resolve problems (Hocker & Wilmot, 1995, p. 133). Similarly, a nonprofit leader who wishes to effect change needs to develop *environmental sensitivity*, my term for being able to size up external pressures and devise the most desirable path for the organization to follow.

Discussion Questions for Section 2

Chapter 4

1. Of the different theoretical approaches to leadership, which one did the YSN board tend to rely on most in selecting an executive director for the agency? What are the likely consequences of depending so heavily on a single approach?

2. What impact has *founder's syndrome* had on YSN? What is the board's role to overcome a founder's strong influence if it becomes clear that change is necessary?

Chapter 5

3. From the information in the first section of the case study, how would you characterize YSN's organizational culture, and on what basis? Is there enough information to get to the deepest level of its culture? Support your position.

4. Is organizational culture shaped by the external environment or vice versa? On what do you base your views?

5. Would you consider YSN's founder a transformative or a transactional leader? Given a choice, with which type of leader would you prefer to work? Why?

6. Since it is unlikely for a top professional to possess all the skills associated with Quinn's competing values model, which attributes are most essential for a nonprofit CEO to be successful in today's turbulent world?

Chapter 6

7. Do you believe a nonprofit leader is better served by developing a variety of decision-making styles or by becoming highly skilled in one particular approach? On what do you base your opinion?

8. Of the three modes of decision-making introduced in chapter 6 (tractable-fluid, vortex-sporadic, familiar-constricted), which one would you use if your nonprofit were considering whether to expand a successful program? To move to a new location? To enter into a collaboration with two other organizations? What steps would you take in each case?

9. How do you anticipate you might use the Six Thinking Hats method in your professional life? In your personal life?

Chapter 7

10. Think about a nonprofit with which you are familiar. At what stage would you place it in the organizational life cycle? How well do you perceive it is handling the organizational tasks associated with that stage?

11. Why do most individuals and organizations find change so problematic? Can someone be an effective change agent for an organization if she or he has difficulty in reaching personal decisions?

12. Which executive assets would be most effective in leading a successful collaborative effort? Some observers believe a leader's trustworthiness is the most important quality to other group members. Do you agree or disagree, and why?

SELECTED READINGS FOR SECTION 2

Chapter 4

Anderson, C. R. (1984). *Management: Skills, functions, and organization performance*. Dubuque, IA: Wm. C. Brown.

Block, S. R. (2004). *Why nonprofits fail*. San Francisco: Jossey-Bass.

Brueggemann, W. G. (1996). *The practice of macro social work*. Chicago: Nelson-Hall.

Houle, C. O. (1989). *Governing boards: Their nature and nurture*. San Francisco: Jossey-Bass.

Kramer, R. M. (1985). Toward a contingency model of board-executive relations. *Administration in Social Work, 9*(3), 15–33.

Mathiasen, K., III. (1983, January). *The board of directors is a problem: Exploring the concept of the following and leading board*. Available from the Management Assistance Group, 1835 K Street, NW, Washington, DC 20006.

Stone, M. M., & Ostrower, F. (2007). Acting in the public interest? Another look at research on nonprofit governance. *Nonprofit and Voluntary Sector Quarterly, 36*, 416–438.

Van Fleet, D. D., & Yukl, G. A. (1989). A century of leadership research. In W. B. Rosenbach & R. L. Taylor (Eds.), *Contemporary issues in leadership* (pp. 65–90). Boulder, CO: Westview.

Wood, M. M. (1992). Is governing board behavior cyclical? *Nonprofit Management and Leadership, 3*, 139–163.

Chapter 5

Edwards, R. L., & Austin, D. M. (2006). Managing effectively in an environment of competing values. In R. L. Edwards & J. A. Yankey (Eds.), *Effectively managing nonprofit organizations* (Rev. ed., pp. 3–25). Washington, DC: NASW Press.

Hofstede, G., & Hofstede, G. J. (2005). *Cultures and organizations: Software of the mind* (2nd ed.). New York: McGraw-Hill.

Hollander, E. P. (1978). *Leadership dynamics*. New York: Free Press.

Howell, J. M. (1997). *Organization contexts, charismatic and exchange leadership* (Transformational Leadership Working Papers, Kellogg Leadership Studies Project). College Park, MD: Academy of Leadership Press.

Kuhnert, K. W., & Lewis, P. (1989). Transactional and transformational leadership: A constructive/developmental analysis. In W. B. Rosenbach & R. L. Taylor (Eds.), *Contemporary issues in leadership* (pp. 192–205). Boulder, CO: Westview.

Schein, E. H. (1985). *Organizational culture and leadership*. San Francisco: Jossey-Bass.

Schmid, H. (2006). Leadership styles and leadership change in human and community service organizations. *Nonprofit Management and Leadership, 17*, 179–194.

Werther, W. B., Jr., Berman, E., & Echols, K. (2005, September–October). The three roles of nonprofit management. *Nonprofit World, 23*(5), 22–23.

Chapter 6

De Bono, E. (1999). *Six thinking hats* (Rev. ed.). Boston: Little, Brown.

Driver, M. J., & Rowe, A. J. (1979). Decision-making styles: A new approach to management decision making. In C. L. Cooper (Ed.), *Behavioral problems in organizations* (pp. 141–179). Englewood Cliffs, NJ: Prentice Hall.

Hickson, D. J., Butler, R. J., Cray, D., Mallory, G. R., & Wilson, D. C. (1986). *Top decisions*. San Francisco: Jossey-Bass.

Janis, I. L., & Mann, L. (1977). *Decision making*. New York: Free Press.

Nutt, P. C. (1989). *Making tough decisions*. San Francisco: Jossey-Bass.

Chapter 7

Galaskiewicz, J., & Bielefeld, W. (1998). *Nonprofit organizations in an age of uncertainty*. New York: Aldine de Gruyter.

Golensky, M., & Mulder, C. A. (2006). Coping in a constrained economy: Survival strategies of nonprofit human service organizations. *Administration in Social Work, 30*(3), 5–24. Article copies available from the Haworth Document Delivery Service: 1-800-HAWORTH. E-mail address: docdelivery@haworthpress.com.

Knowles, M. (1990). *The adult learner: A neglected species* (4th ed.). Houston, TX: Gulf.

Perlmutter, F. D., & Gummer, B. (1994). Managing organizational transformations. In R. D. Herman (Ed.), *The Jossey-Bass handbook of nonprofit leadership and management* (pp. 227–246). San Francisco: Jossey-Bass.

Schein, E. H. (1985). *Organizational culture and leadership*. San Francisco: Jossey-Bass.

Schmid, H. (2004). Organization-environment relationships: Theory for management practice in human service organizations. *Administration in Social Work, 28*(1), 97–113.

Senge, P. M. (2006). *The fifth discipline* (Rev. ed.). New York: Currency Doubleday.

SECTION 3
Securing Material Resources

In this section the emphasis of the book shifts to the management role of the top professional, to functions such as planning, coordinating, and controlling, specifically in reference to obtaining and safeguarding the tangible raw materials a nonprofit organization must have to carry out its mission. This does not mean leadership considerations will be absent from the equation, but the main focus will be on translating vision into processes and outcomes. Similarly, many of the theories and concepts introduced in sections 1 and 2 will be revisited, as they pertain to the practical areas covered in the next several chapters. (The second part of the featured case study is included here as a reference point for chapters 8 to 12.)

Chapter 8 covers the nuts and bolts of strategic planning, from the reasons why an organization ought to engage in this kind of endeavor, to who should be included, to what is the desired end product. It presents issues related to design and structure and details of different planning models.

Chapter 9 moves the discussion of planning from the organizational to the programmatic level, with program development treated as a continuum that includes monitoring as well as both summative and formative evaluation. It considers the place of the logic model in this continuum.

Chapter 10 examines the full spectrum of resource generation as practiced in a nonprofit setting, beginning with the annual fund drive and continuing through the major gifts program, the capital campaign, and planned giving, from conceptualization through implementation. It also addresses ethical issues associated with this area of responsibility.

Chapter 11 is concerned with the performance indicators used by stakeholders in judging organizational effectiveness. A major consideration is the wise stewardship of resources through comprehensive budgeting and sound financial management practices, but nonfinancial elements are also delineated.

Chapter 12 links two important topics, technology and communication. This chapter explores the impact of contemporary technological advances on the ways a nonprofit can choose to interact with its various internal and external stakeholders.

KEY THEMES

Chapters 8 to 12 address these topics and concerns.

- The purpose and design of a strategic planning process: What are the distinguishing features of effective strategic planning?
- The program development continuum, from planning through evaluation: What are the distinguishing features of effective program development?
- The process of securing financial resources: What are the distinguishing features of an effective, ethical program of resource generation?
- The concept of organizational effectiveness: What are the main financial and nonfinancial performance indicators identified by key stakeholders?
- The relationship between technology and communication: How can nonprofits best use technology to interact with key stakeholders?

Conflicting Agendas for the Future of a Youth Agency, Part 2
The Executive Director's Perspective

Margaret Stover, the new executive director, focused on YSN's fiscal problems and soon realized that the decline in the organization's financial position was a symptom of broader issues related to mission and governance. These matters were brought into clear relief through a confidential letter Stover received from a consultant who had been engaged to help YSN promote its sixtieth birthday celebration in 2006:

> The basic problem with YSN is the fact that it has at its core a faulty premise. What we basically are is a neighborhood group . . . with rather large pretensions of being more. This is not to say we don't do a good job—we do in that area. But it's small potatoes, and there must be dozens—maybe hundreds—around the city doing exactly the same thing.
>
> Times have changed, and the fact that we've reached sixty years is more a testament to the good luck of our predecessors than anything existing today. I've told you—perhaps too often—that you have to get rid of the majority of your board. They simply are unimportant people and, mostly, uninspired. The elements of success are simply not there.
>
> I do think you should address these problems as quickly as possible for the continuance of the organization. The competition is just too fierce and severe out there to warrant doing anything else.

While these were harsh words, they had the ring of truth. Beginning with the death of the founder, the organization had begun to slide. During the past ten years, no new programs had been developed, and some of the older programs, such as the tournaments, had been discontinued for lack of support. In addition, no new funding sources had been cultivated. Even though the third CEO had been able to revive the tournaments and had attempted to inject some enthusiasm into the organization, his limited administrative experience and plain bad luck in being caught in the scandal over the direct mail program were his downfall. Furthermore, the board was top-heavy with white males over the age of fifty clustered in a few industries (see table C.1).

The YSN bookkeeper quickly befriended Stover and became a primary source of information. One of the most disturbing revelations concerned the search process. Stover learned that her job had been all but promised to another candidate recommended by YSN's second executive director and that de Marco had tipped the balance in her favor, possibly in order to embarrass the second executive, against whom de Marco harbored a personal grudge.

Stover also received a full report from the agency's bookkeeper about the scandal involving the founder's son. In light of the board members' reactions when the last CEO had brought bad tidings about the direct mail situation, the bookkeeper advised Stover to avoid this issue as much as possible—a difficult task since the lawsuit against the former staff member was still pending—or risk encountering the same fate as her predecessor. Additionally, the bookkeeper was able to provide some insights into the difficulties the third CEO had had with the chair of the Finance Committee at the time, and this information proved valuable when Stover subsequently was invited to lunch by this board member and was treated to his version of the conflict.

In the course of this lunch meeting, the board member suggested that Stover reach out to YSN's second CEO as someone who could provide her with a sense of the organization's history (see table C.2 for a time line on leadership succession). It seemed this trustee wanted to wipe out the last few years, including his disagreement with her predecessor and the direct mail scandal, and renew the ties with the past when YSN was so prominent in the youth services field. Since Stover wanted to establish a positive relationship with the board member, she followed his advice and was pleasantly surprised to discover she rather liked the former CEO, despite his gratuitous criticism of her predecessor's attempts to "modernize" YSN.

All in all, Stover's tenure had an auspicious start. The staff seemed reenergized, and the board appeared to be happy with the choice of their new CEO. Most important, it was possible to put aside monetary concerns for a while when YSN received an unexpected bequest of over $800,000 from a direct mail donor whose average gift never exceeded $100 during her lifetime. In Stover's second year, however, declining revenue again

Table C.2 Leadership succession

Leader and years in office	*Reason for departure*
Founder: 1946–1990	Joined board
Second executive: 1990–2000	Illness
Third executive: 2001–2004	Resignation (semiforced)
Current executive: 2005–	Not applicable

became a central issue. Since she believed the organization had erred historically in putting so much reliance on a single source of income, she began to explore other avenues for generating financial support.

Stover viewed the one remaining community center—down from the three sites YSN had managed some years before—as the organization's biggest resource. Looking for opportunities to expand the center's program, she was successful in obtaining three large grants from three new donors interested in school dropout prevention, which she saw as a link to YSN's original focus on juvenile delinquency prevention.

She was more than a little dismayed, therefore, when the board greeted these funding coups with minimal enthusiasm. For the majority of the trustees, summer camp was still YSN's centerpiece, even though the organization had steadily been losing campers to more modern facilities. Since only a small number of the youngsters attending camp participated in activities at YSN's center, they did not share the loyalty to YSN of campers in the past, when it was common to see the same faces involved in the organization year-round.

Stover was also dismayed by the board's continuing belief that the direct mail program could be revived. She did not share their optimism, but at the urging of the finance committee, she switched consultants in hopes of achieving better results. When there was no appreciable improvement, she made yet another change, which did bring a slight upswing.

Increasingly, Stover believed a complete overhaul of YSN was necessary, and she decided it was time to get at the root causes of YSN's problems and develop a strategy to secure the organization's future. With the support of the board president, she was able to convince the board to enter into a strategic planning process. Although the ostensible goal was the need to strengthen the funding base and to determine which of the current programs were most viable, Stover's long-term hope was to include a serious reexamination of the governance structure. The Strategic Planning Committee was formed toward the end of 2006. It was expected to meet through the first half of the new year and then submit its recommendations to the full board prior to the September 2007 board meeting.

Earlier in 2006, Stover's concerns about governance were heightened when Sal de Marco, who had headed the search committee that selected her, became the new board president. Initially Stover had been very pleased when the Nominating Committee suggested de Marco. With YSN's sixtieth anniversary coming up, naming a former program participant to the top volunteer spot had great public relations potential; moreover, Stover knew de Marco had been very influential in her appointment as executive director and felt they had maintained a cordial relationship ever since. Unfortunately, de Marco's leadership style was very different from that of his predecessor, who had met with Stover at least once a week. Although de Marco did not see the value of frequent meetings with the executive director, he finally agreed to a once-a-month session if Stover would travel to his place of business, which was over an hour's drive from the YSN office.

However, despite the monthly meetings, Stover did not feel she and de Marco acted as a team. Often, when she would bring an issue to his attention and ask for his input, he would respond, "Do what you think is best. After all, you're the girl I brought to the dance." Even worse, when de Marco did consider a matter to be important, he was apt to phone a few of the other board members for their opinions before discussing the matter with Stover. Yet, in his indirect way, the board president was supportive of her, if a bit patronizing. Stover made the best of the situation, but she was certain nothing would change until rotating board terms were adopted and people were selected for the board on the basis of merit rather than personal or business connections.

Much would depend on the outcome of the strategic planning. Stover had influenced the selection of an excellent committee that included the best thinkers and some of the most respected people on the board, although it was a minor setback when de Marco declined to participate, citing business pressures. The group's growing enthusiasm about the process gave Stover confidence they would be able to "sell" the plan to the other trustees. To Stover's delight, the committee even proved receptive to discussing possible changes in governance. When the committee's interim reports were well received at the February, April, and June board meetings, she felt much better about the chances of helping YSN overcome its problems and move forward. The full committee report, with recommendations on changes in programs and services, finances, staff, and plant and equipment, was sent to the board for review prior to the September meeting (see the appendix to chapter 8 for the key provisions). The cornerstone of the plan, and probably its most controversial aspect, was a proposition to use YSN's reserves to cover deficits until new sources of revenue could be cultivated. The crucial vote would take place at the meeting.

Strategic Planning

The term *strategic management* was used earlier to refer to the collective efforts to establish a good fit between an organization and its environment so the former can realize the goals and objectives that are consistent with its mission and available resources while being responsive to the latter's demands. One way to view *strategic planning* then is as the process of achieving the desired ends of strategic management, resulting in "fundamental decisions and actions that shape and guide what an organization is, what it does, and why it does it" (Bryson, 1995, p. 5). Most often the unit of analysis is the entire organization, but departments and divisions may also engage in the same process.

Despite its obvious benefits, strategic planning has not always been viewed as an essential part of organizational life. Some complain about the amount of time and effort required to do the job, and even more, that the report produced through all that work too often ends up as just another computer document, largely ignored. A thorough planning process generally does demand the commitment of considerable human resources and a financial outlay. However, if the process is executed properly and participants fully understand the necessity for it and are committed to seeing that the resulting plan serves as a living document to guide the organization toward meeting present and future consumer needs more effectively, then it is certainly a justifiable use of time, personnel, and money. In recognition of the ever-changing environment in which nonprofits operate, the goal of the process should be what Eadie (2006) calls a "strategic change portfolio" (p. 378) of initiatives, each addressing specific issues of immediate concern along with long-term opportunities or challenges for the organization. Taking such a flexible approach to planning ensures that current, still viable programs will not be discarded on a whim; by the same token, new, exciting service avenues can be readily pursued. Moreover, each organization will determine the period of time for which strategic goals are set by considering the availability of resources, the volatility of the marketplace, and so on. As a general observation, the "planning horizon" (Anderson, 1984, p. 363) has shrunk in recent years; plans for five years and longer used to be fairly common, but today two to three years is more the rule. In any case, goals, objectives, and action steps should be reviewed each year and adjusted if necessary to fit present circumstances.

In the first sections of the chapter, the broad parameters of the strategic planning process are laid out, including its purpose, principal design elements, and the practical aspects to be taken into account in terms of structure, content, personnel, budgeting, and implementation. Next, there are descriptions of different planning models, each with its own underlying philosophy. The chapter ends with an appendix containing excerpts from the strategic plan developed by YSN, the organization in the case study featured in this book.

PRACTICAL CONSIDERATIONS

The preparatory work prior to engaging in strategic planning—the planning for the planning, as it were—is critical to the success of the effort. Often the process is staff initiated, by the top professional or other members of the senior management team; at other times, it may be the board that first senses the organization is not reaching its full potential, through its community ties or during a leadership transition. In some instances the act of an external stakeholder, such as a funder or regulatory body, provides the impetus for an internal reexamination of priorities and practices. Thus, just like decision-making, strategic planning can be broadly characterized as anticipatory or reactive, although now more than ever the proactive organization holds a competitive advantage.

Purposes for Planning

In the for-profit world there are six commonly accepted reasons for strategizing: growth, share increasing, profit, market concentration, liquidation, and turnaround (Anderson, 1984). Each can also be applied to nonprofits.

- *Growth* connotes expansion through the introduction of a new program or service that furthers the organizational mission.
- *Share increasing* refers to improving the position of an already existing "product," perhaps by offering it to a new client group or making it more readily available. Share increasing frequently entails analyzing competitors' offerings to determine what changes would make one's own services more attractive.
- Even though efficiency is important, *profit* for charitable organizations is not just about strengthening the financial bottom line. Rather, it is more often about increasing effectiveness in mission accomplishment and consumer satisfaction.
- For *market concentration* the organization's concern is to focus the lion's share of its resources on promoting what it does best, its core programs and services.

- The aim of *liquidation* is more drastic than it is for market concentration. Here the end result is likely to be the elimination of one or more programs that no longer can justify their existence.

- *Turnaround* involves actions to improve overall organizational performance, for example, by upgrading technological capacity or expanding staff development.

Clearly, these strategic goals are not mutually exclusive. An organization may incorporate several or even all of them in its planning efforts.

Approaches to Planning

One way to approach planning is as a sequential, linear process. Although the details of different planning models may vary, most include the following basic steps: (1) obtaining the commitment of key decision-makers to proceed, (2) identifying formal and informal expectations or constraints that might affect the process, (3) creating the necessary infrastructure to carry out the process, (4) clarifying the organizational mission, values, and vision, (5) gathering pertinent information by assessing the organization's internal and external environments, (6) developing an action plan to address organizational concerns, (7) implementing the plan, and (8) evaluating the results.

In practice, however, planning is seldom truly linear. It is more of a back-and-forth process, with the participants frequently rethinking what they have accomplished. Sometimes the organization is motivated to engage in strategic planning after learning of a new constraint that must be overcome (step 2), in recognizing a key program is no longer viable (step 5), or even at the very end when evaluating the plan's results, if the outcomes fall far short of expectations. Implementation may also begin before the process has been fully completed as long as this does not have a negative effect on subsequent actions (Bryson, 1995). For these reasons, Wolf (1999, pp. 286–287) suggests it may be more useful to view planning in levels, as a roadmap from one place to another:

- Level one, *purpose or mission*, reveals why the organization is making the journey;
- Level two, *goals*, provides the general direction it is heading;
- Level three, *objectives and targets*, reveals the destination;
- Level four, *strategies*, tells specifically how the organization will get there;
- Level five, *actions*, is the trip itself;
- Level six, *evaluation*, determines whether you have arrived.

Table 8.1 illustrates these levels with reference to a specific planning process undertaken by a large human service organization in the rehabilitation field in anticipation of changes in state policy based on managed care principles (Golensky & Walker, 2003).

Table 8.1 Planning levels for an organization in transition

Level	Illustration
1. Purpose or mission	To provide rehabilitation services for people with disabilities in a Christian environment.
2. Goal(s)	To strengthen the organization's competitive position in obtaining state contracts.
3. Objectives and targets	To increase effectiveness through a continuum of care. To increase efficiency by consolidating financial, technological, and human resources services.
4. Strategies and	Adopt a new corporate structure, the management service organization.[b]
5. Actions[a]	Establish a network of affiliates to expand services statewide. Provide management services to affiliate agencies. Work with private-sector vendors in accordance with the state's managed care plan. Adopt a new governance model more in tune with the new corporate structure.
6. Evaluation	Although the MSO initially seemed successful, the discovery of a large deficit brought affiliate concerns to light. Changes were made to restore financial stability and establish a team approach to affiliate relationships. In the end, the organization kept the same model but simplified it.

[a]These two levels have been consolidated for this illustration.
[b]A management service organization (MSO) is formed by one or more nonprofits to achieve greater efficiency and effectiveness by providing management and administrative services to other organizations.
Sources: Adapted from Golensky & Walker, 2003; Wolf, 1999.

By comparison, integrated or holistic planning is based on the idea of strategic fit, with the planning incorporated into the regular organizational operation. In order to create a cohesive whole, all elements of the process are constantly in play to allow for synergy. Thus there are no defined beginning and end points; the information flow must be multidirectional and the planning ongoing. Visually, the integrated process resembles a wheel, with those coordinating the effort in the center and the individuals responsible for the different tasks (formulating goals, setting objectives, and so on) on the perimeter. The coordinators collect information from the task groups and communicate relevant information back to them via the spokes. Ultimately, the various pieces of information come together in a coherent plan. These three activities metaphorically turn the wheel, representing the organization's success in moving the planning forward (Wolf, 1999).

Each approach has its pros and cons. Linear planning tends to be more comprehensive and therefore works particularly well when an organization needs to assess all its strengths and weaknesses and consider changes in a number of operational areas. It is also useful for times when an organization wants to legitimize its decisions to the community at large, such as in undertaking something controversial, risky, or expensive. On the downside, linear planning tends to be a slow process, and once a plan has been developed and approved, it becomes hard to go in a different direction even when circumstances suggest doing so. The main advantages of integrated planning are its emphasis on process, allowing for an immediate response to changing environmental conditions; its ability to keep participants involved over time; and its flexibility in moving quickly to action. However, because of its lack of comprehensiveness, integrated planning can result in hasty, ill-advised strategies, and its emphasis on process may be at the cost of developing a carefully worded, well-documented written plan, which may erode stakeholder confidence in the organization's long-term capacity for addressing key issues. Choosing one approach over the other will depend on the organization's needs, the situation it is facing, and its available resources; it is likely both will be used at some point in the organizational life cycle (Wolf, 1999).

The Nuts and Bolts of the Planning Process

The purpose(s) for the planning and the approach selected influence how the process will be structured in terms of participation, logistics, and use of outside facilitation. For example, an organization that wants to set a more philosophical, global strategy may handle these matters quite differently from one aiming for a highly detailed, broad action plan to address a number of specific concerns. Large organizations often initiate strategic planning at the departmental level, which would then feed into a similar process at the divisional level; the results of the work at these lower levels inform the planning at the corporate level. For smaller nonprofits, a single planning effort for the entire organization should suffice.

Creating a positive climate for planning is key to its success. One way to achieve this is in the determination of who will participate in the planning process. First of all, the board and CEO must demonstrate their commitment by allocating sufficient resources to get the job done and by taking on a defined role in the process. Bryson (1995) refers to those in the leadership core as the "process sponsors," with responsibility for articulating the desired outcomes and stressing the importance of the planning, pledging that the effort will have tangible results, encouraging and rewarding innovative thinking, and keeping the process moving even when conflicts develop.

"Champions" are those responsible for managing the day-to-day aspects of the process, from beginning to end. These individuals ensure that planning stays high on the organizational agenda; attend to the many details related to space, time, and materials; provide a conceptual framework for the process; educate participants about strategic planning if they are unfamiliar with its nature and purpose; involve themselves in the planning without dictating specific solutions; and push the effort forward toward a resolution even when it may seem little progress is being made. If the situation under review is not very complex, it may be possible to have one person do the bulk of the work, but most often, planning is a collective effort. Depending on scope and resources, there may be separate teams for each step in the process or a single group taking on all of the tasks. As for team composition, some organizations choose to use staff only; others include board members and even outside stakeholders. Wherever possible, it is wise to involve organizational members not appointed to the team(s) in the process, to help build broader support for implementing the plan. For example, during the information-gathering stage, have them complete surveys or take part in focus groups, and provide frequent progress updates to everyone.

The length of the planning process will vary as well, based again on the complexity of the issues with which the organization is grappling and the resources at its disposal. A good way to get the process started is with a retreat, which may run anywhere from one to three days; organizations already committed to and familiar with strategic planning may require less time to reach consensus on the design and structure of the process. Asking people to set aside time to attend the retreat, especially board members, signals the importance of the effort. Even the site of the retreat can be a factor in moving things forward. For instance, when the CEOs of four small nonprofits contemplating merger brought their boards together to review the plan drawn up by staff, they selected a space high up in one of the tallest buildings in town, with a panoramic view of the city, to set the right tone about keeping the big picture in mind (Golensky & DeRuiter, 1999). Once the parameters of the process have been set, the champions must set up the schedule of planning meetings and maintain communication with the planning team(s) between meetings via e-mail and the distribution of minutes, briefing papers, and other pertinent materials. It is their job as well to see that the necessary supplies and equipment are on hand at meetings, and to oversee the production of the written plan, from draft stage to the final version, along with its distribution.

Although some organizations may choose to handle the planning process without outside assistance, others will opt to bring in a facilitator to move the process along. An individual known to be impartial about the outcomes of the effort and with proven expertise in managing group interactions can be invaluable, especially when stakeholders with competing interests are involved. To be effective, a facilitator must quickly learn as much as possible about the organization's history, culture, and concerns. However, for this kind of consultation to work, the process sponsors and champions must forge a solid partnership with the facilitator, based on mutual respect and trust. Otherwise there can be unfortunate consequences for everyone involved, which was my experience when facilitating a retreat for an environmental coalition. I learned by chance midway through the second day that the funding for the coalition would not be continued, a fact one of the sponsors had withheld. Since the express purpose for the retreat was to develop a plan for future activities, the entire process was seriously compromised, and my personal relationship with the sponsor was irreparably damaged.

Budgeting and Strategic Planning

A mistake organizations sometimes make is failing to incorporate budgeting into the strategic planning process. Just as it is necessary to consider the costs of entering into a planning process prior to doing so, determining whether there are sufficient monies to implement the plan should not be an afterthought. Management may be more used to associating budgeting with fiscal control than with strategy development and implementation. So it may require a change in the mind-set of organizational leaders to perceive a budget as "the organization's blueprint for the coming months, or years, expressed in monetary terms" (Gross, 1985, p. 11). In this type of financial planning, as goals and objectives are being formulated, it is important to identify past revenue and expense patterns, future financial trends, and the financial impact of proposed new programmatic activities on the monies already on hand as well as the potential for cultivating new funding sources. As part of this effort, it is especially useful to project several scenarios, from the most optimistic to the most pessimistic, to weigh risks and opportunities more accurately. Including a budgetary component in the planning process not only serves as a useful internal reality check, it also can send a positive signal to funders that the organization is prudent in all fiscal matters (Wolf, 1999).

Implementing the Plan

As previously noted, one of the most discouraging aspects of strategic planning is the amount of waste, literally and figuratively, from plans that never get implemented. One reason for this outcome may be that sponsors were not as fully committed to the process as they originally maintained, but more often the practical aspects of implementation were not sufficiently addressed at the planning stage. A case in point: Faculty in a school of social work participated in a two-day retreat to review current practices and consider new initiatives, resulting in a multidimensional plan written out on flip charts. A faculty member was charged with bringing the sheets back to the school so the plan could be entered into the computer. Unfortunately, she became distracted by other matters, put the sheets on a bookshelf in her office, and forgot about them. Shortly thereafter, she took a year's leave of absence as a visiting professor, during which her office was unused, and then transferred to the other university. Since no one had formally assumed or been given the role of process sponsor or champion, a proper follow-through never happened. The sheets with the plan, which everyone assumed had been lost, were discovered two years after the retreat in the move to a new campus.

To ensure successful implementation of the plan, Bryson (1995) recommends these guidelines.

- Put as much time and effort into managing implementation as were devoted to the preceding steps in the process. This is critical when those responsible for implementation are not the same people who served on the planning team.
- Develop explicit strategies to guide implementation through all organizational levels. If this was not completed previously, now action steps must be outlined with specific objectives, a timetable, and clarification of roles and responsibilities.

- Even though it may be difficult to alter the basic design of the plan, take advantage of program staff's firsthand knowledge of client populations to smooth out the rough spots, to the degree possible, to facilitate implementation.
- Provide ongoing support and commit sufficient resources, both human and material, to ensure that implementation is successful but also cost-effective. This implies starting with the actions that are easiest and quickest to introduce.
- Use an incremental approach, linking new initiatives with established programs in a logical way while maintaining stakeholder support internally and externally.
- Make sure planned changes are in compliance with all pertinent legal, regulatory, and funding mandates.
- Recognize that strategic planning is likely to result in changes in the organizational culture, and build in mechanisms to manage any residual conflicts and to celebrate each success.
- Establish procedures for evaluating the implementation process (formative evaluation) as well as the end results (summative evaluation), and adapt strategies as necessary to fit changing circumstances.

STRATEGIC PLANNING MODELS

There are a number of viable ways to engage in strategic planning. In this section, three specific approaches are described in detail. These models were selected because they illustrate very distinct underlying philosophies and perspectives on the design and structure of the planning process, to demonstrate that regardless of size, culture, or stage of organizational development, every nonprofit can identify a suitable approach.

Strategic Business Planning

To some charitable organizations, the idea of business planning may be off-putting, but for those using the corporate model of board governance (for example, referring to their top professional as president/CEO and their top volunteer as board chair), the use of terminology associated with the for-profit world should have instant appeal because such organizations are apt to have a high proportion of trustees with a business background. The case can be made that, like its corporate counterpart, the major challenge facing a nonprofit today is positioning itself effectively for the future; therefore, if the techniques of strategic business planning have worked in one arena, they should be adaptable to other types of organizations (Kluger, Baker, & Garval, 1998).

Underlying Principles
To guide the planning, the organization should adopt a compatible management paradigm. One option would be total quality management (TQM), which stresses the impor-

tance of continuous quality improvement to benefit customers, defined as all service recipients, including staff. Data collection and analysis are a part of every phase of the model, beginning with an organizational assessment and then moving to create the necessary policy documents. Because employees (considered internal customers) are empowered to make decisions on programmatic improvements, staff training is an important ongoing consideration. The final planning phases are service delivery processing and benchmarking: Service delivery processing underscores the need for constant attention to quality improvement and customer satisfaction, as the organization is expected to keep abreast of developments in its external environment and make changes accordingly. Benchmarking, a long-standing practice in for-profits, entails identifying best practices within one's own organization and elsewhere to be adopted or adapted as performance standards. The regular monitoring of customer satisfaction via flow charts and other statistical measures provides documentation of success or, alternatively, triggers a new round of planning (Hawkins & Gunther, 1998).

TQM enjoyed its greatest prominence in the 1980s and 1990s but seems to have lost ground due to mixed reviews of its effectiveness. A newer model is business process reengineering (BPR), defined by Michael Hammer, its leading advocate, as "the fundamental rethinking and radical redesign of business processes to achieve dramatic improvements in critical measures of performance" (cited in Grobman, 2004, pp. 145–146). This is a top-down approach to improving organizational performance. In theory, planning for the future is not based on the past, and so the CEO and other senior managers are asked to consider whether operations should continue as is or undergo significant changes based on present realities. If there is dissatisfaction with the status quo, key operational areas of direct and support services would be redesigned, making use of any new technological advances, with the focus on processes rather than separate work tasks. Given this emphasis on an entire function, specialists either become or are replaced by generalists; with access to all the necessary information, a single employee can take responsibility for achieving a desired outcome, such as meeting a consumer's needs, more efficiently and effectively. Centralizing organizational resources leads to better coordination, which in turn helps to flatten out the traditional hierarchical structure, eliminating much of the bureaucracy and speeding up decision-making (Grobman, 2004).

Steps in the Planning Process

In keeping with the general philosophy of strategic business planning, a first step in the process is to examine current and prospective agency programs and services for commonalities in markets and consumers in order to group them into the primary lines of business. A vision statement, emphasizing ends or outcomes, a summary of programs and services, and a description of the current market served can then be developed for each line of business to increase understanding of the organization among internal and external stakeholders.

Conducting a situational assessment, another key part of the process, leads to identifying the organization's core competencies. It entails collecting and processing data regarding the organization's internal strengths and weaknesses and the opportunities and threats in the external environment, often called a SWOT analysis. The internal review is of the present, and the external review, is of the future. This kind of assessment makes it possible to develop four strategy levels: (1) SO uses current strengths to take advantage of identified opportunities, (2) WO refers to attempts to overcome weaknesses in pursuing possible opportunities, (3) ST means using strengths to avoid threats, and (4) WT involves defensive maneuvers to reduce weaknesses and avoid threats. In addition, the organization may wish to commission an analysis of its current and potential competitors, recognizing that these same entities may at times be collaborators, to see where it stands within its industry (Kluger et al., 1998).

The earlier steps lead to the selection and implementation of strategies designed to maximize the organization's assets, directed at the organization as a whole, a particular line of business, or an individual program or service. As part of this effort, it is possible to be more proactive in the allocation of discretionary funds (those not restricted for a specific purpose), consistent with the strategic business plan, to develop new programs, enhance a current service, or otherwise make an investment in the organization's future. Implementation is often a combination of putting the planned strategies into motion and taking advantage of opportunities that arise unexpectedly. Progress should be monitored to assess the plan's effectiveness, updating it as necessary.

The Strategy Change Cycle

John Bryson (1995) has developed a ten-step planning process aimed at both public and private nonprofit organizations. The rationale for his model is the need to be responsive to the challenges of an ever-changing world, to survive and prosper. While the intent here is not very different from that of strategic business planning, less jargon is used to describe the cycle, making this approach potentially more acceptable to a wider range of organizations. Moreover, Bryson is careful not to make unrealistic promises about what strategic planning can accomplish, noting it does not replace strategic thinking and acting and is not a substitute for dedicated leadership.

Underlying Principles
Bryson contrasts two quite different approaches to decision-making. The rational-deductive method relies on a linear process that, under the most desirable circumstances, leads to consensus on goals, objectives, and strategies to achieve organizational aims, or at least the presumption of consensus. In the inductive, political approach, the emphasis is on issues, recognizing that conflict, not consensus, is more representative of organizational reality, whether "over ends, means, timing, location, political advantage, reasons for change, or philosophy, and the conflicts may be severe" (Bryson, 1995, p. 11). Via compromise and negotiation, efforts are made to resolve differences in a way that is acceptable to all the involved parties, establishing a positive climate for formulating more general policies and programs to address the core issues.

Fundamentally, the strategy change cycle seeks to identify and resolve strategic issues as a reflection of the political approach, but it also draws on the rational method where appropriate. Accordingly, once having used the former to come to an agreement on the best ways to address key issues, the latter can be used to turn the broad principles worked out with the various stakeholders into a concrete plan with specific goals, objectives, action steps, a time table, and so on. Or if there is already consensus on basic matters such as mission and vision, the inductive method can help iron out the remaining areas of conflict, moving the process toward implementation. Developing a common vision early on is essential to the success of the planning effort.

Steps in the Planning Process
Following is a synopsis of the planning cycle.

1. *Initiating and agreeing on strategic planning.* Garnering the support of key internal and external decision-makers to the process is the main purpose of step 1. First the stakeholders must be identified and brought together, often at a retreat site, to receive an overview of strategic planning and then develop agreements about the intent of the process, its design and timing, the role and responsibility of participants, and the necessary resources. For organizations already committed to planning, some of the later steps in the cycle may be part of the retreat agenda.

2. *Identifying organizational mandates.* To decide on the direction to pursue, the planners must be aware of any constraints due to laws and ordinances as well as internal restrictions in the articles of incorporation or the bylaws. There may also be informal mandates resulting from the community's and the organization's cultural norms. Often the most valuable aspect of this step is discovering how few constraints actually exist, which significantly opens up the planning process.

3. *Clarifying organizational mission and values.* The desired outcomes of step 3 are a mission statement (with its underlying values) and a stakeholder analysis. Since everything a nonprofit does should be mission-driven, "clarifying the purpose can eliminate a great deal of unnecessary conflict . . . and . . . help channel discussion and activity productively" (Bryson, 1995, p. 27). Analyzing each interest group's expectations and how well performance standards have been met will provide essential information for ensuring greater stakeholder satisfaction.

4. *Assessing the organization's external and internal environments.* The heart of step 4 is the familiar SWOT analysis. Data may be collected through various means (discussions, surveys, focus groups, interviews, document review, the Internet, etc.). Externally, conducting an environmental scan of forces and trends, key stakeholders, and other nonprofits that may be both competitors and collaborators will be useful. Internally, it is wise to monitor organizational resources (inputs), present strategies (process), and performance (outputs).

5. *Identifying the strategic issues facing the organization.* Bryson defines *strategic issues* as "fundamental policy questions or critical challenges that affect an organization's mandates, mission, and values; product or service level and mix; clients, users, or payers;

or cost, financing, organization or management" (p. 30). The planning team analyzes the identified issues to determine which ones require monitoring, which are likely to require action in the near future, and which need an immediate response. The issues are then arranged to form an action agenda.

6. *Formulating strategies and plans to manage the issues.* To identify the best strategies to deal with the issues identified in step 5, the planners must agree on a set of actions that can maximize organizational strengths and opportunities and neutralize weaknesses and threats. The goal is to have a plan in draft form that furthers the organizational mission, is acceptable to key stakeholders, is doable in consideration of available resources, and is legal, moral, and ethical.

7. *Reviewing and adopting the strategies and plan.* The intent is to secure all necessary approvals from key stakeholders to adopt the proposed plan and proceed to implementation. Depending on the extent of conflicting interests and external regulation, this step may be highly politicized.

8. *Establishing an effective organizational vision.* Although better if done earlier in the process, the planners need to describe what the organization would look like in the future, assuming the plan is successfully implemented, a "vision of success," as it were. Having a description of this nature can motivate all organizational members to do what is expected of them to achieve the articulated goals.

9. *Developing an effective implementation process.* The particulars of step 9 were articulated in the previous section of this chapter. It does bear repeating that a positive outcome for this effort depends on verbal support from organizational leaders as well as the provision of the necessary resources.

10. *Reassessing strategies and the strategic planning process.* Periodically, the strategies put in place should be reviewed to determine whether they have been and will remain effective in consideration of present circumstances, with changes made accordingly. The planning process itself should also be reviewed for strengths and weaknesses, to guide the next planning cycle.

As noted earlier, in practice, this process will not necessarily be as linear as suggested here. For example, with smaller nonprofits and when the issues are less weighty or affect only a single organization, steps 6, 7, and 9 may be combined, and step 8 may be eliminated if regular planning is already an accepted practice within the organization.

The Search Conference

Somewhat less well-known to nonprofits than the previous two planning models is the Search Conference, so named because its principal function is to allow possibilities to surface and then attach meaning to them rather than start with preconceived ideas of organizational reality. Although this methodology was first used in its present form in the late 1950s, its essence has been traced back to certain tribal gatherings and rituals;

also bears some resemblance to the philosophy espoused by the Society of Friends. However, it really began to take root in the United States in the 1990s as organizations came to recognize the impact of operating in a turbulent environment and became attracted to a different way to address strategic planning (Emery & Purser, 1996).

Underlying Principles

To deal successfully with the ups and downs of an unsettled external world, organizations must put aside closed systems thinking, with its linear, operational approach that relies on top leaders and experts to provide all of the answers, and embrace active adaptation, which goes far beyond the mere acceptance of change, as the foundation of strategic planning. "In a turbulent environment, the action of any one system is nested within, and affected by, the constellation of interdependence among all other systems. . . . Dynamic changes occurring in the turbulent environment trigger the need for dynamic changes in organizations and systems" (Emery & Purser, 1996, p. 62).

The search conference therefore takes a more indirect, zigzag course to help an organization reach its desired future, making it possible to maneuver around obstacles and shift direction as needed. One of the first principles is to avoid concentrating resources in one area; a concerted effort is made to tap the knowledge and strengths at all organizational levels by inviting those expected to be affected directly by the changes to be full partners in the planning process. For the same reason, the goal is to develop multiple plans addressing a variety of initiatives, as recommended by Eadie. A second tenet is to use strategies to convert wary stakeholders into advocates by generating enough excitement about the new directions to win over the doubters.

Overall, this model attempts to put open systems thinking into practice by viewing planning as puzzle solving in learning to cope more effectively with uncertainty. It takes a humanistic, holistic view of the world, providing opportunities for creative choice out of the belief that people have a great capacity for purposeful behavior. Furthermore, it explicitly acknowledges the universal desire to live in a more just society by incorporating the search for personal ideals of belonging, nurturance, humanity, and beauty in planning for the future of the organization (Emery & Purser, 1996).

Steps in the Planning Process

The search conference is both the name for the planning model and the event at which planning occurs, usually held in a retreat setting. It is advisable to use an outside facilitator as conference manager, whose responsibilities generally include assisting the sponsors and champions, in Bryson's terminology, with the preplanning and guiding the planning process during the event, such as adjusting the time allotted for the different activities. However, it is best that the facilitator not write the report of what transpired at the retreat or participate directly in implementing the plan, so that group members can take ownership of their work. During preplanning, the purpose for the search conference is established, the participants are selected, and the logistics are worked out. In choosing participants, include those essential to achieving the event's purpose, with

Exhibit 8.1 Search Conference Agenda

RIVERSIDE MUSEUM SEARCH CONFERENCE
February 15–16, 2008

AGENDA

<u>Friday, February 15</u>

3:00–4:00 PM   OPENING SESSION

- Welcome and Statement of Purpose
- Introductions
- Briefing on Search Conference and Overview of Agenda (PLENARY)
- Expectations (SMALL-GROUP SESSION; PLENARY)

4:00–5:00 PM   Scan of Task Environment (PLENARY)

5:00–6:00 PM   History of the System (PLENARY)

<u>Saturday, February 16</u>

8:00–8:30 AM   WELCOME/RECAPPING OF FRIDAY'S WORK

8:30–10:00 AM   System Analysis

- Discussion—SMALL-GROUP SESSION
- Reports and Integration (PLENARY)

10:00–12:00 Noon   System Analysis, continued

- Discussion—SMALL-GROUP SESSION
- Reports and Integration (PLENARY)

12:00–1:00 PM   Lunch (SMALL-GROUP SESSION)

- Discussion: Overcoming Constraints
- Briefing on Strategy Development

1:00–3:30 PM   Strategies and Action Plans (SMALL-GROUP SESSION)

3:30–4:30 PM   CLOSING SESSION

- Reports and Integration Session: Action Plans (PLENARY)
- Next Steps and Wrap-up (PLENARY)

twenty to forty people a workable total. In smaller nonprofits, all board members and senior staff can be invited, with program staff also if desired; in larger settings, it may be necessary to pick representatives of each group. External stakeholders may be included as well. Ideally, the event should run for two and a half to three days, but a day and a half may be more reasonable.

Although each search conference is unique, the event is designed like a funnel, structured into three broad phases: environmental appreciation, system analysis, and strategic action planning. That is, one starts by examining the external environment to identify the broader context and emerging trends, and then you continually narrow the focus by working inward to look at the past, present, and future of the organizational system, leading to the development of the plan. As shown in exhibit 8.1, participants tackle defined tasks in either plenary sessions or small groups. The participants strive to find the common ground within the system that the whole group can support as the basis for future planning. Because a search conference is a democratic process, everyone is seen as an expert by virtue of being part of the system and is encouraged to contribute. In fact, board and staff members are deliberately mixed, which for some organizations may be the first time these individuals have worked side by side. All ideas are considered valid and are recorded on flip charts. As tasks are completed, the flip-chart sheets are taped to the walls of the meeting room, with participants encouraged to walk around to review each other's work. At the end, the sheets are gathered and brought back to the office so the results can be computerized as the official record of what was accomplished.

The last task of the search conference is to identify next steps as the beginning of the implementation phase, a time to start talking about the specifics of who will do what and when. After the event, participants are encouraged to communicate their achievements to other stakeholders to build enthusiasm for the plan throughout the system, which is referred to as *diffusion*. As Emery and Purser (1996) note, "The main challenge after the Search Conference is . . . continuity of organization so that participants retain responsibility and authority for implementation of its action plans." (p. 232). Organizational leaders must be flexible to ensure that sufficient resources are committed to implementation and that bureaucratic constraints do not get in the way of continuing democratic action by the various planning teams. Educating sponsors and champions on these points is a role the conference manager can play during the preplanning phase.

FINAL THOUGHTS

Table 8.2 summarizes the key features of the three planning models just presented. It also makes explicit that effective planning is more than the sum of its parts. When done well, formal strategic planning pays off, for it has been proven to have a much greater impact on achieving high performance than informal planning efforts and seems to offer a competitive advantage to organizations. In particular, this kind of planning results in clearer goals and a greater understanding of what is expected of group members to achieve the desired ends. It also permits the organization to be proactive in responding to perceived opportunities and threats as environmental conditions change, and it focuses attention on the big picture (Anderson, 1984; Grobman, 2004).

Table 8.2 Three strategic planning models

Model	Key features
Strategic business planning	1. Reexamine current and prospective programs and services for common elements; group into lines of business. 2. Conduct a situational assessment of the internal and external environments (SWOT analysis). 3. Select and implement strategies to maximize organizational assets.
Strategy change cycle	1. Gain stakeholder support for process. 2. Identify constraints that might affect the planning process. 3. Analyze stakeholder expectations; clarify mission and values. 4. Conduct a SWOT analysis. 5. Identify, analyze, and order the strategic issues facing the organization. 6. Formulate strategies and plans to address the strategic issues. 7. Gain stakeholder approval for identified strategies and plans. 8. Describe the organization's future (its vision for success).[a] 9. Implement the plan(s). 10. Reassess the strategies and the planning process.
Search conference	1. *Preplanning phase*: Determine the purpose, select the participants, and work out the logistics for the retreat. 2. *Planning phase*: Complete a set of tasks to identify environmental trends; review the organization's past, present, and future; develop one or more action plans for multiple initiatives. 3. *Implementation phase*: Work out the details of who will do what and when; ensure sufficient resources and ongoing leadership support to allow the planning teams to translate broad strategies into concrete actions.

Sources: Adapted from Bryson, 1995; Emery & Purser, 1996; Kluger, Baker, & Garval, 1998.
[a]This step addresses the importance of developing a vision for success. As stated in the text, best practices today suggest visioning should occur early on in the planning process.

APPENDIX
REPORT OF THE YSN STRATEGIC PLANNING COMMITTEE (EXCERPTS)

To the Board of Directors of the Youth Services Network:

The members of the Strategic Planning Committee are pleased to present for your consideration a series of recommendations that offer a vision of the organization that we believe the Youth Services Network (YSN) can become over the next five years.

YSN must step boldly into the future, using all available resources, both human and financial, to make this vision a reality. One of the premises of the five-year plan being proposed is that the organization's reserves will be applied to support its operational needs as long as it proves necessary, that is, until the current income streams can be strengthened and new funding sources developed to make YSN deficit free.

Further, the committee feels board and staff alike must have confidence that what we are doing is good and important, that we know our business and have a firm base on which to build. It must be recognized that an organization cannot stand in place, for surely that leads to mediocrity and then decline. If we are unable to realize our goals by the end of the five-year period, it may be necessary to close our doors, but we will be secure in the knowledge that we have spent our money wisely, and the thousands of young people helped through the years will remain an achievement of the highest merit.

AN OVERVIEW

To achieve its mission, YSN will implement a sequential, developmental program that emphasizes education and employment services.

1. While YSN will continue to serve children and young adults, ages six to twenty-four, our primary target group will be ten- to eighteen-year-olds.
2. To emphasize the developmental nature of the program, there will be an integration of services between the year-round effort and summer camping.
3. There will be a variety of programs to meet the educational, employment, social, recreational, and cultural needs of the service population.
4. YSN will build on its history of successful community-based services by seeking opportunities for establishing additional community centers, using its current site as the model, and for the replication of individual programs, such as the dropout prevention program, in other areas of the city.
5. Because of the emphasis on the integration of services, tournaments will be eliminated as a separate program component. Recreation will continue to be an important part of the community-based and camping programs.

SPECIFIC RECOMMENDATIONS

Programs and Services

The areas of concentration will be community-based services and camping. The initial focus will be on new and/or expanded efforts at the present center. At the same time, there will be an exploration of communities both in the same area of the city and in other sections where a similar type of center might be established. Educational programs and job-readiness training will become part of the camp offerings, along with the traditional activities. The expectation is that for the time being YSN will continue to rent campsites at the state park; however, a feasibility study will be conducted within the next twelve to twenty-four months to determine whether to purchase our own site.

In the early days of the camping program, YSN for the most part served its own youngsters from the various storefront centers we operated around the city. Over the years, this pattern changed as the number of year-round facilities dwindled. Although it could be said that the significant returning-camper population from previous years is "ours," the organization really has minimal impact on these young people even though the program is of very high quality. Given the range of problems experienced by many of the campers such as poor housing, drug abuse within the home and in the surrounding neighborhood, and underachievement at school, a two-week exposure (the typical camp stay) is too short a period in which to make much of a difference. Furthermore, while computers have been introduced at camp, outside of sports and recreation, the activities offered have little connection to the year-round battery of services.

Therefore, the committee recommends that the camping program and year-round effort become more integrated, both in terms of the children served and the types of programs provided. To accomplish this, there will be a move back to the past toward an increase in serving youngsters who also participate in center activities. More educational and employment-oriented activities will be introduced at camp, even to the extent of obtaining Board of Education approval to run a sanctioned summer school, to be combined with traditional camping. The five-year goal is to have almost the entire camp population composed of young people from our year-round effort, perhaps attending in longer time segments, such as a four-week session.

Finances

A broadened base of support is a major goal for this five-year period. Our recent experience with direct mail has taught us that it is unwise to depend too heavily on any one funding source. Therefore, efforts will be made to increase the support derived from foundations, a likely avenue for program start-up assistance, and from all levels of government, where continuation funding might be secured. For center programs, the kinds of support currently in place will be maintained and expanded where possible; this includes the federal grant for the dropout prevention program, the grant from the I Have a Wish Foundation for the special educational effort, and the various grants and contracts with local government.

For the camping program, fees will be raised judiciously over the next several years, and additional income sources will be explored. One possibility is suggested in the program section of this report, contracting with the Board of Education for some kind of summer school program. Finally, board members will be called on to increase their personal efforts to secure financial support, such as sponsoring a special fund-raiser. The following chart provides an overview of the committee's five-year projections.

In the direct mail area, the hope is that the new consultant's approach will result in at least the stabilization of the campaign and even modest growth. However, we must be mindful that the competition from other agencies providing similar services to ours is increasing each year, so our task may be especially difficult in this area.

	Projected revenues ($000)					
	Base year	*Year 1*	*Year 2*	*Year 3*	*Year 4*	*Year 5*
Government	276	283	295	300	312	320
Foundations/United Way	135	150	175	195	200	200
Dues and fees	244	265	275	300	327	340
Direct mail/bequests	400	410	446	501	528	539
Reserves	134	127	111	49	21	9
Total	1189	1235	1302	1345	1388	1408

	Revenues (percent)					
	Base year	*Year 1*	*Year 2*	*Year 3*	*Year 4*	*Year 5*
Government	23	23	23	22	22	23
Foundations/United Way	11	12	13	14	14	14
Dues and fees	21	22	21	22	24	24
Direct mail/bequests	34	33	34	37	38	38
Reserves	11	10	9	4	2	1
Total	100	100	100	99	100	100

Note: The percentages for year 3 do not equal 100, due to rounding.

Adding a special fund-raising event to the overall package should be explored, recognizing that such an approach normally requires three to five years to begin generating a profit. It is for that reason we have elected not to include revenues from this source in our current projections.

Another potential source of support would be corporations. Corporate support will be explored for the educational and employment services we currently provide as well as for the new services that we propose to introduce. A factor to be taken into account here is that success in this area would necessitate a change in our relationship with United Way, since its policies preclude direct solicitation to corporations by member agencies. The committee chose not to include this category in our projections until we have a better sense of what would be gained and what would be lost by our efforts.

The key to the success of this strategic plan is the degree to which everyone can, and does, embrace the underlying growth strategy of using present assets as an investment in the organization's future. Clearly the implementation of such a far-reaching plan will require a board of directors that is fully committed to putting forth the time, effort, and financial support necessary to assist the staff in this undertaking. As its final recommendation, the Planning Committee charges the Executive Committee with the responsibility for developing guidelines on the expectations for a prospective board member and for those individuals already serving as trustees.

Program Development 9

Designing a program is a multiphase endeavor that begins at the point when an idea is first conceived. The next steps are to determine the nature of the program and how it will be implemented, and then to ensure the effort is moving forward as planned. Finally, one must assess its outcomes and impact, that is, whether the program has achieved its intended results and therefore warrants continuation, which brings us back to the starting point. Program development operates as a continuous feedback loop. Its fundamental intent is to address one or more identified social problems in the most beneficial way by making the best use of the available resources.

In this context, a *program* is defined as a discrete set of activities organized to serve consumers in a particular manner to further the organizational mission. For example, an organization whose stated purpose is to enhance the quality of life for the elderly might have a counseling program, a wellness program, a socialization program, and so forth. Clients can avail themselves of all programs responding to their specific needs and interests at any given time and for which they are eligible. Although one sometimes hears the organizational mission, the overarching reason for an agency's existence, referred to as its program, this ignores the real differences between the two terms, with programs being the means to the desired end as embodied in the mission.

Accountability is another significant part of the program development equation, especially in today's challenging environment. To be accountable means being able to justify the value of an organization's offerings to multiple constituencies: consumers, staff, board, funders, other service providers, accrediting bodies, the public at large. It means no matter where you stand in the organizational hierarchy—direct service provider, supervisor, administrator—you cannot escape the need to document the outcomes of the work you do in regard to effectiveness and efficiency and to demonstrate that the work is provided according to high ethical standards.

As noted in chapter 8, the primary purpose of strategic planning is to help the organization determine the optimum direction to fulfill its mission now and in the future. Change often follows this effort, from tweaking current programs to creating new ones, requiring the full support of management and staff to be successful. In their recent research, Trzcinski and Sobeck (2008) found that program development capacity, which encompasses all the activities described above, and readiness for change are mutually reinforcing processes, with the former a statistically significant predictor of the latter.

This chapter covers all of these issues. We first consider the elements involved in developing a project and then move on to the three main components of program development: planning, monitoring, and evaluation.

PROJECT DEVELOPMENT

A *project* is a special kind of program. After being initiated, programs generally are ongoing, with some offered cyclically, that is, activities are repeated over a given period of time (for example, a college course offered every fall for fifteen weeks) and others provided as a constant flow to meet expressed needs, such as hot meals served at a soup kitchen year-round. A project, on the other hand, is time-limited, perhaps offered just once, to test out an innovative treatment approach or in reaction to changing conditions within the community, and is distinctive as to time, place, participants, and desired outcomes. However, successful projects may live on as new programs (Pawlak & Vinter, 2004).

Planning Small-Scale Programs

Schram (1997, p. 4) prefers the term *small-scale programs* for "planning with a small p . . . , on the microlevel of the community" to distinguish these efforts from the much broader focus of strategic or social planning. Such programs generally have low budgets and are coordinated by one person or a few individuals, frequently volunteers with or without the assistance of frontline staff. Examples include producing a resource directory, developing a support group, writing a proposal, holding a staff retreat, and educating legislators about an issue.

One of the advantages of small-scale programs, or projects, as we will call them, is flexibility. They allow stakeholders to become aware of a new concept or service approach in a nonthreatening manner, and just because they are limited in scope does not mean they cannot have an impact. For instance, a human service agency working with the developmentally disabled might want to build support for more community-based programs by mounting a one-year pilot project to establish a group home with supportive services for eight of its highest-functioning clients. If at the end of the year the agency can demonstrate these clients realized measurable gains, it might be possible to obtain funding for an ongoing group-home program.

The steps in planning a project are similar to those for strategic planning: problem identification, project design, implementation, evaluation, and follow-up. During the first two phases, an issue is defined, relevant information gathered, alternatives explored, the commitment of others secured, and, most important, goals are set. As Schram (1997) states, "You may not know which road will take you to your destination when you start a planning process, but you absolutely have to know why you are setting out on the journey" (p. 32). Moreover, without clear goals, evaluating the results would be virtually impossible. Next, the goals must be translated into operational language, specifying the activities to be carried out; sequencing these tasks and assigning the responsible parties are also part of this phase. Given the nature of these projects, it is important to have a contingency plan. For example, if an outdoor site has been picked for the staff retreat, choose a location with indoor space that can be accessed in case of rain. When volunteers are coordinating the project, have others on standby in case circumstances prevent the original group from following through. Records must be maintained on all project details, and the implementation should be closely monitored to ensure the planning unfolds as intended. After the event occurs, follow-up and evaluation lead to writing and disseminating a report documenting the entire process.

The Marketing Approach

For community projects, Boehm (2003) proposes a marketing approach, which emphasizes tailoring services to meet consumer needs and desires. In the development of projects of this type, the first three phases—initiation, planning and design, and implementation—are similar to those noted above, but the last phase, institutionalization or conversion, entails turning the responsibility for maintaining the endeavor over to others, along with evaluating the results of the original effort.

Reflecting a determination of the needs and wants of the target group, marketing consists of the "four Ps": product, price, place and distribution, and promotion. Besides the direct beneficiaries or consumers of the intended project, other stakeholders, individuals and groups with which the organization has ties, may become involved. Some observers, therefore, add a fifth *P*, for people. Even within the target group there are likely to be subgroups with separate expectations, so it becomes a strategic decision how to address these varying needs—as an undifferentiated whole, by segments, or with a concentration on just one subgroup. To illustrate, if the identified issue were teenage pregnancy, the planners could develop a uniform citywide effort to educate all preteens about contraception; or they could target preteens, teen mothers, and teen fathers, with each receiving a different mix of services; or they might focus on teenagers living in low-income neighborhoods.

Product pertains to the services offered. For nonprofits, we are usually referring to nontangible or social products such as changing values and practices, although tangible items may be provided as well. In the teen pregnancy example, the intent may be to help young women gain a better self-image so they will refrain from sexual activity and to teach them techniques to deflect pressure from their boyfriends, but contraceptives may also be distributed. *Pricing* is the value put on what is exchanged between the service provider and the recipients, considering money, time, and effort. Examining the costs and benefits of various service options (individual versus group counseling, for instance) is one way to measure this factor. *Place and distribution* are concerned with service delivery; this discussion may lead to conceptualizing a one-stop service center to provide various kinds of assistance at a single site, which may increase the likelihood of participation in the project. Finally, *promotion* involves the underlying policy and the actual methods used to motivate the target populations to avail themselves of the product. The most common approaches are face-to-face contact, advertising via the media and direct mailings, public relations efforts, and incentives. For the teen pregnancy project, staff might weigh the pros and cons of visiting classrooms and then scheduling individual appointments with interested teens, sending out flyers about the new service center, holding a schoolwide assembly on the effects of early pregnancy, or offering discount coupons for local movie theaters to teens who sign up for the services.

Each project must consider the four (or five) Ps as they relate to the different phases of the planning cycle to achieve the most desirable results. Some elements may be the same throughout, while others could vary significantly from phase to phase.

PROGRAM PLANNING

Planning begins with identifying a social problem or issue and the factors believed to be at the root of the problem. Without some understanding of why the issue occurs and affects a certain population and what this means to society as a whole, planning would be just a random stab at finding a solution. Drawing on assumptions supported by statistics and other kinds of data, a reasonable course of action can be articulated to address the underlying factors, showing a likely pattern of cause and effect (Chambers, 2000; Savaya & Waysman, 2005). Kettner, Moroney, and Martin (2008), who call their research-based, customer-oriented approach *effectiveness-based program planning*, distinguish these two core elements as *theory in* and *theory of planning* (p. 36).

To facilitate the reader's understanding of program development, references will be made in the next sections of the chapter to the Educational Development and Guidance for Employment (EDGE) program, which was created by a national social service organization and carried out by six local affiliates. This was a multifaceted juvenile delinquency prevention program designed for at-risk youth in inner-city communities, to help participants develop a more positive self-image, become acquainted with a range of career opportunities, learn marketable skills and good work habits, and acquire basic life skills. The program also recognized the importance of capacity building at the local level and the need to garner the support of the family and the community for its goals.

Problem Identification and Analysis

Identifying a problem always involves a degree of subjectivity. Until someone or some group labels a phenomenon like juvenile delinquency a problem ("This is bad for our youth and bad for our community"), we are dealing simply with a social condition, a set of facts. To avoid falling back on existing efforts that do little but maintain the status quo, the planner must try to bring a fresh perspective to the situation via a thorough analysis of the problem. This requires knowledge about the nature of the situation obtained from a variety of sources, clarification of terminology to achieve a shared definition, an appreciation of the scale and distribution of the problem (how many are affected and in what geographic areas), the social values that are involved, the level of support for and against taking action, and, of course, the underlying causes, being sensitive to any gender or ethnic considerations. It is particularly important to seek input from all relevant stakeholders at the start to avoid difficulties down the line (Kettner et al., 2008).

Needs Assessment

Once a problem has been identified and clarified, it must be reconfigured as specific needs; measuring their scope and severity, qualitatively and quantitatively, leads to determining the services to be rendered through the program. As a first step, we must recognize the concept of need goes beyond the simple dictionary definition of "a lack of something." *Normative* need assumes there is some standard or criterion for a particular group that is established through custom or general agreement against which it is possible to measure existing levels of service. *Relative* need, on the other hand, takes into account that services are not necessarily distributed uniformly, by comparing services in one community or neighborhood against the level of service provided in a similar geographic area. The third kind of need, *perceived*, refers to what people believe or feel their needs to be; because this is a subjective determination, it can obviously vary from individual to individual but is nonetheless an important consideration in the planning process. Finally, *expressed* need captures the help actually sought from providers, the translation of beliefs and feelings into action (Kettner et al., 2008; Pawlak & Vinter, 2004). By taking all four categories into consideration, the planner is in a better position to develop a program that best fits the client population(s).

Conducting a needs assessment can be costly and time consuming, but its benefits outweigh the negatives, for it increases the likelihood that scarce resources will be used where they might do the most good. Furthermore, an organization can undertake an assessment in cost-effective ways, such as by using volunteers to gather data or reaching out to a nearby college or university to partner on a service-learning project to give students some real-world experience. If the organization has embraced an integrated strategic planning focus, one with no defined beginning and end points, much of the information may already be on hand. Accessing data from government agencies or watchdog groups through the Internet and public documents also saves time and money. Some standard methods used in collecting information include reviewing existing studies; conducting surveys, interviews, focus groups, and community forums; and inventorying the available services of provider agencies. In general, an organization should start internally—using its own service statistics, obtaining staff opinions, conducting exit interviews with clients, canvassing the immediate neighborhood, and so on—before going to external sources. Practicality and accessibility often dictate which approaches are ultimately selected.

Assessment of Assets

Inventorying the services offered by providers can measure both normative and expressed need, depending on the data collected, but it is also a way to determine available resources that might be tapped for a new program. A complete assessment therefore ought to yield information about the strengths or assets of the target population(s) as well as those of the organization and the surrounding community, including its residents and both formal and informal institutions. Two of the most well-known proponents of this viewpoint are John Kretzmann and John McKnight, codirectors of the Asset-Based Community Development Institute at Northwestern University, who believe nonprofits are "much more powerful . . . actors when they are not exclusively focused on needs, problems, and deficiencies" (2005, p. 1). A prevention program like EDGE can be seen as a manifestation of the assets framework, where the emphasis is on fostering the competencies and desired characteristics of those for whom the effort was designed.

Program Design

The structure of the program, the constellation of program activities selected to address the identified problem(s) and how they should be delivered, springs from the theory in planning. For the EDGE program, after reviewing and analyzing the collected data, the planner drew these conclusions: (1) A disproportionate number of the youth who come into contact with the juvenile justice system live in low-income, inner-city communities with large ethnic or racial populations that share such characteristics as substandard housing, inadequate schools, severe unemployment and underemployment, and physical deterioration. (2) When basic support systems (the home, the school, the church) fall short, values and attitudes are shaken, and a sense of hopelessness may set in. (3) To counter these negative factors, a public-private collaboration is needed, for the task is too great and societal issues impacting youth are too complex for private agencies to undertake alone. (4) Prevention offers the broadest framework for positive intervention. (5) Services must address the needs and interests of the youth, their families, and the community, for unless the family and the community understand and agree to support program goals, there will be little chance of success.

Developing Hypotheses

The next step is to develop a series of if-then statements from the theoretical model. As Kettner et al. (2008) note, hypotheses need not be as formal as for a research project; at times, they may be little more than educated guesses. However, the act of crafting hypotheses guides the decisions on program activities and provides the basis for evaluation. Here are some examples for EDGE:

- If youth develop a more positive self-image, and if they obtain some marketable skills and learn good work habits, then they will feel more optimistic about the future, and will be less likely to become involved in the juvenile justice system and more likely to become productive members of society.
- If parents increase their understanding of the needs of youth, then they will be more capable of providing support to their own children.
- If collaborative relationships are forged with other significant community institutions, then current resources will be used more efficiently and effectively and it will be more possible to eliminate service gaps and duplications.

Defining Goals, Objectives, and Action Steps

A *goal* is a broad statement about the ultimate result of the intended program, generally without a specific date for achieving this end; it may be practical or philosophic in tone. A primary goal for EDGE was to improve service delivery to youth at risk and their families, with particular attention to those areas in which services are now inadequate, limited, or nonexistent. In contrast, an *objective* is a specific statement about the expected results for the program expressed in terms of change (outcome objective), or it indicates how the results will be attained (process objective). All objectives should be clear, measurable, time-limited, realistic, and directly related to the program goal(s), and identify the target of the work. Here are some examples from the EDGE program, for the goal identified above.

- To increase the number of services available for youth and their families at each site by at least 25 percent by the end of the first year and by 50 percent by the end of the second year of the program, as measured by service statistics (outcome objective).
- To provide tutorial assistance in mathematics and English as well as preparation for GED tests in order to upgrade educational skills, to begin in the fourth to fifth months of the first year of the program and serve at least twenty youth per site each week, as measured by service statistics (process objective).

The number of goals for a given program will reflect its scope. A program designed for a single neighborhood may have just one goal, whereas a national program could have several. A rule of thumb for both goals and objectives is not to promise more than you are capable of delivering, especially for a new program.

Finally, *action steps* for each objective should be spelled out, assigning the responsibility for their implementation and listing a date, in as concrete terms as possible, when the different activities are to be up and running. Action steps represent the front line of the program, and logic often dictates the order in which they are arranged, for if the program is designed as a progression of activities, certain tasks must be completed before the next segment of the program can begin. To illustrate this point, here are some of the action steps for the process objective given above for the EDGE program.

- Recruit a minimum of three volunteers per site to provide tutoring. Responsibility: facilitators. Due date: Month 2.
- Establish a connection with the local schools serving each program site, to ensure materials used and concepts presented parallel those of the regular classroom. Responsibility: program director. Due date: Month 2.
- Set up a classroom area within each program site to accommodate the tutoring. Responsibility: facilitators. Due date: Month 3.
- Hold a workshop for school personnel at the program site to discuss the progress of the tutoring. Responsibility: program director. Due date: Month 7 or 8.

The Logic Model

A useful tool for all phases of program development is the logic model, which "is a systematic and visual way to present and share . . . the relationships among the resources you have to operate your program, the activities you plan to do, and the changes or results you hope to achieve" (W. K. Kellogg Foundation, 2004, p. 1). The logic model enables planners to see the connections between the identified problem, what you intended to accomplish, and the actual unfolding of the effort over time. It is usually presented in a linear, columnar format to emphasize the causal linkages believed to exist between program components. Here are its standard elements.

- *Inputs.* The resources necessary to run the program (staff, clients, facilities, supplies, equipment, collaborative partnerships, etc.).
- *Throughputs* (also called *activities*). The methods used to carry out the program (trainings, role-play, counseling, groups, data collection and analysis, etc.).
- *Outputs.* The immediate, quantified results of the program (number of clients served, number and types of groups conducted, number of counseling sessions, number and types of training provided, etc.).
- *Outcomes.* The short- or intermediate-term effects of the program on the target population(s) (greater knowledge of career and educational opportunities, acquisition of marketable skills, decreased number of truancies, ability to set realistic goals, increased level of self-confidence, etc.).
- *Impacts.* The longer-term effects of the program on the target population(s) and perhaps society (reduction in service gaps and duplications, fewer youth involved with the legal system, increased collaboration among community agencies serving the target group, ongoing parental support, etc.).

There are three main categories into which logic models fall: *theory*, for conceptual or planning purposes, taking into account the rationale for the strategies selected, with an emphasis on the underlying problem or issue; *activities*, for monitoring purposes, showing in some detail for each objective how the program is being implemented; and *outcomes*, for evaluation and reporting purposes, with a focus on program details to show how inputs and activities will lead to the expected results, both short and long term.

Table 9.1 represents a theory logic model for the EDGE program. The intent at the conceptual stage of program development is to make a case for your proposed solution to the identified problem by showing the connections between the assumptions about causal factors and the program approach that has been selected, presented in broad strokes (Savaya & Waysman, 2005). Later on in the chapter, an outcomes logic model for the same program is provided.

The reader will note that expected outcomes and impacts are identified. The place to formulate the evaluation of program results is at the beginning of the planning process, not as an add-on. In fact, Lackey (2006) maintains program failure can often be traced back to not thinking about evaluation during the planning phase. By being clear

Table 9.1 Theory logic model for EDGE program

Assumptions	Inputs	Activities	Outputs	Outcomes	Impacts
Youth with a more positive self-image are less likely to become involved in the juvenile justice system.	Youth	Youth-oriented services	More participating youth not affiliated before with local agency	Positive self-image for youth	Reduction in number of youth involved in juvenile justice system
Youth with good work habits and marketable skills feel more hopeful about the future.	Parents	Parent-oriented services	More parental involvement	Marketable skills for youth	Reduction and/or elimination of service gaps and duplications
Parents with a better understanding of youth needs are more capable of supporting their children.	Volunteers	Community networking	More hours and service options at local level	Parental support of youth	
Collaborative relations among community institutions will ensure resources are used more effectively and efficiently.	Staff		More interest in youth issues by community agencies	Increased capacity to deliver services at local level	
	Facilities				
	Equipment				
	Community partners				

about the desired outcomes early in the process, we can build in the necessary steps during implementation to collect data that show the linkages between the concrete results of the effort and what was expected to be achieved, and to help us understand any gaps between the two so that future planning can be refined.

PROGRAM MONITORING

The purpose of program monitoring is to determine whether the effort is proceeding as intended and is serving the targeted population(s). Thus, it occurs while the program is operating and provides continuous feedback to management and staff that allows for changes in implementation if necessary. Monitoring of this type may be referred to as a *formative* or a *process evaluation*; it is distinguished from a *summative evaluation*, which occurs after a program is completed and is externally driven, to demonstrate how well the endeavor achieved its stated goals and objectives (Unrau, Gabor, & Grinnell, 2001). Summative evaluations will be discussed in the next section.

A key aspect of monitoring is quality assurance. This implies the existence of certain standards against which program practices can be measured and then improved should they not be up to par. Quality standards may be set externally by an accrediting body or another objective source. In the past, such groups put great emphasis on operational compliance but seemingly were less concerned about program outcomes. Today, this is no longer the case. Accordingly, we will address accreditation and licensing in the section on evaluation.

Quality standards may also be set internally based on best practices as reported by like organizations or even comparing one department to another within the same setting. This is called *benchmarking*. Through the systematic collection and analysis of program data, an organization can track the degree of compliance with relevant standards, to see if actions are consistent with beliefs about what constitutes effective service. Many nonprofits, especially the larger ones, have a full-time quality assurance officer on staff to oversee such activities.

Design Fidelity

In developing a program, as indicated above, objectives and action steps are written with as much specificity as possible to reflect the expected number of people to be served and the array of services to be provided, along with a time frame for implementation, to achieve the program goals. To ensure the effort is progressing as designed, at set intervals a more senior staff member is generally charged with obtaining from program staff data that are considered to be indicators of reaching the predetermined quantitative and qualitative performance levels. Reports can then be prepared to keep top management informed and to comply with the requirements set by the funder, if the program is externally supported. Most important, assuming a climate of mutual responsibility for the quality of the program has been established, effective monitoring allows program staff to receive constructive feedback on all aspects of implementation and guidance to make improvements in any areas found wanting. In addition, maintaining detailed records creates a programmatic history for purposes of continuity, for instance, in the event of staff turnover, and for future program development.

Typically, program-specific instruments are developed for data collection. Completing forms and compiling reports is still tedious but much easier now with the availability of computers. For the EDGE program, the national program director, operating out of the organization's headquarters, created a manual for use by staff at the six local sites, with definitions, an array of monthly and quarterly forms, and instructions on their completion. Some of this material was dictated by the funder, a federal agency; the rest was her own invention, to help those at the direct service level understand a vital part of their job was tracking the delivery of program services.

Definitions included client eligibility guidelines and clarification of a service unit in each program component. A flow chart, a diagram that shows progression in a system through connecting lines and symbols, provided a way to depict client movement from the point of intake until termination from the program. Exhibit 9.1 is a section of a completed Client Activity Record for one of the program sites; the purpose of this form was to track outputs or quantity of service on a month-to-month basis. Exhibit 9.2 is a completed Participant Evaluation Form for a client at one of the sites, which reflects qualitative measurement of progress. Client files containing all applicable documents were maintained at each site; the national office kept on file all reports submitted by local staff and copies of all reports sent out to the different stakeholders.

Benchmarking

As previously indicated, benchmarking is concerned with identifying best practices, most often those of similar organizations considered leaders in their field, and then using this information to establish internal standards. The main challenge is to find a good balance between setting desired performance levels so high that it will be difficult if not impossible to meet expectations and setting them so low that they are virtually meaningless. According to Mordock (2002): "Maintaining staff adherence to standardized . . . protocols requires continued staff training, support, and encouragement. . . . [However,] staff cannot be forced to apply effective interventions; they must want to do so" (p. 79). The national program director of EDGE attempted to foster a positive relationship with staff at the local level by bringing everyone together at least twice a year for training, producing a quarterly newsletter featuring site achievements, being available anytime for phone consultations, and sending frequent memos updating staff on pertinent matters. In the third year of the program, participants and local staff worked with the national office to hold a youth conference showcasing the participants as both presenters and session chairs. Two of the youth, elected by their peers, subsequently presented the conference findings in Washington, DC, before a blue-ribbon panel. Such activities kept staff and client enthusiasm for the program at a high level.

Through benchmarking, an organization can identify more effective and efficient ways to achieve the desired results, thereby improving program output as well as product

Exhibit 9.1 Client Activity Record for EDGE Program (Partial)

Site: EDGE in Town, State   **For Month of** _____

1. Number of Clients ENROLLED in the Program (Youth only)

Number of Clients	Total Enrollment from Previous Month (Col. 4, last report)	New Clients Enrolled This Month	Client Cases Closed This Month	Total Enrollment at End of This Month (Cols. 1 + 2 – 3 = 4)
Previously Served	35	2	3	34
New to Agency	75	23	2	96
Total	**110**	**25**	**5**	**130**

2. Number of Clients SERVED by the Program (Youth only)

Components	Total Served Prior to This Month (Col. 5, last report)	Clients Previously Served by Agency # / units	Clients New to Host Agency # / units	Total Clients Served during Month (Cols. 2 + 3 = 4) # / units	Total Clients Served to Date (Cols. 1 + 4 = 5)
Indiv. Counseling	80	10 / 27	12 / 18	22 / 45	102
Group Work	150	22 / 39	31 / 48	53 / 87	203
Tutoring/GED	125	8 / 32	23 / 51	31 / 83	156
Paid Employment	26	3 / 25	1 / 3	4 / 28	30
Volunteer Service	15	4 / 4	4 / 4	8 / 8	23
Field Trip—Job	80	12 / 12	3 / 3	15 / 15	95
Field Trip—Cultural	50	8 / 8	4 / 4	12 / 12	62
Rec. Activities	100	24 / 77	42 / 98	66 / 175	166
Youth Council	35	5 / 5	2 / 2	7 / 7	42
Other	6	2 / 3	— / —	2 / 3	8
Total	**667**	**98 / 232**	**122 / 231**	**220 / 463**	**887**

Note: Numbers represent individual clients served for the month by each component. A unit of service equals a client contact for that component; therefore, for example, if the same client participated in a group two times in the month, that would equal two units of service. Similarly, the same client might participate in several components and would be counted for each one.

Exhibit 9.2 Participant Evaluation Form for EDGE Program

Name of Participant: Alice Jones   Age: 14
Date Enrolled in Program: _____   Source of Referral: Parent

     Evaluated by: Carol Franks   Date: _____
     For Period: Sept.–Dec. 201_

1. Record of Participation

Activity	Attendance Record	Contribution
Tutoring	Excellent	Received service
Field Trip	Excellent	Bus Ride Monitor

2. Behavioral Assessment

Rating Category	Rating Level	Comments
Acceptance of Responsibility	High	_____
Interactional Skills	Average	_____
Leadership Ability	Average	_____
Enthusiasm	High	_____
Flexibility	Average	_____
Maturity	Average	_____
Assertiveness/Aggression	Low	A little too timid.

3. Strengths: Quickly perceives areas in which she can help others. Logical approach to problem solving.

4. Areas for Improvement: Overcoming hesitancy in being assertive; overcoming tendency to be involved in negative activities for peer approval and recognition.

5. Overall Assessment (Current Level of Functioning): Beginning to develop trust in own decision-making capabilities. Relying more on self than others for approval. Beginning to feel more competent as intellectual skills are strengthened through tutoring and career exposure (field trips).

6. Next steps: Assist Alice in forming more appropriate friendships during the next report period; encourage her to rely even more on her own judgment.

       Signature of Evaluator: _____

---

or service quality and streamlining operations. The following are some standards established for EDGE for the process objective on tutoring:

- Each site will enroll 75 percent or more of the targeted number of youth for daily tutorial assistance by month 5.
- Each site will establish an ongoing interface with 100 percent of the school systems serving the client population by month 3.

- Each site will recruit at least five school dropouts to take part in GED preparation by month 6, replacing successful candidates thereafter with likely
prospects.

If a benchmark value cannot be determined for certain program areas, which may be true
particularly with new, innovative services, staff are advised to establish their own baseline measures by tracking client progress during the first year of the program and then
developing a benchmark based on this data for year 2 (Unrau et al., 2001).

Of special concern is a major departure from the agreed-upon benchmark, that is,
when program staff introduce a practice totally different from what is prescribed, as
opposed to simply not reaching the standard. Efforts must be made to understand the
reason(s) for not abiding by the protocol, with appropriate follow-up action by the program monitor. Sometimes this results in discovering a method that appears to be more
effective than the one in the original program plan, and the decision may be to adopt the
new practice. In other cases, staff may require additional training to increase their comfort level with the desired practice. At the end of the day, for monitoring and evaluation
purposes, design and performance must be in sync.

Budgetary Implications

Since budgeting is part of the planning process, it should also be one of the elements
reviewed during program monitoring. Much can be learned about how a program is progressing from the monthly expenditures, especially from the narrative accompanying the
figures. On the one hand, if expenses related to a specific activity continually exceed the
amount allocated in the budget, this may indicate a greater level of participation than
had been anticipated, which would be a positive development. On the other hand, the
explanation for the overage could be that the cost to provide the service is greater now
than when the budget was developed. For both scenarios, some adjustment of the budget is probably warranted, but for different reasons: dollars may be shifted from a line
item that is under budget to accommodate the higher service use, or a less costly yet still
effective activity may be substituted for the one whose cost has accelerated.

Program staff should be held as accountable for adhering to the budget as for being
faithful to the program design. For a program like EDGE that was developed at a national
level but implemented locally, direct service staff were hired just prior to implementation
and obviously had no input into the budget. Each site had a copy of the budget and was
required to submit expense reports quarterly. Where possible, then, it is wise to include
those who will be responsible for delivering the services in the discussions on program
content and budget construction so that they will have a sense of ownership not only for
what is offered but also how the program plays out.

PROGRAM EVALUATION

At the point of evaluation, the focus shifts to the identified program outcomes, and now
the likely audiences will be those most concerned with whether the program achieved

what was promised, its outcomes and impacts, and whether it did so in a cost-effective manner. Ideally, the fundamental purpose of this activity is to improve the quality of services provided to consumers, but other reasons also dictate its being an integral part of program development. A thorough and unbiased evaluation, one that tests out theory, adds to the knowledge base on how to more effectively address social problems, yields data that can strengthen decision-making by both internal (top administrators) and external (funders and policymakers) stakeholders, and demonstrates sufficient and appropriate services were delivered to those in need as efficiently as possible (Unrau et al., 2001).

In a less-than-ideal world, evaluation may be introduced after the fact to make linkages that do not really exist between intentions and outcomes. Lackey (2006) uses the expression "paper programs" for situations where "formal documents . . . specify the services or other resources they are supposed to provide, and their routine documentation suggests they are providing what they claim, but in reality the programs are providing none or a mere fraction of these services" (p. 1). In such cases, written reports become a substitute for true accountability. However, ethical practitioners and administrators, by putting the client first and treating the evaluator as part of the team, along with knowledgeable funders and consumers, are the best defense against sham efforts.

In this section, we will consider the issues associated with implementing the evaluation process as well as the different forms of summative evaluation.

The Mechanics of Evaluation

When evaluation is not an afterthought, at the onset of program development, planners must take into account various stakeholders' interests in proving that the connections between the assumptions and the suggested course of action are valid and the program activities as designed do in fact lead to the demonstrated results. These intentions point up the significance of ongoing monitoring, for if the effort does not unfold as intended, then evaluation cannot attribute outcomes to the program. The most crucial decision pertains to the type of evaluation, which will dictate what information needs to be collected, how, when, and by whom. A related concern is the manner in which the results will be presented to the different audiences. Possible approaches include exploratory (pre-experimental), descriptive (quasi-experimental), and explanatory (experimental) designs; each provides valuable information, but only the third option attempts to demonstrate causality. Although space limitations prohibit a detailed discussion of each design, practical considerations regarding complexity, cost, feasibility, and so forth must be taken into account before selecting one rather than another (Kettner et al., 2008).

For discussion purposes, we will assume the single group pretest/posttest approach has been chosen, which does establish a baseline for comparison purposes but is insufficient to say with any certainty that the program was the only cause of client change. Because it is relatively easy and inexpensive to implement, this pre-experimental design is used quite often by smaller and midsized nonprofits.

Working backward from the stated goals and objectives, staff can build protocols into the organization's management information system for collecting and analyzing the kinds of data necessary for a summative evaluation. Capturing quantitative data is not usually a serious problem once line workers have been trained in how to enter the information, but if some data are obtained through qualitative methods such as observation and interviewing, as is likely, management must decide whether to do content analysis by hand or use one of the specialized software packages on the market. For EDGE, staff tracked each client from intake through termination, using basic information forms as well as component-specific, individualized attendance sheets to record every aspect of participation. As noted earlier, other forms were more evaluative in nature. For example, staff met quarterly one-on-one with the enrollees to discuss their progress in meeting personal goals, recording the results following each meeting. Data entry was expected to be done in a timely manner and had to be completed by close of business every Friday.

Typically, program staff are the primary data collectors, but the "who" question extends to whether the evaluator should be an insider or outsider. The former option has the advantage that the individual already knows the organization and is known to other staff, but impartiality may be hard to achieve. While the pros and cons would seem to be reversed in using an external person, the potential exists for a conflict of interest when the organization running the program is also paying the evaluator's fees. Lackey (2006) suggests one way to combat this problem is to involve the evaluator from the preplanning stage, building an open working relationship with all stakeholders and maintaining this connection throughout, as a kind of checks-and-balances system. The risk here, however, is that the evaluator may become too invested in the program and so lose objectivity.

Government funders, and other external stakeholders, often hire an outside evaluator to work with grantees, which takes the decision out of the hands of the sponsoring organization. As for presenting the outcomes, funders may also resolve this issue by specifying when and how they wish to receive feedback. Otherwise, the organization should consider the best and most accurate way to convey to its various publics what occurred. Thus, while the board may receive a full written report, other interested parties may be directed to a more scaled-down version online, and a community forum might be held to reach an even wider audience.

Forms of Evaluation

The numerous approaches to program evaluation range from the very formal to the fairly casual, from ones controlled by external stakeholders to others in which staff and even consumers participate in decision making. Here we will look at a selection of these approaches, chosen to show the variety in philosophy, intent, and implementation.

External Validation

Many nonprofits see value in voluntarily seeking and receiving accreditation as "a way to ensure their own quality and to ensure that they are comparable to similar organizations in other places. It is also a condition for receipt of some funds and, in some places, for the legal right to provide services" (Ginsberg, 2001, p. 76). Although accreditation touches on the entire organization, a significant part of the evaluation is an examination of each program offered.

The process, which tends to be industry specific and fee based, usually begins with the organization completing a self-study consisting of a lengthy narrative and supporting documentation to show compliance with all the different standards. Next a site visit is scheduled so the review team can observe the operation, during which management, staff, consumers, and sometimes others may be interviewed. Subsequently, the applicant receives a preliminary report of the findings and may refute any claims of noncompliance on one or more standards. Following a period of negotiation, a final determination is made. Accreditation is typically granted for a certain number of years, after which reaccreditation may be sought.

In similar fashion, licensing bodies, which are usually state government agencies, provide validation of an organization's compliance with quality standards. The principal difference here is those nonprofits that must be licensed, such as nursing homes, foster care agencies, and day-care centers, cannot legally operate without this credential, and the review process is not voluntary.

Quantitative Analysis

To help determine effectiveness in a more objective manner, one nonprofit developed a planning and assessment tool, the Program Evaluation Grid (PEG), "to survive these challenging economic times and proactively manage the situation" (Kluger, 2006, p. 34). Programs are numerically ranked on twenty-four factors in five value areas: strategic, effectiveness/quality, financial, program importance to key stakeholders, and marketing. The individual factors address both internal and external concerns (for example, under marketing, the cost-effectiveness of the program and how it compares to local competitors). Ratings may be assigned by one or more staff. The agency has used PEG not only to eliminate weak performers but also to strengthen a program whose pluses outweigh the minuses.

A more widely used diagnostic tool is Event History Analysis (EHA), which offers a longitudinal picture of program outcomes by estimating when clients are at greatest risk for success or failure during periods of change. By statistically tracking how a client moves through a given program, EHA yields valuable data to determine which factors (personal qualities of the consumer, specific services, and so on) affect whether and when change may occur. An *event* is an identifiable change in an individual's status; keeping a record of the time before the client experiences a change provides the *event history*. Using this type of tool enables a nonprofit to make programmatic changes to increase effectiveness and can help practitioners assess, and make more congruent, their expectations and actual program results (Unrau & Coleman, 2006).

Outcomes Measurement

The outcomes approach to evaluation differs from the previous one in that both quantitative and qualitative measurements are used to assess performance. Compared with EHA, effectiveness, productivity, and efficiency are equally important parts of the equation. Inputs, throughputs, outputs, and outcomes are all subject to examination, and the driving forces seem to be increased pressure for accountability and competition for scarce resources. Hence, although the data are provided by the individual organization, the process is often dictated by external stakeholders, for instance, by funders such as United Way, which in recent years has made a dramatic departure from its former method, mainly using outputs to evaluate those seeking its support.

For social workers and other professionals providing direct client services, the transition to performance-based evaluation has not always been smooth. Staff may be required to go through extensive training in how to provide the necessary data, and the sheer amount of paperwork involved can be daunting, especially for smaller nonprofits. As Neuman (2003) notes, "The difficulty in studying outcomes for social service agencies is due in large part to the challenges of operationalizing and controlling for the outcome variable" (p. 8). Moreover, participating in this kind of intensive effort does not always result in a commensurate amount of dollars; management therefore must weigh the benefits in improved program quality against the costs in deciding whether to continue seeking funds tied to outcomes measurement (Zimmermann & Stevens, 2006).

Table 9.2 is an example of an outcomes logic model based on the EDGE program. Its intent is to show through a detailed rendering of each step of program development the organization's perceptions of the interrelationships between the selected activities and the expected results.

Stakeholder Participation

Philosophically different from the previous approaches is what is broadly known as stakeholder evaluation. The basic premise is to involve all those who have an interest in the program in every phase of the evaluation process, from conceptualization through implementation to reporting the outcomes. A range of quantitative and qualitative data collection techniques may be used. Proponents of this approach point to the benefits of encouraging the participation of a representative group of people with a stake in the program outcomes, which allows as broad a perspective as possible to be built into the process. Doing so can also increase the program's legitimacy and level of community support. On the downside, it is possible to manipulate this approach in order to stave off outside criticism of the program (W. K. Kellogg Foundation, 1998).

As a subcategory of stakeholder participation, empowerment evaluation, in recognizing consumers as *the* primary interest group, strives to be democratic and collaborative, with self-determination and personal capacity building as the core values. For this approach to work, clients must be trained in evaluation practices so they can make critical decisions on what will be evaluated, the data to be collected, and so forth (Andrews, Motes, Floyd, Flerx, & Lopez–De Fede, 2005). Another variant is design evaluation, which bears a resemblance to formative evaluation in its focus on process and a close working relationship between the evaluator and program staff but also provides useful information, primarily qualitative, for a subsequent outcomes evaluation. One of its main features is obtaining client feedback on effectiveness to refine program logic and practices (Gardner, 2000).

Table 9.2 Outcomes logic model for EDGE program

Inputs	Activities	Outputs	Outcomes	Impacts
Youth between 12 and 18 residing in low-income neighborhoods	One-on-one and group counseling	1,200 youth receive group counseling	More positive self-image for youth	5% reduction in youth contacts with juvenile justice system (per site)
Parents of participating youth	Life skills groups	600 youth receive individual counseling	Increased level of marketable skills for youth	Significant progress toward elimination of service gaps and duplications (all sites)
Volunteer group	Tutoring/GED preparation	900 engage in tutoring or GED preparation	Expanded level of parental interest and support for youth	
Project director; two group workers, secretary at each of six sites	Paid employment for older youth; volunteer experience for under 16	180 provided with paid employment; 140 given volunteer work experience	Increased agency capacity to deliver services at local level	
Facilities/equipment necessary to deliver identified services	Field and cultural trips	600 participate in job-related field trips; 360 go on cultural field trips		
Community network of youth-serving agencies	Parental skill-building & Parents Club	150 parents enrolled in Parents Club; 120 parents participate in various volunteer roles		
	Neighborhood Beautification Corps	Community networks established at all sites		
	Community network			
	Program Advisory Council			
	Community Volunteer Program			

Note: This model represents the program in Year 1.

FINAL THOUGHTS

Even though the steps in the planning phase of program development have been laid out in a very linear, rather prescriptive fashion, in practice there must be some flexibility built in so when unforeseen obstacles arise that cause a delay in implementation—and they will—staff do not become immobilized or overly discouraged. Keep in mind that more than one stakeholder is likely to have an interest in a new program, but their agendas may not be the same. In addition, even after conducting a thorough needs and assets assessment, at best this provides the planner with information of the moment "and what [service demands] may be at some time in the future if attitudes, expectations, conditions, and values do not change dramatically" (Kettner et al., 2008, p. 56).

As for the other two major components of program development, monitoring seems to be well established and, for the most part, accepted by staff and management as a beneficial use of resources. Regarding evaluation, however, especially the performance-based approach, organizational acceptance is more mixed. As Campbell (2002) notes, "Promoted as a way to create objective standards for evaluating programs, the actual work of specifying outcomes by measurable indicators often raises as many questions as it answers, due to data limitations, methodological disputes, or value conflicts" (p. 244). Yet when the feedback results in higher-quality services to consumers, everyone wins.

Resource Generation

Nonprofit organizations face a variety of challenges in striving to fulfill their mission. They must be able to operate effectively and efficiently in a highly complex and ever-changing environment characterized by "heightened demands for . . . services, higher expectations for accountability, and increased competition for funding" (Edwards & Austin, 2006, p. 3). Of these different challenges, none may cause more concern for organizational leaders than the seemingly never-ending responsibility for securing sufficient revenue to carry out their work. Unlike their for-profit counterparts, who derive most of their funds from consumer purchases of goods and services, nonprofits typically rely on a range of financial support, such as government contracts, foundation and corporate grants, private donations, and fees for service, each bearing its own benefits and constraints (Gronbjerg, 1993; Martin, 2001).

In considering the different revenue streams, reflecting a combination of donative (contributed) and earned income, the broader term *resource generation* is probably more appropriate than simply talking about fund-raising. Organizations that are successful in obtaining necessary financial resources understand that a key component of the process is developing personal relationships with their funders—"friend-raising," if you will—an endeavor that is part strategy, part psychology, and part a certain attraction between the fund seeker and the donor that transcends the inherent power differential. Resource generation then is both an art and a science. And do not discount luck; sometimes it is simply a matter of being in the right place and making the right request at the right time. One thing is clear: The role of the staff person charged with oversight of this area of operations, often called the *fund-raising manager* or the *development officer*, has certainly become more complex.

In this chapter, we first consider some basic principles that apply to the decisions, strategies, and activities associated with bringing in the personal and material resources an organization must have to implement its mission. Then we review the major components of a resource generation program: philanthropic support, government support, and earned income (see Appendix A for a glossary of terms related to this specialized field).

BASIC PRINCIPLES OF RESOURCE GENERATION

Just as with strategic planning and program development, a nonprofit organization needs to create a comprehensive plan for its resource generation efforts and then execute the plan as effectively as possible. In addition, especially with regard to philanthropic support, there is an expectation by key stakeholders that these efforts will be conducted in an ethical manner, meaning, above all, the monies are being raised to meet important community needs and will be put to the purpose identified in the request.

It is important therefore to distinguish between the funds required for daily operations, to pay staff salaries and benefits, to cover rent or mortgage payments, to purchase office and program supplies, to enable staff to travel to see clients at home or to attend a professional conference, and so on, versus the dollars put toward capital outlays such as constructing or refurbishing a building, obtaining a new van, or upgrading the management information system. The latter group of expenditures differs from the former in its intent, which is to build the organization's assets. Office supplies are used up in a matter of weeks or months and must be replenished, but capital purchases have more lasting value and generally are authorized only when something has worn out, becomes obsolete, or is essential for a new service. Both types of expenditures are critical to the organization's ability to fulfill its mission, but each has its own rationale.

Diversification

A fundamental principle in a highly competitive environment is to build a broad network of support that includes individuals, foundations, corporate donors, and government. Keep in mind the basic tenets of resource-dependency theory. The more an organization has some control over the acquisition of resources, the greater its ability to exercise a degree of control in its relationships with funding sources; however, when an organization is dependent on a limited number of external resources, it is in a much more vulnerable position. Having allowed its government contract to become too large a portion of the budget, a statewide association of nonprofits found itself in this bind. The funder wanted to change the contract in ways that might compromise the organization's mission, but resistance could have resulted in a nonrenewal for the following year.

Regardless of the circumstances, if a major funding source suddenly dries up, it can be difficult to find a likely substitute on short notice. The same holds true for limiting the strategies employed. Consider the difficulties experienced by Youth Services Network (YSN), the organization in our featured case study, due to the board's insistence that direct mail remain the primary fund-raising activity even though strong competition from other local nonprofits providing similar services was making it difficult to maintain the same market share as in years past. Instead of praising the executive's success in obtaining grants from several new sources, the out-of-touch board criticized her for not finding a solution to the decline in direct mail income.

Diversification may mean moving in directions that are contrary to long-standing traditions. Since the early 1990s, there have been significant changes in the makeup of the resource generation program in many nonprofits. For instance, one of the growing trends in the field of human services is deriving a larger portion of the annual operating budget from earned-income strategies such as fees for service, sales of products, and other commercial ventures, with some observers estimating as much as 40 percent or more of total revenues from these sources. This kind of commercialization has drawn criticism from certain quarters although it has long been common practice for nonprofits in the education and health arenas, and there is little proof it has negatively affected the essential character of human service providers (Gronbjerg, 2001).

The Saliency of Planning

Planning to obtain necessary resources is a multifaceted undertaking best "approached in a . . . strategic manner that places long-term benefit over short-term gain" (Benefield & Edwards, 2006, p. 65). First, there must be clarity about why a nonprofit merits support, which is the cause that defines the organization's reason for being. We call this the *case*; a *case statement* sets forth all the reasons that donors should want to contribute to an organization. Pertinent information is collected and organized in a resources file, often referred to as the *internal case*. The *external case statement*, derived from this file, brings the story to prospective donors. Case elements include how the organization intends to address the community problem(s) reflected in its mission, through clearly articulated goals and objectives as well as well-constructed programs; the costs related to service delivery; the quality of the leadership and staff charged with carrying out the activities; the manner in which the efforts will be evaluated; and the nonprofit's history of successes (Seiler, 2003a).

Once the internal case is in place, the actual planning begins. A key decision at this point is the composition of the revenue mix; it is important to determine which income streams are consistent with the organizational mission and culture, are acceptable to stakeholders, will best support programs and services, and are feasible. For example, some nonprofits elect not to seek government support because they dislike the red tape and close oversight that is usually part of the deal. Moreover, the strategies for securing the different sources of revenue cover a wide range, and certain ones may work better for staff and volunteers than others. A third consideration is organizational age. Being a newly formed nonprofit can be a plus or a minus to funders when compared with more established organization that have a solid track record and high community recognition.

Securing Philanthropic Gifts
A key step in the planning process is translating the internal case into specific funding goals, objectives, and action steps for the programs offered by the organization, based on the implementation costs attached to each one. With regard to philanthropic gifts, this necessitates identifying the potential donor groups (individuals, foundations, and corporations) that are most apt to be interested in the cause and understanding what these donors expect to gain through their support. Asking board members and other key vol-

unteers to vet these ideas helps create a sense of ownership for the plan and lays the groundwork for their direct participation as gift solicitors.

Next, strategies for obtaining the revenue must be articulated, matching the different possible approaches with each desired gift market. As we will consider in more detail below, there are many methods from which to choose, including face-to-face solicitations; direct mail; special events, such as golf tournaments and benefit dinners; phonathons and telethons; and grant proposals. Newer techniques include the use of e-mail via the Internet and text messaging (see chapter 12). Each method should be analyzed and evaluated through the organization's past experience as well as the expected payoffs related to costs, to determine the ones that are most likely to work well for the markets to be tapped (Seiler, 2003b).

Efforts involving both staff and volunteers, sometimes acting alone and at other times in concert, will be needed to execute the plan. Lists of prospective donors for all markets should be drawn up and reviewed, with priority given to those who most closely meet the LAI criteria: "*linkage* to the organization, *ability* to give gifts at the level being sought, and *interest* in the organization's work" (Seiler, 2003b, p. 28). As noted earlier, relationships are critical to success in this arena. Once having formed the corps of volunteer solicitors, ideally individuals with strong ties to and knowledge of the community in general but also of its pockets of wealth, a useful exercise is to have the volunteers rate their own ability to be effective in approaching the names on the donor lists from one to four, from highest to lowest level of familiarity, and then use these rankings in assigning responsibility for solicitations.

The final steps are to make the solicitations, track the results, recognize the donors' contributions, ensure the gifts are used for their intended purpose, evaluate the entire process in terms of strengths and areas for improvement, and make the necessary adjustments. The organization is then ready to begin the entire cycle again (see table 10.1 for a summary of the process).

Thoughts on Other Income Streams

In contrast with obtaining philanthropic gifts, earned-income ventures and government contracting tend to be more market based, that is, testing whether there are sufficient customers willing to pay for the services and products the organization can offer at an appropriate level. This does not mean planning is less important; it just entails different considerations. For instance, the organization must give greater attention to how it stacks up against its competitors, who may well be for-profits. For these income streams, relationships are more apt to be based on organizational performance, on effectiveness and efficiency, than on who knows whom. Even though the connection between a government liaison and a provider's executive director may become very tight over time, the ability to offer quality services at the best price may be the deciding factor in contract renewal. When it comes to selling products and services, issues of promotion, inventory, and distribution must be taken into account. Thus, management will have to call upon a different set of skills to be successful.

Table 10.1 The planning process for securing philanthropic gifts

Element	Pertinent questions
1. Clarify the case.	What community need(s) does this organization address? How are these needs addressed?
2. Determine the revenue mix.	Which income streams are compatible with the organizational mission and culture? Which ones will provide sufficient income for both operational and capital needs?
3. Define funding goals, objectives, and action steps.	What are the specific programs and services to be offered? What financial resources are needed to support these activities?
4. Identify potential donors.	Which individuals, foundations, and corporations are most likely to support the cause? What will donors gain through their support?
5. Match strategies with gift markets.[a]	What is the likely cost-benefit ratio for each strategy? What can be learned from past experience to guide these decisions?
6. Form the corps of volunteer gift solicitors and prioritize prospects.	Which donors most closely meet the LAI (linkage-ability-interest) criteria? How can the volunteers' knowledge of the community best be used?

Source: Adapted from Seiler, 2003b.
[a]Gift market refers to individuals, foundations, and corporations.
Note: The final steps in the fund-raising cycle are to execute the plan, track the results, evaluate the process, and make adjustments for the next time.

Ethical Practices

Public outrage has been justifiably high over stories of nonprofit leaders, professional and lay, who have violated donors' trust by using monies for personal gain that were obtained to fulfill the organizational mission. A flagrant example involved the Association of Community Organizations for Reform Now (ACORN). It came to light in 2008 that the brother of the founder and longtime CEO, then on staff, had embezzled almost $1 million some eight years earlier and, worse, senior officials had covered up the matter, not even informing the board until the story broke (Strom, 2008a & c). Also in 2008, an internal investigation showed two board members of the Shriners Hospital for Children had violated the organization's conflict-of-interest policy by putting undue pressure on the fund-raising manager to hire the direct mail company they favored (Strom, 2008b).

It is a fundamental principle of resource generation that dollars raised be used for the purpose identified in the solicitation process. The term *stewardship* in this context refers to "the concept of being responsible for something of value . . . and the recognition that what is cared for actually belongs to someone other than the caretaker" (Conway, 2003, p. 432). To exercise stewardship in a nonprofit organization requires a full appreciation by the leadership core and all relevant staff of the importance of clearly articulated policies and procedures related to securing support, however achieved, and transparency in regard to their implementation.

PHILANTHROPIC FUND-RAISING

Developing a comprehensive strategy for maximizing the organization's potential to obtain philanthropic gifts from individuals, foundations, and corporations is akin to building a three-story house. First, there must be a solid foundation; here it would be the annual giving campaign. Its primary purpose is to initiate contact with prospective donors to raise the cash needed for the programs and services, but also, when done well, it can attract dedicated volunteers, identify new consumers, and increase market share along with public recognition. The second level is the major gifts program, whose goal is to increase donor commitment in order to bring in larger contributions for both operations and capital projects. At the top is the planned giving program for securing bequests and other long-term donor investments in the cause. As the effort moves upward from the foundation to each successive tier, the intent is to nurture donor relationships to yield an ever-growing interest in and enthusiasm for the mission that will translate into a concrete demonstration of support on a sustained basis while returning to the donor a sense of personal satisfaction for contributing to the public good (Greenfield, 1999).

The Annual Giving Campaign

A well-designed annual giving campaign, the starting point for virtually all resource-generation programs, should bring in a steady flow of revenue to avoid crisis fund-raising whenever a shortfall occurs. For most organizations, multiple solicitations spaced throughout the year will be necessary. With so many possible campaign strategies, each nonprofit must determine the ones that are best suited to realize its financial goal(s) in the most cost-effective manner. For example, a telethon normally requires a media sponsor, a celebrity spokesperson, and other resources that make it more appropriate for a larger organization with fairly broad name recognition, whereas a phonathon is within the reach of even the smallest agency since only a bank of phones and some volunteers may be involved. Experience will help increase the accuracy of predictions about financial needs, productive fund-raising vehicles, and timing. Some of the more frequently used methods are discussed briefly below.

Direct Mail

A very common technique used in annual fund drives is direct mail. Although many of us toss out the unsolicited envelopes we receive almost daily, this approach continues to be popular because, for a lot of organizations it works, not only to capture new donors but also to obtain repeat gifts from past supporters in response to each mailing. Professional advice is recommended, to help tailor the packages to different categories of givers and guide the rental, purchase, or exchange of mailing lists, a necessary step to build the numbers of prospects. While once seen as a way to reach first-timers for fairly small gifts, direct mail is now used frequently to secure higher-end or major gifts through personalized appeals. Telemarketing and online solicitations may supplement the traditional mailings (Warwick, 2003).

Special Events

Sometimes called *benefits*, special events are cultural, educational, recreational, or purely social activities that link an organization with its community in support of the mission. The type of activity can range from the very simple, such as a bake sale or a car wash, to the very elaborate, which might be a dinner-dance honoring a corporate leader or political figure. Frequently volunteers, whether an ongoing group or a committee formed for this express purpose, organize and run the event on behalf of the organization, with or without staff assistance, or a civic organization like the Rotary Club may undertake a project for a charity. A new event is often more about friend-raising than fund-raising; it may take years before a benefit becomes established on the annual community calendar. However, in time a well-planned and executed event can become a solid money-maker that also educates the public about the organization: A small midwestern youth agency where local police officers are significantly involved as both staff and volunteers struck gold its first time out with a "Kids and Cops Ball," a perfect marriage of mission and message.

Further Options

Arts organizations, colleges and universities, churches, and other kinds of nonprofits may be linked to a support group, variously called an auxiliary, an alumni association, "friends," or an advisory council. These groups provide financial support through membership dues, contributions, and benefits; members may also serve as volunteers, advocates, and community boosters. A related strategy is forming donor clubs to recognize individuals at different giving levels, each with a unique name to convey a special status and conferring certain privileges such as an invitation to meet privately with the CEO, reserved seating at events, or a separate newsletter. Just as it is common practice to ask a current direct mail donor to consider increasing the next gift, by publicizing the advantages for every club level, the organization can encourage a move to a higher tier (for example, from the Gold Club to the Platinum Club).

For some nonprofits, participating in a federated campaign, in which fund-raising and marketing are done jointly, is another possibility. United Way of America's annual appeal, with its focus on workplace giving through payroll deduction, is probably the most familiar example (Greenfield, 1999). Face-to-face solicitations of individuals and requests to foundations and corporations are also key elements of many established annual fund drives, using techniques described in the next section.

Major Gifts Program

One of the payoffs for hard work on the annual campaign is being in a position to solicit larger contributions from supporters already familiar with your cause, as well as from new sources, to build an endowment, the organizational equivalent to a personal savings account; to secure underwriting for new and expanded programs; and to mount a capital campaign to meet the organization's highest-ticket needs. Individuals provide about 80 percent of philanthropic gifts, but foundations and corporations are also key markets for major giving, and all three often play a role in a single campaign.

Individual Solicitations

According to Schervish (2006), people of wealth are motivated to use their capacity to give to achieve a desired social end that accords moral purpose to their lives. Another perspective on donor motivation is provided through the framework of the "seven faces of philanthropy" (Prince & File, 1994).

- *Communitarians*, who are frequently local business owners, believe supporting their community makes sense because everyone benefits.
- *The Devout* donate for religious reasons, as a moral obligation, and channel most of their money to churches and related institutions.
- *Investors* "give with one eye on the cause and one eye on personal tax and estate consequences" (p. 43).
- *Social elites* use their personal networks on behalf of favorite causes, often by putting on special events that allow them to do good while having fun.
- *Altruists* are selfless, giving out of a moral imperative and to achieve spiritual growth; they may prefer to remain anonymous.
- *Repayers* often support institutions through which they or family members have personally benefited, such as hospitals and schools, but also insist on effectiveness.
- *Dynasts* use inherited wealth to carry on the family philanthropic tradition but may do so in ways that differ from their elders.

To develop donor constituencies, an organization should identify the segments of society it influences, beginning with the groups most closely associated with the cause, such as current board members, staff, program volunteers, and clients, and then moving on to those with some kind of past relationship, including former trustees, consumers, and volunteers. Next it can try to cultivate people who might be positively disposed toward the organization due to similar interests; an environmental nonprofit might therefore purchase the mailing list for a magazine focusing on outdoor activities for its direct mail program. Beyond that are the long shots, sometimes referred to as *suspects*; each organization must weigh the expenditure of money and staff and volunteer time to make the necessary connections against the probability of forming productive relationships (Murray, 1994).

Following the rating of prospects by the cadre of volunteer solicitors, the organization may elect to use some form of donor research (a computerized search perhaps) to learn more about the less familiar individuals and their families in hopes of finding a link to justify their inclusion. Appointments can then be set up for personal visits either at the prospective donors' place of business or at home. Experience suggests a two-person team composed of the volunteer who knows the individual best and the CEO or another senior-level staff member is most effective in these types of solicitations since volunteers sometimes are uncomfortable making the financial request, the *ask*, on their own. The organization should keep detailed records of all contacts and their results to establish a giving history of the donors. Also remember to thank every contributor in a suitable manner; for those with the greatest potential for subsequent and larger gifts, consider ways to increase their involvement with the cause, such as an invitation to join the board. Equally important is to keep the volunteers motivated by celebrating each success and bringing out the positives of visits that ended with no immediate return, as every contact is one step further in building a relationship.

Institutional Supporters

Foundations and corporate giving programs are alike in that both tend to have specific areas of interest, guidelines, and procedures to govern their funding decisions. With the increased level of competition for private support, most now place a heavier emphasis on measurable results and on grantees' demonstrating effective management and leadership. In addition, they may limit grants to shorter time periods and gravitate more toward program or project grants than general operations, although there are exceptions. A key difference is that foundation support is derived primarily from interest on investments, whereas corporations, outside of company foundations, link their philanthropy to profits, meaning the amount available for gifts can fluctuate from year to year. Corporations also are driven by their commercial interests, and therefore many limit their support to "safe" nonprofits in fields like the arts and education. All of these factors are important when it comes to determining which institutional funders to approach and for what purpose.

There are four main types of foundations: (1) *independent* foundations are private entities, with assets generally derived from gifts by individuals or families; (2) *corporate* foundations are also private, obtaining assets from their respective for-profit companies but maintaining a degree of independence on grant making; (3) *operating* foundations are private funds that conduct research and other programs to benefit nonprofits but seldom make grants; and (4) *community* foundations, most classified as public charities and serving a specific geographic area, are permitted to both receive gifts, which come from many donors, and award grants. Foundations are recognized by the IRS as 501(c)(3) organizations whose primary purpose is to make grants to other charities and to individuals. Under current federal laws, to maintain tax-exempt status, each year private foundations must pay out at least 5 percent of the average market value of their assets; since they normally pursue their own agenda, operating foundations are mandated to spend at least 85 percent of their income to support their programs (Perry, 2003).

Although not all corporations have foundations, there are other avenues to pursue for both annual and major gifts. Most companies have a corporate giving program, which tends to be closely tied to business interests and annual profits and is controlled by senior officers, often reflecting the CEO's personal interests. This kind of giving is not subject to the same reporting or payout restrictions imposed on private foundations. In addition, many for-profits provide in-kind contributions, nonmonetary gifts such as equipment, office supplies, furniture, space for a benefit, and even property. Best of all may be the loan of an employee, to the annual United Way campaign, perhaps, or to help revamp a charity's computer system. Yet another philanthropic area is a matching gifts program, whereby the company equals or exceeds employee contributions. Especially when a solid donor relationship has been established, it is possible for a nonprofit to successfully tap all of these potential sources within a single company each year. (Cause-related marketing is addressed in a later section of this chapter.)

Haphazard fund-raising should be avoided. It is a waste of time for everyone concerned when a nonprofit requests something totally outside the funder's identified interests and types of support. A good source of information on foundations' giving patterns is the annual IRS Form 990-PF; many are available through GuideStar (www.guidestar.org). Another key resource is the Foundation Center, a nonprofit headquartered in New York City that maintains a broad range of online and hard-copy materials on philanthropy and reaches grant seekers directly through its cooperating collections across the country. Many funders today have Web sites as well as printed materials describing their giving program, and larger institutional donors often have full-time staff available to answer questions.

Solicited and Unsolicited Requests

A donor may have an idea for a project and then invite applications from interested parties (solicited request). Since this approach is used frequently by public agencies, it will be discussed in the section below on government support. An unsolicited request starts with the organization, as the result of strategic planning, staff discussions, consumer expressions of unmet need, and so forth. Here donor research becomes critical in order to find a promising fit. Monetary awards from institutions are typically called *grants*, and the primary vehicle for submitting a request is a *proposal*, a written application accompanied by supporting documentation. In recent times, prior to consenting to receive a full proposal, many grantors have begun requesting a *letter of inquiry*, in which a prospective applicant identifies an issue or problem and how it hopes to address it with the funder's assistance. This is a wonderful opportunity for a nonprofit to make a good first impression by showing it has done its homework.

Submission procedures and formats vary widely. Accordingly, an organization should obtain the funding source's published guidelines before preparing the proposal. However, a completed application is likely to include these components.

- *Cover letter.* A brief overview of the project, including the requested amount, on agency letterhead and signed by the CEO and/or board chair.
- *Executive summary* or *abstract*. No more than a page containing every element of the proposal captured in a sentence or two.

- *Organizational background.* A statement of the applicant's history and qualifications for carrying out the project.
- *Need* or *problem statement.* A clear articulation of the issue and the proposed solution, backed by carefully chosen documentation.
- *Objectives.* An indication of the expected outcomes of the project, stated in specific, measurable terms, flowing logically from the identified need.
- *Methods* or *procedures.* A detailed description of how the project will be carried out (participant recruitment, staffing, timing, location, equipment needed, etc.).
- *Evaluation.* The process for collecting and analyzing data to assess project outcomes, now often presented in a logic model (see chapter 9).
- *Budget.* A presentation of anticipated/actual revenue and all costs for the project, by category, with justification for the figures.
- *Appendices.* Attachments as requested; most private funders ask for the applicant's IRS determination letter, a board list, and the latest audit.

The grantor may also request a plan for continuing the project after the initial funding ends. In place of a multipage application, some funders, especially corporations, prefer a letter proposal for a fairly simple or time-limited project (see appendix B for a sample). In several states, a common application form has been adopted to simplify the process.

Capital Campaigns

As part of the overall resource-generation program, the organization may elect to initiate a capital campaign to raise money for large-ticket items, with donors frequently pledging support over a period of years. Once thought of primarily for construction or renovation of a building, and thus called a bricks-and-mortar campaign, often now such efforts are more comprehensive, including funds for an endowment, scholarships, program development, and similar long-term needs. It is also no longer true that capital campaigns are a rarity; universities and other large nonprofits seem to run perpetual campaigns, with a new one scheduled right after the completion of another. An organization considering this type of campaign for the first time is strongly advised to conduct a feasibility study before proceeding, to ensure that its cause is well enough known to garner the support of likely donors. Hiring an outside consultant to conduct this activity, and to subsequently guide the entire enterprise, can be a wise investment, as one nonprofit discovered. Even though the organization had been in existence for many years and had a loyal consumer base, the feasibility study indicated a lack of broad recognition and support in the community as a whole. On the advice of its consultant, the agency tabled the campaign until it could establish a better foundation for success.

Careful preparation for such a large endeavor entails validating and prioritizing the needs that justify the campaign, accurate goal setting, enlisting board members and other top-level volunteers as solicitors and advisors, identifying prospects, setting time lines, and selecting the most effective solicitation strategies. A gift-range chart is a technique used to help determine the quality and quantity of gifts as well as the number of prospects required to meet the campaign goal. A capital campaign operates on the premise that 80 to 90 percent of the total funds will be obtained from the top tier, or 10 percent, of the givers. To set the tone of the entire campaign, aim to secure a lead gift of at least 10 percent of the total, for the remaining prospects tend to look at the first gift as the de facto ceiling, and few if any will contribute more. As an example, if a campaign has a goal of $10 million, the lead gift will be put at $1 million, with three to five prospects identified who would be capable of giving at this level (Pierpont, 2003).

A compelling case statement is a must. Ideally, an organization ought to have several statements, each meant for a specific market. For a large national organization mounting the biggest capital campaign in its history, the materials designed for the lead donor were so strong that after further study, he increased his pledge from $20 million to $50 million. Traditionally, the effort begins with a *quiet phase*; its goal is to demonstrate the campaign's viability by obtaining an impressive number of commitments, including most of the top gifts, from those closest to the organization. Face-to-face solicitations by peers of the prospects are the norm. The *public phase*, to raise all the remaining monies, often starts with a kickoff event to announce the total to date, recognize donors who have already made commitments, and energize staff and volunteers to finish the job. During the public phase, direct solicitations continue, and proposals may also be submitted to institutional donors. To motivate the lowest tier, the last 5 percent on the gift chart, Lindahl (2008) suggests adding a third phase when the goal is in sight, a particularly sound idea in a difficult economy.

Planned Giving Program

The top tier of philanthropic giving is an effort to secure various kinds of intentional gifts as permanent investments from committed donors. The underlying theory is that decisions must be made in the present to benefit both the donor and the organization over the long term. Accordingly, an organization may enlist an accountant or a tax attorney to assist in setting the parameters of the program to ensure good stewardship of all funds received. In addition to outright gifts of stock, real estate, artwork, and the like, some of the other common methods used for estate planning include bequests through a will, insurance policies naming the charity as beneficiary, and various kinds of trusts, some of which distribute a certain percentage of the donor's assets immediately to the charity, with the rest reverting to the donor or the designated beneficiary at the end of a set time, and others that provide annual income to the donor or beneficiary for life, with the charity receiving what is left at the donor's or beneficiary's death (Greenfield, 1999; Regenovich, 2003).

Smaller nonprofits may question the wisdom of including a planned giving program, believing it is an approach better suited to organizations that already have wealthy individuals as steady supporters. However, this ignores the reality that bequests often come from donors who during their lifetime never gave the organization more than $100 in response to each direct mail appeal. In fact, recent research indicates "that bequest fund-raising should not be limited to a specific segment of the database and that there may be considerable utility in seeking such gifts across the file" (Sargeant, Wymer, & Hilton, 2006, p. 401). This would seem to argue for every nonprofit to at least consider planned giving, choosing the methods that best suit its constituency.

GOVERNMENT SUPPORT

Despite the red tape, relatively high formality of the application process, and changes in priorities to reflect current political considerations, for many segments of the nonprofit sector, government funding continues to be sought as a major share of total support. In general, this support is manifested in two ways, through grants and through contracts, although in-kind gifts such as surplus food are also available.

Government Grants

As noted earlier, many government agencies solicit applications for grants to operate programs already deemed vital to the public. Here a need has been clearly identified and documented, and the funder is seeking organizations that can meet its criteria to provide the services. The agency may issue a *program announcement* in which it spells out the type of project it wants in fairly general terms, leaving some room for the nonprofit to design the actual program. Some private donors also use this approach to get the word out. However, when an agency has a much more specific idea of what it wants and how it expects the program to operate, it will use a *request for proposal* (RFP) to delineate all of the details of the population to be served, the geographic area in which they can be found, the methods to be used, timing, and so forth. Obviously, in these instances applicants strive to demonstrate how closely they can adhere to the stated requirements.

Program announcements can be found on the federal government's Web site, whereas at the state or local level, they may appear in daily newspapers as well as via the Internet. Nonprofits can also contact agencies that have previously supported them or seem compatible with their interests and request to be placed on the mailing list for future announcements. Information on RFPs issued by the federal government can be found online in the *Federal Register*, a daily publication that lists grants by category. The *Catalogue of Federal Domestic Assistance* is more comprehensive but very complex, so it may be helpful to review the print version before going online (www.cfda.gov). Other Internet sites include FirstGov (www.firstgov.gov), Grants.gov (www.grants.gov), Fundsnet Services (www.fundsnetservices.com), and Federal Gateway (http://fedgate.org). The latter two are nongovernmental sites, and are very informative (Hall & Howlett, 2003). Because federal categorical and block grant monies are passed through to states and cities, nonprofits intent on securing public support should also become familiar with state and local government Web sites and seek to make personal connections where feasible.

The proposal format for government grants basically follows the outline provided above for institutional donors, but again it is important to obtain the specifics directly from the prospective funder. Government agencies are famous for being very particular about the submission process; an application arriving a minute after the stated deadline or omitting a requested document may put the organization out of the running. Once a submission has passed these first hurdles, it often will be given to a peer review board that rates each component on a point system the agency has set. Applications that achieve a certain overall ranking are then given further scrutiny to make the final grant decisions. The written notice of the award normally contains instructions for when and how progress reports should be submitted. Successful applicants can also expect that an unannounced audit of program funds may be conducted sometime during the grant period and should therefore be sure to handle the monies exactly as directed.

Government Contracts

A contract represents a kind of business arrangement between a government agency and a nonprofit to deliver specified services to a particular population in a certain manner over a given time period as articulated in an RFP. Sometimes the announcement is called an RFQ, or *request for a quote,* because awarding a contract can be a highly competitive process in which cost-effectiveness is critical. That is, if one nonprofit maintains it can do the job just as effectively but for a lower cost than another, all things being equal, it is likely to get the contract. On the other hand, once a nonprofit has secured a contract, unless its performance is truly unacceptable, it will normally continue as the provider of record until political pressure is applied to engage in a new round of open bidding.

Some contracts use straight-cost reimbursement, based on actual expenditures, while others set a fixed price within which the nonprofit must function even if costs are higher. Increasingly, government has turned to performance-based contracting, which "focuses on the outputs and outcomes of service provision and may tie contractor payment, as well as contract extension, to their achievement" (Martin, 2000, p. 32). Many observers believe this trend reflects the high interest in accountability as defined by measurable outcomes, to demonstrate change in the target population, rather than simply by inputs or outputs. One result of this development is that complacency on the part of the government agency or the provider may become a thing of the past, to the ultimate benefit of the consumer.

COMMERCIAL VENTURES

For many nonprofits the move toward earned-income strategies may be a consequence of need in the face of declining government support and increased competition for private dollars, but once having taken this step, they often find the ability to generate revenue through selling services and products and engaging in other sorts of commercial ventures provides a degree of independence from external funding demands that justifies any criticism of such activities as somehow contrary to the traditional view of charities. However, any organization considering this avenue must understand that it entails more than hoping for a quick infusion of capital. Rather, the decision to move forward here really depends on compatibility with the mission and a dispassionate assessment of organizational strengths and weaknesses (Massarsky, 1994).

Business Opportunities

Program-related products are items closely linked with the organization that prove to be moneymakers. The Girl Scouts of the USA, arguably the most widely known nonprofit product seller, has always maintained that its very profitable cookie sale teaches skills directly related to its mission and has successfully defeated legal efforts to characterize the monies earned as unrelated business income. Other types of program-related products might include educational materials marketed to elementary and middle schools by an organization specializing in interventions with at-risk children and pre-teens, and publications on management topics produced by a state association of non-profits.

Nonprofits may also provide program-related services to closely associated groups like members, volunteers, and alumni as well as to the general public. Examples include museum gift shops and parking garages, bookstores at universities that sell sweatshirts and souvenirs along with classroom texts, and food sales and beverage vending machines, from which the organization receives a share of the profits. In the same vein, many statewide associations of nonprofits offer their member organizations the opportunity to purchase different types of insurance at a group discount rate.

A third option draws on staff, organizational, and client resources. Charging fees for service falls into this category. While asking those who can afford it to pay all or part of the fee is not unethical, and some would say is actually empowering, turning clients into consumers, an agency must be careful to maintain fair, nondiscriminatory practices so as not to violate its basic purpose. Other examples are a nonprofit providing the counseling for the employee assistance program at a local corporation, and an organization that serves the mentally disabled selling the products from its sheltered workshop. To make more efficient use of land and buildings, colleges and universities often rent space to programs such as Road Scholar (formerly Elderhostel) in the summer. Similarly, a summer camp operated by a youth-serving nonprofit in Michigan becomes a retreat site for businesses and other nonprofits in the spring and fall. Finally, Massarsky (1994) identifies "soft property" as "income-earning assets that include copyrights, patents, trademarks, art and artifacts, and even mailing and membership lists" (p. 385).

Cause-Related Marketing and Sponsorships

Both cause-related marketing and sponsorships involve a corporation linking itself to a nonprofit in ways that hopefully help both parties. To the for-profit such ties, particularly with charities that have high name recognition or with a popular cause, combine good business with an opportunity to gain positive publicity by demonstrating corporate social responsibility. For the nonprofit it can mean additional funds, of course, and greater public exposure, but care must be taken to ensure the tie-in will be beneficial. As an obvious illustration, an organization involved in smoking cessation programs would certainly refrain from allowing its name to be used for marketing purposes by a cigarette company.

A common and relatively simple vehicle is a product discount coupon stating that a percentage of each purchase will be donated to the named charity. In contrast, some companies do elaborate research before adopting a cause and determining the best ways to support it. When the marketing team at Jones Apparel Group learned that employees and consumers identified children and education as top priorities, a multilevel initiative called Jones New York in the Classroom (JNYITC) was launched in several major markets to raise awareness of the need to identify and retain new teachers. The effort focuses on engaging employees, the trade, the press, its retail partners, and customers in promoting the cause. For example, employees have been given paid leave to hold local fundraisers, and in the initiative's first year, retailers sold a special T-shirt and a car magnet, with all proceeds going back to JNYITC (Nobles, 2006).

Steps in Establishing an Earned-Income Program

The strategies just described do not exhaust the possibilities, but before engaging in any of these kinds of activities, an organization must look at the matter from many angles. Although research has shown that bringing in high levels of commercial income can be positive for an organization's self-sufficiency, reputation, and ability to attract and retain staff, it can also result in a loss of donative revenues and does not appear to lead to any significant improvement in service delivery (Guo, 2006).

Massarsky (1994) has outlined the steps to be taken before proceeding with business ventures: (1) explore every aspect of the issue, including ethical considerations; (2) conduct an audit of organizational assets, including staffing, the physical plant, and finances; (3) brainstorm possible strategies, keeping in mind interests and capabilities; (4) carry out feasibility studies of the potential businesses identified in step 3, which involves analyzing the marketplace for likely consumers and developing an operating plan; (5) secure the commitments of staff, management, and the board to the operating plan; (6) develop a business plan spelling out the entire venture and the capital needed to make it a reality; and (7) seek capitalization appropriate for businesses that remain part of the organization as well as any for-profit subsidiaries that are spun off. Note that for any commercial activities not linked to the mission, the organization will have to pay the appropriate tax, and therefore gains must be sufficient to offset expenses.

FINAL THOUGHTS

As indicated in table 10.2, a summary of the options for the major components of a resource generation program featured in this chapter, there is something for just about every size and type of nonprofit. It is unfortunate the YSN board was not more open to developing a full-scale effort, because the organization had the potential through its long-standing direct mail program for generating major gifts from individual donors as well as a diversified planned giving program. In one way or another, it all comes back to relationship building with current and prospective donors and consumers. Readers may

Table 10.2 Overview of resource generation strategies

Income stream	Strategies
Philanthropic fund-raising	
Annual giving campaign	Direct mail solicitations
	Special events (benefits)
	Support groups
	Donor clubs
	Federated campaigns
	Face-to-face solicitations
	Requests to foundations and corporations
Major gifts program	Individual solicitations
	Proposals to foundations and corporations
	Capital campaigns
Planned giving program	Gifts of stock, real estate, art, etc.
	Bequests
	Charitable instruments (e.g., trusts, insurance policies)
Government support	Grant proposals
	Contracting
Commercialization	Business opportunities:
	Program-related products
	Program-related services
	Fees for service
	Employee assistance programs
	Rentals
	Cause-related marketing and sponsorships

therefore be surprised to learn that one of the most common mistakes organizations make is forgetting the simple courtesy of thanking each supporter in a manner commensurate with the gift.

Looking ahead, what does the future hold for nonprofit leaders and development personnel? One challenge, in light of the growing percentage of the operating budget derived from earned-income strategies, will be to maintain the philanthropic tradition that has long been viewed as a basic characteristic of the nonprofit sector in the United States. A promising avenue still in the early stages is venture philanthropy through foundations established by wealthy individuals, giving circles, and other organizational forms, which applies to grant making some of the same thinking that has fueled start-up businesses (Moody, 2008). Two other key challenges are to find creative ways to keep active contributors interested in programs and services while identifying new sources of revenue to underwrite both operating and capital expenses and to practice transparency by putting in place accountability measures to ensure the ethical, effective, and efficient use of resources.

APPENDIX A: GLOSSARY OF SELECTED RESOURCE GENERATION TERMS

Term	Definition
(the) Ask	The solicitation for support, with specific reference to the dollar amount of the request.
Capital campaign	A special drive to secure larger gifts for expenditures with more lasting value (e.g., constructing or renovating a building).
Case for support	The rationale for why the organization merits support, starting with the mission.
Cultivation	The process of developing a more involved donor relationship.
Direct mail	A strategy used to attract first-time donors and encourage/upgrade repeat gifts but also to secure major gifts.
Donor	An individual or institution that has previously supported the organization.
Donor club	A group of donors organized by level of support, with specific "insider" privileges.
Earned-income strategies	Fees-for-service, product sales, and other commercial ventures.
Endowment	A permanent fund that functions like a savings account; interest may be used for operational needs.
Income stream	A source of financial support.
LAI principle	A method for determining the most likely donors, based on linkage, ability, and interest.
Letter of inquiry	A requirement of some funders prior to accepting a full proposal, to determine the fit in organizational priorities.
Prospect	An individual or institution that offers higher potential to become a donor.
Request for proposal (RFP)	A funder's solicitation of applications to address an issue of interest, with specifics about the preferred type of program, desired outcomes, selection criteria, etc.
Special event (or benefit)	A cultural, educational, recreational, or social activity that is often part of an annual campaign; may be more about "friend-raising" than fund-raising initially.
Suspect	An individual or institution whose interests may be compatible enough to warrant some attention. The aim is to turn a suspect into a prospect and eventually a donor.

APPENDIX B: SAMPLE LETTER PROPOSAL

[Month, day, year]

Mr. John Q. Smith
Corporate Foundation Director
XYZ Company, Inc.
Any Street
Detroit, Michigan [zip code]

Dear John:

The ABC Organization is grateful for your company's ongoing support of the Educational Development and Guidance for Employment (EDGE) program at our local affiliate and your personal involvement as a member of the Program Advisory Council. Knowing of the XYZ Company's long-standing interest in youth-related concerns, we are writing to request a contribution of $5,000, toward the total estimated cost of $8,000, to become the lead sponsor of the National Youth Conference that will be held in Detroit on October 5–7 at the Hotel _____.

This event will be different from most such conferences in that youth along with volunteers and professionals from the six participating EDGE sites are working with national staff to plan the program. The teenagers will also play a key role at the conference as presenters and session chairs and/or discussants. By structuring the planning process so the program participants have a major voice in shaping the conference, we are providing yet another means to foster their sense of self-worth and develop leadership skills, which are key goals of the EDGE program. Moreover, the intent is to have youth be the largest group in attendance; the planning committee has decided there must be two youth for every adult who comes to the event. The attendance goal is to have a minimum of 100 young people, including representatives from all the EDGE sites as well as from other nonprofits across the country serving the same constituency, and 50 adults. The conference theme will be "The Rights of Youth," with a focus on assessing the local response to teenagers in each community represented at the conference in the areas of education, employment, juvenile justice, and health/recreation, and how services might be improved to further the welfare of youth. Accordingly, specialists in these areas from across the country will be invited as resources, to provide expert testimony on what exists today and what might be developed for the future, which will supplement local fact-gathering by a team of youth and adult investigators.

There will be no fee to attend the conference, but airfare, hotel accommodations, and some food costs must be borne by attendees. Although program participants and staff will be conducting fund-raisers to secure as much of the money for their expenses as possible, some deserving youth and adults will fall short in these efforts, and we do not wish to exclude anyone on the basis of cost. Therefore, $4,000 of your contribution will be for conference scholarships. We will use $500 to underwrite the reduced fee and expenses for bringing in Dr. Martin L. Brown, a nationally recognized motivational speaker based in San Francisco, who will address the attendees on the topic "Becoming an Effective Advocate." The final $500 will cover the hotel charges for audiovisual equipment and snacks throughout the program. The federal grantor for the EDGE program has already agreed to provide the remaining $3,000, to underwrite the invitations and other mailings to youth organizations outside of the EDGE program, travel and hotel expenses for the national staff, and ground transportation, some of the food, and conference materials for the attendees.

The board of the ABC Organization believes this conference will garner national recognition of the issues facing low-income youth living in inner-city communities and is fully behind the effort. Also keep in mind that for many of the youth participants, attending the conference will be a wonderful learning experience on many levels, for it will likely be the first time they have ventured far from their immediate neighborhoods. We hope you will join us in making the conference a reality. The National Director of EDGE, Michael Peters, will contact you in a few days to answer any questions you might have about the event.

Sincerely,

Mary C. Jones, Executive Director
ABC Organization

Note: EDGE was an actual program offered by a national social service organization through six of its local affiliates, underwritten by the federal Office of Juvenile Justice and Delinquency Prevention. Although this letter is fictional, the conference referenced here was held in Detroit at the end of the second year of the grant.

Organizational Performance Indicators

11

In this age of accountability, key stakeholders are looking for indicators of organizational effectiveness. This concept is difficult to understand in nonprofits because of the diversity of missions, programs, and services both across and within the various subsectors. Many interested parties, especially funders, seem to equate program effectiveness with effectiveness in the organization as a whole, but other respected observers of the nonprofit world maintain there are multiple criteria of effectiveness that frequently operate independently. In the absence of an agreed-upon bottom line for all voluntary organizations, *responsiveness*, however defined, may come the closest to filling the bill (Herman & Renz, 2008).

One element often cited as a useful way to measure effectiveness is how well the organization manages its financial resources. In meeting this standard, nonprofits must be scrupulous in honoring the intent behind philanthropic gifts, and they should be equally as attentive to establishing clear policies and procedures for oversight of all monies entrusted to them, regardless of the source. As with so many aspects of administration, good financial stewardship entails careful planning, monitoring, and evaluation, and it goes far beyond budgeting and proposal writing to involve "a variety of concepts, principles, and tools designed to improve the use of resources to accomplish in an efficient and effective manner the [organizational] mission, goals and objectives" (Martin, 2001, p. 1).

Unfortunately, organizational leaders, whether the top professional or board members, depending on their past experience in dealing with numbers, sometimes view this fiscal responsibility with a certain amount of anxiety and self-doubt. Even though it may be tempting to allow most of the burden in this area of management to fall on the chief financial officer (CFO) and the board treasurer, to do so can have serious negative ramifications. Too many of the scandals that have beset nonprofits in the past have been linked to the failure by an overly trusting executive director or board to carry out their fiduciary duties. So, while it may never be one of your favorite parts of the job, just consider financial management a necessary undertaking to further the greater good.

The discussion of performance indicators in nonprofits begins with a consideration of some fundamental principles regarding responsible oversight of resources. It moves on to examine organizational decisions in a time of tight money, and concludes with a review of different perspectives on the connection between performance and effectiveness.

FISCAL FUNDAMENTALS

Financial planning and record keeping for nonprofits coincide with each organization's fiscal year, a twelve-month period designated in the bylaws for keeping track of all transactions related to revenues and expenses, roughly equivalent to the program year. For many organizations the fiscal year parallels the calendar year, but it is not uncommon to choose the same fiscal year as that of a major funding source to simplify the reporting process, which would be October 1 to September 30 for the federal government and July 1 to June 30 for most state and local governments.

A key part of financial management is constructing the annual budget and then striving to live within its parameters. As defined in the dictionary, a *budget* is "a statement of . . . financial position . . . based on estimates of expenditures during [a specified] period and proposals for financing them"; "a plan for the coordination of resources and expenditures"; and "the amount of money that is available for, required for, or assigned to a particular purpose." Thus, a budget is variously a plan of action, a mechanism for allocating resources, a device to control the actions of others, a monitoring tool, and a prediction of the future based on current actions (Brueggemann, 1996). However, budgeting should never be done in isolation but as a part of the overall planning for the organization, so that the end result reflects resources currently on hand as well as a strategic determination of the organization's future. Long-range planning is the board's responsibility, aided by the chief professional officer, and therefore, board members must be directly involved in both the development and the monitoring of the budget, often through a standing financial committee.

Types of Budgets

To sum up, the main purposes of budgeting are for control, to ensure expenses do not exceed revenues and both are properly documented; for management, to make sure monies are expended efficiently to provide as many clients as possible with the services they require; and for planning, to determine the revenues to be allocated to achieve the organization's goals and objectives. These three purposes are in turn operationalized through three major budgeting systems: *line-item*, *functional*, and *program* (Kettner, Moroney, & Martin, 2008).

Line-Item Budgeting
Line-item budgeting is concerned with inputs (resources) and activities (expenditures) during a single fiscal year, with control as its principal purpose. It is also the format used most often for program and project proposals. It takes its name from the manner in which it is constructed, the listing of all the budget categories and subcategories, which are meant to be comprehensive and mutually exclusive, and the associated amounts, in columns, divided between revenues and expenses. Each category has been preset, sometimes according to a commonly accepted definition, such as employee-related expenses; sometimes internally by the organization, such as job classifications by

title; and sometimes by a funding source, such as the distinction between equipment and supplies. Generally a miscellaneous category is included to ensure there is a place in the budget for every revenue source and every expense. The expectation is that the budget will be balanced between anticipated revenues and proposed expenses, and so it is preferable to address this when the budget is first developed.

Once a basic line-item budget has been constructed, the same principles can be applied to each distinct programmatic or administrative unit of the organization. The term *cost or expense center* is widely used for an individual unit, to emphasize the importance of living within the budget (Martin, 2001). However, to get a truer picture of total expenditures, one additional step is necessary, making a distinction between *direct* and *indirect* costs. The former refer to expenses incurred by a single unit (for example, salaries and wages for staff of program X, travel costs for those staff as they carry out their duties, and so forth); the latter pertain to expenses that benefit more than one unit, often called *overhead costs* (for example, rent and janitorial services for the entire facility). It is not very difficult to determine each unit's direct costs, and not much harder to identify the organization's indirect costs, once you understand the underlying concept, but determining the distribution of the indirect costs to individual units is a bit trickier. There are four basic methods of *cost allocation*: by total direct costs, direct labor costs, direct labor hours, and direct costing (Kettner et al., 2008).

To illustrate the allocation process, direct costing has been selected, even though it is the most difficult of the methods to implement, because it is considered the most accurate approach and, perhaps more important, is the one mandated by many funding sources. Table 11.1 represents the expense side of a line-item budget for a statewide nonprofit, divided into cost centers. With direct costing, a different but appropriate basis is used in making allocations for each budget category. For example, while the work of the top professional is seen as benefiting the entire organization, from the CEO's time sheet it is possible to count the number of hours spent on behalf of each cost center and then use this information to arrive at a percentage that can be applied to the executive director's annual salary to distribute to the various units. The result is 40 percent to Management and General, 20 percent to Fund Raising, and 10 percent to each program area. Conversely, the membership director spends virtually all of her time running the Products and Member Services program, with the remainder given to general management tasks. Rent generally is allocated by distributing the total amount according to the square footage each unit occupies, postage by the number of pieces of mail processed for each unit, printing by the number of pages or jobs handled for each unit, telephone by the number of phones used by each unit, and so forth (Kettner et al., 2008; Martin, 2001).

Functional Budgeting

The focus of functional budgeting is at the program level, on inputs (resources) and outputs (units of service) and their related costs, for management purposes in regard to productivity and efficiency. The starting point is the line-item budget, with the allocation of indirect costs to each unit, and the key concern is the cost for delivering the amount of service provided by each program as measured by predetermined objectives for the fiscal

Table 11.1 Partial line-item budget with cost centers

Account	1	2	3	4	5	6	Total
Executive director	$ 7,151	$ 7,151	$ 7,151	$ 7,151	$28,603	$14,302	$ 71,509
Assistant director	4,040	0	0	22,122	12,078	2,020	40,260
Communications director	4,000	20,000	14,000	0	0	2,000	40,000
Membership director	37,000	0	0	0	813	0	37,813
Secretary	3,672	4,896	5,000	4,180	4,407	2,672	24,827
Travel	0	500	300	2,080	700	312	3,892
Rent	4,278	3,422	3,141	6,702	3,563	1,567	22,673
Maintenance	315	302	84	494	286	189	1,670
Telephone	1,315	972	910	1,904	1,610	729	7,440
Equipment[a]	997	898	366	2,064	1,364	599	6,288
Supplies	250	300	250	500	450	250	2,000
Postage	100	100	200	200	200	300	1,100
Printing	75	200	90	300	200	100	965
Total	$63,193	$38,741	$31,492	$47,697	$54,274	$25,040	$260,437

Notes: 1 = Products and member services; 2 = Advocacy; 3 = Public education and information; 4 = Technical assistance; 5 = Management and general; 6 = Fund-raising.

This is an approximation of the annual budget for a statewide nonprofit organization that uses the direct costing method of allocating indirect costs, for the cost centers as defined above. The organization is real; the figures were calculated by the author.

One way that sometimes is used to judge how a nonprofit manages its resources is the 80/20 test, that is, when expenses for all programs are totaled, they should be approximately 80 percent of the total budget, leaving about 20 percent for management and general and fund-raising. This organization's ratio is 70/30, which would still be considered acceptable, especially in light of its programmatic cost centers.

[a]Equipment includes rentals, purchases, and maintenance on the items.

year. The first task is to identify the output measure for the program. Referring to the organization depicted in table 11.1, we will concentrate on the second largest program, Technical Assistance. Let us assume that the unit of service is one hour of technical assistance, whether delivered at a single recipient's offices or in a group setting. Next we must consider how much service was expected to be provided in the current twelve-month period. Typically, each individual consultation requires anywhere from two to four hours, so we will use three hours as the standard, with thirty nonprofits slated for assistance during the year, for a total of ninety units. Each of the workshops is also three hours long and averages twenty-five attendees. For the current year, four workshops have been scheduled, which calculates to 300 total units. Overall, then, the program objective is to deliver 390 total outputs. When divided into the program's total expenses of $47,697, this means the unit cost is $122 per hour of direct client time.

In analyzing this result, the question is whether sufficient services are being provided and in an efficient manner. Technical assistance is very labor intensive and in most cases must be tailored to the needs of the specific recipient. Another factor would be the average fee charged by a private consultant for the same services. Taking everything into consideration, the likely conclusion is that the Technical Assistance program is pretty much a bargain.

Program Budgeting

Planning is the main purpose of program budgeting, which is concerned with inputs (resources) and outcomes (the expected changes in the target population[s] as expressed through the program goal and objectives), to address effectiveness. The process is virtually the same as for performance budgeting: Start with a line-item budget, determine the measure for the desired outcome, and calculate the cost per outcome.

In the Technical Assistance program (see table 11.1), the most important result for a client agency is to use the tools it has been given to overcome an obstacle that was interfering with its service delivery. For the organizations receiving on-site help, the policy is that the technician or consultant does not leave until the problem has been resolved, so all thirty organizations scheduled for assistance during the fiscal year would be considered outcomes. For the 100 workshop attendees, even though they are all given the knowledge to address their problems, based on past experience just half will actually apply what they have learned. Thus, for eighty total outcomes, the cost per outcome is $596.

In each situation, an organization has to assess the results to see if its own standards for effectiveness have been met. For both functional and program budgeting it also make sense to benchmark outputs and outcomes, respectively, against those of similar nonprofits. The advantages in using these approaches are that it may be easier to demonstrate the quantity and quality of the work to funding sources and other key stakeholders, administrators should be in a stronger position to control costs, and if engaged in performance contracting, organizations will be less apt to underprice their services. The major disadvantages are that the organization must have the financial know-how to set up and maintain such sophisticated systems, and it can be challenging to define accurate measures of both outputs and outcomes (Martin, 2001).

Budget Development and Approval

Generally, there are two separate but related organizational budgets to prepare each year: The *operating* budget shows the expected revenues and expenses to provide day-to-day activity, while the *capital* budget indicates the anticipated purchases of equipment and other large-ticket items with a longer shelf life that will support the organization's programs and services. Thus, buying a new van to transport older, frail adults to their medical appointments and to the senior center for socialization might be a line item in the capital budget; hiring a part-time driver for the Older Adults program would be the corresponding item in the operating budget.

Ideally, both line staff and board members will participate in budget development, but it is the top professional who ought to play the lead role. Today, even without an accounting background, a nonprofit executive must be conversant enough with numbers to guide the budget process from creation through monitoring and final assessment. This includes hiring competent professionals, either as staff or consultants. In larger nonprofits, there may be a full business department headed by a CFO; in smaller settings, the responsibility for crunching numbers and maintaining accounts may fall to a single individual, possibly with the title of bookkeeper, aided by an outside certified public accountant to advise on the more complicated transactions. Regardless of size, every organization can benefit from having an annual audit, an examination of its financial records and practices, performed by an independent accounting firm, to ensure its fiscal health and protect against fraud as well as unintentional errors.

The Budget Cycle
Wolf (1999) has identified the steps necessary to complete a successful budget cycle.

1. Make a wish list of what the organization hopes to accomplish in the coming year to force people "to think systematically about . . . [its] activities, its mission, and its programs" (p. 188).

2. Factor in actual expenses of the past year's programs, projected expenses for the current year, and a realistic estimate of the likely expenditures for new services.

3. Allocate the revenue expected from each activity on the wish list, being conservative in estimating both restricted and unrestricted funds (monies earmarked for certain purposes versus those used at the organization's discretion).

4. Compare the results of steps 2 and 3, revealing that expenses exceed revenues and therefore some activities will need to be discarded to balance the budget.

5. Set priorities, not based strictly on dollars and cents but taking into account the organization's mission and the activities best able to help realize that purpose.

6. Adjust the budget to put it into balance, with enough leeway to accommodate unexpected expenses or revenue shortfalls that may arise, to the extent possible.

7. Allocate time for the board to exercise its fiduciary responsibility by thoroughly reviewing the proposed budget and being clear about the figures before giving approval.
8. Monitor the budget throughout the fiscal year, making adjustments only when necessary in light of new information or circumstances.

Although the reader may wonder about the advisability of creating a wish list, knowing that ultimately not everything on it will end up in the budget, Wolf maintains it is an essential step to ensure the organization will continue to seek new and better ways to meet client needs. At the same time, it would be irresponsible to undertake more than the organization can support. In addition, differing stakeholder interests may come into play during the decision-making. All of this suggests budgeting is not entirely the rational process it may first seem to be.

Practical Considerations

Whenever possible, those responsible for delivering programs and services should be active participants in steps 1–6 of the budget process just described, particularly if these same individuals will also be held accountable for their expenditures. Depending on organizational size, each staff member can be invited to draw up a wish list for the coming year and submit it directly to the executive director, or the separate lists can be compiled into one representing each department and then sent on. At this point a composite draft version would be constructed with expected costs and revenue projections and circulated to staff, who would be asked to offer suggestions of what activities to keep and what to discard, with a rationale for their recommendations. With this information in hand, a final draft can be prepared and circulated once more to make sure nothing has been overlooked.

Approval of both the operating and capital budgets is a board responsibility. It therefore is prudent to go through an exercise similar to that for securing staff input either with the whole board or just the finance committee, to increase the trustees' comfort level so they can make informed judgments about the contents of the budgets and then be effective monitors of the anticipated revenues and expenditures throughout the fiscal year. Once a final draft has been developed, the CEO, accompanied by the CFO or bookkeeper, is ready to meet with the board treasurer to go over the numbers and answer any questions about the budgeting process. Modifications of the budget are possible at this point. Next the board treasurer should convene a meeting of the finance committee to review and approve the financial statements. For this meeting an explanatory narrative is prepared to accompany the budget drafts. Again, it is important that board members' views be respected and accommodated, for this committee's support will go a long way in guaranteeing smooth sailing when the budgets go to the full board. The last step is presenting the proposed budgets, with the narrative, to the board, clarifying items as necessary; with all the groundwork just described, the savvy executive should not have much difficulty obtaining the required formal approval of the documents.

Budget Monitoring

The board's responsibility for oversight of the budgets continues throughout the year. One way to exercise this responsibility is by formulating policies and practices to govern financial transactions. For example, checks for expenditures over a certain amount may require the signature of certain trustees in addition to that of the top professional. Whether to have an annual audit, which is highly recommended, and, if so, the choice of the auditing firm are also board decisions, as are investment considerations and the size of the reserve fund, an amount put away to cover unexpected expenses that may arise.

Financial Reports

For each finance committee and board meeting, staff must prepare different kinds of documents for review and approval. The two most important documents for ongoing monitoring purposes are a comparison of revenues and expenses to date against the budgeted amounts and the previous year's actual figures, with an explanation of major variances, and a report on the organization's cash flow position, which projects month-by-month inputs and expenditures in all budget categories.

Table 11.2 illustrates what a budget variance report might look like for a hypothetical nonprofit providing mental health and substance abuse counseling; it represents the organization's financial position at the end of the second month of the fiscal year. Many board members, especially those coming from the for-profit sector where projections of monthly sales figures tend to be more consistent, find the variability of nonprofit finances somewhat disconcerting. It is therefore important for the board to understand, for instance, that government agencies often are late with their reimbursements. As shown in this example, contract monies are running a month behind schedule. On the positive side, the organization appears to be taking seriously the importance of diversifying revenue sources and has secured a new foundation grant.

A cash-flow report reveals patterns of inflows and outlays for the year; for the same nonprofit, it might show a double payment by the contracting agency at the end of each quarter, which would reconcile the current year actual amount with the current year budget to date. This pattern would also serve as justification for opening a revolving line of credit at the bank holding the organization's accounts, a common strategy for nonprofits that rely heavily on government funding sources to ensure meeting the weekly or biweekly payroll. Although revisions of the budget should never be done without compelling reasons, monitoring the variance and cash flow reports over time may indicate unanticipated changes in circumstances that warrant such modifications.

Other Financial Statements

Periodically, the board should also be provided with a statement of financial position (also known as a balance sheet), a presentation of the organization's finances for the current year and the previous year at a fixed point in time, which could be the end of a month, a quarter, or the fiscal year. This statement shows all assets balanced against all liabilities. Assets are categorized as cash and cash equivalents (certificates of deposit, for

Table 11.2 Budget variance report for February 2____

Line item	Current month				Year to date				Total current yr. budget
	Prior yr. actual	Current yr. budget	Current yr. actual	Variance	Prior yr. actual	Current yr. budget	Current yr. actual	Variance	
Public support									
Contract	$28,375	$29,900	0	($29,900)	$ 56,750	$ 59,800	$ 29,900	($29,900)	$ 358,799
Grant	18,266	18,266	54,798	36,532	36,532	36,532	54,798	18,226	219,195
Subtotal	$46,641	$48,166	$ 54,798	$ 6,632	$ 93,282	$ 96,332	$ 84,698	($11,634)	$ 577,994
Other revenue									
Membership dues	$13,500	$15,000	$ 16,000	$ 1,000	$ 27,000	$ 30,000	$ 31,500	$ 1,500	$ 180,200
Fees for service	10,000	11,000	13,000	2,000	21,000	22,000	26,500	4,500	120,560
Individual donations	6,700	7,500	7,000	(500)	12,100	13,000	11,500	(1,500)	98,639
Foundation grant	0	4,200	4,200	0	0	8,400	8,400	0	50,000
Corporate support	3,600	4,000	4,700	700	7,600	8,000	9,000	1,000	47,678
Interest income	1,555	1,700	1,600	(100)	3,200	3,400	3,200	(200)	20,925
Subtotal	$35,355	$43,400	$ 46,500	$ 3,100	$ 70,900	$ 84,800	$ 90,100	$ 5,300	$ 518,002
Total support & revenue	$81,996	$91,566	$101,298	$ 9,732	$164,182	$181,132	$174,798	($ 6,334)	$1,095,996

Expenses

Salaries	$ 67,680	$ 72,000	$ 70,500	$1,500	$ 95,880	$102,000	$ 99,000	$3,000	$ 641,243
ERE[a]	17,001	18,260	17,945	315	20,608	21,893	21,263	630	132,361
Travel	920	1,000	1,003	(3)	9,049	9,500	9,050	450	53,543
Printing	5,344	5,500	5,308	192	9,944	10,600	10,405	195	62,400
Postage	3,906	4,100	4,156	(56)	9,568	10,000	10,093	(93)	61,600
Supplies	427	450	421	29	839	875	871	4	5,166
Telephone	471	500	491	9	4,098	4,250	4,600	(350)	28,200
Rent	4,700	5,000	5,000	0	14,269	15,180	15,180	0	91,080
Utilities	607	675	684	(9)	1,206	1,300	1,227	73	7,590
Lease contracts	550	570	570	0	1,101	1,140	1,140	0	6,845
Misc. expenses	483	500	485	15	902	975	1,002	(27)	5,968
Total expenses	**$102,089**	**$108,555**	**$106,563**	**$1,992**	**$167,464**	**$177,713**	**$173,831**	**$3,882**	**$1,095,996**

Notes: On the support and revenue side of the budget, when the actual amount is lower than the budgeted amount, the variance is in parenthesis; on the expense side, when the actual amount is higher than the budgeted amount, the variance is in parenthesis.

Although it appears the organization was relatively conservative in its projections for the current year compared to the previous year's actual figures, it is worrisome that the government contract is expected to provide about 33 percent of the total budget. However, since expenses have been kept in check, mainly due to not filling a part-time, entry-level position, and assuming the cash-flow problem with the government contract is resolved, the overall budget remains on target.

[a]Employee-related expenses (ERE) include Social Security payments, payroll and other required taxes, retirement contributions, health insurance costs, and any additional benefits the organization chooses to provide. Many agencies use a percentage of the total salaries cost to arrive at the total for ERE.

example), investments, monies pledged to the organization but not yet collected (accounts receivable), product inventories, prepaid expenses (for rent, perhaps), property and equipment, and an aggregation of miscellaneous items, such as a deposit on leased space. Liabilities include monies owed to vendors (accounts payable), monies received for services to be rendered (deferred revenues), mortgage(s), notes payable on other long-term debts, and any other monies owed, lumped together, such as for property taxes or health insurance premiums. To determine the accumulated worth of the organization, you subtract the liabilities from the overall assets to get the net assets, which may be unrestricted, temporarily restricted as to purpose or time, or permanently restricted according to the donor's specifications (M. S. Thomas, 2006).

In addition, the organization must prepare an income statement, or more formally, a statement of activities or of revenue and expenditures, a representation of inputs and expenses for the entire year, compared with the previous year. The various types of financial support are listed by source—contributions, government grants, fees for service, and so on—and, like net assets on the balance sheet, by donor restriction or lack thereof. Expenses are presented as line items by function (salaries, rent, travel, and so forth). At the bottom of the statement of activities, there will be an indication of whether total revenues have exceeded expenses, and the surplus, which by custom in nonprofit accounting is never called a profit, or deficit is combined with the net assets at the beginning of the year to yield a new figure, the net assets at the end of the year. When an income statement is produced for a shorter period, it often takes the form of the budget variance report discussed earlier, for the explicit purpose of summarizing and comparing financial activity for a month or a quarter in relation to the budget.

Communicating with External Stakeholders

Some financial reports are mandated, such as the annual Form 990 all charitable nonprofits must file with the IRS on their activities for the fiscal year and the latest independent audit, which most funding sources today expect to receive as part of the solicitation. Others are distributed at the organization's discretion. When deciding what to share and with whom, keep in mind that certain documents provide a snapshot of financial conditions at a specific point in time while others give more of a historical perspective on how resources are being managed. Since it may take all of the reports examined together to convey a true picture of fiscal health, an organization needs to be careful about what message it wishes to send (Wolf, 1999).

THE "NEW" CUTBACK MANAGEMENT

For a good part of the twentieth century, it was established policy that the federal government should play a major role in helping to solve social and economic problems, and funding for programs was relatively easy to obtain. However, public sentiment toward government began to change in the 1970s due to the Vietnam War, the Watergate scandal, and the recession brought on by the oil embargo, and by the time Ronald Reagan took office in 1980, government was viewed as the problem rather than the solution (Lebold & Edwards, 2006).

Conservatism became the dominant philosophy, meshing with President Reagan's personal belief that anyone who worked hard could succeed and that private philanthropy and help from family and friends were sufficient to assist those in need. The new government policy, based on supply-side economics, was to give large tax cuts to the private sector to stimulate economic growth; at the same time, the federal government severely reduced spending for social programs other than popular entitlements like Social Security and Medicare. State and local governments now had to pick up the financial burden to deal with homelessness, AIDS, substance use, and so on, causing a severe strain on budgets that continues today in many jurisdictions (Jansson, 2005). Although the nonprofit sector grew extensively during the mid-1990s and into the new century, this expansion began to level off as the economic climate soured, and simultaneously, attention, and funding priorities, shifted to address the war on terrorism, the growing international AIDS problem, the aftermath of Hurricane Katrina, and other such crises.

Organizational Vulnerability

As we look at the current state of affairs for nonprofits, a line from a song comes to mind: "Everything old is new again." During and even before the Reagan years, the term *cutback management* found its way into common nonprofit parlance, and much was written about developing effective strategies to cope successfully in a challenging environment. And here we are again "entering into an era of increased uncertainty when funding patterns are in decline or fragmented and demand for services and accountability is on the rise. . . . Those [nonprofits] that are surviving—or thriving—are organizations with leaders who have acquired the necessary skills to effectively navigate these turbulent fiscal times" (Lebold & Edwards, 2006, p. 433).

There seems to be general agreement that when faced with the prospect of having to do more with less, organizational leaders must be prepared to make difficult choices about what to cut while continuing to offer high-quality services, maintaining positive staff morale, attracting and keeping highly productive people, and retaining the trust and support of key stakeholders. In fact, it may appear to be counterintuitive, but being innovative is perhaps even more essential when resources are declining, and it is often easier to overcome resistance to change in this kind of environment (Behn, 1996).

In purely financial terms, a nonprofit organization may be considered vulnerable if there is a strong likelihood it would cut services immediately following a setback affecting its resources, such as an economic downturn or the loss of a major donor. One indicator of financial vulnerability is a lack of diversity in funding sources; organizations with a number of income streams are in a better position to withstand a crisis. Other key indicators are an inadequate equity balance, low administrative costs, and a low operating margin, all of which reduce the options for finding solutions beyond cutting programs (Greenlee & Trussel, 2000). Programmatically, organizational decline may occur as the result of mismanagement or imprudent expansion of activities, with a concomitant and unwarranted increase in staffing, as a national nonprofit discovered when it accepted government grants for several new programs without having a plan for continuation funding. Once the original monies were depleted, all the new efforts had to be discontinued, compromising the organization's relationship with its financial supporters and the clients who no longer were being served. A decline may also be the result of a failure to maintain a competitive edge in a particular service niche or of a scandal, which can diminish credibility and contributions. Furthermore, organizations can stagnate as they mature unless steps are taken to sustain creativity (Lebold & Edwards, 2006).

Coping in a Turbulent Environment

One of the more prevalent strategies for controlling expenditures is to reduce, phase out, or even eliminate one or more programs. However, this presupposes we can accurately determine what each program contributes to fulfilling the organizational mission, both qualitatively and quantitatively, that is, in terms of effectiveness and efficiency. Otherwise, emotion, instinct, or political pressure may make the decision for us. For Moore (1995) the key is understanding the relationship between costs and outcomes in order to maximize the output from every input, to the extent possible in a real-world situation. As shown in figure 11.1, programs high in outcomes but low in costs are the "bright stars" for the organization, its bread and butter. "Rising suns" are programs high in both outcomes and costs; since they have already proven to be effective, it is now just a matter of expanding their reach or reducing the input costs to turn them into bright stars. In the third category are the "space" programs, ones with low costs but also low outcomes. Even though it may be tempting to keep such programs because they seem harmless and have some benefit, they represent mediocrity and therefore should be targeted for elimination. Finally, there are the "black holes," programs high in costs but low in outcomes that are simply a drain on organizational resources and must go. In practice, though, the perceptions of major stakeholders such as funders may trump this kind of logical approach in setting organizational direction, forcing the continuation of certain otherwise dispensable services.

Figure 11.1 Outcomes-to-Costs Efficiency Matrix

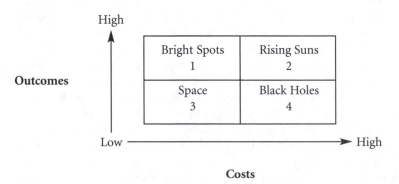

Source: Reprinted with permission from S. T. Moore, Efficiency in social work practice and administration, p. 603. Copyright 1995, National Association of Social Workers, Inc., *Social Work*.

Another perspective is provided through a three-dimensional portfolio model developed by Krug and Weinberg (2004) to measure the contribution of each program to advancing the organizational mission, the revenue it generates as well as its costs, and its performance value, which they summarize as mission, money, and merit. From their research to test the model, they found it went beyond the original purpose to highlight the importance of clarifying managerial assumptions about programs, revising unclear mission statements, strengthening inadequate financial systems, and being more rigorous in evaluating programs to improve overall strategic decision-making. In many regards, this model is similar to the balanced scorecard, a diagnostic tool designed for use in the corporate sector but now often applied to nonprofits as well.

In adopting a downsizing strategy, organizational leaders must guard against the negative effects of an across-the-board approach, which can result in disproportionately punishing programs that are actually efficient and effective rather than those needing to make major changes. Similarly, when a program is cut, the result can be less efficiency because the ratio of fixed costs to outcomes is changed, as the same overhead is now distributed across fewer expense centers. Therefore, it often makes more sense to eliminate administrative staff or to consolidate facilities. Hiring freezes and refusing to accept new clients may also end up being counterproductive; the net effect is a lower level of service delivery (Moore, 1995; E. C. Thomas, 2002).

Furthermore, programmatic cutbacks are not the only answer. The following coping strategies are proactive and may have the additional benefit of increasing staff morale: Seeking additional revenue from new sources, turning to an influential stakeholder who might be able to ward off a proposed funding cut, deferring planned activities such as building renovations to a later date, making quality improvements in standard procedures, using part-timers and volunteers to fill new positions to lower labor costs, increasing the use of technology and other laborsaving approaches, providing incentives for resource conservation and performance improvement, collaborating with other nonprofits on projects of mutual interest, and instituting selective cost reductions, such as asking employees to stay in less expensive hotels when attending conferences (Lebold & Edwards, 2006; E. C. Thomas, 2002). The bottom line is that before choosing a strategy, an organization must weigh both intended and unintended consequences.

PERFORMANCE AND EFFECTIVENESS

Effectiveness, whether at the program or organizational level, seems to be one of those concepts that, like power, we recognize when we see it as opposed to having a way to measure it that works in all situations. In the same vein, Herman and Renz (2008) suggest effectiveness in nonprofits is a social construction that becomes viable only after key stakeholders respond to the written or verbal accounts of various activities, having formed judgments based on their interpretations of the data presented and subsequently conveyed to others that what they have in hand is evidence of effectiveness. Further, the more credible and influential the person sitting in judgment, the more weight is likely to be accorded to that person's actions.

Even though there may not be consensus on a single measure of effectiveness, the financial health of the organization is perceived by many people as a very important indicator. In a study of nonprofit board governance in one county in Michigan, regardless of the type of organization, when asked to identify the biggest challenges facing the sector, most of the more than 500 trustees who responded put funding issues at the top of the list, which included resource generation, financial management, and competition with other nonprofits (Golensky, 2000). Yet, it can rightly be argued that focusing only on what has monetary value and on funding sources ignores other equally important social concerns, such as the organization's impact on its natural environment, and fails to consider the views of staff, consumers, volunteers, and the general public (Richmond, Mook, & Quarter, 2003). We will now explore some of the specific attempts to come to terms with nonprofit effectiveness, both quantitatively and qualitatively.

The lack of clarity as to how financial performance is linked to effectiveness in nonprofit organizations is a problem for both researchers and practitioners: "The researcher finds it difficult to develop normative conclusions regarding the activities and attributes of NPOs that lead to higher (or lower) performance. The practitioner's difficulties arise from an inability to effectively assess performance" (Ritchie & Kolodinsky, 2003, p. 368), especially when engaging in benchmarking, the comparison of one's own organization to similar entities in the same industry. In response to these concerns, factor analysis, a statistical technique used to uncover the correlations among a large number of variables by combining related items into a single factor, was applied to selected financial measures for a group of university foundations to test for relevance and distinctiveness. Three categories emerged as significant indicators: fund-raising efficiency, a ratio of total dollars raised to monies spent in the process; the level of public support; and fiscal performance, defined as either the ratio of all revenues or just contributions to total expenses. Further work with other types of nonprofits will determine the broader applicability of this research (Ritchie & Kolodinsky, 2003).

Crittenden (2000, Supplement) also looked at financial performance, in this case in social service organizations, but with the larger concern of exploring how financial success relates to strategic management, funding, and growth. Two surveys conducted three years apart were supplemented with case studies. Financial performance was equated with balancing the budget and meeting targeted funding goals. Organizations were classified as *successful* if they achieved both criteria, *unsuccessful* if neither standard was met, and a *tweener* if only one goal was reached. The more successful organizations were financially savvy (for example, they projected likely revenues and expenses before making decisions), had a diverse funding base, were strategic in targeting potential funders, recognized the importance of marketing, and sought growth principally through increasing clients rather than programs.

A third approach is based on a multidimensional and integrated model of organizational effectiveness that applies statistical analysis to both programmatic and management elements. The model is hierarchical in that it focuses on decisions made by top-level managers regarding organizational capacity as well as by individual staff at the program level on activities, but also suggests the interrelationship of the two. That is, service outcomes alone do not define effectiveness; structure and operating processes must also be understood as contributing to or hindering those outcomes. Moreover, the assumption is made that indicators of managerial effectiveness such as the existence of a formal mission statement, a strategic plan, and up-to-date human resources policies will be relatively stable while program indicators will vary within a given system, and that both objective and perceptual measures are probably needed to fully capture effectiveness (Sowa, Selden, & Sandfort, 2004).

The relationship between the nonprofit and for-profit sectors, as collaborators and competitors, has been discussed at several points in this book, highlighting their similarities and differences. With regard to performance measurement in nonprofits, of the different concepts used in the corporate world, the balanced scorecard is the crossover tool that appears to be the best fit, at both the programmatic and organizational levels, because it acknowledges the existence of multiple stakeholders whose views matter and uses a variety of indicators, considered generally from four perspectives, financial, customer, internal, and learning and growth (Speckbacher, 2003). The challenge is for the organization to identify quantifiable measures of its operations, with the starting point, as always, being the mission. For example, in the customer arena, a nonprofit providing education services could specify desired goals for the number of training courses offered and the progress made by clients who complete the training in finding paid employment, and then monitor the results during the year. From the financial perspective the main concern would be adding value for consumers and donors, while controlling costs; internally it would be determining the operating processes most necessary to meeting client needs; and for learning and growth, it would be to consider where changes could be made to improve service quality (Pokrant, 2004). Again, in each case, concrete ways to measure progress toward goals would have to be found, perhaps using benchmarking. A related approach is the development of an organizational report card, which employs techniques similar to those for the balanced scorecard, with two key differences: the efforts in the focal organization are compared with achievements in at least two other organizations, and the assessments are managed by and designed for external parties (Gormley & Weimer, 1999).

In conducting performance evaluations in nonprofits, a perceived problem has been the difficulty in quantifying outcomes consisting of modifications in behavior and attitudes, increases in knowledge, and so forth. In truth, virtually all outcomes can be measured using qualitative data and descriptive statistics, the mainstays of social accounting, which is another term more associated with for-profits and refers to a systematic analysis of items that do not have an established dollar value (Richmond et al., 2003). For instance, for the clients of a human service organization helping those with substance use issues, an increase in self-esteem represents a major step forward on the road to sobriety. As part of an organizational review, you would assess the different modalities used with the clients, with groups led by peer counselors being one. In this case, clients can be asked to complete a self-administered questionnaire to probe their sense of self-worth when they enter and again upon leaving the group, and the results can be compared pre- and posttreatment. Ideally, you would want to use an externally validated instrument, but if one is not available to fit the situation, the organization can develop its own. As long as the instrument is consistently administered and interpreted, valuable information can be obtained for planning and evaluation purposes. As a secondary source, a key informant, such as a close family member or a clergyman, could complete a related questionnaire on the client or be interviewed (Mordock, 2002).

To sum up, even though we may not be able to define organizational effectiveness in precise terms, there is agreement on the three major approaches to conceptualizing and measuring this phenomenon, the attainment of specified goals, the procurement and management of resources, and the opinions of key stakeholders, with elements of each often used in combination as multiple frames of reference (Balser & McClusky, 2005).

FINAL THOUGHTS

Kettner (2002, p. 8) has identified the main themes emerging from studies of excellence, which in many ways is simply a synonym for effectiveness.

1. Establishing a purpose and mission for the organization and ensuring that all systems are consistent with the mission;
2. Creating an organizational structure that is consistent with organizational purpose and maximizes flexibility;
3. Designing jobs in a way that will permit staff to use their expertise and creativity;
4. Demonstrating commitment to high performance by rewarding productive staff;
5. Collecting data and information about services that will permit evaluation and continuous program improvement;
6. Budgeting and financing the organization in a way that is consistent with the mission;
7. Recruiting and retaining the best qualified and most productive staff; and
8. Monitoring, evaluating, and providing feedback about staff performance in a way that leads to continuous improvement and high levels of productivity.

In the end, what those of us working in, studying, and observing the nonprofit sector—all interested parties in one capacity or another—want is to see these organizations move closer and closer to achieving excellence. Incorporating the practices embodied in these eight themes, or at least striving to achieve that goal, may be the true test of accountability.

Technology and Communication

In the mid-1980s the registrar for the camping program run by a small nonprofit organization kept the campers' records on 3 × 5 cards filed alphabetically in a shoebox. How far we have come in a relatively short time! Today, even the smallest of nonprofits is likely to have at least a basic level of technological capacity, for it is generally understood that no voluntary organization can be competitive without this essential tool. "For organizations able to use information and communication technologies (ICTs) effectively, the benefits extend beyond conventional enhancements of administrative and operational efficiency and effectiveness" (Burt & Taylor, 2000, p. 132). Access to these technologies may make it possible not only to reshape operations but also to redefine all internal and external relationships.

The key is how ICTs are used. As might be expected, budget size does have an impact on capacity and infrastructure; smaller organizations are less likely to have networked computers, a broadband connection to the Internet, or a formal technology plan with goals and dedicated resources (Manzo & Pitkin, 2007). This disparity between the haves and the have-nots, sometimes referred to as the *digital divide*, seems to be even more problematic for organizations serving communities of color (Schneider, 2003). However, research indicates that many nonprofits, large and small, do not take full advantage of the tools at their disposal. Manzo and Pitkin (2007) have identified six primary barriers to ICT development: (1) insufficient funding for upgrades and maintenance, often exacerbated by donor restrictions on contributions to program needs; (2) inadequate time spent mapping out the best ways to integrate technology strategically within the organization; (3) external pressures, especially by funders, to upgrade technology in a specified manner that may not fit the organization's priorities; (4) a lack of staff whose main responsibility is managing ICT, possibly reflecting limited support for technology by organizational leaders; (5) little or no training for staff in the use of the various technologies, despite the generally accepted rule that 70 percent of the monies set aside for this purpose should go to training and maintenance; and (6) an inability to identify or gain access to expert assistance and reliable information, which may be aggravated by gender or cultural differences between staff and consultants.

Above all, it is important to avoid goal displacement by keeping in mind that technology is always a means to an end. In nonprofits, the mission should be the driving force behind the decisions on hardware and software, to the extent possible. From this perspective, most of the common applications, for fund-raising, advocacy, marketing, volunteer management, record keeping, and so forth, are in essence a form of communication with one or more of the organization's stakeholders.

THE BASICS OF EFFECTIVE COMMUNICATION

Because internal and external relationships may begin, be modified, or end through communication, it is one more skill that an organizational leader must master. Communication is both a science and an art. It is possible to learn various techniques and how to apply them to different scenarios, but even though we may be able to anticipate the dynamics of a particular situation, such as a staff meeting or a negotiation with a major funder, each interaction is unique. Despite the thoroughness of our preparation, people seldom follow the script we may have mentally laid out for them, and there will always be circumstances we cannot control. This is where the art enters into the equation: it means developing the capacity to adapt to what is rather than what was expected while still moving toward the desired outcome.

Whether communication is used to convey a simple message, for problem solving, or to effect change, the process always has *content*. That is, A is usually talking to B about something, the aspect we tend to notice first when tuning in to a conversation. Further, it is possible to distinguish specific categories of content, for example, fact versus feeling. Second, some exchanges occur in a quiet atmosphere and others in the presence of a considerable amount of *noise*, which refers to things that interfere with the transmission of ideas and emotions, like static on a telephone line. There are also psychological noises: A supervisor may be meeting with a new employee to discuss the first days on the job, but the worker is thinking about her child's difficulties in mastering long division and therefore finds it hard to concentrate on what is being said to her. Or the worker may believe she is going to be reprimanded for how she interacted with a particular client, and her fear gets in the way of focusing on what the supervisor is actually saying. Language can be a kind of code noise when the two parties do not have the same understanding of the words being said. For instance, the supervisor may describe the new staff member's counseling style as "interesting," meaning it as a compliment, but the worker takes it as a criticism.

In the presence of noise, A is likely to use redundancy to improve the communication process, by repeating the message in the hope B will hear it better the second time or by trying to say the same thing but in different words. Redundancy can be an efficient technique if the message is then received as sent, but it can also be inefficient in the sense that repetition is wasteful of time and energy and may not succeed. In the scenario described above, the supervisor, realizing the meeting is not being very productive, might get farther by saying, "I'm not sure I'm being clear in how I see your work to date. Is this a fair assumption?" In combining two techniques that often help to avoid miscommunication, using an "I" statement, to take responsibility for one's own ideas and feelings, and perception checking, by asking for a clarification of the other person's position, the supervisor gives the worker an opportunity to address her concerns without feeling attacked.

A third dimension of communication, especially in organizations, is the *network*, which defines how individuals can speak to each other. In a hierarchical setting, A (a line worker) may not be permitted to speak directly with B (the executive director) but has to go through C (program supervisor), who in turn must pass on the message through D (department head). Conversely, in an organization using a flattened, matrix structure, it is much easier to interact across levels. The organization chart, a diagram showing the formal roles and relationships in a given environment, delineates the division of work, the chain of command, areas of responsibility, and levels of management; it not only conveys the expected information flow but also tells us a lot about the speed and accuracy of members' communications with one another.

A final consideration is the *direction* of communication. In one-way communication, A talks and B can only listen, whereas in two-way communication, A and B engage in a real dialogue. The initial reaction may be to view the second style as better than the first because it seems more humanistic. However, it is important to recognize that both have their pluses and minuses, and therefore the most efficient and effective approach to use is the one that best fits the specific circumstances. Research has shown one-way communication is considerably faster, so it would probably be preferred in an emergency (directing the orderly evacuation of a burning building, for example). On the other hand, two-way communication tends to be more accurate because the receiver can ask clarifying questions as needed. An individual concerned about maintaining power and appearing in control is more likely to use one-way communication, while the person valuing interpersonal relationships may opt for two-way communication, despite knowing the task can become more complicated. Thus, one executive whose organization is facing major financial setbacks may elect to send a memo announcing the decision to downsize, but another in the same situation will prefer to discuss the plan and its rationale with staff even though she may be challenged on the decision, in hopes of keeping the loyalty of those remaining after the cutbacks (Brueggemann, 1996; Leavitt, 1972).

Although the widespread use of e-mail for internal communications in organizations may seem to provide a compromise on direction, as recipients can reply instantly to the sender, there is no guarantee the responses will have the desired effect when they can so easily be ignored or deleted. Furthermore, excessive reliance on e-mail can actually increase the noise factor, with nonessential messages clogging up the channels of communication, and limiting the message to specific addressees can be a way to narrow the scope of the communication network. Like any good management tool, e-mail certainly has its place, but sometimes there is no substitute for the low-tech, face-to-face conversation, especially when the content involves emotions.

TECHNOLOGY AND INTERNAL COMMUNICATION

In the organizational setting, technology offers a way to communicate vertically and horizontally, namely, from level to level as well as intradepartmentally. Along with carrying messages through the system, computers are used extensively in nonprofits for word processing, Internet access, financial accounting, program monitoring and evaluation, and basic record keeping on clients, staff, and members. For the most part, ICT capacity appears to be greater for larger nonprofits and those located in metropolitan areas, but it is less a function of type of nonprofit, although organizations in the fields of education and public and social benefit do seem more advanced in the use of technology than those in the human services (Clerkin & Gronbjerg, 2007).

Practical Considerations

To address the barriers to ICT development noted earlier, we must recognize that before selecting a particular system, there are some basic steps an organization has to take to plan and manage technology effectively (Zimmerman & Broughton, 2006).

- *Assessment.* First, it is important to establish the goals for automation at all levels of the organization, but an assessment should also include an inventory of the hardware and software currently in use as well as a determination of the computer skills of the staff, especially as they relate to the identified goals, information that can then guide the development of a training plan.
- *Strategic planning.* As part of the organization's overall strategic thinking and planning, attention must be given to how technology fits into present and future needs to further the goals set during the assessment. This plan should be reviewed annually and updated in accordance with any changes in practices.
- *Personnel.* Factoring in at least one staff person to support the network is strongly advised, especially in the early stages of introducing technology into the organization. In larger settings, two individuals may be needed, a network administrator and someone to handle the application software.
- *Staff training.* The training plan should be comprehensive enough to address all skill needs. When this component is ignored to save money, the costs to the organization due to less efficient and less productive work are generally comparable to what would have been spent on training staff in the first place.
- *Budgeting.* Include line items for purchasing and maintaining both hardware and software, along with monies for tech staff and training. Choose equipment capable of supporting the applications currently needed by the organization but also powerful enough to be upgraded to handle future requirements.

Given the costs associated with technology, at each of these stages organizational leaders must make sure to weigh all the relevant factors to support their subsequent decisions (see table 12.1).

Table 12.1 The planning process for managing technology effectively

Step	Pertinent questions
1. Assessment	What are our automation goals?
	What are the dimensions of our current hardware and software capabilities?
	How do staff rate in terms of basic computer skills? On more advanced skills?
2. Strategic planning	What are our technology needs to meet current goals?
	What upgrades and other changes in technology can be anticipated to meet projected goals for the next 1 to 3 years?
3. Personnel Small organizations	Do we have a qualified staff member to provide general technical support or must we hire someone for this position?
	Is it a part-time or full-time responsibility?
Large organization	What are the job requirements for the position of network administrator? For the support technician?
4. Staff training	What kind of core curriculum is needed to bring staff skills up to the desired level?
	How should we implement the training (i.e., in-house or external courses, hire an outside trainer or train a staff member to train the rest, etc.)?
	How should advanced skills training be addressed?
5. Budgeting[a]	What specific line items must be included to cover hardware, software, personnel, and training needs, and for upgrades/additions as required?
	Are there sufficient monies available to meet our technology needs? If not, should we prioritize or seek a capacity-building grant?
	What computer brand and model is best suited to meet current needs but also to handle future requirements?
	What are our software needs, now and in the immediate future?
	Should we purchase and adapt an existing system or customize one in-house to fit our needs?

Source: Adapted from Zimmerman & Broughton, 2006.
[a]A good rule of thumb is to allocate at least 5 percent of the total annual budget to technology considerations.

Management Information System

An organization's information system (IS), usually electronic, is intended to be the central repository for inputting administrative, financial, and program data that can then be analyzed and manipulated in various ways to provide a variety of outputs for different stakeholders. It is therefore dismaying to learn that the failure rate for productive utilization of these systems has been put as high as 50 to 75 percent, with the suspected cause a lack of fit between what system users need and want and the actual design of the system, which often ignores the role of decision-making (Fitch, 2007).

Moreover, characterizing this extensive database as a *management* information system is somewhat misleading in terms of utilization, especially in a human services organization, for in general, three important kinds of decision-making occur on a regular basis: *operational*, at the direct service level; *tactical*, at the middle-management level; and *strategic*, at the executive level. Unlike in the business sector, where line workers tend to follow directives from above, counselors, therapists, and other frontline staff in a social agency often function autonomously when interacting with consumers, and their overriding interest is knowing whether they are making a difference in the lives of these individuals. Managers, on the other hand, are seeking to determine whether the programs offered are having a positive impact on clients, while the top decision-makers may be concerned about the organization's place in the larger community. Given the specific needs at each organizational level, the discussion on configuring the system must shift to "what the most meaningful design is based upon the decisions a person has to make in the course of performing his or her work" (Fitch, 2007, p. 137).

Traditional Information-System Design

Too frequently, with the traditional approach to design, the emphasis is on the tasks to be accomplished through the system and the desired end products. For instance, since resource generation is a common information-system application, the organization might be asked to identify its main sources of revenue and other support, what information it needs on individual and institutional donors, and the types and timing of reports the different funders expect. Although accommodating major stakeholders is important, this approach fails to get to the core issue of decision making, which is how the system will facilitate reaching operational, tactical, and strategic decisions.

In their effectiveness-based approach to program development, Kettner, Moroney, and Martin (2008) maintain that producing data is intended to support decision-making in the broadest sense. Yet it appears they are most interested in the tactical and strategic levels. To determine which programs work best with respect to certain types of clients and problems, they identify these primary considerations: "(1) What questions do I need the system to answer? (2) What data elements must be included in the system to answer the questions? and (3) What types of routine reports do I want the system to generate?" (p. 179). These *are* key questions, especially to those responsible for program planning and evaluation, and for obtaining the material resources necessary to implementation, but they may not go far enough in overcoming underutilization at the operational level. When direct service workers are not included in the development of the system yet are asked to provide most of the data for reports that are unhelpful to them, they may rightfully feel imposed on and never take full advantage of the system's capabilities (Savaya, Spiro, Waysman, & Golan, 2004).

Systems Theory and Information-System Design

Fitch (2007) suggests that the traditional approach to design, by focusing on management concerns, in effect disempowers those employees whose informational needs are not recognized as equally valid. Instead, he proposes using an emancipatory design that takes into account decision-making at all staff levels and promotes open communication channels throughout the organization. Too often in social agencies, the detailed notes on clients recorded by line workers for their purposes must be reduced to a summary for a supervisor to enter into a spreadsheet, which cannot capture observations and other nuanced comments regarding the intervention. As a result, the information on the real work being done is lost. An alternative that may overcome these problems is System Design Modeling (SDM), a methodology for identifying the full range of organizational functioning by allowing "practitioners, managers, and directors in human service organizations to analyze their current information flows and processes, identify barriers to optimal performance, and design information system solutions to meet their organizational needs" (Fitch, 2007, p. 138).

System design modeling is based on general systems theory. Therefore, it has the potential to be used by nonprofits and for-profits because both are a collection of processes that use information to explain their nature. As for Activity-Based Management (ABM), this technology originated in the business sector and has now moved to nonprofits, both public and private. Here the focus is on determining efficiency and effectiveness by studying how inputs, processes, outputs, and outcomes relate to each other (Menefee, Ahluwalia, Pell, & Woldu, 2000), much like the logic model's emphases discussed in chapter 9. The primary goal is continuous improvement in the delivery of high-quality services in the most cost-effective manner to maintain a competitive edge. Analysis, usually done monthly, is based on the resources consumed (staff salaries, for example) and time spent on a given activity, the units of service delivered, and outcomes as measured by performance indicators constructed to fit each program. Considering the present climate for nonprofits, ABM has a certain appeal since it is clearly related to outcomes-based evaluation, but it also requires a major commitment on the part of organizational leaders and staff to make a successful transition to such a complex system.

ICT Impact on the Nonprofit Workplace

No one disputes that technology has transformed the workplace across all sectors. To understand the effects of ICT on nonprofits, it is helpful first to consider some core characteristics of the sector, for instance, the predominance of women among staff and volunteers, whose values are then reflected in the importance given to such nonmonetary concerns as the mission of the organization, relationships with colleagues, and work-related opportunities for personal and professional growth. Within this broad framework, Saidel and Cour (2003) explored the ways technology has changed work and workplace interactions in the voluntary sector with regard to autonomy and flexibility, learning challenges, the distribution of power, and overall job satisfaction (see table 12.2).

Table 12.2 The impact of technology on the nonprofit workplace

Impact area	Kinds of changes
Job transformation	
Upward migration	Professional staff are more likely to prepare their own reports, memos, presentations, etc.
Lateral migration	Tasks may be handed off by middle managers at the central office to their counterparts in satellite locations.
Circular migration	Tasks are sent back to the central office if decentralization proves less efficient.
Task expansion	Support staff are taking on higher-order administrative and non-administrative tasks in addition to their regular clerical work.
Learning opportunities	Gaining new technical skills is seen as a form of career development and an incentive to stay with the agency.
	Some staff become in-house coaches and informal tech support for their colleagues.
	New tech positions may be created, allowing for lateral job moves and new career directions for current staff.
	Staff may gain new interpersonal skills as a result of technology demands.
Distribution of power	Senior-level staff often feel they have delegated power to subordinates due to technology.
	Support staff are more likely to feel they have gained expert power rather than delegated authority.
	In general, the ability to access new kinds of information and expand communication outlets is a source of power at all levels.
Job satisfaction	
Positives	Technology may offer new challenges, more variety in tasks, greater autonomy, and continuous learning opportunities.
	Acquiring new skills increases staff marketability (internally and externally) and chances for promotion.
	Having a personal computer at each workstation gives employees a greater sense of independence and control in carrying out assignments.
Negatives	There is potential for a mismatch between new job requirements due to technology and the person holding the position (over- or underqualification).
	Some staff experience frustration when the organization fails to provide sufficient tech support and training.

Source: Adapted from Saidel & Cour, 2003.

Job Transformation

Relatively speaking, direct service and management staff in nonprofits tend to be highly professional and well-educated, which means they are likely to be able to adapt to using technology on a regular basis to prepare reports, draft memos, and so forth. Now, "tasks that were once performed separately and in sequence first by a manager with follow-up by administrative support staff are . . . compressed into virtually a single function and performed by the manager" (Saidel & Cour, 2003, p. 10), which is referred to as *upward migration*. In addition, there is evidence of *lateral migration*, when scheduling, client tracking, and similar tasks are handed off from middle managers in the central office to professionals at the same job level in satellite locations. A third variation, *circular migration*, is possible; this would occur if decentralizing a task proved to be less efficient than expected and the job was routed back to headquarters.

Although certain routine matters may now be handled directly by professionals, along with the remaining clerical work, support staff are expected to take on higher-order administrative and nonadministrative tasks such as preparing databases and spreadsheets, coordinating client services, and managing survey research. *Task expansion* also is occurring for professionals and executives, as just noted. In both cases, some see this as job enrichment while others find it stressful.

Learning Opportunities

Many staff perceive the opportunity to learn new technical skills as a form of career development and an incentive to stay with the organization. In nonprofits that lack the resources to hire ICT staff, professionals and clerical personnel who gain technical know-how become valued informal coaches and tech support for their less-adept colleagues. In other settings, new positions in technology have been created, allowing for lateral job moves and new career directions by current employees. In fact, it may be fairer to characterize the career path in nonprofits as spiral rather than linear. Besides, it is certainly more cost-effective to develop talents in-house.

In addition, technology may lead to unexpected side benefits, such as developing new interpersonal skills. For example, discussing business via e-mail with someone you have never met requires learning how to negotiate effectively and to trust a person you cannot see. Similarly, the support staff member asked to train a group of professionals in the use of a complicated spreadsheet needs to practice diplomacy and patience.

Distribution of Power

The different views of how technology has influenced power shifts within the organization depend on position. Executives and other senior-level professionals often feel they have delegated much of their power to subordinates due to technology, giving them more autonomy to work independently, be innovative, and make their own decisions. Support staff, however, are more apt to refer to an increase in expert power rather than delegated authority. Being able to access new information and engage in new forms of communication is also a source of power in today's competitive environment. Since many nonprofits already lean toward a more participatory structure, the availability of e-mail, an in-house Listserv, or a Web-based discussion group only increases the possibility of direct involvement in decision-making and planning for all organizational levels.

Job Satisfaction

As indicated earlier, nonmonetary incentives, such as mental challenges, variety of tasks, and autonomy, are important in voluntary organizations. The opportunity for continuous learning of ICT skills is identified as an important contributor to job satisfaction. The acquisition of these new skills also enhances an individual's marketability and chances for promotion, internally and externally. For many, having a computer at the ready provides a sense of control over certain aspects of the job and reduces the need to rely as much on others. On the whole, although increases in workload and skill expectations due to technology might be expected to cause dissatisfaction, most staff appear to be taking this in stride by looking on the positive side of the impact of ICT on their work lives. However, some staff do become frustrated at the rather slow pace of their organization to reach full technological capacity, including a lack of sufficient technical support and training.

A potential concern is that, as technology transforms the workplace, there could be a mismatch between the new expectations of a position and the individual holding that job. Skill requirements could increase or decrease, resulting in the worker being overqualified or underqualified. Women, whether staff or volunteers, may be more affected under these circumstances due to the often erroneous perception that they have less technical know-how than their male counterparts. In practice, when training in the use of technology is offered in nonprofits, it is generally made available to all who need a particular skill set, which would tend to level the playing field.

TECHNOLOGY AND EXTERNAL COMMUNICATION

Turning to the use of technology to communicate with the external world, Internet connection, providing access to the World Wide Web, and e-mail come immediately to mind as tools that have become ubiquitous in the nonprofit sector, with some variations in capacity again due to budget size and by field (Clerkin & Gronbjerg, 2007; Manzo & Pitkin, 2007). Employees can now exchange information with their counterparts locally and globally, obtain data on almost any subject imaginable, participate in online discussion forums, take continuing education courses, and even deliver certain client services, to name just some of the possibilities with modern technology (Zimmerman & Broughton, 2006). A term that has found its way into the general lexicon is *e-commerce*, which refers in general to business that is conducted electronically. In nonprofit organizations, it describes using the Internet "to generate donations, increase membership, market products and services, and respond to customer inquiries and complaints" (Grobman, 2004, p. 264). We will now focus on these and other electronic applications that are becoming a standard part of the operations of many nonprofits.

Advocacy

Over the past two or three decades, the use of *e-advocacy* by nonprofits to impact the direction and development of public policies has evolved from efforts at the local or regional level that complemented established social-change methods like community organizing, lobbying and petition drives, to much broader campaigns with national and even international targets (globalization, for example), using newer techniques such as a blog, wireless cell phones or pagers, and instant and short text messaging. The latter two techniques can lead to the formation of a *smart* or *flash mob*, a spontaneous gathering of like-minded individuals, perhaps to stage a demonstration. It is also possible to use the Web to set up physical meetings, with advance registration, for advocates at restaurants or other specified areas to organize around an issue (McNutt, 2007).

Despite these advances, not all nonprofits have adopted the new techniques. For smaller organizations, cost may be a factor, although some believe technology may actually allow such groups to compete more effectively with wealthier organizations. Moreover, e-advocacy is not generally a substitute for the more conventional approaches but is likely to be integrated into one overall strategy. The choice of a particular method, whether low- or high-tech, will often depend on the intent of the communication, one to one, one to many, or many to many (McNutt & Boland, 1999).

Fund-Raising

Another term enjoying wide recognition today in nonprofits is *e-philanthropy*, referring to the use of the Internet to obtain donations and other forms of philanthropic support, especially from individuals. Although this approach had already been in place for over two years, it became a major vehicle to promote charitable acts after the terrorist attacks of September 11, 2001. People were almost desperate to respond in a positive way to these tragic events, and the Internet provided the mechanism, once several for-profit Web sites linked their credit card processing systems so that visitors to the sites could donate to the relief efforts (Hart, 2003). More recent disasters (Hurricane Katrina, for one) have sparked the rise of *mobile philanthropy*, or the use of text messaging, to solicit gifts.

As organizations have begun to create their own effective and informative Web sites, e-philanthropy has evolved to encompass the full range of development activities, starting with the initial effort to reach and educate potential donors. In addition to seeking online gifts, a nonprofit can use the Internet for all levels of resource generation up to and including planned giving, as well as to engage supporters in other ways to help the charity, such as through membership, volunteering, and advocacy. There are also online services that focus just on organizing and managing every aspect of special events, from sending out invitations to surveying participants in the previous year's fund-raiser, and others for conducting prospect research. While it is always critical to protect information about donors, it is doubly so for giving via the Internet; sites should employ encryption technology to ensure that credit card information is secure (Hart, 2003).

Even though e-philanthropy is still small, relatively speaking, with just a few organizations raising more than 10 percent of their total revenue in this manner, it is definitely growing in popularity: With regard to the Philanthropy 400, a list of the top 400 fund-raising charities in the United States published by the *Chronicle of Philanthropy*, at present 95 percent accept online gifts (Waters, 2007). For most nonprofits, however, this approach is likely to remain just one component, albeit an important one, of the overall strategy for securing material resources for some time to come.

Interorganizational Relations

As Austin (2002) points out, "The increased pressure to integrate services, facilitate organizational change, foster interdisciplinary practice, and identify best practices is forcing middle and top managers to . . . add . . . 'managing out' to their expertise in managing down and managing up" (p. 35). In practical terms, this means expending time and energy on boundary-spanning activities as well as on internal issues to ensure the fulfillment of the organization's mission and remain competitive in securing essential resources. A key strategy is engaging in both formal and informal networks with other organizations in the community.

Although nonprofits have varied in the degree to which they have embraced ICT in the past, some of the emerging technologies may encourage broader usage to improve networking capacity both internally and externally. Social service agencies, for instance, could benefit from "Web services," which use a specific standard protocol so that other computers on the Internet can access them and obtain the data they need to, say, create a treatment plan to move a child in foster care through the delivery system more effectively and efficiently. To achieve this goal, the data must be specially formatted to enable computers to do much of the work. XML, standing for extensible markup language, is an approach capable of turning documents into minidatabases; by agreeing to mark up the text in a certain way to allow their computers to read the same material, service providers with a common interest can share the information, thus fostering both intra- and interagency coordination. Refinements of XML by means of more advanced technologies known as the Semantic Web can move this process to an even higher level. Furthermore, the Health Insurance Portability and Accountability Act (HIPAA), although initially a potential barrier to sharing data across organizations due to its strict privacy requirements, may in the long run make interagency communication more feasible once HIPAA-compliant networks to protect confidentiality are the norm (O'Looney, 2005).

Marketing

At one time a popular camera brand was advertised on TV with the slogan "Image is everything." Some leaders of voluntary organizations may still be under the impression that marketing is mostly about manipulating an image. However, this is a short-sighted view. According to Wolf (1999), "in the nonprofit sector, marketing is the engineering of *satisfaction* among a variety of groups including users of an organization's services, funders, trustees, regulators, and others who can influence the success of the organization— such as the media and even the general public" (p. 152, emphasis in original). In other words, it is a form of exchange with key stakeholders through targeted and varied means of communication to educate and enlighten them, and to ensure their support of the organization's mission. This support may be manifested as gifts or grants, favorable legislation, the purchase of services, a featured article in the local newspaper, or a positive opinion expressed by an average citizen about the organization's work. Seen from this perspective, marketing is as vital a management function as planning and resource generation, and not to be easily dismissed as simply self-promotion.

A basic concept in this arena is *market segmentation*, which refers to identifying the different constituencies or stakeholder groups and planning strategies accordingly. To maximize the effective use of scarce resources, it is important to focus on the groups deemed most critical to the enterprise's overall success. Obviously, there are many claims on any constituency's loyalty, so to help figure out what motivates someone to make a charitable gift or purchase a service, we must consider the elements of a standard *marketing mix*, commonly referred to as the four P's: *product* (for nonprofits, the programs and services provided), *promotion* (making people aware of the available programs and services), *price* (the costs to use the programs and services), and *place* (the locations where programs and services are provided). To be competitive, a voluntary organization must take all four elements into consideration, blending them strategically to meet its own needs and those of its target market(s). For example, a nonprofit may have developed an innovative after-school program for youth ages twelve to fifteen, but if the area schools and parents in the community do not know the program exists, if the price is too low or too high compared with the costs of similar services, if the program is not offered in a convenient location and transportation issues have not been addressed, it is unlikely the new program will attract enough youth to make it a success. Conducting research on the external environment to obtain sufficient customer-related information to develop the optimum marketing mix is an essential first step in the process; it is equally important to periodically survey consumers to gauge their satisfaction with the product to allow for continuous quality improvement (Moyer, 1994; Wolf, 1999).

Marketing vehicles should include both low-tech and high-tech approaches. An e-mail newsletter distributed to all constituents every other month may be perfect to convey general information about the organization's activities and solicit small donations, but it is not a substitute for a print mailing with details about new initiatives sent only to top-level supporters, designed to make these individuals feel special and to pave the way for a major gifts campaign. In online marketing, a key initial step is to create an e-mail file and then continually build it up by gathering new addresses offline, running "Forward to a Friend" or viral campaigns, and uploading your traditional donor file. A recent survey of electronic marketing in nonprofits (Bhagat, Hauf, & Donovan, 2007) concluded that success in this arena entailed, in addition to having a large e-mail file, the ability to attract visitors to the Web site by offering compelling content and promoting the site through other media, and the establishment of effective mechanisms to convert Web traffic into registered users and ultimately donors.

Volunteer Management

Although we will examine the management of program volunteers in more detail in chapter 16, it is important to note here that technology has been adapted for use in volunteer programs. There are now Internet-based services such as Idealist.org and Volunteermatch.org that can connect potential volunteers and organizations, and some larger nonprofits have created their own Web-based services for this purpose. Online volunteering refers to "activities that are completed, in whole or in part, via the Internet on a home, work, or public access computer, usually in support of or through a mission-based organization" (Cravens, 2006, p. 16). While it is often assumed these volunteers will never be seen by their nonprofit sponsors, in fact many of the same people also volunteer locally and in person. Moreover, ICT appears to create new possibilities for volunteering on both sides of the equation: smaller or startup organizations, and those in remote locations, may find it easier to attract and involve volunteers online, and for the volunteers, participating electronically can overcome the potential barriers of limited time, distance, and physical disability (Dhebar & Stokes, 2008).

Nonprofit leaders and managers considering an online volunteer program are advised to plan carefully, starting with what the organization hopes to accomplish by this approach and then articulating how these objectives could be translated into specific opportunities within its programs and services. Being able to post clear, detailed descriptions of assignments is the best way to ensure a positive response. Good and frequent communication is vital to encourage volunteer retention and performance, and regular monitoring and evaluation may be even more essential for these programs. Some of the attributes for successful online volunteering are well-developed people- and project-management skills, a solid and stable infrastructure, and an appreciation for diversity (Cravens, 2006; Dhebar & Stokes, 2008).

FINAL THOUGHTS

Some barriers to ICT development, such as insufficient funding for upgrades and maintenance, clearly pertain to material resources, but it is important not to lose sight of the personal element. Line staff may be apprehensive about having to acquire new skills and adopt new practices that seem contrary to their professional ideology and even require learning a new vocabulary (see table 12.3). At other times, it is top-level managers who, in their concern for efficiency, focus on the costs involved, failing to see the larger picture of what could be accomplished in improving service delivery with a more technologically capable environment. Since cultural change is generally accomplished only when leaders perceive a need to move the organization in a different direction, the first step would appear to be educating the CEO and other senior managers about the strategic advantages associated with effective ICT use.

Brainard and Siplon (2004) approach the question of technology usage by first identifying two nonprofit organizational models, one emphasizing businesslike methods (the economic model) and the other, participation and membership (the voluntary spirit

Table 12.3 Glossary of selected technology terms

Term	Definition
Blog	A list of entries posted on a Web page that can serve many purposes, from an online newsletter to a personal journal, to share experiences, opinions, and feelings. Some invite feedback.
Chat room; discussion forum	Both provide online exchanges on specific topics, using the Web or the Internet, between parties with a common interest. Chat rooms allow for communication in real time, while forums accept postings but have no capacity for interactive messaging.
Database	A collection of organized information often containing software used to sort, select, and track the information rapidly. An example is the Raiser's Edge.
E-mail	A means or system for sending, receiving, and storing messages electronically; the message itself.
Hypertext markup language (HTML)	A system for creating a document on the Web that indicates its layout in terms of text, graphics, etc.
Internet	An electronic communications network that connects computers around the world through a standardized protocol.
Listserv	A computer program that automatically sends an e-mail message to all the subscribers on a list.
Local area network (LAN)	A means to link personal computers in the same locale for communications and sharing of software and hardware.
Mobile philanthropy	Use of text messaging to cell phones to raise gifts for a specific cause, such as disaster relief. Some charities are now recycling old handsets or selling their own branded phones, using the profits to support programs.
Search engine	A type of software that indexes millions of sites on the Web, based on titles, keywords, and the text in the pages. Examples include Google and Yahoo.
Spreadsheet	A document produced on the computer, set up in rows and columns, that is often used to store financial data. This structured data can be analyzed and printed as charts.
Viral marketing	A method of facilitating and encouraging messages to be passed along from person to person via the individual's social network. "Viral" refers to the speed with which such messages can spread.
World Wide Web (the Web)	A way to organize information on the Internet. A user may access a *site*, which is a collection of pages put together by an individual or organization, using a computer program called a *browser*. Most sites are coded to provide links to other pages of interest.

model). For the economic model, efficiency is viewed as a higher value, while those oriented toward the second category are much more interested in promoting democracy and building relationships. The Internet is a useful tool in both instances, but the desired ends obviously are quite different. In advocating for a return by nonprofits to their voluntary roots, the authors cite the examples of three groups that each have, in addition to their formal structures, a cyber-organization developed and run by volunteers that is much more than a Web site to promote fund-raising on behalf of the cause: "The interactions themselves become valuable for the sense of solidarity they engender, the sense of mutual obligation that pushes people to contribute to the attainment of purposive goals, and the information sharing they facilitate" (Brainard & Siplon, 2004, p. 449).

The one constant is that technology and its applications continue to evolve, so we might speculate on what lies ahead for nonprofit organizations in this regard. On a practical level, management information systems may be retooled as knowledge management systems (KMSs) that have the capacity to be much more than excellent data accumulators and can actually bring together the collective intelligence of an entire organization. The next logical step is to expand beyond the boundaries of a single agency to create networks of providers engaged in mutual problem solving through virtual intelligent collaboratives (Schoech, Fitch, MacFadden, & Schkade, 2002). The citizen cyber-organization already exists but has yet to have wide currency; the virtual intelligent collaborative is a concept still to be realized. Although separate in their intent, these ideas share the common bond of improving communication through the wiser use of technology.

Discussion Questions for Section 3

Chapter 8

1. In light of the ever-changing external environment, what adjustments would you make in the basic approach to strategic planning to keep it relevant? Why?

2. What are the strengths and weaknesses of YSN's strategic plan (as presented in the appendix to chapter 8)?

3. Which of the models introduced in chapter 8 was most likely used to develop this plan? Given what you now know about the organization, would one of the other models have been more appropriate? Justify your opinion.

Chapter 9

4. What are the pluses in using a logic model for program development? What are the minuses?

5. Of the four perspectives on need (normative, relative, perceived, expressed), which might present the greatest challenge in data collection and analysis? Why?

6. How does benchmarking contribute to improving organizational performance?

7. Why has outcomes measurement become the preferred approach in evaluation for United Way and many other funders? Conversely, why are many nonprofits less enthusiastic about this approach?

Chapter 10

8. Seiler (2003b) notes that "effective fund raising depends on effective planning and rigorous execution—actually more planning than execution" (p. 23). Do you agree or disagree, and why?

9. What are some of the arguments for and against the trend in nonprofits toward greater commercialization?

10. Since diversification of funding sources seems so logical, why do some nonprofits still resist going in this direction? How would you overcome this resistance?

11. If you had to choose between starting a direct mail effort and introducing a new special event for the annual fund drive, which would you select? Justify your decision.

Chapter 11

12. Why is it important for a nonprofit CEO to know the basics about financial management?
13. What is the budget's role in organizational planning?
14. Is it more critical today for a nonprofit to live within its budget or to continuously seek new and better ways to meet client needs? On what do you base your response?
15. Why is it more difficult to measure organizational effectiveness in a nonprofit than a for-profit?

Chapter 12

16. The underutilization of information and communication technologies (ICTs) in nonprofits is a concern. What are the major barriers to effective use? What are some specific issues impacting technology use in human service organizations?
17. How does each of the four identified dimensions of communication (content, noise, network, and direction) figure into promoting effective exchanges in nonprofit organizations? What is the role of the leader in improving communication in the organization as well as externally across organizations?
18. Technology has had a major influence on the nonprofit workplace. In what ways have ICTs improved the quality of work life? How have they changed the dynamics in less positive ways?
19. Of the different current external applications of technology discussed in chapter 12, which ones are likely to have staying power in the future? On what do you base your opinion?

SELECTED READINGS FOR SECTION 3

Chapter 8

Bryson, J. M. (1995). *Strategic planning for public and nonprofit organizations: A guide to strengthening and sustaining organizational achievement* (Rev. ed). San Francisco: Jossey-Bass.

Emery, M., & Purser, R. E. (1996). *The search conference*. San Francisco: Jossey-Bass.

Golensky, M., & Walker, M. (2003). Organizational change: Too much, too soon? *Journal of Community Practice, 11*(2), 67–82.

Kluger, M. P., Baker, W. A., & Garval, H. S. (1998). *Strategic business planning: Securing a future for the nonprofit organization*. Washington, DC: Child Welfare League of America Press.

Wolf, T. (1999). *Managing a nonprofit organization in the twenty-first century* (Rev. ed.). New York: Simon & Schuster.

Chapter 9

Ginsberg, L. H. (2001). *Social work evaluation: Principles and methods.* Boston: Allyn & Bacon.

Kellogg, W. K., Foundation. (2004). *Logic model development guide.* Battle Creek, MI: Author.

Kettner, P. M., Moroney, R. M., & Martin, L. L. (2008). *Designing and managing programs: An effectiveness-based approach* (3rd ed.). Thousand Oaks, CA: Sage.

Lackey, J. F. (2006). *Accountability in social services: The culture of the paper program.* New York: Haworth.

Unrau, Y. A., Gabor, P. A., & Grinnell, R. M., Jr. (2001). *Evaluation in the human services.* Itasca, IL: Peacock.

Chapter 10

Benefield, E. A. S., & Edwards, R. L. (2006). Developing a sustainable fundraising program. In R. L. Edwards & J. A. Yankey (Eds.), *Effectively managing nonprofit organizations* (Rev. ed., pp. 61–82). Washington, DC: NASW Press.

Greenfield, J. M. (1999). *Fund raising: Evaluating and managing the fund development process* (2nd ed.). New York: Wiley.

Hall, M. S., & Howlett, S. (2003). *Getting funded: The complete guide to writing grant proposals* (4th ed.). Portland, OR: Portland State University, External Studies.

Massarsky, C. W. (1994). Enterprise strategies for generating revenue. In R. D. Herman (Ed.), *The Jossey-Bass handbook of nonprofit leadership and management* (pp. 382–402). San Francisco: Jossey-Bass.

Schervish, P. G. (2006). The moral biography of wealth: Philosophical reflections on the foundation of philanthropy. *Nonprofit and Voluntary Sector Quarterly, 35,* 477–492.

Seiler, T. L. (2003b). Plan to succeed. In H. A. Rosso and associates & E. R. Tempel (Eds.), *Hank Rosso's achieving excellence in fund raising* (2nd ed., pp. 23–29). San Francisco: Jossey-Bass.

Chapter 11

Herman, R. D., & Renz, D. O. (2008). Advancing nonprofit organizational effectiveness research and theory: Nine theses. *Nonprofit Management and Leadership, 18,* 399–415.

Lebold, D. A., & Edwards, R. L. (2006). Managing financial uncertainty. In R. L. Edwards & J. A. Yankey (Eds.), *Effectively managing nonprofit organizations* (Rev. ed., pp. 431–456). Washington, DC: NASW Press.

Martin, L. L. (2001). *Financial management for human service administrators.* Boston: Allyn & Bacon.

Moore, S. T. (1995). Efficiency in social work practice and administration. *Social Work, 40,* 602–608.

Thomas, M. S. (2006). Managing the finances of nonprofit organizations. In R. L. Edwards & J. A. Yankey (Eds.), *Effectively managing nonprofit organizations* (Rev. ed., pp. 255–274). Washington, DC: NASW Press.

Wolf, T. (1999). *Managing a nonprofit organization in the twenty-first century* (Rev. ed.). New York: Simon & Schuster.

Chapter 12

Austin, M. J. (2002). Managing out: The community practice dimensions of effective agency management. *Journal of Community Practice, 10*(4), 33–48.

Fitch, D. (2007). Designing information systems around decision making. In M. Cortes & K. M. Rafter (Eds.), *Nonprofits and technology: Emerging research for usable knowledge* (pp. 135–147). Chicago: Lyceum.

Manzo, P., & Pitkin, B. (2007). Barriers to information technology usage in the nonprofit sector. In M. Cortes & K. M. Rafter (Eds.), *Nonprofits and technology: Emerging research for usable knowledge* (pp. 51–67). Chicago: Lyceum.

Saidel, J. R., & Cour, S. (2003). IT and the voluntary sector workplace. *Nonprofit and Voluntary Sector Quarterly, 32*, 5–24.

Zimmerman, L. I., & Broughton, A. (2006). Assessing, planning, and managing information technology. In R. L. Edwards & J. A. Yankey (Eds.), *Effectively managing nonprofit organizations* (Rev. ed., pp. 255–274). Washington, DC: NASW Press.

SECTION 4
Maximizing Human Resources

To complement the information on securing material resources presented in the previous section, we now turn to the human side of the equation. One of the common observations about the nonprofit sector is that most of the programs and services offered by voluntary organizations are initiated and delivered through the efforts of individuals, paid staff and volunteers, working separately or together to address consumer needs. Accordingly, such organizations are described as "labor-intensive." The main challenges in this arena are to establish and maintain high standards of performance, to motivate and build cohesiveness, and to foster loyalty and commitment. (The third part of the featured case study is included here as a reference point for chapters 13–16.)

Chapter 13 returns to the topic of leadership, but with a focus on the leader as the moral and ethical compass of the organization. This entails a dual responsibility to set a personal example of values-based conduct and to protect the organization against internal and external risks that might compromise its good name.

Chapter 14 explores the policies and procedures that must be put in place and enforced to create a dedicated, effective, and productive workforce, with special attention to issues related to diversity. Human resources management encompasses all of the activities pertaining to paid staff and their work environment.

Chapter 15 covers the practical side of nonprofit board governance, from recruitment through self-assessment. Understanding the value of this organizational resource justifies the time and effort necessary to develop and nurture a board that is fully capable of assuming its rightful leadership role.

Chapter 16 provides a detailed account of the process for introducing and maintaining a high-quality volunteer program. Recognition is given to the different types of volunteerism as well as to the wide range of individuals drawn to assisting nonprofits in carrying out programs and services.

KEY THEMES

Chapters 13 to 16 address the following topics and concerns.

- The ethical dimensions of leadership: What are the professional leader's responsibilities in promoting a values-based organization?

- The human relations side of nonprofit organizational life: What policies and practices need to be in place to build and retain a competent, dedicated workforce?
- The effective nonprofit board: How should a governing board be structured and sustained to ensure high-level performance?
- The organizational value of a dedicated corps of program volunteers: What are the essential elements of a strong volunteer program?

Conflicting Agendas for the Future of a Youth Agency, Part 3
The Board President's Perspective

Sal de Marco could not remember a period in his life that he was not connected with YSN. He was only five when his father died and Uncle Lou stepped in as the man of the family. Since his uncle was director of programs for YSN, young Sal was enrolled at camp during the summer and busy at the community center the rest of the year. He was still close with several boys—men—who had participated with him in these activities.

There were many good times in those early years. De Marco remembered the excitement of taking part in the citywide track meets sponsored by YSN and then seeing his picture in the paper the next day for anchoring the winning team in the relay race, his specialty. And he loved camp. Getting out of the hot city for the summer, swimming in the lake, and watching the Indian ceremony where Uncle Lou played the chief were wonderful memories.

Yet de Marco also associated one of his worst experiences with YSN. When YSN's founder, Trevor Clinton, announced his plans to retire, Uncle Lou confided to the then-teenage de Marco that he wanted the job and submitted his letter of interest. Shortly afterward, de Marco came home from school to find his uncle in the living room, crying. Clinton had sent a memo to the YSN staff stating that the associate director of the agency would succeed him; Uncle Lou was never even interviewed for the position. De Marco considered this a great injustice, for the associate director, in his opinion, did not match his uncle's skills.

Although Uncle Lou remained with YSN until he retired some years later, de Marco resented what had happened. He turned his attention more and more to his studies, and ultimately became a banker, an accomplishment that his uncle did not live to see. De Marco's main connection to the organization at this point was small gifts in response to direct mail appeals. It was thus a surprise when the third executive director, who had followed Clinton's hand-picked successor, reached out and invited him to join the YSN board. With mixed feelings, de Marco agreed.

Old habits die hard. De Marco discovered his belief in the importance of the agency's work was still strong. Furthermore, he felt he had something to prove to the other trustees, although he was never quite sure what that was. As YSN neared the milestone of its sixtieth birthday, the nominating committee decided it would be fitting to name a former program participant to be board president, and de Marco was selected. He wished that Uncle Lou could have been there to see his nephew receive this honor.

In the time since Margaret Stover had been hired, de Marco had not had much contact with her outside of board meetings. Overall he was pleased with her performance, although he had hoped she would have achieved more success in reviving the direct mail program by now. One quirk of hers did bother him, though: Stover always seemed to be waiting for the board to show overt approval of her actions and had difficulty hiding her disappointment when the trustees failed to acknowledge her efforts to her satisfaction. For example, when Stover announced to the board that she had obtained a government grant of $75,000 a year for the next two years, she obviously felt it was a major achievement. True, it was the first federal grant YSN had ever received, but the amount was chicken feed compared to what the direct mail program generated. In the best years, direct mail had raised close to $800,000 annually, and even now it brought in over $400,000. When there was little reaction from the board, Stover looked crestfallen. De Marco took this show of emotion as a sign of weakness; he'd never let his board at the bank see his feelings so openly.

After becoming board president, de Marco discovered that Stover expected to have frequent meetings with him to discuss agency business, as she had done with his predecessor, Ben Shank. She didn't seem to realize that he couldn't be as free with his time as Shank, who owned his own company and could come and go as he pleased. In the spirit of compromise, de Marco agreed to monthly meetings if Stover would drive to the bank early in the day so that his schedule was not disrupted. Yet these needs of Stover's were minor irritants. She had been his choice for executive, and he still felt she brought many strengths to the organization. Therefore, when she suggested the idea of strategic planning, he saw no reason not to go along with her or to question the process once it began, as long as it would not make additional demands on him.

Upon receiving the Strategic Planning Committee's report, however, he wondered whether he should have been more directly involved in the effort. Some of the recommendations were fine, such as trying to integrate the programs and involve the kids on a year-round basis. That arrangement had worked well for him, certainly. On the other hand, he had trouble with the heavier emphasis on the community-based programs at the center. Even though camping was discussed, it appeared to him that the program was of secondary concern. Moreover, the plan's suggestion of combining schoolwork with camp activities had no appeal to him at all—camping was about having fun!

Being a fiscal conservative, de Marco also had trouble with the concept of dipping into the reserves in the hope of realizing future gains. This seemed to him a dangerous step to take because the implication was that if YSN could not identify and secure new monies, the organization might not survive. Perhaps to Stover, whose history with the agency amounted to only a couple of years, it was sensible to consider such a possibility, but de Marco knew that for himself and the majority of the board members with long-standing ties to YSN, no plan implying the end of the organization could be taken seriously.

Recognizing he would not be able to support the committee's report, de Marco dialed the YSN number to inform Stover he would be making a statement at the board meeting advising that no sweeping changes be introduced at this time. Really, he didn't think the organization's problems were so great; more direct mail revenue would resolve a lot of the present concerns. Maybe they could develop the center programs along the lines suggested in the report, but camp should keep its traditions. As he well knew, a two-week stay was long enough to provide memories for a small child that would last forever. His message to the board would be that the winning formula of the past was just as viable today. Tampering with the basic structure of YSN was not a direction he could endorse.

Presentation of the Strategic Plan

After a night of tossing and turning, Stover made her way to the office on the day of the board meeting, still perplexed by de Marco's reaction to the proposed strategic plan. Unfortunately, she was still no clearer than she had been the night before about the best course of action to take. After drinking two cups of strong coffee, she sat down at her desk to think through her options, knowing that, as is often the case in such situations, no solution would be perfect.

One possibility would be to contact the chair of the Strategic Planning Committee, Joan Ardway, to talk about the board president's concerns and how that might affect the discussion on the plan at the meeting and the full board's decision regarding it. This would prevent Joan from being taken by surprise when de Marco made his statement against the plan and allow for some strategizing in advance by the committee members to respond to his objections. However, Stover feared Ardway would take de Marco's position too personally, as an attack against her work as chair of the committee, and give in to her tendency to get very defensive when she felt she was being criticized. At such times, Ardway seemed to lose her ability to present an effective and logical case to support her views and even was known to become overtly emotional, which was somewhat surprising given that she was a first-rate systems analyst for a major corporation and had a well-deserved reputation in her field for her ability to handle complex situations.

If Ardway lost control, this would play right into de Marco's hands, whose rather condescending opinion that most women were not constitutionally suited for leadership had been voiced more than once to other board members, usually on social occasions after he had had a couple of drinks. In truth, Stover privately thought that with YSN's history, this kind of attitude toward women was probably shared by several of the male trustees. All in all, it might be best not to give Ardway too much time to think about a worst-case scenario. It was possible de Marco could change his mind and decide not to oppose the plan, and then Ardway would have been upset for nothing. Also, the committee as a whole had never showed anything but satisfaction with the results of their work; Stover felt certain they would back up the committee chair and not allow de Marco to bully her.

A second option was for Stover to take the lead in presenting the plan. Even though it had been a group effort from the start of the planning process, many of the issues addressed by the plan had been raised first by the executive director, and she had the best command of the facts underlying the various recommendations. Perhaps it was time to demonstrate to de Marco, and the rest of the board, that she was a forceful leader and dispel any doubts that she had been the right choice for her job. It was tempting to picture herself in this way, but fundamentally Stover believed it was necessary for the strategic plan to be embraced by the board through its own actions. If the board approved the plan simply to please her, she would be perpetuating the very tradition established by YSN's founder that she hoped the plan would begin to change. Stover remained convinced that the organization could not move forward and be competitive in today's environment without a strong board. All of her training and experience would be directed toward helping the board achieve this desired end once the plan was ratified.

For the same reason, Stover decided against calling board members who were not on the Strategic Planning Committee to lobby for the plan. She did not in any way want to suggest she did not have full confidence in the committee. Furthermore, making such calls could be tricky: if she did not mention de Marco's intention to oppose the plan, once this was revealed at the meeting, some board members might feel they had been manipulated and swing over to his side just on principle, and if she did bring up the board president's concerns, she might inadvertently plant seeds of doubt about the plan's merits.

Sometimes it was best just to let matters take their own course. After weighing the different options open to her, Stover decided to wait for the meeting and let the process play itself out. At bottom, she believed the strategic plan was sound, and most important, the members of the Strategic Planning Committee stood behind it 100 percent. She also believed that the board members cared a great deal about YSN and would see that the proposed plan was the right way to go. Turning to the pile of papers on her desk, Stover busied herself in her work and tried not to keep looking at her watch. Six o'clock would come soon enough.

Leadership by Example

Life is full of contradictions, unresolved problems, and seemingly uncontrollable circumstances. In uncertain times, we often look to our leaders to make sense of it all; think of President Roosevelt's fireside chats during the Great Depression and World War II. Organizational life is no different. Viewed within a symbolic frame, organizations resemble "complex, constantly changing, organic pinball machines" (Bolman & Deal, 1991, p. 245). Myths, rituals, ceremonies, and stories become vehicles through which meaning and order can be restored. In regard to the concept of organizational culture, further reflection suggests the artifacts, values, and deep-seated assumptions associated with any organization may be its most powerful symbols. To fully understand why group members perceive and react to situations as they do, it is necessary to identify the pattern that ties everything together in some kind of coherent whole (Schein, 1985).

One of the responsibilities of a leader most suited to interpretation from a symbolic perspective is how that individual establishes and enforces an ethical approach to practice. Many nonprofits provide services to highly vulnerable populations, to those with mental or physical illnesses or limited cognitive abilities, to those suffering from substance use disorders that cloud their judgment, to those too young or immature to be able to make critical decisions on their own and who lack appropriate adult supervision, and so on. Who is best placed to speak for those who cannot represent themselves? How do you reconcile client needs with managed care limitations on the amount of care? When important stakeholders disagree on the balance between effectiveness and efficiency, whose perspective deserves more consideration? In all of these and other similar circumstances, it is the top professional who must not only verbalize what is expected of organizational members but also act as the moral and ethical compass for that organization. In other words, inspirational rhetoric is not sufficient: "Leading by example is how leaders make visions and values tangible. . . . Actions, then, are the *evidence* of a leader's commitment" (Kouzes & Posner, 1995, pp. 210–211; emphasis added). If the CEO fails to live up to this obligation, as we have seen in some well-publicized scandals that have rocked the nonprofit world, the fallout for the organization in terms of staff, consumer, donor, and public disillusionment can last for many years.

To set the stage for the remaining chapters in section 4, we will explore a nonprofit leader's responsibility to create and sustain a values-based culture. First, we will review some basic ethical principles. Next, we will delineate the general parameters of an ethical culture as well as the particular expectations for faith-based organizations. Last, we will consider the steps a leader must take to protect the organization against threats from within and without that could negatively impact its reputation as a provider of high-quality services and its ability to secure necessary resources.

BASIC ETHICAL PRINCIPLES

Given the pressures for accountability and quantifiable outcomes placed on nonprofits today, it may seem almost quaint to focus on ethics, but in truth, it may be even more important now than in the past to reaffirm what is the essence of a voluntary organization, the values underlying and shaping its mission. This is the central attraction for the majority of those who seek to work and volunteer in this arena, and the more clearly we articulate this fundamental truth, the more closely we can align purpose and practice (Rothschild & Milofsky, 2006).

As defined in a standard dictionary, both *morals* and *ethics* refer to conforming to standards of right and wrong in behavior, but some observers suggest ethics may go farther in confronting more subtle issues or questions pertaining to rightness, fairness, and equity. Brueggemann (1996), for one, maintains morality is more about not breaking conventional rules and laws, whereas ethical behavior is driven by coming to terms with values that transcend time and place and can be applied to all societies. Thus, if people wish to act morally and ethically, they must try to practice core values such as justice and righteousness in their personal and professional lives and also work to institutionalize them in society at large.

Two primary ethical theories have evolved that look at doing the right thing in very different ways (see table 13.1). According to *deontological theory*, the emphasis is on the means to achieving a particular good; it holds that actions are fundamentally right or wrong based on universal laws, regardless of the consequences and the situation in question. The Golden Rule (do unto others as you would have them do unto you) is a good illustration. On the other hand, *teleological* or *consequentialist theory* focuses on the ends. A particular course of action is chosen because it is likely to lead to the desired results, and under the doctrine of utilitarianism, the right action is the one producing the greatest good for the greatest number of people, or put another way, more benefit than harm for those affected, based on some measurable standards (for example, instituting cost-effective practices derived from economic criteria). However, both theories present some obvious difficulties as a guide to effective decision-making. Deontology deals in absolutes, to be applied in all circumstances, but in the real world, things are not always so clear-cut. With the utilitarian approach, some desirable outcomes (the quality of life, for instance) cannot be measured objectively. In addition, it is possible to justify inappropriate or even immoral actions undertaken to achieve a positive end (Manning, 2003; Rothman, 2005).

An egregious example of disregard for basic ethical principles is the Tuskegee Experiment, in which poor African American males were recruited for a study on the effects of syphilis, conducted by the U.S. Public Health Service (PHS). The participants

Table 13.1 Ethical theories and related concepts

Theory	*Concepts*[a]
Deontological theory: Emphasis on the means; actions are fundamentally right or wrong.	*Religious texts*: E.g., the Ten Commandments, the Golden Rule.
	Natural laws: E.g., categorical imperatives or moral obligations that are unconditional and universal in their application (Kant, 1963).
	Social contract: E.g., a real or hypothetical agreement among people defining and limiting rights and duties binding on all members (Rawls, 1971).
	Common sense: E.g., self-evident obligations guide actions unless there are other over-riding moral issues (Ross, 1930).
Teleological theory: Emphasis on the ends; actions serve a desired purpose	*Utilitarianism*: E.g., the moral worth of an action is to achieve the greatest good for the greatest number or more benefit than harm for those affected (Bentham, 1961; Mill, 1861/1998).
	Applied ethics: E.g., one's own interests cannot count for more than the interests of others; do what has the best consequences for those affected by the action (Singer, 1993).
	Pragmatism: E.g., values are considered hypotheses about what actions will bring satisfactory results (Dewey, 1929; James, 1907).

Sources: Adapted from Manning, 2003; Rothman, 2005.

[a]The concepts identified here represent a selection of the ideas that have been derived from the two major ethical theories. The cited authors are some of the more prominent thinkers associated with the concepts.

received free food, transportation, and medical examinations but were not told they had syphilis and were not treated for the disease. Tuskegee University, a historically black institution, then known as Tuskegee Institute, was enlisted by PHS to encourage local African Americans to take part in the study and received in return money, training for its interns, and employment for its nurses. The agency also sought help from black church leaders, community leaders, and plantation owners. The project was finally stopped in

1972, over forty years after it was initiated, due to the efforts of a whistle-blower working for PHS. Following congressional hearings, the regulations governing the use of human subjects in publicly funded projects were rewritten, and a class-action lawsuit was filed in U.S. district court on behalf of the study subjects, resulting in a $10 million out-of-court settlement by the U.S. government (Tuskegee University, n.d.)

Prudent leaders wishing to demonstrate ethical behavior through their actions must exercise great care to explore both means and ends, with the hope of finding just the right way to obtain the desired goal. This requires weighing the practicalities of expending precious resources to achieve a particular end versus other opportunities that will not be pursued. Politics also enters into the equation, as leaders have many forms of influence at their disposal, from persuasion to coercion. Choosing an ill-advised means, such as placing undue pressure on key stakeholders, may lead to attaining the identified goal but at a high cost in regard to ongoing relationships (Manning, 2003). The CEO of a small youth agency discovered this when he forced staff members to contribute to a pet cause of dubious reputation and word of his actions reached the board. The executive was dismissed because the board felt his credibility with staff had been irreparably harmed, and his behavior raised serious questions about his professional judgment.

As a final consideration, Rothman (2005) notes that while ethical theories provide a conceptual structure for examining issues, they are often too general in their orientation to be very helpful in providing direction for everyday decision-making. Thus, it becomes necessary to derive principles from these theories that can be operationalized as guidelines for practice to ensure some kind of consistency and equity in carrying out the organization's work, such as might be found in a professional code of ethics.

PROVIDING ETHICAL AND MORAL LEADERSHIP

In their efforts to be competitive, by adopting certain businesslike practices and conforming to the external expectations of funders and regulatory agencies, too many nonprofit organizations, especially the larger, more bureaucratic ones, seem to have forgotten their origins and strayed from their core. However, it is this very essence that distinguishes nonprofits from their counterparts in the public and for-profit sectors (Rothschild & Milofsky, 2006). Although volunteers, whether at the policy or programmatic level, can and should play a key role in refocusing nonprofits on values and ethics, it often falls to the top professional to show the way, keeping in mind that for many organizational members, the journey is as important as the destination. Accordingly, to establish an ethical climate, which is fundamentally a psychological construct, leaders need to be very aware of how decisions are made and of their general behavior (Malloy & Agarwal, 2001).

Creating a Values-Based Organizational Culture

To ensure that ethical ideas and expectations go beyond the surface, a leader has to create an organizational culture in which these principles become deep-seated assumptions for all group members (Jeavons, 1994). The top executive must first model the key values and then establish the mechanisms essential to translating the values into practice, along with the rewards to reinforce the desired behaviors.

Taking into account both moral obligations and social or community standards, Jeavons (1994) identified five essential ethical attributes of nonprofit leaders and the organizations in which they function that are consistent with expectations placed on the voluntary sector to serve the public good.

- *Integrity*, which speaks to the "continuity between appearance and reality, between intention and action, between promise and performance" (p. 192) in all aspects of individual and organizational existence.
- *Openness*, often called *transparency* today, about what the organization does and how it generates support for its endeavors as well as the rationale behind these decisions in order to build trust.
- *Accountability* to all the different stakeholder groups associated with the organization for the manner in which resources are used and receptivity to constructive feedback on improving these processes.
- *Service*, as the fulfillment of the purpose for which the organization was established and in recognition of the tax benefits enjoyed through nonprofit status.
- *"Charity,"* as rooted in a sense of caring about the well-being of others, beginning with the interactions between top management and staff and the CEO and the board, as a reflection of the generosity of everyone who supports the organization and as a means of transmitting societal values from this generation to the next.

Assuming there is agreement that the five values just described represent the ethical obligations that ought to guide the ways in which nonprofits and their leaders operate, the practical question remains how to move from an ideal state to everyday practice. Schön (1983) coined the term *reflective practitioner* to describe a professional who develops the capacity to face the complexities of modern society by applying previous experience to new situations as they occur, which often requires reconfiguring the knowledge drawn from the past in the moment to address a current problem, rather than analyzing the issue after the fact to gain a better understanding of it. In today's turbulent world with all of its conflicting demands, CEOs who can think on their feet are going to be better equipped to help organizational members deal effectively with ethical concerns. Table 13.2 illustrates how a reflective practitioner might apply the core values described above to both common organizational activities and unexpected developments.

Some professions, such as social work, have a very well-defined code of ethics that provides a strong foundation for creating a values-based organizational culture, but the top executive must still take responsibility for ensuring that group members remain true

Table 13.2 Ethics in practice

Core value	Applications[a]
Integrity	A standing board committee meets at least three times a year to review programs and services for compatibility with the expressed organizational mission.
	The executive director informed the board of a staff member investigated by Child Protective Services for alleged inappropriate behavior toward a client. Although no proof was found, the agency developed a remedial retraining plan for the worker as a preventative measure.
Openness or transparency	The organization routinely reports on how monies obtained through government contracts and individual gifts, its main financial sources, are used to fulfill its mission.
	The organization participates with other groups and has its own campaign to educate external stakeholders about the need for more resources to address child abuse.
Accountability	The board annually evaluates the executive's job performance; he reports monthly on key issues at board meetings and meets weekly with the board president.
	The organization voluntarily sought, and was granted, accreditation through the Council on Accreditation of Services for Families and Children.
Service	The organization has adjusted its programs in recognition of the declining age of its clients.
	The organization is an active member of a local consortium whose aim is to develop a cost-effective college program for direct-care workers to improve hiring standards and retention.
"Charity"	Senior managers maintain an open-door policy so that line staff can bring suggestions for changes in agency practices and clients can raise their concerns; there are weekly unit meetings, case conferences, and administrative staff meetings.
	The executive has identified a group of clients with severe family problems (e.g., drug abuse) that present barriers to reunification as "functional orphans" in order to bring this issue to the surface.

Sources: Adapted from Jeavons, 1994; Schön, 1983.
[a]The applications represent actual occurrences in a nonprofit providing residential care to children and youth unable to live at home.

to the core values in all interpersonal dealings both within and outside of the organization. It starts by the CEO showing the way through actions that are consistent with being a person of high moral character: "The challenge is to be a light, not a judge; to be a model, not a critic" (Covey, 1991, p. 25).

Servant-Leadership

The obligation to serve as the moral and ethical compass of the organization is perhaps most fully embodied in Robert Greenleaf's concept of *servant-leadership*, a model that places serving employees, consumers, and community, which is synonymous with society at large and encompasses the other major stakeholders to whom the organization is accountable, as the number-one priority of a true leader. In 1964 Greenleaf founded the Center for Applied Ethics (now headquartered in Indianapolis, Indiana, and renamed the Robert K. Greenleaf Center for Servant-Leadership in his honor). Ever the pragmatist, Greenleaf summed up his approach in one fundamental question: "How do we get the right things done?" Out of the founder's writings, the center's current CEO, Larry C. Spears (2002), has identified ten characteristics that capture the essence of this type of leader.

1. *Listening.* The servant-leader attempts to capture and refine the will of the group by paying close attention to what others say as well as practicing self-reflection on a regular basis.

2. *Empathy.* The servant-leader recognizes and is sensitive to what is unique in others by understanding group members' and consumers' expectations.

3. *Healing.* The servant-leader embraces the spiritual side of organizational life by responding to problems and crises in a caring manner.

4. *Awareness.* The servant-leader makes a concerted effort to stay in touch with what is going on with others as well as with the inner self.

5. *Persuasion.* The servant-leader relies on convincing arguments and dialogue rather than coercion to build consensus among group members.

6. *Conceptualization.* The servant-leader is able to think beyond present needs and provide a longer-term vision for the organization.

7. *Foresight.* The servant-leader seems to have an innate ability to anticipate the likely consequences of a decision for the future.

8. *Stewardship.* The servant-leader acts responsibly for the greater good of society in fulfilling the organizational mission.

9. *Commitment to the growth of people.* The servant-leader is dedicated to nurturing the personal, professional, and spiritual development of group members.

10. *Building community.* The servant-leader strives to promote social capital, or a sense of connectedness, within the organization so that group members can in turn be socially responsible to the community at large.

Young (2002) describes foresight as a critical element "in helping the organization move from a survival outlook, reacting to the immediate events, to being proactive, moving with an incremental plan" (p. 245). It is a quality most likely to develop over time as the leader gains an almost intuitive understanding of the patterns of organizational life. Having foresight means being able to anticipate the opportunities that the future may offer by drawing on the past, to grasp the meaning of events that may seem obscure to others, and to articulate a vision for the organization in a way that enables group members to willingly embrace change. The final step is to translate vision into action through a creative, measurable plan. Thus, foresight, which is really an ongoing process, can be viewed as the central ethic of servant-leadership.

Managing Faith-Based Organizations

Kosher products, such as the meats produced by Hebrew National, a part of ConAgra Foods, Inc., are made according to Jewish dietary laws. For many people, buying kosher has nothing to do with religion but instead reflects a perception that such food is of higher quality and more healthful (Severson, 2010). *Branding* is the process used by companies like Hebrew National to position their products and services as having characteristics consumers consider special. Similarly, faith-based nonprofits represent a specific brand or kind of organization, one often held to especially stringent standards. Historically, organizations operating under the auspices of a particular religious denomination played a significant role in the development of social services in the United States and were among the earliest to serve the needs of the poor (Gibelman, 2003). Although many of these organizations now rank among the largest nonprofits here and abroad, a substantial number continue to operate with modest budgets and limited staff who believe their rewards come mainly from doing God's work.

These traditions of selflessness factored into the Bush administration's much-discussed Faith-Based Initiative, which was intended to level the playing field in competing for federal funds and increase the involvement of religious groups in a broad range of social services. Unfortunately, implementation of the plan was hampered from its inception by fears that it was really a way to promote a conservative political agenda and by concerns over maintaining the separation of church and state, exacerbated by the administration's decision that organizations receiving government support could use faith as a hiring criterion. In the early days of the Obama administration, officials signaled an intention to revisit the initiative.

A fairly widespread view of faith-based organizations is that they are "hubs of trust and islands of peace and support within their communities," providing concrete services as well as spiritual and moral guidance and a unifying presence (Cnaan, Sinha, & McGrew, 2004, p. 57). However, an unanswered question is whether it is fair to expect more ethically of these organizations than of secular groups. Certainly, a misstep by this type of nonprofit engenders a high level of anguish and recrimination, as was evident in the scandal involving the American Bible Society (ABS) in the spring and summer of 2008. After it came to light that the CEO had paid over $5 million to improve the organization's Internet presence to a consultant with ties to online pornography and gambling, the board initially suspended the executive and subsequently decided not to renew his contract. Perhaps the reaction was so negative because of the allegations of poor management at ABS over the past decade. As one person commented, "The people who are sitting in high positions in the religious world must be extra cautious about their call and responsibilities" (Kwon, 2008). However, the reality is that leaders of faith-based organizations appear to be susceptible to the same temptations to engage in managerial and financial wrongdoing as are leaders of secular groups, suggesting accountability measures need to be in place and enforced for all nonprofits but particularly for those funded by public dollars, regardless of auspices (Gibelman & Gelman, 2002).

The other critical issue pertains to the capacity of faith-based organizations to provide high-quality services. As noted above, many have limited budgets and staffing. In addition, religious values often dictate how services are delivered even when there are policies against outright proselytizing. For instance, in the area of reproductive health care, clients seeking help from an organization like the Salvation Army may not receive an appropriate assessment of their needs or be fully informed about their options. For social workers and other professionals guided by a clear code of ethics, this can present a real dilemma and conflict of values, especially for those staff members who do not adhere to the same religious doctrine as their employing agency. Faith can also have more practical ramifications. For example, Jewish organizations often are closed on major religious holidays celebrated by that denomination but do not officially recognize Christmas and Easter, putting them at odds with the more standard community calendar. In practice this may not present an obstacle, because clients tend to select a provider based on the availability of specific programs, and as long as these are offered when needed, the clients may be unaware of decisions not directly affecting them (Lewis, 2003).

Despite the challenges, it is likely that religious groups will continue to play a major role in the social services in partnership with the public sector and, just as they have for decades, will find ways to accommodate their religious principles with more secular values to achieve mutual benefit. In fact, it is because the leaders of faith-based organizations believe their work is part of God's purpose that they are comfortable doing what they must to further the organizational mission. Evidence points to finding common ground around issues of openness, inclusiveness, and the promotion of broader social and community obligations, such as seeking justice for the poor through working to change local neighborhoods and institutions (Campbell, 2002; Vanderwoerd, 2004).

RISK MANAGEMENT

The management of risk through the exercise of judicious monitoring and coordination technically falls within the internal-control quadrant of the competing values model described earlier in this text (see table 5.3), but with the ever-increasing emphasis on accountability, its importance is felt throughout the organization. We live in litigious times, and "as nonprofit organizations come of age, they find that maturity involves new risks and responsibilities" (Kurzman, 2006, p. 276). While true of all types of nonprofits, there may be a disproportionate burden on human service organizations (HSOs), particularly those serving vulnerable populations. For example, any entity involved in health care that transmits data in electronic form, such as health plans, clearinghouses, and direct providers, must comply with the provisions of the Health Insurance Portability and Accountability Act (HIPAA), as originally enacted in 1996 and modified in 2002, which is designed to protect the privacy of individuals' health information while permitting the flow of information needed to ensure high-quality care and protecting the public's health and well-being. HIPAA violations can have serious consequences in the form of monetary penalties and even prison for certain acts of noncompliance.

An Overview

Just as leaders are expected to set an example and create a climate for ethical practice, they also have the responsibility to take appropriate steps when the organization is at risk. *Risk* is defined as anything that could compromise the organization's ability to carry out its mission by endangering one or more of the organization's primary assets: people, including consumers, staff, policy and program volunteers, and the general public; physical and intellectual property (for example, buildings and original materials); donative and earned income (for example, grants and fees for service); and goodwill, as reflected in the organization's stature and reputation in the community (Alliance for Nonprofit Management, 2003–2004).

To address risk proactively, organizational leaders should review current insurance policies on a regular basis and make adjustments to the coverage as seem warranted. Suggested types of coverage include premises liability insurance for all areas where services are provided and staff are based; professional liability insurance for the activities of all staff, volunteers, and consultants carried out on behalf of the organization; directors and officers liability insurance, as discussed in chapter 4; vehicular insurance, at a level higher than the mandated state minimum; and bonding for anyone with authority to sign contracts or handle organizational finances. Every nonprofit should also have access to legal counsel to advise on matters such as reviewing leases, signing contracts, entering into formal agreements with others, and modifying the organization's bylaws (Kurzman, 2006). In addition, establishing a positive working relationship with the accounting firm that prepares the annual audit can ensure that internal fiscal policies and practices are in keeping with current standards for nonprofits. However, some types of risk are not insurable, such as the loss of public support, and therefore prevention is the wisest course of action, with the first priority being to avoid doing harm to any of the people associated with the organization.

Establishing a Risk Management Program

Managing risk entails systematically identifying the operational areas in which the potential for a threat to the organization is relatively high, determining the likelihood of the occurrence of these threats, and then taking necessary action to prevent the problem from happening or, for unanticipated situations that arise, to mitigate any negative consequences. The size of the organization may affect how the process is carried out, with larger nonprofits perhaps having a separate risk management department while smaller entities might rely on a committee of staff and volunteers (Alliance for Nonprofit Management, 2003–2004).

Tremper (1994) recommends writing down all of the possible risks that come to mind and then using checklists available from various sources, including insurers and accrediting bodies. To cover less obvious threats, there should be an examination of all procedures manuals for legal compliance, a review of safety records over the past year, a physical inspection of the premises to look for hazards, and a comparison of job requirements with the actual skills and judgment of staff. Although some risks are generic, such as a client slipping and falling on a wet floor, others are more site-specific: the issues of concern for a nonprofit providing residential care would be very different from those at an agency whose main service is information and referral, and so on. The next step would be to assess the probability of each identified risk becoming a reality and attaching the likely cost; risks can then be prioritized based on the frequency and severity of the threat. Finally, a decision must be reached on the actions to be taken, which could include eliminating the activity, modifying it to reduce the risk to an acceptable level, accepting the risk because there is no good alternative, or shifting some of the risk, at least the financial aspect, through insurance or contracting with another provider.

Ethical Considerations

The actions of employees are a major source of risk for nonprofits, both as a result of interactions with consumers that result in dissatisfaction or worse and as litigants against the organization due to issues related to compensation, promotion, and many other matters associated with human resources (HR) management. Furthermore, as will be discussed more fully below, nonprofits seem to be very susceptible to occupational fraud, which includes the misappropriation of the employing agency's assets by a staff member or the use of one's position for personal gain (Greenlee, Fischer, Gordon, & Keating, 2007).

Concerns Related to Staff Performance

According to Watkins and Watkins, "professionals are held to a higher standard of behavior in their professional capacities than that of the general population" (cited in Kurzman, 2006, p. 276). Unfortunately, the subject of ethics is not fully explored in most graduate education programs, especially the legal aspects, but organizations like the Association of Fundraising Professionals and the American Evaluation Association generally provide this kind of guidance for their members. The National Association of Social Workers (NASW, 1999) has developed a very comprehensive code of ethics identifying detailed standards of conduct in six different areas of responsibility: to clients, to colleagues, in practice settings, as professionals, to the profession, and to the broader society. However, although virtually all the issues a worker might encounter in everyday practice are addressed, many of the standards are aspirational rather than prescriptive, and some seem contradictory, which often leaves it to the individual to determine the most ethical action. For instance, in the first section of the code, promoting the well-being of clients is established as the primary responsibility, but it also states loyalty to the client may be superseded under special circumstances, such as when the worker becomes aware the client is abusing a child and is then required by law to report this information. Maintaining client confidentiality is another strong belief, except when there are compelling reasons not to comply (for example, if the client makes a credible threat to harm himself or another person), and so on.

Obviously, even with a broad professional code, there are opportunities for wrong interpretations and simple mistakes in judgment that may lead to lawsuits by irate consumers or their families. This suggests nonprofit leaders should be more proactive in their communications with employees by putting in place site-specific internal procedures that provide clear guidance to staff, especially recent hires, regarding lines of accountability and performance expectations, without circumscribing individual decision-making to the degree that workers are reduced to mere automatons. Moreover, it is not just those dealing directly with clients who must be educated about legal obligations and possible areas of organizational vulnerability; supervisors and senior managers may be equally in need of direction on these subjects (Kurzman, 2006).

HR management is the focus of chapter 14, but it should be noted in this context that employee lawsuits over salaries, working conditions, opportunities for advancement, and so forth are another area of potential risk to the organization. Consequently, organizations must be conversant with all applicable laws and regulations and aware of current societal trends. They must then take the necessary steps to ensure that personnel policies are fair, up to date, and enforced uniformly, to avoid or at least discourage litigation but also to be in a stronger position to respond effectively to any charges of discrimination or harassment. Nevertheless, despite taking all possible precautions, a nonprofit may still fall victim to retaliation by a disgruntled staff member, as a regional child-care agency discovered. An employee who had injured herself as the result of allegedly slipping on ice in the agency's parking lot decided to sue for damages after being fired for poor performance unrelated to the accident. While it was obvious to the nonprofit's leaders that the suit was frivolous—no one had witnessed the accident and therefore it was only the litigant's word as to the circumstances of her fall—with legal fees mounting, the organization elected to come to a financial settlement with the former staffer.

Concerns Related to Fraud

The dictionary definition of *fraud* is "an act of deceiving or misrepresentin, intentional perversion of truth in order to induce another to part with something of value or to surrender a legal right." This definition captures the basic elements of fraud under common law, although it is worth emphasizing that the victim is disposed to accept the statement or the act at face value and responds accordingly, which suggests why occupational fraud is so easy to perpetrate in a nonprofit. If you think that most people electing to work for a voluntary organization do so because of a belief in its mission rather than for monetary reasons, then trust in the integrity of your colleagues is virtually a given, and the sense of personal violation is all the stronger when fraud does occur. Even though the organization itself may commit fraud through improper acts (for example, falsifying financial statements or miscoding services rendered in order to increase Medicare reimbursements), most of the cases of occupational fraud involve bad behavior by individual employees, motivated either by external circumstances, such as financial problems at home, or by internal factors such as a real or perceived experience of having been treated unfairly on the job (Greenlee et al., 2007; Holtfreter, 2008), as illustrated in the following actual cases.

- The chief financial officer of a statewide nonprofit, believing herself to have been denied a deserved raise, decided to take the increase anyway by giving the CEO supporting documents when checks were signed to make it appear a dormant account originally set up to encourage staff to continue their education was still active. Her duplicity came to light after she had taken a similar position elsewhere, during the annual audit. Although the CEO felt the new employer should be made aware of the theft, the board president decided that because the total amount taken was under $1,000, he would handle the matter discreetly by making arrangements directly with the former staff member to repay the money.

- After resigning as top executive of a national organization, the CEO admitted to having embezzled more than $870,000 from the charity during the previous decade due to resentment over perceived unfair treatment by the board in regard to his salary and benefits. He concealed the theft by intercepting donations to the charity and depositing them in bank accounts set up for his personal use. Former colleagues and key volunteers expressed shock and anger at this news. The ex-CEO was prosecuted for his crime, receiving a prison sentence; he was also required to make restitution to the charity. Yet he continued to blame the board for his actions.

The Ethics Audit

Weak internal controls, a lack of business and financial expertise, overreliance on poorly prepared volunteer boards, and the previously mentioned atmosphere of trust seem to be contributing causes of fraud. However, with scandals, big and small, occurring all too frequently, the general public is no longer as willing to accept the good intentions of nonprofits but now expects charitable organizations to demonstrate that appropriate systems and policies have been established to ensure that contributions and other resources are being prudently maintained, managed, and deployed (Greenlee et al., 2007).

Whereas annual financial audits are well established by now in the nonprofit sector, far fewer organizations make use of an equally useful mechanism, an ethics audit, "to review and assess the adequacy of current practices, modify . . . practices as needed, and monitor the implementation of these changes" (Reamer, 2000, p. 356). Two broad areas ought to be addressed: staff awareness of known risks related to practice and the manner in which ethical concerns are presently being handled within the organization. This kind of audit is applicable to any nonprofit, with a simple Internet search providing guidelines for creating a suitable instrument. For purposes of illustration, we will focus on the audit as is might be used in a social service agency; it was originally conceived for that purpose, drawing on the NASW code of ethics and common law as sources (see table 13.3).

Table 13.3 Conducting an ethics audit

Step	Pertinent questions
1. Committing to the process	What are the likely benefits to the organization?
	Is there a downside to pursuing an audit?
	What impact would an ethics audit have on our resources (people, time, money)?
2. Assigning oversight responsibility	Should the process be handled in-house or by an outside consultant? If in-house, who should be in charge?
	What are the pros and cons of forming a standing ethics committee?
3. Identifying areas of risk	What current practices constitute a potential threat to our organizational and professional values?
	Which of the available objective checklists and protocols should we use to ensure that we are not overlooking anything?
4. Developing the instrument	Which stakeholder groups should be involved to help produce the most effective instrument?
	What is the most efficient way to produce an appropriate instrument to meet our needs?
5. Collecting and analyzing data	What sources need to be tapped to collect all the relevant data?
	What is the fairest and most practical way to prioritize the potential risks as reflected in the data?
6. Using the findings	What is the best plan for making constructive improvements in agency policies and practices?
	What safeguards should be put in place to ensure that the plan is implemented in the most ethical manner?

Source: Adapted from Reamer, 2000.
Note: The findings of an ethics audit should be treated as a living document, as the first important step in an ongoing process.

Once an organization's leaders have made a commitment to initiating an ethics audit, the first step is to assign primary responsibility for overseeing the process. Depending on the size of the organization, the CEO might take on the job personally, it could be delegated to other management staff, or a standing ethics committee might be formed. For maximum impartiality, an outside consultant could be hired for the entire review. The second step is to prepare a list of likely topics to be covered in the audit, divided into client-specific issues (for instance, client rights, confidentiality and privacy, informed consent) and more general issues pertaining to the agency as a whole, such as service delivery practices, maintenance of boundaries, conflicts of interest, defamation of character, supervision and training, use of consultants, fraud, referral policies and procedures, grounds for termination of services, and practitioner impairment. A key area to address is the ethical dilemmas encountered by social workers in direct practice due to conflicting professional duties and obligations, as discussed previously in this chapter. Human services administrators also face ethical dilemmas over the allocation of scarce or limited resources, telling the truth, and adhering to the relevant policies, regulations, and laws governing such organizations. For example, in serving the elderly, should priority be given to the many or the few, that is, to those well enough to participate in day programs at the agency or to the frail, home-bound clients? In the vignette above about the CFO who stole a small amount of money by manipulating documents, which position on handling the situation was more beneficial for the organization, the executive's or the board president's?

Once the specific topics have been determined for a given setting, a structured instrument should be developed to systematically collect data and rate the level of risk in each category, from the lowest point, which would pertain to a practice needing no modification, to the highest ranking, for something deemed to be seriously flawed and in need of immediate attention. As part of this effort, likely data sources must be identified. After the data have been collected and analyzed, the results should be prioritized by the degree of risk, and a plan should be delineated for implementing the findings, starting with the most significant concerns (Reamer, 2000). Although a thorough review of this nature may not be warranted every year, senior management must remain vigilant, ready to identify any new potential threats and take appropriate action, and periodically it may be advisable to conduct another full audit, especially if the organization experiences anything out of the ordinary, such as an incident of occupational fraud, or when there is a change in the top leadership.

FINAL THOUGHTS

For the most part, in this discussion on ethical leadership, the focus has been on the actions of the top professional, but it is important to keep in mind that leadership in nonprofits is a shared responsibility, with the board an equal partner and therefore also a possible source of risk to the organization's reputation and steady flow of resources. In the case of the board of directors of the Charles M. Blair Family Museum in Martindale, Montana, the issue was failure to execute the duty of care, a basic responsibility of a nonprofit board (see chapter 4). As the result of a suit brought by a group of community volunteers, the Montana Supreme Court dismissed the trustees for breaching their fiduciary duties in not spending enough of the money left in trust by the donor at her death to establish the new institution, resulting in its closing. The court's ruling has been seen as a victory for the principle of honoring the wishes of the donor except in those rare instances when the intentions cannot be fulfilled or are deemed too frivolous. The court ordered that a new board be formed to reopen the museum (Strom & Robbins, 2008).

Elected officials have also weighed in on board responsibilities. In response to accounting frauds at Enron and other large corporations, which revealed the weaknesses in board oversight of resources, in 2002 the U.S. Congress enacted the American Competitiveness and Corporate Accountability Act, better known as the Sarbanes-Oxley Act after its two primary sponsors, Senator Paul Sarbanes and Representative Michael Oxley. The intent of this law is to ensure financial accountability in the corporate community by strengthening governance policies and procedures (Thomas, 2006). Even though the principal focus of this act is publicly traded entities, it already has affected governance practices in nonprofits as well, with many states using the Sarbanes-Oxley regulations or passing similar legislation to ensure that board members are qualified to serve and understand their fiduciary duties (Snyder, 2005).

Snyder maintains that one of the best ways to restore public confidence in nonprofits is to create a board-staff partnership committed to the fulfillment of the organizational mission according to the laws governing voluntary agencies and accepted standards of practice, and guided by a code of ethics to form and maintain a values-based culture. For even in cases of wrongdoing resolved through legal measures, there is almost always an ethical principle of one magnitude or another that has been violated. Snyder also would encourage nonprofits to work together to regulate the sector from within, in a consortium comprising foundations, state associations of nonprofits, umbrella groups, and other interested parties, to forestall the imposition of regulations via external means. Independent Sector, a Washington, DC–based nonprofit, is a good example of such a consortium.

Human Resources Management

For nonprofits and other organizations that focus primarily on the delivery of services rather than on producing goods, a competent, dedicated workforce is perhaps the most critical resource in carrying out the organizational mission. To find, prepare, and retain a well-qualified staff requires careful attention to "all of the choices and actions that take place in the life of an organization's employees" (Strom-Gottfried, 2006, p. 141), from recruitment through performance appraisals, including disciplinary measures when needed, falling within the broad function of human resources (HR) management. In larger settings, there may be a separate department to oversee these areas; in smaller organizations, they may be included within the executive director's responsibilities or delegated to another member of the senior staff. Regardless of who oversees HR management, the policies and procedures guiding the process must be implemented with skill and an even hand. As noted in the previous chapter, many of the risks to a nonprofit stem from disputes arising from personnel issues, so there can be a lot at stake both financially and in terms of the organization's reputation in the community.

From a broader perspective, the value of the nonprofit sector as an employer has become increasingly important to the overall economy of the United States. Based on recent data from the U.S. Bureau of Labor Statistics, American charities employ between 9.5 and 9.7 million workers, which is more than 10 percent of the country's total workforce. Although nonprofits can be found in many fields, over half of the employment is in health care, with education second; in the years to come, job opportunities are projected to be highest in the health and human services. Moreover, the number of nonprofit employees has doubled in the last twenty-five years, representing a higher average annual growth rate than business and government are experiencing. In dollar terms, for 2004 nonprofit workers were paid $322 billion in wages, significantly outpacing the wages paid by the utilities, construction, and wholesale trade industries (Independent Sector, 2004; Salamon & Sokolowski, 2006).

This chapter examines the topic of HR management in nonprofits from many different angles. Addressing the issue of job satisfaction and commitment sets the stage for considering all of the practical details associated with the decisions that must be reached, and their ramifications, in regard to an organization's workforce. Last, we will focus on the special challenges of managing diversity in the workplace.

PROMOTING JOB SATISFACTION AND COMMITMENT

To be successful, an organization must not only find ways to hire the best people to provide its programs and services but also be mindful of what it takes to retain these individuals. Staff turnover can be measured both financially and psychically; in addition to the actual costs of replacing an employee, clients may be inconvenienced while a new person is sought, hired, and trained, and the remaining staff members may feel a personal sense of loss. For those attracted to working in nonprofit settings, the general perception is that they are drawn initially by the nature of the work and are most likely to stay on when their personal beliefs and organizational values coincide and when they feel their efforts contribute to mission fulfillment (Brown & Yoshioka, 2003).

Intrinsic versus Extrinsic Motivations

According to Taylor's classic theory of motivation, which was developed in reference to the for-profit sector, monetary rewards are the major incentive to achieve greater productivity, but regardless of the sector, few today believe money is the only factor to bring about increases in work output. For instance, Likert maintained the most significant motivating element is supportive relationships with coworkers and the supervisor, who is encouraged to send out as many positive signals as possible, such as involving staff in decision-making. These two very different perspectives are captured in McGregor's X and Y theories, with the first suggesting human beings have an inherent dislike for work, valuing security above everything, and therefore require a considerable amount of direction and control to perform well, while the second posits individuals have a natural capacity for creativity, want more responsibility, and so need a work climate encouraging democratic participation. Theory Z, developed some years later, is a kind of compromise position, encompassing aspects of both theories X and Y. Along these same lines, Maslow proposed a hierarchy of needs, starting at the physiological level (food, clothing, and shelter) and proceeding to four higher levels: safety needs, social needs and the desire for love, the need for esteem, and the need for self-actualization (as cited in Skidmore, 1995).

Maslow's theory serves to underscore the importance of perceiving workers as individuals. It takes into consideration both personal and group needs in order to provide appropriate working conditions and challenges, particularly with respect to the highest-level need of self-actualization, which involves the desire for achievement along with social approval and recognition. The contract renewal and promotion process used by most U.S. colleges and universities reflects this theory; for many academics, the benefits of achieving tenure include job security and peer approval, but even more important is the freedom to pursue research areas that are personally meaningful even when they may be outside the mainstream of one's discipline. Workplace studies by Hofstede and Hofstede (2005) comparing people in different occupations provide evidence that those in fields demanding education well beyond the basics, such as professionals, are more likely to be motivated by intrinsic factors—the nature of the work, achievement, responsibility, recognition, and advancement—and those with less education, such as clerical staff, by extrinsic factors, that is, working conditions, supervision, salary, and company policies and procedures. However, "collective practices . . . depend on organizational characteristics like structure and systems and can be influenced in more or less predictable ways by changing these organizational characteristics" (Hofstede & Hofstede, 2005, p. 308).

Key Factors

As noted earlier, a general theory cannot account for all individual behaviors, which may vary by occupational level, age, length of employment, job scope, and so on. One way of understanding how individuals view their work is through Schein's concept of *career anchors* (2006), the specific preferences each person has regarding the kind of work they do, which are believed to exist prior to accepting full-time employment but then evolve over time and with experience. Haley-Lock (2008) focused on five of the anchors that seemed relevant for nonprofits, especially HSOs, to study how career orientations might affect job satisfaction: (1) dedication to a cause (the desire to have an impact on larger social issues); (2) lifestyle (the desire to strike a balance between work and nonwork responsibilities); (3) autonomy (the desire to be able to choose how and when to complete tasks); (4) managerial competence (the desire to have advancement opportunities and hold a leadership position); and (5) entrepreneurial creativity (the desire to develop or reshape programs according to one's own vision). She found that newer employees placed much more value on entrepreneurial creativity than those with a longer history at the organization, but the reverse was true for lifestyle balance. Both groups expressed a similar interest in autonomy, serving the cause, and having opportunities for promotion and leadership. Yet in terms of job satisfaction, surprisingly, although lifestyle orientation was not statistically significant for the "veterans," it was for the relative newcomers even though the veterans valued this career anchor much more than the newcomers. In addition, while dedication to a cause was positively related to job satisfaction for all workers, this was not true for the three remaining anchors, further reinforcing the idea that managers must consider individual needs and wants to promote a sense of well-being in the workplace.

The ability to retain staff is a kind of referendum on organizational efforts to promote job satisfaction. Thus, finding ways to reduce work-related stress, frequently a strong predictor of the intention to leave, should be management's goal. Support from supervisors and coworkers is particularly important, with family support acting as a buffer to lessen the effects of conflict between work and home obligations. It stands to reason then that implementing policies and procedures to increase social supports and decrease stress on the job should be encouraged (Nissly, Mor Barak, & Levin, 2005). Interestingly, Giffords (2003) found that in general social service workers in nonprofits and for-profits demonstrate more commitment to the organization and the profession than do those in public settings. Moreover, professional commitment, but not organizational commitment, appears to increase with age and for those in more responsible positions that allow greater flexibility in decision-making. This suggests a need to find better incentives to bring about a higher level of commitment to the organization. Nevertheless, worker loyalty can be a mixed blessing, for staff in nonprofits often come with a strong belief in the mission, as noted above, but may also hold their organizations to higher ideological standards. One result might be an informal or even formal grievance when a job-related problem is encountered and a decision to leave if the situation is not resolved in a manner consistent with the individual's personal values (Hoffmann, 2006).

PRACTICAL CONSIDERATIONS IN HR MANAGEMENT

In establishing the policies and practices necessary to manage the workforce, a nonprofit must consider both internal and external aspects of the environment. First and foremost, the mission, the guiding force for all programmatic decisions, ought to determine the types of jobs as well as the skill levels of employees to fill these positions. Another critical internal factor is the organization's financial health, which obviously has considerable bearing on the number of staff and the reward system. Finally, the culture of the agency, by setting the tone for expectations and work style, dictates hiring individuals who will fit in and also influences the degree of formality of HR procedures.

Externally, the composition of the labor pool and general economic conditions may represent opportunities or constraints in setting personnel policies. As part of this process, some or all of the following pieces of legislation will have direct bearing on both policies and practices (Strom-Gottfried, 2006).

- The Social Security Act of 1935 and the Fair Labor Standards Act (FLSA) of 1938 established the basis for federal and state unemployment programs, minimum wages and hours, and overtime pay provisions. Nonexempt staff must receive overtime pay and so forth under FLSA, but exempt employees (usually managers, executives, and professionals) are not covered.
- The Equal Pay Act of 1963 mandates equal pay for employees holding the same jobs, except when seniority, merit, and factors other than sex dictate otherwise. It addresses both direct and indirect (benefits, for instance) compensation.
- Title VII of the Civil Rights Act of 1964 (amended in 1991) bars discrimination on the basis of sex, race, color, religion, or national origin for organizations with at least fifteen employees working twenty or more weeks per year. The Lilly Ledbetter Fair Pay Act of 2009 clarifies the timing of unlawful discriminatory behavior.
- The Age Discrimination in Employment Act of 1967 (amended in 1978 and 1986) protects individuals forty and older from arbitrary discrimination.
- The Equal Employment Opportunity Act of 1972 extended Title VII coverage to more kinds of organizations. In 1980 sexual harassment was recognized as a form of sex discrimination by the Equal Employment Commission.

- The Pregnancy Discrimination Act of 1978 identified pregnancy as a disability qualifying a person to receive the same benefits as given for other disabilities.

- The Americans with Disabilities Act (ADA) of 1990 prohibits discrimination on the basis of physical or mental disability by organizations with at least fifteen employees and requires reasonable accommodations for such individuals.

- The Family and Medical Leave Act of 1993 requires organizations with at least fifty employees to grant up to twelve weeks of unpaid leave for the birth or adoption of a child, for the care of any member of the immediate family with a health issue, and if an employee cannot work due to a major health problem.

Compensation and Benefits

Many factors dictate the nature of the compensation and benefits program, including the prevailing trends in the community, in order to be competitive in attracting and retaining the best people. In determining salaries and wages, depending on the organizational structure and strategic goals, an egalitarian philosophy may dictate little differentiation by staff level, or the approach, as in many larger settings, may be more hierarchical. With the latter strategy, however, the organization can open itself to criticism from key stakeholders if the disparity from level to level is too great and the CEO's salary is much above that for executives in comparable agencies. United Way, a nonprofit academic center at a local university, the state association of nonprofits, and the Internet are possible sources for salary studies to use as a general guide.

An important policy decision is whether compensation will increase automatically according to a predetermined schedule or by merit, or some combination of the two. As for benefits, some, such as paying into the state unemployment insurance fund, are mandatory while others are up to the organization. Historically, nonprofits were known to provide strong benefits packages, partly to offset less-than-stellar salaries, but economic pressures now often necessitate other arrangements. For example, health care has become so expensive that many organizations have had to reduce the coverage and increase employee copayments. Vacations, paid holidays, sick leave, personal days, staff development, and retirement plans are other examples of discretionary benefits.

Job Design

The components of a job ought to reflect the client and/or organizational needs that a particular constellation of services is expected to meet. Accordingly, the duties and responsibilities of a direct-care worker in a residential facility will be markedly different from those of a middle manager in the same setting. The first step in job design is to collect and analyze relevant data to determine the best configuration of jobs to carry out the mission, not just for the present but also in anticipation of future demands. With this information in hand, the specific tasks and behaviors attached to a given position can be identified as well as the desired characteristics and qualifications of the person to fill that slot, the appropriate rewards (monetary and nonmonetary), and the physical accommodations necessary to do the work, often referred to as *ergonomic concerns*, to eliminate or at least minimize risks and injuries. The ultimate aim of job design is to improve organizational effectiveness and efficiency and increase employee job satisfaction.

Recruitment and Selection

Job descriptions must be written for each open position, with as much detail as possible on duties and responsibilities; the required knowledge, skills, and abilities; and the reporting relationship. Any specific physical requirements should be noted as well. Except when hiring the top professional, a board responsibility, this task generally falls to senior management, who must also specify the procedures for filling vacancies to ensure the process is fair, meets all legal requirements, and is consistent with the board-approved salary range. The aim is to identify the most critical tasks and qualifications so that applicants can judge whether to submit their credentials without making the job seem undoable and thus prematurely limiting the pool of candidates. To that end, some expectations may be stated as absolute while others are open to negotiation. For instance, the educational preference for program director of a large HSO might be a master's in social work, but a master's in public administration or education could be an acceptable alternative. Periodically, all job descriptions should be reviewed to ensure they still reflect organizational needs and realities, and revised accordingly (see exhibit 14.1 for a sample job description).

Hiring procedures should define who will be involved in personnel decisions, how openings will be advertised, what records need to be kept and by whom, and how the selection process will unfold. A job announcement is generally prepared for each opening; to meet affirmative action guidelines, it should include job title and classification as exempt or nonexempt; location; a description of the most essential duties; the minimum acceptable qualifications; the starting date; and the application procedures, covering what, where, and to whom materials should be sent and by when. Announcements may include the salary range or just state that salary is negotiable. As Pecora (1998) notes, "The recruitment and selection of employees is a form of public relations. The quality of recruitment materials and the respect and professionalism shown to applicants shape the image of your organization" (p. 157). Thus, the venues for advertising or posting a position must be chosen carefully so all likely candidates are made aware of the vacancy, with particular attention to reaching women and people of color, especially for management openings. A copy of each announcement with a list of how and where the position was advertised or posted should be stored in a permanent file.

Even when an announcement is clearly worded to discourage unqualified candidates, applications are apt to be received from individuals lacking the stated criteria. Having screening guidelines, weighted to emphasize the most important qualifications, date-stamping applications as received, and keeping a log to record their disposition will

Exhibit 14.1 Sample Employee Job Description

Youth Services Network, a 60-year-old nonprofit organization supported by individual donations, United Way, and foundation and government grants

Job Title: Program Director

Responsible for oversight of current programs, consisting of a variety of activities housed at the agency's youth center, a summer camping program, and two grant-funded programs also housed at the youth center.

Essential Duties and Responsibilities

- Monitors all programs to ensure they are implemented as designed.
- Supervises center director and director of camping services.
- Evaluates current programs and prepares reports for key stakeholders.
- Assesses client needs and recommends new programs as warranted.
- Develops and secures funding for approved new programs.
- Represents agency on citywide youth council.
- Performs all other duties as assigned by the executive director.

Qualifications

- Knowledge of youth programming trends and stages of youth development.
- Proven skill in fund-raising with private and government donors.
- Strong supervisory skills, including the ability to design individual professional development plans.
- Expertise in program monitoring and outcomes-based evaluation.
- Skill in forging collaborative relationships with peers.

Education and Experience

- Master's degree in social work preferred; graduate degree in public administration or education will also be considered.
- At least five years' experience in youth work at a nonprofit organization, with a minimum of one year in a management capacity.
- Must be a self-starter and detail-oriented.

Reporting Relationship: Reports directly to the executive director.

Salary and Benefits: Negotiable.

---

provide concrete proof that everyone has been treated fairly and consistently. For those who meet the minimum job qualifications, it will be helpful to have some kind of systematic way to distinguish the best candidates from the others; Camp Fire USA (n.d.) has developed an executive director's rating criteria worksheet to compare applicants' strengths, which could easily be modified for other positions. Individuals eliminated at this point should be sent a letter thanking them for their interest but indicating they will not be receiving further consideration, with copies retained in the permanent file.

The next set of decisions concerns the selection process. Depending on the nature of the position and the number of individuals on the short list, many organizations will conduct brief telephone interviews to make further reductions. A key decision is whether to consider current employees for the opening and, if so, how to ensure they are treated in the same manner as any other applicant. Whether interviews will be conducted by a single person or a committee, careful attention must be paid to the process to avoid violating rules and regulations on discrimination. All interviews should be scheduled for the same length of time, and the same list of job-specific questions must be posed each time. The Department of Statistics at the University of Washington provides guidelines on what information may be legitimately requested and what is unlawful, drawn from the Equal Employment Opportunities Commission's regulations, via its Web site (www.stat.washington.edu/jobs/questions). Here are some sample questions.

> Subject: Family—*Unlawful inquiries*: How will your husband feel about the amount of time you will be traveling if you get this job? What kind of child-care arrangements have you made? *Lawful inquiries*: Can you work overtime? Is there any reason why you can't be on the job at 7:30 a.m.?

> Subject: Arrests & Convictions—*Unlawful inquiry*: Have you ever been arrested? (An arrest does not necessarily mean the party is guilty.) *Lawful inquiries*: Have you ever been convicted of any crime (excluding minor traffic violations)? If so, when, where, and what is the disposition of the case?

To help determine whether past experience is relevant to the position in question, a useful technique is the Patterned Behavior Description Interview, which delves more specifically into the individual's qualifications. For example, you might ask how the applicant handled the need to make a significant change in the way work got done within the organization (Pecora, 1998). A related technique is the situational interview. This entails presenting hypothetical but likely scenarios pertaining to the job and/or the organization and asking the candidates to indicate what they would do under those circumstances. In both cases, a rating scale can be established to judge the responses, say, 5 = much more than acceptable to 1 = much less than acceptable, with supporting comments. With a selection committee, the candidate's answer can be compared to those of group members for the same vignette (Golensky, 1995).

Although much more common in the for-profit sector, testing is used by some nonprofits as a screening device to ascertain skill levels, knowledge, personality, and technical capabilities but also before making the final selection. However, the validity of such tests is not universally accepted; as a general rule, testing should never be the only hiring criterion, and the results must be viewed with great caution. Finally, before offering the job, the organization should conduct background and reference checks. The reasons for a background check vary with the position. For example, criminal checks are required in virtually all states for anyone who will be working with children, the elderly, or the disabled. In addition, due to the events of September 11, 2001, the possibility of terrorism has become an issue, and the fear of litigation remains an ongoing concern. Areas to investigate include driving record, Social Security number, bankruptcy, property ownership, and credit rating (Privacy Rights Clearinghouse, 2008). The person's legal right to work in the United States should also be checked. Misrepresentation of any information provided may be grounds for immediate disqualification of that candidate.

Reference checks are still considered an important piece, but since the applicants indicate whom to contact and therefore can be expected to choose only those apt to provide positive comments, the insights from these sources must be taken with a grain of salt. Furthermore, with the increase in the number of lawsuits filed by individuals against former employers suspected of sabotaging efforts to obtain a new position, even though anything truthful about the person's performance legally can be shared, many organizations have adopted policies strictly limiting the information to affirming the title of the job held, the dates of employment, the most recent salary, and whether the person would be eligible for rehire (potentially the most telling bit of information). A verbal request for a reference may prove to be more fruitful than a written request, because it is often possible to convey certain reservations by a voice inflection or choice of words.

The job offer should precisely state the responsibilities of the position, salary, benefits, starting date, and the date for accepting or rejecting the offer. Contact may first be made by phone, followed by a confirmation letter. Until everything is definite, the other finalists should not be notified, so that if the deal falls through, it may be possible to go to the next-best applicant and avoid having to restart the entire process. Once the decision is certain, a letter should be sent to those not selected, expressing the organization's thanks for their time and interest, with some wording to the effect that the background of the person chosen more closely fits the agency's current needs and the requirements of the position. It is very important to handle any internal candidates with delicacy; keeping their goodwill should be the goal, for they are likely to remain at the organization. In fact, this may present an opportunity for career counseling on obtaining further education or work experiences to increase their chances in the future.

Staff Development and Supervision

Staff development, encompassing various forms of training, career counseling, and personal accommodations, is part of the overall reward system and is intended to benefit both employees and employer. Landsman (2008) found two primary pathways to building loyalty and fostering retention, through job satisfaction and perceived organizational support, the first representing an emotional response and the second, a more cognitive appraisal of how much value the organization places on the employee's contributions and well-being.

Opportunities for professional growth start with the first day on the job via an orientation, whose purpose is to make new workers aware of the organizational structure and how they fit into the whole enterprise, and to help them begin building relationships with their colleagues. For line staff, their immediate supervisor, the primary person charged with ensuring quality in job performance and enforcing agency rules, is generally given the responsibility for conducting the orientation. After a tour of the facility, the new employees should be shown their workstation and introduced to the other members of the unit. Most important, ample time must be set aside for the supervisor and each new employee to review the tasks associated with the job and to discuss the individual's interests and aspirations. By the end of this first meeting, mutually agreed-upon goals for the first evaluation period and a basic outline for a staff development plan should be set. A similar process can be followed for new managers, with the executive director or another senior person doing the honors. In addition, every new hire must be given a copy of the agency's personnel manual, the key document spelling out all relevant policies and procedures; many organizations require newcomers to read the manual and then sign a form attesting to their understanding of and willingness to comply with its provisions. Exhibit 14.2 illustrates some key policies found in a typical personnel manual.

Exhibit 14.2 Selected Personnel Policies

AT-WILL EMPLOYMENT

All agency employees are employed on an at-will basis. As such, employment can be terminated with or without cause, and with or without notice, at any time, at either the option of the employee or the employer. No supervisor, program manager, manager, or other representative of the agency (other than the executive director) has the authority to enter into any agreement or contract for employment for any specified period of time or to otherwise modify the employee's at-will status. Any modification to the employee's at-will status must be in writing and signed by the executive director.

CONFLICTS OF INTEREST

Secondary Employment

It is recognized that some employees will involve themselves in outside employment over and above agency responsibilities. Any employee intending to engage in other paid work must submit to the executive director, in writing, pertinent information as to these activities and secure prior authorization. Activities related to outside employment cannot occur during the employee's regularly scheduled business hours and may not interfere with the employee's effectiveness in the provision of services for this agency. Agency equipment or facilities may not be used when engaged in outside employment.

Ethical Behavior

Employees are to conduct themselves in a manner that will reflect credit on themselves and the agency. All personnel have a primary commitment to our customers. It is further the responsibility of all personnel to uphold the code of ethics adopted by her/his professional organization and the agency. [Subheadings address confidentiality in general and specifically in regard to customers, gifts or other special considerations, special privileges, and financial interests.]

PARTISAN POLITICAL ACTIVITY

Employees may not use their agency authority to influence or interfere with the result of an election or a nomination for office; nor may any employee coerce, attempt to coerce, command, or advise another employee to pay, lend, or contribute anything of value to a party, committee, organization, agency, or person for political purposes. An agency employee is not, however, precluded from engaging in political management or political campaigns in her/his personal capacity.

PERFORMANCE EVALUATION

All employees' performance and potential shall be evaluated on a continuing basis in order to improve the employee's effectiveness, assess training needs, and make decisions on placement, promotion, separation, compensation, and other actions that affect the employee. Performance evaluation is an ongoing process and is part of everyday supervision. No evaluation or review in any way alters the at-will status of an employee.

Supervisors shall evaluate all regular employees at least annually. Employees are expected to participate in their evaluation, will receive a copy of their evaluation, and will review the written summery with their supervisor. All evaluations will be based upon quality and quantity of duties, as outlined in the employee's job description and goals mutually agreed to by the employee and supervisor. All evaluations will include performance goals for the next year and for professional development, when needed. All employees will sign their own evaluation and have the opportunity to add comments to the document.

PERSONAL DAYS

All regular employees [i.e., those working full-time or who work on a scheduled part-time basis] shall be credited with a total of three (3) "personal" days at the beginning of each calendar year. A prorated portion will be available to new employees hired after the beginning of the fiscal year. These days can only be used singularly. They may not be used in succession. Personal days cannot be used in less than one (1)–hour increments. Personal days may be used for sick leave, but they may not be added to vacation or holiday leave.

Employees must use personal days in the year in which they earn them or they will lose them. Employees may not carry unused personal days over into the next year, and will not receive pay in place of unused personal days. The agency will not pay an employee for unused accrued personal days upon termination of employment.

Note: These policies are from the personnel manual of a nonprofit providing employment services to women.

The specifics of a staff development plan will vary, taking into consideration the needs and wants of each employee as well as the organization's expectations and available resources. For the employee it may entail financial support and release time to earn an advanced degree or to attend a workshop that fulfills licensing requirements for continuing education. From the organization's perspective there may be an interest in having staff acquire additional training in a particular discipline so a new program can be offered in response to consumer demand or to update computer skills to handle new technologies; the requirements of accrediting or regulatory bodies will also be a factor. After weighing all factors, an organization can choose from several types of development activities, including on-the-job training, mentoring, coaching, skills training via videos and DVDs, teleconferencing, and Web-based instruction (Strom-Gottfried, 2006).

As mentioned previously, the supervisor plays a critical role in fostering job satisfaction and organizational commitment. To do so effectively necessitates balancing the three main supervisory functions: education, management, and personal support. In many cases, the same person wears all three hats, at one point counseling workers on client intervention techniques, then explaining changes in the employee benefit package, and upon learning about a spouse's illness, providing words of comfort and concrete assistance if needed. Given these potentially conflicting duties, a central dilemma for supervisors is to find the best approach to empower those reporting to them, but at the same time respond to organizational pressures for greater efficiency and accountability (Perlmutter, Bailey, & Netting, 2001).

One continuing challenge for supervisors is helping to create an organizational culture promoting collaboration in general and the use of teams in particular. Informal interactions between staff members to share information or bring a task to completion have always existed, but at present there is much greater emphasis on the idea of working together, both internally, often across disciplines, and externally, in more formal ways, in the belief that dividing up responsibilities allows each person or entity to contribute from a position of strength and with respect to specific talents. At the intraorganizational level, once it has been determined that group process is the best course of action, the supervisor, acting as team leader, must carefully select the other group members, clearly articulate the assignment and desired outcome(s), provide the necessary resources to get the work done, create an atmosphere of open communication, help build trust and manage any differences that arise within the team, and bring the project to a productive end. In short, according to Bailey and Dunlap (2006): "Effective task-oriented teams are best understood as collections of people who are held together by a common purpose, a sense of loyalty and accountability to themselves, a culture of trust and confidence that attends to results but does not require certainty of consensus, a concomitant agenda for a positive experience for all its members, and a clear understanding of measures of success" (p. 198).

Performance Review

As a general rule, all employees should receive a formal evaluation at least annually, often on the anniversary of their date of hire, to gauge progress in achieving their goals and determine the future direction of the staff development plan. However, the basic content of the review ought not to come as a surprise. It is good supervisory practice to meet regularly with each supervisee throughout the year to discuss job-related matters, including performance. Doing so allows for remedial action as warranted well before the annual review. A staff member whose performance is judged to be deficient during the formal evaluation will then be reviewed at set intervals until the problems have been corrected or the individual is terminated. Organizations mandating a three-month or six-month probation for new staff will also conduct evaluations at those times.

Because employment-related issues remain the primary area of litigation by staff, with allegations of wrongful termination the most common and charges of sexual harassment and discrimination the next leading causes (Alliance for Nonprofit Management, 2003–2004), organizations must take particular care in developing the language of their personnel policies. Asking an attorney to review the policies periodically to ensure compliance with the various applicable rules and regulations is advisable. Many nonprofits now have an at-will employment policy, allowing either the organization or the staff member to break the work relationship with or without cause, which refers to misconduct as defined by the organization and may include such things as failure to follow policy, the commission of an illegal act, or insubordination, as long as there is no explicit contract between the parties and no agreement with a union (see exhibit 14.2). Although several states recognize exceptions to this rule, in practice the burden is on the discharged employee to prove there has been a violation. While inadequate performance may be a listed cause for dismissal, it is usually not invoked unless the employee is unwilling or unable to follow the organizational procedures for corrective action.

A key step is determining both the criteria and the process for evaluation. A good evaluation system should be *valid*, meaning the instrument measures what it is supposed to address; *reliable*, which refers to the consistency of the evaluation over time and from individual to individual; and *practical*, in terms of ease of administration within a reasonable time frame and its acceptability to both management and staff. Assuming the intent of the appraisal is positive and nonpunitive, the process can be structured to benefit everyone involved. Ideally, the evaluation instrument should include both generic and job-specific elements, confine its content to actual dimensions of the job, and be realistic in its expectations, in recognition that not everyone will or can improve on every dimension each year. In fact, for both personal and professional reasons, it is not uncommon for people to reach a plateau or even decline from one year to the next. Therefore, a benchmarking approach is recommended, by which the most desirable behavior might be rated a 7 and the least desirable a 1, with the midpoint of the scale still representing an acceptable level of performance (Millar, 1998).

For these reasons, it makes sense to have staff participate directly in the construction of the instrument, using their job descriptions as the starting point to identify specific situations and the standards for judging them. Not only will this increase the perception that the process is fair, it may also forestall later legal challenges. In addition, there will be items that reflect organizational expectations of all employees; these may be behavioral in nature, such as measuring dependability or maintaining good relationships with colleagues. In the end then, there may actually be several instruments, all sharing the same core elements but differing on the job-specific items by position. The approach described above uses a *behaviorally anchored rating scale*. Other options include (1) a simple list of statements describing a worker (for example, "takes initiative in carrying out responsibilities"), with the evaluator checking any item that is true and leaving the others blank; (2) a *graphic rating scale*, which provides statements on performance like the checklist, but here a scale is used to rank the person, perhaps from 1 = seldom to 5 = always; (3) an *essay*, an open-ended narrative describing the employee's strengths and areas for improvement; (4) *critical incidents*, statements capturing highly effective and ineffective behaviors that critically affect doing the job; and (5) a *management-by-objective review* based on specific, measurable goals set for a given period of time, say six months or a year, relevant to an individual's job, with agreed-upon indicators of quality to reflect the level of performance rated from superior to acceptable (for example, again using the item on initiative, superior = employee shows initiative 90 percent of the time when presented with opportunities, acceptable = 75 percent of the time, and unacceptable = less than 50 percent of the time). The essay or critical incidents might be used with a scale to offer a more nuanced view (Strom-Gottfried, 2006). Exhibit 14.3 shows examples of some of these options.

Exhibit 14.3 Performance Evaluation Options

OPTION 1: BEHAVIORALLY ANCHORED RATING SCALE

Job-Specific Dimension: Recommending New Programs

This dimension addresses the ability to be responsive to current and future client needs while being cognizant of trends in youth development and sensitive to organizational and community priorities regarding the allocation of resources.

7   This staff member demonstrates a superior ability to respond to current and future client needs in light of trends in youth services and resource availability.

6   This staff member demonstrates an excellent ability to respond to current and future client needs in light of trends in youth services and resource availability.

5   This staff member demonstrates a very good ability to respond to current and future client needs in light of trends in youth services and resource availability.

4   This staff member demonstrates an ability to respond to current and future client needs in light of trends in youth services and resource availability.

3   This staff member demonstrates some ability to respond to current and future client needs in light of trends in youth services and resource availability.

2   This staff member demonstrates limited ability to respond to current and future client needs in light of trends in youth services and resource availability.

1   This staff member demonstrates no ability to respond to current and future client needs in light of trends in youth services and resource availability.

OPTION 2: CHECKLIST

For the following items, place an X before each one that is characteristic of the staff member you are evaluating.

_____ Effectively assesses current and future client needs.
_____ Stays abreast of trends in youth program development.
_____ Develops strong program designs to address the identified needs.
_____ Demonstrates skill in seeking and obtaining new funding as warranted.
_____ Effectively monitors ongoing programs.
_____ Effectively evaluates current programs.
_____ Effectively supervises all staff with a direct reporting relationship.
_____ Demonstrates strong writing skills in preparing reports and other documents.
_____ Effectively represents the agency in the community.
_____ Is a consistent team player within the organization.

OPTION 3: GRAPHIC RATING SCALE

For each of the following items, rate the quality of the employee's work performance, as reflective of the individual's job description, using this scale:

1 = Poor   2 = Fair   3 = Average   4 = Good   5 = Excellent

[The same list as in option 2 would work here. This approach can also be used to rate frequency of performance, with a different rating scale, such as 1 = Never, 2 = Infrequently, 3 = Sometimes, 4 = Usually, and 5 = Always.]

Note: The examples are derived from the sample job description shown in exhibit 14.1, for a program director of a youth agency.

Prior to the evaluation conference, the supervisor and each supervisee should complete the performance review instrument independently and as objectively as possible so their time spent together can be used productively to note both strengths and areas for improvement. Except with regard to goal setting and the individual development plan for the next evaluation period, it is not essential that the parties agree on every dimension of the assessment (Millar, 1998). In fact, the dialogue over disagreements often becomes the most important aspect of the evaluation, providing an opportunity for the supervisor to clarify expectations and the supervisee to raise any job-related concerns or personal issues that might be affecting performance. The form should also include space for the supervisee to comment on the appraisal. Fairness in the process is the primary goal. To that end, a number of organizations have adopted what is known as a "360-degree" review, an approach that allows all members of the staff to evaluate each other in a formal but anonymous manner. Depending on the position of the person being evaluated, other stakeholders such as consumers, funders, and community partners may also be contacted for their input. Even though this kind of review is rather time consuming, the benefits in obtaining a more well-rounded perspective on the competencies of every employee can be worth the investment. The final step is to make sure all evaluative data are properly recorded and submitted in accordance with set deadlines, because other HR decisions (bonuses, promotions, and so forth) may be affected by these results.

Voluntary and Involuntary Separations

In general, there are four primary ways an employee and an organization may part company: resignation, retirement, termination, or layoff. The first two actions are typically initiated by the individual and the latter two by the organization, but in practice the actions of the organization may influence the decision to resign or retire, and the individual's contributions to mission fulfillment, real or perceived, may have some bearing on terminations and layoffs. Especially if unanticipated or forced under circumstances deemed invalid by other organizational members, an employee's departure can have negative consequences, such as disappointed clients, derailment of a program, or dismay over a valued colleague's fate by those remaining. At other times, the result may be quite positive: When someone leaves who was ineffective or had difficulties in working collaboratively, it can actually improve service delivery and staff morale. And although layoffs are never a happy occurrence, this difficult decision may enable an organization to continue valued programs and preserve other jobs.

While staff may resign to continue their education or to spend more time on child rearing, a voluntary resignation often signals some level of dissatisfaction over the nature of the job or working conditions. For example, in smaller organizations, the only route to a promotion or higher salary may be going to another setting. It is therefore advisable to hold an exit interview to explore the reasons why an employee has chosen to leave, even if it reveals a few painful truths. Retirement, on the other hand, usually comes toward the end of one's career and, unless motivated by a serious health issue, can be an occasion for celebration. Since there is no mandatory retirement age by law, an organization must set its own policies as to timing; to keep particularly valuable senior staff, certain organizations now offer incentives such as the option to work part time but still remain eligible for full medical coverage. Other retirement policies should address pensions, the payment of accrued benefits, and rights to continue participation in employer-sponsored benefit programs (Kettner, 2002). As of January 1, 2009, new IRS regulations for administering 403(b) retirement plans went into effect, with stiff penalties for non-compliance. Essentially, there are two types of plans, actively sponsored and non–actively sponsored, each with its own detailed requirements (Unser, 2008).

Moving on to involuntary separations, a distinction needs to be made between problem employees and employees with problems affecting performance, arising from family, mental health, substance abuse, or financial issues. In the latter case, help may be offered via health insurance or an employee assistance program, with dismissal the last resort (Rivas, 1998). As indicated above, termination of problem employees may be for cause (violation of policies, insubordination, and so on), but inadequate performance is probably the most common reason. When concerns arise over how an employee handles work assignments, most organizations initiate a progressive disciplinary process, moving from verbal warnings to written warnings, and finally to dismissal if there is no change. Even though this is the least enjoyable part of a supervisor's job, such concerns must be addressed immediately and in a respectful manner. The first step is to develop a plan together that spells out the expectations for improvement, with dates for subsequent evaluative meetings to monitor progress toward these objectives. At each stage the supervisor should make every effort to help the staff member correct the problem areas, perhaps by modeling the desired technique or providing opportunities for additional training. It is also very important to document all the steps to demonstrate that personnel policies have been followed to the letter and applied fairly.

Layoffs, however, typically are a result of budgetary constraints, as one organizational strategy used in difficult times (see chapter 11). Sometimes it is possible that these individuals will be rehired if circumstances change, but often the separation is permanent. In truth, this may be a way to remove problem employees without having to go through the progressive disciplinary process. Here "the issue of fairness can be addressed through some type of formula that uses such factors as seniority, performance appraisal, and the employee's contribution to critical programs and services" (Kettner, 2002, p. 353). To avoid charges of discrimination, the reductions should be applied across the board and with appropriate consideration for those in protected classes (due to color, race, disabilities, gender, age, and other similar factors).

Even in dismissal, the dignity of the staff member should be preserved, to the extent possible, during a private, confidential, and uninterrupted meeting between supervisor and supervisee in which the specific reasons for the decision are stated. While the employee may dispute the decision, the supervisor must make it clear there is no room for negotiation but should inform the individual of the appeal or grievance process if there is such a policy. Also be sure to spell out the procedures regarding final salary, accrued vacation time, benefits, completion of any outstanding work, and the disposition of property belonging to the organization, like files and office keys. To alleviate some of the tension and provide corroboration of the facts of the meeting in the event the employee subsequently challenges the termination, it may be helpful to invite another manager or an HR professional to be present at the interview.

ADDRESSING DIVERSITY IN THE WORKPLACE

There are compelling reasons for organizations, whether for-profit or nonprofit, to find effective ways to manage a staff representing differences with regard to ethnicity, race, gender, age, sexual preference, and disability status. First, it is a matter of demographics: Reflecting the current and projected shifts in the U.S. population, women, people of color, and immigrants will be the majority of new workers entering the workforce in the twenty-first century. The same changes will be manifested in the clientele, who are likely to prefer communicating with someone who knows their culture and speaks their language and who may select a provider based on these factors alone. Thus, building and maintaining a diverse staff is an imperative that makes sense out of a concern for both efficiency and effectiveness. For nonprofits, we might take it a step further to say that diversity embodies many of the basic values of the sector.

Yet, for all of its pluses, diversity also brings many challenges, especially in terms of communication, collaboration, and conflict management. Due to legal prohibitions, discrimination is apt to be more subtle. While it is no longer a question of keeping women and people of color out of the workplace, too often they are still excluded from the real circles of power and influence. Moreover, Mor Barak (2000) suggests the need for an expanded definition of diversity that distinguishes "observable or readily detectable attributes ('visible diversity') such as race, gender, or age . . . [from] less visible or underlying attributes ('invisible diversity') such as religion, education, and tenure with the organization" (p. 51). The latter characteristics may not be so obvious but may be just as significant a barrier. A good example would be sexual preference; although it may remain invisible when an individual chooses to keep his or her orientation secret, if word gets out, because of cultural assumptions and prejudices about masculinity and femininity, the result may be a less comfortable relationship between coworkers.

A Question of Age

In the workplace of the twenty-first century, there are three dominant age cohorts: the Baby Boomers, Generation X, and Generation Y, also known as the Millennial Generation. Such labels, having captured the imagination of the general public, have led to a good deal of theorizing about the alleged differences from one generation to another. For instance, GenXers have been characterized as more pessimistic, cynical, and self-centered than Baby Boomers, who are perceived as goal-oriented, highly dedicated to their work, sometimes to the point of overidentification with the job, and comfortable in hierarchical settings. In contrast, GenYers are supposed to be more optimistic, patient, and tolerant of others, and see themselves as change agents.

However, it is not clear how accurate these generalizations are, nor are they particularly useful in understanding how best to deal with the three age groups. In fact, Kunreuther (2003), who researched social-change nonprofits, found that despite some differences across the generations, there were more similarities than one might expect. The commonalities included a deep commitment to the mission of the organization, a high level of job satisfaction and dedication to the work, and a strong desire to make an impact on the lives of their clients. They differed in that the younger staff were more anxious about maintaining a balance between work and family and were more apt to have chosen this type of work due to a personal experience, such as being a victim of violence or discrimination. For GenXers and GenYers in leadership roles, the main difference was their attempts to alter traditional organizational structures, such as by using teams and flattening the hierarchy. One clear message was the need for Baby Boomer directors to actively prepare the younger staff to be the future leaders.

Before leaving this topic, it is important to note that some nonprofits, like their business counterparts, have been discriminatory in their HR practices toward older workers by finding reasons to terminate their employment, especially those in more senior positions and therefore with higher salaries. On the other hand, colleges and universities seem to be much more cognizant of the value derived from the most experienced faculty, instituting flexible workload policies that enable these individuals to continue being effective teachers and scholars long after the traditional retirement age.

Women in the Workplace

Women constitute a large portion of the nonprofit workforce, particularly in the human services, where leaders such as Jane Addams and Mary Richmond helped define the profession of social work. It is ironic then that as salaries in social agencies have improved, more men have gravitated to upper management positions, and fewer women have been selected for these top spots, except in organizations devoted to women's and girls' issues (for example, rape crisis centers and Girl Scouts), which tend to be almost exclusively staffed by females (Gibelman, 2000). Indeed, the glass ceiling remains a real barrier as "women managers continue to receive lower organizational rewards such as pay, promotion, desirable work assignments, and training opportunities than their male counterparts" (Chernesky, 2003, pp. 13–14). The contrast can be stark: a 2005 survey of western Pennsylvania nonprofits revealed women leaders earned an average of $27,861 less than male leaders ("Women Running Nonprofits," 2005).

The issue does not seem to be overt discrimination, as most organizations abide by federal policy guidelines; at the same time, few appear to do anything specific to ensure women enjoy equality with respect to promotions and the like. For instance, women may be passed over for plum assignments that might showcase their talents and let them grow professionally, or they may not have the same access as male staff to mentors. To combat such discrepancies, a promising program worth emulating has been initiated by Philadelphia's Valentine Foundation, working with the Nonprofit Center at La Salle University's School of Business, to create peer-to-peer support groups of women in management in local nonprofits for joint problem solving and knowledge sharing; a second component involves helping emerging female leaders map out personal career-development plans (University of Notre Dame, 2009).

One explanation for the disparities in work-related opportunities may be sex-role stereotyping. As illustrated in the case study featured in this book, the board president is conflicted about the executive director, whom he believes is well qualified but disparages for too openly seeking board accolades for her achievements. However, his real feelings may be more evident in his tendency to discuss important matters with some of his board colleagues before addressing them with the executive director, requiring her to cater to his schedule for their meetings, and referring to her as "the girl [he] brought to the dance," which demonstrates a lack of respect for her position. In short, if perceptions remain that women lack the necessary traits to be effective leaders, succeed more by luck than skill, or cannot be fully devoted to their work due to family responsibilities, the glass ceiling is not likely to disappear anytime soon (Chernesky, 2003).

Ethnic and Racial Groups in the Workplace

As indicated earlier, the twenty-first-century nonprofit workplace will be dominated by men and women of diverse races, ethnicities, and cultural backgrounds. Thus, there are economic incentives for learning how to manage diversity effectively, but also there are legal mandates governing affirmative action as well as ethical reasons to spur putting ideals into practice (Parish, Ellison, & Parish, 2006). Nevertheless, as for women, evidence exists of inequities toward people of color in terms of advancement, salary, and so forth, driven by historical patterns of decision-making, traditional power structures, and lack of appreciation for the value of diversity. Three patterns are evident in hiring practices: (1) *discrimination and fairness*, a strategy to increase the numbers, motivated primarily by the desire to comply with government mandates, with the expectation that these individuals will blend into the dominant culture of the organization; (2) *access and legitimacy*, an attempt to strengthen connections and enhance outreach efforts in niche markets, such as hiring African Americans to work with African American consumers; and (3) *learning and effectiveness*, the most desirable approach, which views a diverse workforce as a way to achieve a more vibrant and productive organization, reflecting a major attitudinal shift by top leaders (Allison, 2001).

Although a number of organizations have attempted to establish new social norms of inclusion for their employees of color through diversity-training programs, even when successful, such efforts appear to result only in change at the individual level. To achieve a true pluralistic environment across the board in which individuals from all cultures are valued and respected, more comprehensive measures are required that include equitable hiring and promotional policies, ongoing training, and mentorship (Findler, Wind, & Mor Barak, 2007). Moreover, if substantive and lasting change is to occur, it must begin at the top through helping administrators and senior managers see that diversity enhances the organizational mission and then securing their personal commitment "to create an institutional culture that rewards the differences while honoring the similarities among staff" (Perlmutter et al., 2001). Proactive strategies, such as seeking and hiring applicants from diverse backgrounds for HR positions, should be encouraged; at the same time, managers must be prepared to step in and deal with conflicts that arise, to reaffirm the organization's pledge to its stated values (Parish et al., 2006).

Other Diversity Concerns

As noted earlier, both visible and invisible diversity can present workplace barriers. The disabled obviously fall into the first category. While the Americans with Disabilities Act makes it illegal for employers with at least fifteen employees to discriminate due to physical or mental disabilities, the legislation does not set numerical goals for hiring or promotion. This means a position can be denied to a disabled person who is deemed unable to carry out the essential functions of the job. The key word here is *essential*, defined as the basic components of the work that have to be performed, with or without reasonable accommodation. For example, a requirement for a camp counselor could be to lead frequent hikes over rough and hilly terrain, which is likely to eliminate from consideration someone who is wheelchair-bound or uses crutches. In contrast, the director of camping services may design the summer program but is unlikely to be leading the hikes, so a disability should not be a factor in hiring for this position. Furthermore, advances in technology have made the modern nonprofit more accessible to people with a wide range of disabilities, adding yet another element to enrich the organizational landscape.

Gays and lesbians who choose not to make their sexual preference known fall into the invisible category. In this case, discrimination tends not to become a concern unless their orientation becomes general knowledge, at which point they may be harassed by coworkers or denied promotions and other organizational supports. Accordingly, such individuals may need to tread carefully as to what they reveal and to whom. For nonprofit managers, addressing the specific issues for this group can be complicated because there is no federal legislation to set a national standard; instead, there are various state and local laws, judicial rulings, and executive orders barring certain kinds of discrimination. Public opinion is also somewhat contradictory: polls show that opposition to equal rights for gays and lesbians is on the decline, but in many quarters there is still strong disapproval of marriage and legal adoption by same-sex couples. As a consequence, stakeholders may hold views ranging from total acceptance to a desire to exclude homosexuals of both genders from all organizational roles. The best advice for top management is to be sensitive to internal and external norms as well as the applicable laws in setting HR policies (Hostetler & Pynes, 2000).

FINAL THOUGHTS

In the end, for most organizations the overarching goal in HR management is to instill in all employees a common vision about the important work to be done and their collective responsibilities in achieving the mission. To do so requires a thorough understanding of the emotional needs and professional interests of each staff member and then making every effort to see that policies and procedures are designed to take both driving forces into account, to foster job satisfaction, productivity, and loyalty.

The Nonprofit Governing Board

In the United States, as in many other countries, a nonprofit seeking incorporation must have a set of bylaws and a board of directors, a group of community volunteers who pledge to ensure fulfillment of the stated mission by providing oversight of the organization's programs and services and the management thereof. In meeting these responsibilities the board exercises a special kind of authority, *governance*, composed of *accountability*, being responsive to key stakeholders' expectations and abiding by pertinent legislation and regulations; *transparency*, openness in sharing information with various interest groups about organizational activities and finances; *predictability*, carrying out a clearly defined role in a uniform and fair manner; and *participation*, active involvement in planning, decision-making, and evaluation of the organization's work to promote effectiveness and efficiency in the use of available resources (Gill, 2005).

With respect to participation, there is a general belief that effective boards lead to effective organizations, although the exact nature of the relationship remains unclear (Herman & Renz, 2008). Much of the literature designed for practitioners is prescriptive and maintains that governance and management should operate as separate functions, which often leads to reducing the issue to a list of responsibilities expected of the board and another for the staff. While this approach may be useful to a frustrated executive director coping with a board that insists on being included in all the day-to-day minutiae or the opposite extreme, one so uninvolved that it contributes virtually no guidance or support, it provides little real assistance in motivating the board to perform to its highest potential. A promising new direction is laid out by Chait, Ryan, and Taylor (2005), who believe that as CEOs have become more sophisticated leaders, boards have actually been left with many of the operational details: "The real threat to nonprofit governance may not be a board that micro*manages*, but a board that micro*governs*, attentive to a technical, managerial version of trusteeship while blind to governance as leadership" (p. 5, emphasis in original). The issue then is how to establish a meaningful division of labor between the board and top management to maximize the talents and expertise of both.

Chapter 4 painted in broad strokes a picture of the concept of shared leadership prevalent in most nonprofits, identifying the board's responsibilities as stated in the prescriptive literature and exploring the nature of the board-executive relationship, including descriptions of the most common governance models. Here, in contrast, the emphasis is on the nuts and bolts of forming and sustaining a high-functioning board.

AN OVERVIEW OF EFFECTIVE GOVERNANCE

According to the dictionary, something is effective when it produces a definite or desired result. In the nonprofit world, with its emphasis on mission as the cornerstone of all activities, means are typically given as much attention as ends, and therefore a systemic view of board effectiveness may be more relevant than one oriented toward mere goal attainment. To this end, Herman and Renz (2008) maintain that an effective board has a high degree of collegiality along with strong interpersonal ties. Similarly, Preston and Brown (2004) found a positive relationship between board members' emotional commitment to the organization and performance: such boards tended to be more actively engaged, as reflected in better attendance at meetings, willingness to serve on more committees, larger financial gifts, and so on.

Given the shared leadership model prevalent in most nonprofits, the top professional's perception of the board is a key variable in any discussion of effectiveness. In the Preston and Brown study, for instance, it was no great surprise that the executives rated their best-performing board members as very valuable to the organization. As indicated by Kramer in his classic 1985 article on governance, the CEO's behavior toward the board may be guided by a view of the trustees "as a nuisance or unnecessary burden, a group to be overcome rather than an indispensable resource whose development is an essential part of professional responsibility" (p. 22). He labeled the belief that most of the power in organizational policymaking should be vested in the professional as "technocratic ideology" and the opposite position, that the executive has an obligation to nurture the leadership abilities of the board, as "democratic ideology." Since executives often are directly involved in board recruitment, or at least strongly influence the process, how they see their relationship with the board may have great bearing on whether it plays a substantive role in policy and decision-making or is more of a rubber stamp.

Motivation and Performance

One simple fact about board members is often overlooked, or not taken into account as fully as it should be: Namely, they are volunteers, albeit with different responsibilities than those in direct service or support roles, but with the same needs and expectations, and requiring the same outlay of time and energy. Although the stereotype of a nonprofit board member is the altruist, someone who serves unselfishly out of a moral imperative, both logic and experience tell us that individuals who agree to be on a nonprofit board do so for a variety of personal and professional reasons. Some kind of exchange process occurs, whether materially, psychically, or both. Moreover, once in place, board members demonstrate a great deal of variability in their capacity and willingness to fulfill the responsibilities commonly assigned to them in the nonprofit management literature.

In an early but still significant study of motivation for board participation, Widmer (1989) proposed four discrete categories of incentives: material, social, developmental, and ideological. In addition, some of the reasons given by the trustees she studied were labeled "service" incentives. In the material category are both employment- and client-related incentives, gaining skills that might lead to a job in the first case and ensuring access to services for self or family in the second instance. Social incentives include meeting new people, working with friends, and wanting to spend time with those already on the board. Learning new skills or having a chance to exercise current talents, training, and experience would be examples of developmental incentives, and participation due to a belief in the cause or in the work of the agency would fall into the ideological category. Virtually all of her study subjects also reported some kind of service incentive, ranging from a desire to repay a debt to society or the organization, to more altruistic motives, such as to fulfill a civic duty or contribute to the well-being of the community. Interestingly, these findings closely parallel those of Prince and File for donor motivation, as discussed in chapter 10.

Building on this work yet going a step further to consider the effects of the incentives for board participation on the actual behaviors of trustees after their selection, a study of nonprofit board members and executives in one Michigan county pointed to a direct link between motive and performance (Golensky, 2000). The data indicated a significant relationship between serving on a board out of a belief in the organization's work and two of the most desired behaviors for boards cited in the literature, contributing funds and advancing the organization's image. In addition, the developmental incentive of being able to contribute skills and experience was closely associated with the two behaviors just mentioned plus three other expected responsibilities: selecting and supporting the executive, reviewing the executive's performance, and planning for the organization's future. Equally important, the findings showed certain service reasons given for board participation, for example, out of a sense of civic duty or to repay a debt to the agency or society, did not appear to translate into a disposition to carry out the duties we might expect of trustees. One possible conclusion to draw is that for these individuals, simply being on the board and attending meetings represented what they felt obligated to contribute. Table 15.1 presents the results of this research, which suggests a practical application for board composition and recruitment, that is, to seek out and cultivate those whose incentives to serve are closely aligned with organizational expectations and therefore more likely to result in effective performance.

One important gap in helping us understand board behavior is the absence of a single unifying theory on governance. After examining the various options used to describe corporate governance for their relevance to nonprofits, Miller-Millesen (2003) developed a typology of three separate theories to explain how boards function. From her analysis, agency theory, which stresses the importance of ensuring that management operates in a manner congruent with stakeholder expectations, was linked with the board's monitoring role in determining mission and purpose, assessing the CEO's performance, overseeing programs and services, exercising fiscal control, and strategic planning. Resource dependency theory focuses on the organization's ability to secure the resources essential to its survival; the logical connection here was to the board's boundary-spanning role in

Table 15.1 Motivations for participation as related to performance

Motivation	Level of performance
Having skills or experience to contribute	High
Belief in organization's work	High
Belief in the cause or mission	Moderate
Meeting new, interesting people	Moderate
Civic duty	Moderate
Opportunity for personal development	Moderate
Expected for business/professional reasons	Moderate
Repayment	Low
Advocacy for clients	Low
Opportunity to work with friends	Low
Making business/professional contacts	Low

Sources: For data, Golensky, 2000; for terminology, Widmer, 1989.
Note: The ratings are based on chi-square scores of study participants in testing the association between motivation and areas of board responsibility as prescribed in the nonprofit management literature.

raising funds, enhancing the nonprofit's image in the community, advocating on the organization's behalf, and protecting its interests with external constituencies. Finally, institutional theory, with its emphasis on conforming to societal norms and values, may influence board structure and processes (for example, operating through committees and ensuring adherence to relevant laws and regulations). Nonetheless, the author concluded that many of the board behaviors could be interpreted by using any of the three theories, leaving us still unclear why what boards actually do frequently bears little resemblance to what the prescriptive literature dictates.

The Board-Executive Relationship Revisited

According to Gill (2005), "selecting, supporting and regularly evaluating the performance of the CEO is the board's most important responsibility" (p. 57). However, meeting this governance responsibility is often problematic. When the time comes for a change, depending on the circumstances of the executive's departure, the board may consciously or unconsciously look for someone with exactly the same qualities and strengths as the outgoing individual or seek a totally different skill set. Instead, this should be viewed as an opportunity to reexamine values and analyze needs for both the present and the future (Golensky, 2008). As for evaluating the executive's performance, some boards find the process uncomfortable and therefore shy away from it; others believe it is unnecessary. Even in those nonprofits that do conduct an annual review, the process may be less than satisfactory for both parties (Golensky, 2000).

Whether overtly or covertly, issues of power and control do emerge in considering the board-executive relationship in nonprofits. Ideally the two halves of the leadership core should work together in harmony to carry out the organizational mission, but this ignores the very real tensions that can arise because the board selects and can fire the executive while the executive controls the flow of information to the board and has the professional know-how and credentials on which the board depends. Although the most common governance models, as described in chapter 4, suggest some kind of accommodation in which each party has its defined role and responsibilities, in practice organizational patterns vary widely, on a continuum from board domination at one end and staff dominance at the other. Furthermore, as outside observers, we must guard against the temptation to judge as dysfunctional a particular arrangement that departs from the prescriptive literature, for the central concern is whether it works for everyone involved. For example, in a small nonprofit focusing on child abuse, the board showed little inclination to be involved in most of the traditional governance tasks, deferring to the executive director on virtually all decisions. Yet this seemed to have no bearing on the organization's stability or reputation in the community.

Nevertheless, it is possible to identify good practices that can greatly increase the chances for success. A critical relationship is that of the top professional and the board president (also known as board chair in certain settings), whose roles in many ways are complementary, one managing the staff and the other, the remaining trustees. If these two powerful individuals have mutual trust and respect, the CEO's interactions with the board as a whole tend to be much smoother. Conversely, "the greatest source of friction and breakdown in voluntary organizations of all types, sizes, ages, and relative degrees of sophistication and excellence relates to misunderstandings and differing perceptions between the volunteer president and staff director" (O'Connell, 1993, p. 54). Failing to recognize these dynamics can bring unintended consequences. During its search for a new executive director, a nonprofit allowed the board president to take a leave of absence rather than resign after she decided to be a candidate for the job and then to return to her original position when she was not selected, putting the new executive at a considerable disadvantage from the beginning of her tenure. Similarly, in the YSN case study featured in this text, we have seen the unfortunate impact on the entire organization of the male board president's clear disdain for the female executive director despite his protestations to the contrary. On the other hand, a too-close relationship between the board president and the CEO can result in resentment by the other trustees, who may feel left out of the real action. With this scenario, the professional can become the target of these negative feelings, and long-term board development may also suffer.

Determining the best division of labor between the board and staff remains a bone of contention for many nonprofits, especially in smaller settings with limited personnel. Much of the hard evidence continues to show a discrepancy between what the board actually does and what it is supposed to do as described in the prescriptive literature. Moreover, boards and their top professionals often disagree in regard to the functions and activities each believes the other should and does perform, with fund development, long-term financial planning, and fiscal oversight among the areas where there are significant gaps between expectations and performance (Golensky, 2000; Green, Madjidi, Dudley, & Gehlen, 2001). Even though, by necessity, board members appear to be taking a more active role in fund development now than in the past, many trustees still express feelings of discomfort over donating money and seeking it from others. Rather than accepting this situation as the norm, it may be time to take concrete steps to help the board become more at ease with the world of finances, such as by providing training on different kinds of fund-raising techniques or using a team approach for securing major gifts, pairing a less confident trustee with either the CEO or a more confident peer. One nonprofit asks board members annually to select from a list of fund-raising activities the ones they prefer to do, which range from sending thank-you notes to donors to personally seeking capital campaign contributions, without passing judgment on the choices made.

Bradshaw (2002) proposes a creative solution to the division-of-labor question, reframing the discussion by using the metaphor of storytelling to emphasize the functions of governance, leadership, and management rather than specific roles assigned to the board or the staff. If we accept the premise that nonprofits are socially constructed, it is the leadership function to create the *story*, which refers to forming a coherent sense of the past and a vision for the future in a compelling version of the activities and decisions shared by organizational members. The management function then is to implement and enact the reality established by the story, while the governance function is "to question, challenge, test, and refine the organizational story" (Bradshaw, 2002, pp. 475–476) so that the narrative does not become overly entrenched and prevent the organization from adapting to new environmental demands. Who carries out the governance function—in most cases, it would be the board—and how, whether in a supportive, collaborative, or confrontational manner, as circumstances dictate, is less important than that this function is performed.

PRACTICAL CONSIDERATIONS

As noted above, trustees are volunteers, arguably the most important component of the nonprofit volunteer corps. They apply their talents as a group, through full board and committee work, and individually, taking on special assignments. In today's turbulent and competitive world, there appears to be little justification for viewing the board as anything but a critical resource that, when helped to perform effectively, can and will make a major contribution to the organization's continued success. Sadly, some nonprofits and their top professionals still ignore this reality, learning their lesson the hard way when a crisis occurs and the board is too weak to be of much use. In this section we will examine the structures and processes that give shape and direction to the nonprofit governing board, highlighting proven practices designed to foster effectiveness.

Board Structure

As in most enterprises, form ought to follow function. In other words, the structure of a particular board is derived from its legal mandate and the general policies established in its bylaws and incorporation documents to carry out the defined organizational mission. One important consideration is size, reflecting the governance model that has been chosen. For example, with the policy governance approach, since the trustees act on all matters as a committee of the whole, a small board of about seven is considered sufficient

(Carver, 1990). Most of the other models use some sort of multiple-committee system, so the number of board members must be high enough to do the work in an efficient manner. In the case of a very traditional nonprofit that has twelve working committees, its large size of forty-four members is viewed as a necessity.

Typically, board leadership consists of a president (or chair), one or more vice presidents, a treasurer, and a secretary. These officers and usually the chairs of standing committees, perhaps with a few other trustees for more balance, constitute an executive committee, a group that provides governance oversight and may make certain decisions between regular board meetings. The CEO usually sits with the executive committee, but rarely as a voting member. The president is responsible for seeing that the board operates as a team, conducting meetings, assigning members to committees and keeping them accountable, and for working closely with the CEO on such matters as meeting agendas and ensuring that key stakeholders are kept abreast of organizational developments. The vice president stands in when the president is absent or unavailable but may also head a major committee or lead a project. The primary responsibilities of the treasurer and secretary are, respectively, to manage the organization's financial affairs and to maintain complete records of all board business as well as to handle all types of communication.

Besides an executive committee, there may be permanent committees to cover finances, fund development, HR or personnel, programs and services, marketing/PR, and nominations (today often called the board development committee). Other committees are common for certain types of nonprofits, such as buildings and grounds for an organization owning property or collections management for a museum. The main responsibilities of a committee, as spelled out in the bylaws or a written charge, are to study issues pertinent to its assigned area and recommend policies for adoption by the full board. When specific, time-limited needs arise, ad hoc committees or task forces are frequently formed; their duties expire once the assignment is done.

Some might say the board president's most important responsibility is to make committee assignments and select the chairs, frequently with input from the CEO and the executive committee, from among those on the board or the community at large, depending on the committee's charge. Ideally, these decisions are based on an assessment of skills, interests, support of the organizational mission, and for current trustees, evidence of meeting the expectations of board members, although cronyism can be a problem. Choosing officers is generally an internal process; individuals are named from within the board, using much the same criteria as for committee chairs, and are elected to their positions as specified in the bylaws. Quite often, there is a more-or-less formal succession plan whereby people move up through the organizational hierarchy to eventually become president. However, it is wise to observe how someone performs as a board member and on committees before considering him or her as an officer.

The length of board service is another structural concern. It is strongly advised to institute some kind of limitations on board terms to ensure that fresh viewpoints and talents are always part of the mix, but some organizations (YSN, for one) see a greater value in continuity and loyalty and therefore allow trustees to serve as long as they wish. In most instances this is a mistake, for board members can get too complacent and fail to carry out their duties in an effective manner or become simply a rubber stamp of the executive's decisions. Accordingly, many nonprofits set a two-term limit, of two, three, or four years each, for board members and require at least one year off the board before again being eligible for consideration. Another recommendation is to stagger the terms, with perhaps a third of the board turning over every year, to maintain some stability but also allow for growth. Term limitations ought to be placed on board officers as well, to prevent leadership from being the province of just a few.

Board Composition

There is an old saying: Act in haste and repent at leisure. It directly applies to building a board, as we have seen in the YSN case study. The founder installed his friends and business associates on the board because it was expedient to do so. Moreover, it ensured that people would ratify his actions without question and not get in the way of his vision for the organization. To his successors this became their worst nightmare, for the board proved unwilling and unable to rise to the occasion when new environmental demands and challenges threatened YSN's long-term survival.

One viewpoint on forming an effective board is to strike an even balance of people who bring *wisdom*, the knowledge related to the organization's programs and services; *wealth*, the ability to contribute or obtain funds, or both; and *work*, the time, energy, and skill to carry out the typical governance responsibilities. Although the concept's origin is uncertain, it has been used widely for over twenty years (Herman & Block, 1990). Today we might add *wallop*, my term for having connections and influence with external stakeholders that can pay off for the organization in securing necessary resources, obtaining favorable legislation, and so forth. While this formulation is a bit simplistic, it does convey the important message that a strong board needs diversity of abilities and strengths. Another perspective is that the makeup of the board should reflect the community and clients served by the organization. A number of funders have taken this position; the Ford Foundation, for one, has long required grant applicants to describe the demographic breakdown of the board.

Many boards struggle with diversity, especially regarding ethnicity and culture. In fact, the typical profile of a trustee remains a forty-year-old white male who works in the business sector or the professions. Even though board members profess to want broader representation in their ranks, in practice the emphasis seems to be more on diversity of skills. One problem is that, depending on the depth of the pool of available candidates, nonprofits may end up vying with each other for those perceived to be the most desirable. For instance, in one midwestern city, the same African American female, a well-known professional with extensive background in HR management, was recruited heavily by both for-profits and nonprofits and thus had her pick of organizations while other, less prominent individuals were overlooked. Although informal networking may prove fruitful, the best way to change board composition is to make diversity a priority by adopting a systematic plan for recruitment and retention that is supported by both professional and lay leaders (Bradshaw, Inglis, & Purdy, 2004; Daley, 2002).

Recruitment and Selection

Despite the rhetoric on the desirability of a diverse board, standard recruitment practices suggest it is likely that new trustees will closely resemble those already serving. All too often, filling empty positions becomes an issue only as the date set in the organizational bylaws for board elections nears, and then time limitations prevent doing a thorough search. Just as with YSN, those approached are frequently friends, neighbors, or business colleagues; moreover, the process may be very informal, consisting of a telephone conversation, and lacking in specificity about duties and expectations. As one respondent in a research study (Golensky, 2000) noted, his organization tends to invite the participation of anyone proposed by a current board member who seems to have something to contribute and is willing to join, as long as the person is not diametrically opposed to the agency's philosophy.

However, there are several easily adopted practices to help build an effective board. First, as in hiring staff, the starting point should be job analysis and design, the expectations and responsibilities deemed generic to all trustees, from which a job description can be developed (see exhibit 15.1 for a sample). The job description is discussed with each board prospect, so that when individuals agree to come on the board, there is no question about the duties for which they will be held accountable. To create a board diverse in all of the areas judged to be important by the current trustees, a grid (also known as a skills inventory) can be constructed as a computer document. Along the left-hand side, specific qualifications, such as geographic location, age, ethnicity, gender, areas of expertise, community relationships, and fields of employment, with drop-down menus, are listed. The second step is to enter the names of current board members at the top and then put an X in every appropriate box; the empty cells result in a recruitment profile. Finally, because recruitment is too vital to leave to the last minute, establish a standing board development committee charged with working year-round to identify prospective trustees and manage the whole selection process, leading to preparation of a strong slate of candidates for the annual election. The same committee can also be responsible for identifying opportunities to increase board knowledge and awareness and oversee board assessment, both of which will be discussed in more detail below.

One further point on recruitment and selection: Although we cannot ignore the possible value to the organization of having a trustee with extensive financial resources or the kind of name recognition that easily opens doors, if that individual has no desire to be a full member of the board, attending meetings regularly and serving on committees, it might make more sense to create an advisory board for the social or business elite of the community. Their association would still be useful to the nonprofit, but there would be no false expectations of the role they would play and no resentment on the part of the other trustees for having to carry more than their share of the workload. The nonprofit with the extensive number of active committees referenced earlier established two such groups, with a very positive effect. First, they formed a board of counselors, to assist with fiscal matters, real estate transactions in particular, and second, a group for former board members who choose to stay involved, who are expected to contribute to the agency's annual fund-raising campaign. Each of these advisory groups meets once a year

Exhibit 15.1 Sample Job Description for Board Members

Position Title: Member of Board of Directors

Responsible to: Entire Board of Directors

General Description

Board members have the overall responsibility for the organization. They are charged with supervision and oversight, which is the process by which they make decisions, delegate work, and assure decisions are carried out as intended.

Responsibilities

- Attend all board meetings.
- Serve on at least one committee and attend all of those meetings.
- Support and participate in fund-raising activities.
- Be aware of and take all responsibilities seriously (i.e., legal, financial, planning continuity, evaluation, selection, and evaluation of Executive Director).
- Be a goodwill ambassador for the organization.
- Actively participate in decision-making.
- Be willing to assume leadership positions.
- Be a team player.
- Contribute financially according to one's means.

Qualifications

Interest in and willingness to support the goals of the organization. Initiative, integrity, analytical ability, leadership, good decision-making ability, planning skills, and the ability to organize and monitor work.

---

on a formal basis, but at least two of the counselors serve regularly on the standing investment committee, and former trustees are often asked to work on particular tasks, depending on their areas of expertise.

Board Meetings

For local nonprofits, monthly or bimonthly board meetings are the norm. However, in one survey of governance practices (Golensky, 2000), over 13 percent of the respondents indicated the board met just quarterly, which is fairly common for regional, statewide and national organizations, with some of the largest ones whose members reside all across the country holding semiannual meetings. While the trustees participating in the 2000 survey generally felt the frequency of meetings was about right, many of the CEOs whose boards met every other month or quarterly questioned whether this was sufficient to accomplish the necessary business. The dilemma is that attendance is often a problem, so holding more frequent meetings may not resolve the issue and could make it worse, even resulting in the loss of some members, especially for boards that have recruited heavily from the top corporate or professional ranks. A possible solution is alternating virtual and face-to-face monthly meetings.

The most commonly cited reasons for missing a board meeting are conflicting obligations at work (another meeting scheduled at the same time, for example) or home (a child's or spouse's illness, out of town on vacation, and so forth). Some of the strategies adopted to increase attendance include changing meeting times, with early morning and lunchtime popular options; shortening the length of meetings; and having a more focused agenda to stimulate increased discussion on important matters. This last choice is particularly interesting because so often the agenda is overlooked as a strategic tool. In fact, this seemingly innocuous piece of paper can be a real source of power for the person who determines the topics to be covered, as much by what is left out as what is included. Ideally, this task should be handled jointly by the board president and the executive, ensuring that critical matters requiring the trustees' involvement are addressed proactively. It might seem obvious that the agenda and accompanying material ought to be sent out enough in advance of the meeting that board members can be well-prepared to participate in the discussion; since the mailings are a management responsibility, when the agenda is received at the last minute or distributed at the meeting, this may be a sign of an executive who is trying to control the decision-making process.

To increase the efficiency and effectiveness of board meetings, some nonprofits use a *consent agenda*, grouping routine business such as approval of the minutes of the last meeting, summaries of recent committee meetings, and any other item considered primarily informational, that is, not necessitating discussion and action by the board, to be voted on together, usually at the start of the meeting. In this way, the bulk of the time can be spent on more substantive issues pertaining to the present and future of the organization. For this approach to work, sufficient information must be provided in a timely fashion so board members understand what is included in the consent agenda. This permits anyone who feels further consideration should be given to an item to ask, prior to or at the meeting, that it be removed and accorded separate attention.

To achieve much the same ends, Tropman (2006) emphasizes structuring board meetings to produce high-quality decisions, drawing on his research into the ways nonprofit executives who are masters of promoting good group decisions go about the task. Many of these experts follow the rule of the *agenda bell*, a system of organizing the meeting time into seven parts. Shaped like the classic bell curve showing normal distribution, this agenda accords major attention to decisions, divided into modest, moderate, and the most difficult items, which fall in the center of the curve and consume around half the total time. The meeting starts with about ten minutes for approval of the previous meeting's minutes and brief announcements; the last half-hour or so is spent brainstorming about a particular issue before adjourning. This allows board members to work up to the hardest issues and then finish with a "fun" activity that unites the group in planning for the future. It is also clear this approach asks trustees to do their hardest work when energies and attendance are at their peak. Other related practices include the "no-new-business" and the "no-more-reports" rules, to emphasize the need to submit items in advance in order to make the best use of time at the meeting itself (p. 232).

Exhibit 15.2 illustrates another useful governance tool, this time looking at the entire year, that was developed by a nonprofit organization providing child-care services to a multicounty area in west Michigan. The intent of this calendar is to reinforce the timing of critical decisions, linking them to ongoing organizational goals and objectives. When the organization undertook an extended search for a new executive director, the

Exhibit 15.2 Board of Directors Calendar for FY 20__

October 5, 20__	November 2, 20__	December 7, 20__
New Board Members Marketing Presentation	Review Human Resources Policy	Board Members' Get-Together
Quality customer service, fiscal responsibility and professional staff development are standards for agency.	The diverse child-care needs of families are met.	
January 4, 20__	**February 1, 20__**	**March 1, 20__**
Audit Report Board Evaluation Community Input	Discussion of Strategic Planning	Strategic Planning Continues
The community is educated on all aspects of quality child care.	Partnerships are maintained to meet our mission.	The agency is viewed by the community as the lead child-care resource.
April 5, 20__	**May 3, 20__**	**June 7, 20__**
Nominations for New Board Members	New Board Members Begin Marketing Presentation	Community Input Board Member Activity
A comprehensive child-care system is established.	The diverse child-care needs of families are met.	The community is educated on all aspects of quality child care.
July 12, 20__	**August 2, 20__**	**September 6, 20__**
Begin Director's Evaluation Salary & Benefit Review	Director's Evaluation Written; Salary Approval. Board Officer Nominations Calendar Planning FY Succession Plan & Annual Authorizations	Nominations for New Board Members Officer Elections Meeting with Director Next Year Budget Capital Budget
Partnerships are maintained to meet our mission.	The agency is viewed by the community as the lead child-care resource.	A comprehensive child-care system is established.

Source: Adapted from Golensky, 2008.
Note: Many nonprofits elect not to hold board meetings in July and August.

different tasks associated with the process were also listed on the calendar to remind the board members of the added obligation and to ensure they kept to the schedule set for the search. The result was a meaningful and logical context for addressing all board actions.

The Educational Component of Governance

The cycle of board development begins with recruitment, continues through a process of education to help trustees carry out their work, and ends with monitoring the board's performance, with the possible removal of those not meeting expectations (Brown, 2007). Since recruitment has already been addressed in a separate section and board assessment follows, here the focus will be on the efforts to educate and train trustees.

It is ironic that even though both CEOs and board members embrace the idea of an educated board as an important step toward board effectiveness, board training is not always made a high priority by either. In some settings the training consists primarily of an orientation for new board members and little thereafter; other nonprofits incorporate education in the regular board meetings by having staff members present short overviews of the programs and services offered, with outside speakers brought in on occasion to address governance topics; still others hold annual or every-other-year, all-day board retreats during which training is given a prominent place. A possible explanation for these varying approaches can be traced to ambivalence about the importance of clarifying board roles and responsibilities. Board members may acknowledge they are not as well versed in organizational matters as they should be but then cite time constraints as a barrier. For executives, especially those subscribing to the technocratic ideology discussed earlier, underlying the stated desire not to overburden their very busy trustees with further demands on their time is often a fear that better-educated board members might then feel empowered to micromanage (Golensky, 2000).

To an outside observer, these perceptions can seem like mirror images of each other. In truth, a clearly articulated program of board training and education often results in greater commitment to the organization as trustees gain more confidence in their ability to handle the business of governance and thus take more pride in their work, reducing their need to rely so heavily on the executive. Orientation should begin at the point of recruitment as prospects are informed about the nature of the organization and its mission. Once individuals have accepted the invitation to join the board and preferably before they take up their duties, a time needs to be set for a formal orientation, during which the executive and board president, with other staff and board members included as seems warranted, discuss the organization's history, programs, finances, and personnel structure, and review the expectations of trustees in terms of attendance at meetings, service on committees, fund development, public relations, and so on. Ideally, each new board member will be given a manual with the same information presented during the orientation, the calendar of meetings and other board-related events, the organization's bylaws, and any other useful materials pertaining to governance and management. Some organizations also assign an experienced board member to each new person as a mentor or a "buddy" for the first year, a way to help the newcomers feel more comfortable in taking up their responsibilities (Gill, 2005).

Although devoting some time at every regular board meeting to a topic that will increase the members' understanding of their governance obligations is certainly a positive step, many nonprofits find this is insufficient to achieve the goal of a well-educated board. Consequently, they may encourage trustees, especially those being groomed for current or future leadership roles, to attend conferences and organize study groups or seminars for them. In addition, an annual (or biannual) retreat may be scheduled to consider bigger issues with longer-term implications that require extensive discussion. This special event is often held at a location away from where the board generally meets, to emphasize its importance and to signal a focus on nonroutine matters. When the purpose of the retreat is board development, the resources devoted to it can be considered a wise investment to accomplish the following objectives:

- Strengthening performance through a review of governance processes and the board's roles and responsibilities;
- Assessing the board's contributions to the organization and identifying ways that it can add greater value;
- Establishing priorities for the board and identifying strategies and actions to achieve them;
- Enhancing collegiality and working relationships among board members and between board and staff; and
- Determining the next steps in board development and in the implementation of overall action plans. (Holland, 2006, p. 360)

Information for planning and conducting a retreat may be obtained online from several sites. One of the best resources on this and other aspects of governance is the nonprofit BoardSource (formerly known as the National Center for Nonprofit Boards), established in 1988 and located in Washington, DC; its Web site is www.boardsource.org.

Board Self-Assessment

Frequently, one of the agenda items for a board development retreat is self-assessment, a task that many trustees find as disquieting as evaluating the performance of the executive. In this age of accountability, however, when external stakeholders such as accrediting bodies, funders, and regulatory groups are examining virtually every aspect of organizational life, the majority of boards now accept the necessity of conducting some form of evaluation of their own contributions, collectively and individually. For those that have embraced the Policy Governance model, it is a built-in obligation to systematically look at the manner in which the board manages its time and actions; others may come at the process with less enthusiasm but no less a commitment if for no other reason than a realization that the board ought to lead by example.

More and more, the definition of an effective board has come to include monitoring its own progress and evaluating its performance. Having a board president and top professional who understand the importance of the assessment process is critical to its success; by their calling attention to the need for regular evaluation, they accord it legitimacy and establish a behavioral norm. One reason trustees have not taken self-assessment very seriously is that organizations are often reluctant to tie personal consequences to the process. Many nonprofits include in the bylaws a provision for removing a board member, such as the following as instituted by a statewide association of nonprofits: "Any Trustee may be removed from office for 'cause' by the affirmative vote of two-thirds of the Trustees. For purposes of this Section 6(b) 'cause' shall mean (i) misconduct, or (ii) failure to attend any three consecutive regularly scheduled meetings of the Board of Trustees during any one calendar year without being excused therefrom by the Chairperson of the Board of Trustees." Unfortunately, such policies are seldom if ever invoked even for poor attendance, which here is pretty clear-cut, so removal for "misconduct," which is not spelled out at all, is likely to come into play only for the most egregious reasons. However, if unsatisfactory performance were well defined, added as a cause for removal, and then applied when appropriate, this could go a long way toward strengthening these types of evaluation.

The starting point is to develop some kind of work plan for trustees, with goals and objectives, similar to the one established for the organization as a whole. Earlier in this chapter, the annual board calendar created by a west Michigan nonprofit was used as an illustration of a method for keeping trustees focused on the work at hand. It may not be very surprising to learn that this same organization also prepares a board action plan at its annual governance retreat for the coming year that reflects its evaluation of the progress made collectively toward the outcomes set the previous year. Some time back, this nonprofit adopted the Policy Governance model, which has as a core principle the concept of *moral ownership*, namely, that a board is responsible to those stakeholders who have a special interest in the work of the organization. For a community-based organization the ownership would be the community at large (Carver, 1990). Thus, the first outcome for the annual work plan is linkage with its owners; the process for evaluating the action steps under this goal is shown in exhibit 15.3. One tool for individual assessments is the Director's Self-Evaluation Checklist (Gill, 2005), consisting of twenty-two statements (sample item: "I have a good understanding of my role and duties as a board member" [p. 149], with a scale ranging from 4 = agree to 1 = disagree). The stated purpose of the checklist is to "assess the 'added value' that [individual board members] bring to the organization, whether they have met the expectations set by the board when they took their place at the boardroom table and whether they continue to be committed to serving on the board" (p. 148). At the bottom of the form, the trustee may offer suggestions for improving board performance and his/her ability to make an effective contribution; it is also indicated on the form that the responses will be used by the board chair in a face-to-face discussion with the individual about past efforts and future service. Other evaluation instruments of this type can be accessed through the Internet.

Exhibit 15.3 Board of Trustees' Self-Assessment Tool (Partial)

As the Board of Trustees of XYZ Agency assesses its own performance with governance, it should do so in the context of its own job description and outputs in these areas of governance: Linkage with Its Owners, Policy Development, Monitoring CEO Performance, and Board Governance Process.

In addition to individual and full board assessment of its performance, the Board may also seek input from the Executive Director.

On a scale of 1–5, 5 being the *highest* level, please check the column that best reflects your assessment of the collective board's performance in the following areas:

Progress with Board Outcomes	1	2	3	4	5	Improvement Opportunities and Comments
Linkage with Its Owners: In the past year, the Board communicated with and/or interacted with key policymakers, the community, and other stakeholders.						
In the past year, the Board met with the boards of agencies whose missions intersect with this agency to learn more about ways for the boards and staffs to coalesce on mission-related activities.						
In the past year, Board trainings or meetings addressed appropriate community relations and advocacy roles and means to be embraced.						
The Board assisted in introducing the new CEO to the community and key stakeholder groups.						

Note: This is an actual tool used by a regional child-care organization in west Michigan.

FINAL THOUGHTS

According to Senge (2006), when people are asked what it is like to be part of a great team, their responses express the meaningfulness of being fully connected with others in generating a new reality for the organization while growing as individuals. What does it take for a group to get to this place? One of the primary requirements is to bring the members into alignment: "When a team becomes more aligned, a commonality of direction emerges, and individuals' energies harmonize. . . . There is . . . a shared vision, and understanding of how to complement one another's efforts" (p. 217).

This is the perfect recipe for what the ideal nonprofit board should be, and it is an achievable goal when both the executive and the board president are of one mind about the roles and responsibilities of an effective board. It is safe to conclude that it is not the particular model of governance that makes the difference but the level of commitment brought to the enterprise. In this context the answer to the question posed above on how to build a great team is to devote the necessary energy and resources to the full gamut of board development, from recruitment through education to assessment.

Direct Service Volunteers

Volunteers are a vital part of the life of many nonprofit organizations, giving time and often money in support of their favorite causes. Some nonprofits, such as the Girl Scouts, could not function without the volunteers who fill positions like troop leader for which there is no paid staff equivalent. In other cases, such as museums, hospitals, or soup kitchens, volunteers render services, that otherwise would have to be provided by paid staff. These individuals assist the organization through two distinct roles: *Direct service* volunteers work with the paid staff on tasks such as walking the dogs housed at a rescue shelter, staffing emergency hotlines, and giving guided tours of a public arboretum, and generally have a fair amount of consumer contact. *Indirect support* volunteers are the ones putting together mass mailings, answering phones, and delivering supplies, with limited client contact. Board members and community people serving on board committees also fall into this second classification (Hartenian, 2007).

Volunteering, defined as any kind of unpaid effort, freely given, whether in more formalized ways in organizations or informally (helping out a neighbor, for example), has been a part of the American tradition since colonial days. According to the Corporation for National and Community Service (2007), in 2006 over 61 million adults, ages sixteen and older, volunteered nationally, representing 27 percent of the population. Even though the numbers are slightly down from 2005 figures, the U.S. volunteer rate is still historically high when compared to previous decades and almost at the rate during the year after September 11, 2001. The growth in volunteering between 1974 and 2006 has been driven primarily by three age groups, young adults, sixteen to nineteen years old; midlife adults, forty-five to sixty-four years old; and older adults, ages sixty-five and over. Volunteers contributed 8.1 billion hours of service in 2006, with religious organizations the most popular choice (35%), followed by educational or youth service (27%) and social or community service (13%). To put a monetary value on volunteering, Independent Sector (2009), a national umbrella organization of nonprofits, has estimated each hour contributed at $19.51 for 2007, up from $18.77 in 2006, using average hourly earnings for nonmanagement, nonfarm workers and estimated fringe-benefit costs. Multiplying the 2006 contributed hours by the hourly rate for that year gives some idea of what volunteers are worth but does not account for the intangibles, such as demonstrating community support of a cause.

In this chapter, the primary focus is on the direct service volunteer rather than the individual providing indirect support (see chapter 15 for information on boards). We will first consider various conceptual and practical aspects of volunteerism and then examine the elements of an effective volunteer management program.

AN OVERVIEW OF VOLUNTEERISM

From the information on numbers and the dollar value of volunteers, the reasons behind the widespread use of volunteers in nonprofit organizations may seem obvious. Indeed, the conventional wisdom is that volunteers represent a considerable cost savings for their organizations and, at the same time, make it possible to offer more services. On the downside, there is also a general belief that volunteers may be used to displace paid workers, and thus relationships with staff can be problematic. However, recent evidence suggests this kind of conflict is not as prevalent as previously assumed, especially when organizational leaders introduce the volunteer program by including salaried staff in the decisions on its design and implementation. In most cases it is no longer legal to substitute volunteers for paid employees in either private or public sector agencies. Moreover, overworked staff seem to appreciate having the extra help and recognize that volunteers can be effective advocates for the organization (Brudney & Gazley, 2002).

Another possible misconception about volunteering was addressed by a survey of giving and volunteering practices in California. It revealed much higher levels of informal or person-to-person volunteering, such as offering emotional support, transportation, and assistance with household chores to needy neighbors, friends, and extended family members, than had been reported in earlier national research (O'Neill, 2001). This trend was confirmed in the study by the Corporation for National and Community Service (2007) noted above; for 2006, in addition to those involved in organizationally based volunteering, more than five million people engaged in informal activities with their neighbors to improve the community.

Forms of Volunteerism

Direct service volunteerism can be categorized as informal or formal. The first category, also called *unmanaged volunteering,* includes spontaneous and sporadic efforts between friends and neighbors; the second category may be called *managed volunteering* and is normally conducted through organizations.

In addition, it is possible to address the different forms of volunteerism by the length of the involvement and the nature of the assumed tasks. An increasingly popular option is *episodic volunteering,* which tends to be short term and time limited and is ideal for those who cannot make more extensive commitments, perhaps because of family or job constraints but often simply out of personal preference. Some may offer their services for a specific project on a temporary basis, for a few hours or a day at most (a one-time neighborhood cleanup effort, for example), while others show up at a given site at regular intervals as their schedules permit, such as at a community food bank to sort contributions. A third approach involves service that may be provided regularly but for short periods, usually less than six months: volunteering to assist victims of a natural disaster would be a good illustration. As discussed below, such individuals present very different challenges from managing more traditional volunteers.

With *recurring volunteering*, individuals generally exhibit a greater level of commitment, although it may still be of relatively short duration. Examples would include tutoring adults who are illiterate and being a mentor to a child. In these cases, a person is likely to follow a set schedule, say, every Wednesday afternoon from three to five, and his or her absence would leave a void, whereas at a food bank several people are apt to be on site on any given day so one absentee will not hinder completion of the task.

There are also volunteer opportunities for groups. To promote greater cohesion, a family, however defined, might elect to participate in an activity as a unit. This could involve serving dinner on Thanksgiving at a homeless shelter or organizing a fund-raiser to benefit the neighborhood or a particular nonprofit. This kind of participation is an excellent way to instill the value of community service in young people and create a new generation of volunteers. Finally, there is *team volunteering*; individuals from the same company or religious institution working together to build a house for the local Habitat for Humanity or entering a 10K race sponsored by a charity as a single entry would be illustrations of this form (Korngold, Voudouris, & Griffiths, 2006).

Motivations for Volunteering

Just as there are many reasons why individuals seek to serve in indirect support roles in nonprofits, the motivations for direct service volunteering cover the spectrum from satisfying purely altruistic purposes to addressing self-serving interests. As reported by Wolf (1999), volunteers themselves have identified the following motivators:

- Sense of satisfaction in feeling needed and making a useful contribution to the community.
- Altruism, as an outgrowth of religious beliefs and/or family traditions and upbringing.
- Companionship, as a way to widen one's circle of acquaintances and develop personal connections that may extend beyond the volunteer setting.
- Learning about a field of interest, such as the arts, for personal enrichment.
- Pride in being a successful entrepreneur through creating a nonprofit and helping it grow.
- Developing contacts that may prove useful in one's business or professional life.
- Getting ahead in a for-profit that expects up-and-coming executives to volunteer.
- Obtaining training and experience that may pave the way for seeking a paying job in the field.

- Providing access to a particular organization for either future employment or board service.
- Social status through associating with those who are part of the community elite.

For some individuals a single motivation may be influencing their volunteering while for others a combination of factors is at work. The key to successful recruitment and retention of volunteers is to understand what they hope to gain from the experience and to enhance their sense of self-esteem through the assigned activities, for when people believe they are fulfilling a meaningful and effective role within the organization, their commitment to their volunteer efforts is likely to increase. Mayer, Fraccastoro, and McNary (2007) found those with higher levels of self-esteem volunteered more days per year and for a longer period than those with lower self-esteem. One useful tool to promote these desirable ends is the *psychological contract*, an actual or implied reciprocal agreement between two parties. It is applied most often in understanding employee behavior but seems to have equal validity for volunteers. The premise behind the psychological contract is to identify each individual's goals and needs and then, to the extent possible, attempt to meet their expectations. Although people do not volunteer in exchange for financial rewards, they do have expectations of the entity to which they contribute their time. Accordingly, at first contact, organizations should pay attention to what motivates particular individuals to volunteer in selecting from the available activities, to try to satisfy those driving forces, and endeavor to provide some clear indication via timely feedback and a system of rewards and recognitions "that their work is actually contributing to the overall mission and goals" (Farmer & Fedor, 1999, p. 363).

As mentioned earlier, volunteering to help religious organizations is the most popular choice. Through telephone interviews with more than 500 Indiana residents, Gronbjerg and Never (2004) found that frequent attendance at religious services was a strong predictor of involvement in any type of volunteering and directly related to participation in providing religious services, with a significant association as well to helping with fundraising and the maintenance of facilities and grounds for religious institutions. However, they remind us that factors influencing certain kinds of volunteer activity may have no relevance with regard to other volunteer work, thus reinforcing the need to take into account the differential impact of the various psychological motivations on individual decisions for effective volunteer management.

Age as a Factor in Volunteerism

In considering all age cohorts, those falling into the 35–44 range volunteered at the highest rate nationally (33 percent) in 2006, followed closely by individuals ages 45–54, at 32 percent. Yet in terms of time, it probably is no surprise that volunteers 65 and older were at the top of the list, averaging 100 hours per month, with the 55–64 age group next, at 60 median hours (Corporation for National and Community Service, 2007).

The data from the Corporation's 2007 report reveal some important developments with respect to young people. Between 1989 and 2006 the percentage of individuals ages

16–19 engaged in volunteering nearly doubled, from 13.4 percent to 26.4 percent. In fact, the report notes the percentage of entering college students today who express the belief that it is very important to help others in difficulty has reached a twenty-five-year high. One possible factor contributing to the increased interest in volunteering among young adults is the growth in service-learning programs that, in many communities, begin with kindergarten. Simply defined, *service-learning* (S-L) is a way to connect academic goals with community service through age-appropriate projects; students are provided with real-world experiences specifically designed to bring classroom learning alive. A lot of middle schools, high schools, and institutions of higher education across the country now include some kind of volunteer community work as a graduation requirement. In a study of S-L as a predictor of future volunteerism, prior involvement in service projects emerged as the most powerful determinant. Other key factors were the personal gain to the students from acquiring communication, leadership, and interpersonal skills through participating in S-L and the project's perceived value to the community organization and its clients (Tomkovick, Lester, Flunker, & Wells, 2008).

At the other end of the age spectrum, adults ages 65 and older have substantially increased their volunteer participation over the past three decades, from 14 percent in 1974 to 24 percent in 2006 (Corporation for National and Community Service, 2007). Using a broader definition of seniors as individuals 55 and above, Independent Sector (2004) found these older volunteers gave on average 4.4 hours per week to their favorite causes, or approximately 5.6 billion hours annually, at a value of $77.2 billion to non-profits and other beneficiaries. Any way you slice it, seniors are a major force in volunteerism. But what accounts for this extraordinary contribution? Some plausible reasons, such as improved health, more free time, or the desire to fill the void left by the death of a spouse or some other form of family disintegration, have been, by and large, ruled out. We are left with two partial explanations for this phenomenon: advances in education and the significant involvement of women, with a third possibility being changed attitudes toward retirement from a time for relaxation to an opportunity for new activities and adventures (Goss, 1999). Support for the relationship between perspectives on retirement and volunteerism is provided by Smith's study of midlife workers (2004), ages 50–64, on their future plans, but with some unexpected results. When asked to describe their ideal retirement lifestyle, close to 60 percent of the respondents saw volunteerism as a significant part of the equation, but even more (63 percent) connected retirement with living a life of leisure. Moreover, those within five years of retirement were less likely to view volunteering as part of the plan than those farther away from leaving the workforce, which suggests that in the end personal needs may take precedence over societal expectations.

Gender and Ethnicity as Factors in Volunteerism

Although men volunteer slightly more hours per month on average than women (fifty-two versus fifty), women tend to offer their services at a higher national rate, at 32 percent versus 24 percent for men (Corporation for National and Community Service, 2007). Taniguchi (2006) focused on the effects among white adults of employment and family characteristics to help explain gender differences. Consistent with previous studies, the majority of the respondents had done no volunteering, but of the men and women who had participated in some kind of volunteer work, employment status made a big difference. Women working part time or who were unemployed contributed many more hours than men with the same status, but among full-timers, men spent more hours volunteering than women. In addition, women spent significantly more time caring for aging family members, which, as one might expect, appears to limit the time available for volunteering. These findings are important "because of their implications not only for the overall supply of volunteers but also for women's opportunities to get involved in the community, cultivate social networks, attain personal growth, and gain life satisfaction" (Taniguchi, 2006, p. 97). Research by Rotolo and Wilson (2007) on how women's volunteerism is affected by children and employment status yielded fairly similar results: Homemakers and then part-timers are more apt to volunteer than are full-time workers. However, they also discovered that whereas mothers of preschoolers are less likely to be active volunteers, having school-age children has a positive effect on volunteering, especially for homemakers. If nonprofits wish to increase the involvement of young women with children, it may require some rethinking of how best to use such volunteers, perhaps by providing more avenues for family volunteering.

With respect to ethnicity, participation patterns for people of color seem to differ from those of whites, but there is little empirical research to tell us exactly how. Some evidence does indicate personal and social resources, such as education and amount of discretionary time, contribute to the likelihood of volunteer participation and that women are more apt to volunteer than men among native-born African Americans, Asians, Hispanics, and whites and among immigrants from these same groups except for Asians. We also know the way formal volunteering is viewed in immigrants' native cultures may affect volunteer behavior in their new culture (Sundeen, Garcia, & Raskoff, 2008). For instance, focus groups involving Latino adults in Oregon revealed that their volunteering occurs mainly in the context of the family and secondarily in the neighborhood and church rather than in mainstream community-based organizations. They consider what they do as simply "helping" others. In many Latin American countries, volunteering means activities by the rich to help the poor, so volunteer work as defined in the United States is not really part of their experience. Thus, the best route to connect with the Latino community is to build trust by establishing personal relationships, slowly, respectfully, and unobtrusively (Hobbs, 2001). For many African Americans, volunteer participation takes place through the church, but black sororities and fraternities are a major outlet as well for their members, who may engage in team volunteering.

Measures of Satisfaction and Discontent

Macduff (2006) has identified the central dilemma for many volunteer programs, namely, they have not kept pace with the changing landscape of volunteering to accommodate the needs of the increasing numbers of people who do not wish to or cannot participate in more traditional ways. For example, the "serendipitous volunteer" (p. 34) may show up at an agency offering a few hours of her time and wanting to be put to work on the spot, and then not return until weeks or even months later. Whereas traditional volunteers crave stability, the serendipitous volunteer's main concern is flexibility.

Failing to understand such differences affects both recruitment and retention. Just as with paid staff, organizations make an investment in recruiting, training, and placing volunteers and so have an interest, both monetary and programmatic, in what prompts individuals to continue to volunteer or drives them away. Moreover, when volunteers leave out of disappointment or frustration, depending on their role within the organization, it can have a negative psychological effect not only on staff and clients but even on the larger society. As indicated earlier, satisfaction with the volunteer experience is derived from the activity itself but also from the rewards the tasks provide, which may be intrinsic, such as the feeling of accomplishment after mastering a new skill, or extrinsic, perhaps through social interactions with other volunteers. At the other end of the spectrum, volunteers may burn out due to the stresses caused by their assignments.

Often the responses to volunteering can be traced to individual personality traits; those with better coping skills seem able to overcome any negative aspects of their assignments and maximize the positive side. Satisfaction also is derived from family support, legitimating the time spent away from home, and the quality of the supervision, reflecting the value placed on the personal commitment (Kulik, 2007). Indeed, there is a strong connection between individual motivations for volunteering and the organizational responses in terms of the tasks assigned and the rewards available to meet these expectations in fostering satisfaction as well as the desire to remain a volunteer. A newly developed Total Match Index (TMI), which measures the overall fit between motivations to volunteer and what its creators refer to as "environmental affordances" by the organization, offers an exciting possibility for predicting whether the experience will be positive for both parties, taking into consideration that no tool can perfectly capture all the nuances of any situation (Stukas, Worth, Clary, & Snyder, 2009).

It is also useful for program managers to gain a better sense of the factors leading to volunteers' dropping out. On one hand, individuals make the decision to volunteer at a particular organization of their own volition and are free to leave at any time, so it may seem a bit of a paradox to focus on why they decide to discontinue their services, but the burnout phenomenon is very real and, as previously stated, potentially costly. On the other hand, volunteers may leave for reasons that have nothing to do with a negative experience, such as when their circumstances change due to relocation or a new job. Therefore, Yanay and Yanay (2008) suggest that, to understand perseverance and dropout, it may be more fruitful to look at the discrepancies between volunteers' expectations and their actual experiences within the organization rather than on their reasons for volunteering. For example, a social service agency dealing with clients in crisis may want their volunteers to act independently in managing their tasks, whereas the volunteers are feeling abandoned when expected to handle on their own the anxiety and pain arising from their work. In other words, the problem may be less psychological than contextual and relational.

ELEMENTS OF EFFECTIVE VOLUNTEER MANAGEMENT

There are many similarities between creating and maintaining a dedicated workforce (see chapter 14) and an effective program of volunteer management in a nonprofit. In both cases the process starts with assessing organizational needs and continues with close attention to planning, recruitment and screening, orientation, supervision and training, rewards, and evaluation. However, in volunteer programs, because people often pick an organization for its mission rather than for a specific position, matching individual expectations with available opportunities is critical. In addition, scheduling the hours of service to accommodate both the volunteer and the organization is almost an art form. Korngold et al. (2006) identify the key elements of a high-impact program: (1) visible and consistent support from senior managers; (2) staffing by one or more professionals for whom this is their primary if not sole responsibility; (3) adequate resources in the annual budget, with a cost-benefit analysis each year to determine the program's value; and (4) sound written policies to govern all aspects of the effort, including risk management.

Assessment and Planning

For any new enterprise, what goes into its formation often has a major influence on the end result. The starting point is to assess the "why" of the program; each nonprofit will determine whether and how volunteers can contribute to fulfilling its mission, from carrying out an indispensable function (the Girl Scout troop leader, for example), to supplementing the work of paid staff, to providing an extra hand for special occasions, such as preparing a large mailing. In making these decisions and then designing the actual program, it is wise to obtain as much input as possible from administrators, staff, board members, other policy-level volunteers, and even consumers, as appropriate, perhaps through a series of focus groups.

As part of the assessment, potential problems should be considered—the extra time demands in providing volunteer supervision, for one—and then weighed against the likely benefits before moving forward, so the worth of the investment of organizational resources can be clearly delineated to both internal and external stakeholders. Involving staff early on in major decisions is probably the best way to avoid later difficulties. If staff feel threatened by the volunteers' presence or are indifferent to them, the diversity of opportunities and the quality of the supervision will certainly be affected, diminishing the overall experience for the volunteers and, as a result, the success of the program. Conversely, when staff feel empowered by their inclusion in developing the program, they are much more apt to see the positive side of using volunteers (McCurley, 1994).

Once the decision has been made to develop a volunteer program, policies should be written, and approved by the board, to explain its purpose, goals, and objectives; the roles volunteers are likely to fill; and the general management of the endeavor, including applicable personnel procedures, insurance coverage, and budget implications. A key step is establishing oversight responsibility of the program. Ideally, this person, who may be either a current employee or a new hire, will be at the managerial level to demonstrate organizational commitment and, if resources permit, will serve full time as *volunteer manager, director,* or *coordinator* (the most common titles). Depending on the size of the organization and the program's projected scope, there may be additional staff needs, for both professional and clerical support. While personnel will be the largest budget item, sufficient monies should also be set aside for other likely expenses, which may include advertising, transportation, meals, and recognition events. In addition, training may be necessary to upgrade the volunteer manager's skills, to prepare paid staff to assume their supervisory duties, and to help the volunteers perform effectively in carrying out their assignments. Exhibit 16.1 illustrates policy statements suitable for a volunteer program at a hypothetical multiservice nonprofit organization.

Creativity must be used in designing assignments to fit the varying needs of the types of volunteers encountered today. For traditional volunteers, after an analysis of the recurring roles that individuals could fill within the organization, a job description should be written for each one, with a clear indication of duties and responsibilities, the reporting relationship to paid staff, and other pertinent details about the position. Once aware of an individual's strengths and aspirations, the volunteer manager can use the job descriptions as a guide in matching the right job with the person's expectations to achieve the best fit, modifying the final dimensions of the job as warranted. For nontraditional volunteers it is still useful to do this kind of analysis in order to have an overall understanding of the various opportunities within the organization as the foundation for an open-ended discussion about the possibilities for meeting both individual and organizational needs.

Recruitment

Most organizations rely on a combination of formal and informal approaches to recruit potential volunteers for both recurring roles and more time-limited assignments. The analysis of organizational needs, conducted prior to the program's start, points to the most likely sources. A nonprofit serving young teens through recreation and tutoring might view the local colleges and universities as the primary target, whereas an agency helping women gain employment via training and counseling is more apt to turn to the community's business sector. At the same time, the appeals must be effective in drawing individuals who are qualified for the available positions. Having a surplus of people who cannot be placed, for one reason or another, is a problem because it may create negative feelings toward the organization and make poor use of staff time to interview and screen unsuitable candidates.

McCurley (1994) proposes three different ways to conduct recruitment efforts to ensure the organization obtains the number and types of volunteers it needs.

- *Warm-body recruitment.* This approach works best when a relatively large supply of volunteers is needed for a short period of time to do fairly simple tasks, such as to act as judges and huggers for a Special Olympics event or to sign in participants for a charity golf tournament. Techniques like

Exhibit 16.1 A Sample of Policy Statements for a Volunteer Program

The Multi-Activity Service Centers (MASC) is committed to the principles that guided the settlement house movement. First and foremost, the organization is deeply connected to the communities it serves and sees its purpose as nurturing all the potentialities of the residents in these areas, from young to old. To achieve this end, there must be an exchange of experiences and talents through bringing together the resources from within and outside of each community. One of the most effective strategies for realizing our mission is to institute a comprehensive volunteer program.

1. *Defining Who Is a Volunteer*. A volunteer is an individual who engages in any kind of unpaid effort, freely given, on behalf of our clients, whether on a recurring basis or to meet short-term needs. We welcome diversity in age, gender, ethnicity, socioeconomic status, educational background, sexual preference, and ability level, as long as the person subscribes to our mission, is willing to take appropriate direction, and has no legal or physical impediments to carrying out assigned tasks.

2. *Recruitment and Screening*. MASC will use all suitable methods for locating volunteers to help in the various programmatic and administrative areas identified through our assessment as needing this assistance, and we are prepared to commit the necessary resources to ensure we can attract the number of people needed to fill these positions. All prospective volunteers must be willing to give the organization permission to conduct background and reference checks as warranted by the positions in which they have expressed an interest.

3. *Program Administration*. A full-time staff member will oversee the program, with the title of "Program Manager." This person may be a current employee who is reassigned to this position or a new hire, based on who best fits the job description. She or he will supervise a half-time clerical person and one of the two AmeriCorps participants currently at MASC, and be responsible for managing the program's budget. Depending on the growth of the program, the board and executive director are committed to a commensurate increase in the staffing and budget in future years.

4. *Personnel Policies*. Volunteers will be required to wear name badges while working at any MASC facility. They must also sign in and out each day. Those filling recurring positions are required to attend an orientation prior to starting their duties and to take part in all trainings deemed essential to their work. Each volunteer will report to the staff person designated as his/her supervisor and follow this employee's directions as they pertain to the job; in turn, each paid staff member serving as a supervisor must treat the volunteer as a full member of the team and attend a special training before assuming supervisory duties as well as any subsequent identified trainings. This assignment will be considered during the employee's annual performance review. Volunteers may park in the staff lot and will be reimbursed for gas (or public transportation), meals, and any other approved expense incurred in the course of carrying out their assignments.

Note: MASC is a hypothetical nonprofit, a composite of three actual social service agencies.

distributing brochures, putting up posters, using public service announcements on local radio and television stations, issuing press releases, and talking to civic groups are used to disseminate information about the organization and activity to as many people in the community as possible.

- *Targeted recruitment.* Unlike the previous method, here the focus is on a predetermined and limited group of volunteers who can provide particular skills, based on a profile of the ideal person for the job. The recruitment campaign will be shaped by clearly establishing what talents are needed for the task, to identify the most likely locations for finding these people and the best ways to capture their interest by tapping into their psychological needs. Being a "friendly visitor" to an older adult who is homebound, and fielding calls to a crisis hotline are good examples of jobs that require a high level of empathy and compassion.

- *Concentric circles recruitment.* The intent of this approach is to secure a small but steady flow of volunteers, with word of mouth as the primary vehicle. It relies on the goodwill of staff, volunteers, consumers, and people living in the immediate vicinity of the organization to convey the need for additional help to their friends, family members, and neighbors. Just about every nonprofit with a volunteer program uses this method at some point because it has proven to be very efficient in achieving its objectives. It is well suited to episodic volunteering, such as tending to a community garden.

Sometimes the volunteer pool already exists and the need is for organizational partners. This would be the case for colleges and universities mandating internships or service-learning as a graduation requirement. For students in schools of social work, fulfilling a field placement in a local social service agency is the most critical part of the program; thus, considerable effort goes into the process of finding the right match. The AmeriCorps national service program, created by the passage of the National and Community Service Trust Act in 1993, is a special case because its participants receive government financial support to help meet their living expenses and future educational needs. A study of a sample of AmeriCorps members bore out expectations that the initial goals of these "stipended volunteers" influence attitudes and subsequent behavior in carrying out their assignments. Those experiencing high self-esteem due to feeling needed and believing they were accomplishing something worthwhile were more inclined toward altruistic ends, which supports the importance of identifying the interests and needs of all potential volunteers at the time of recruitment and selection, and using this knowledge for effective placement (Tschirhart, Mesch, Perry, Miller, & Lee, 2001).

Even though the statistics on the number of active U.S. volunteers are impressive, the reality is that two-thirds of the population do not become involved in formal volunteering. Perhaps the most easily overcome barrier is simply to be asked, for like donors, the majority of people invited to volunteer will do so. Of other potential barriers, lack of time, lack of interest, and ill health are the ones most often cited. Interestingly, there is some evidence that higher social and economic status may be associated with lack of time as a barrier, while those with a lower status are more apt to cite lack of interest in organizational volunteering, although they may participate in informal efforts. These findings suggest the need for adopting a variety of recruitment approaches, especially for nonprofits wishing to broaden the diversity of their volunteer program (Sundeen, Raskoff, & Garcia, 2007). Organizations hoping to eliminate or at least mitigate the barriers to participation must become more flexible in their expectations and their outreach by increasing the number as well as the scope of their volunteer opportunities. As noted in chapter 12, online or virtual volunteering is one option worth pursuing to widen the pool of individuals who can, and want to, contribute their talents, recognizing this is often a first step toward a greater personal connection, perhaps starting with a combination of online and on-site tasks.

Screening and Placement

For many nontraditional forms of volunteering, as when warm-body recruitment is used for simple assignments, it may be sufficient to screen respondents by phone or even online, but in most cases, if resources permit, there is no substitute for face-to-face interviews to do a proper evaluation.

Screening of direct service volunteers must be handled as diligently as for paid staff, particularly when an organization serves vulnerable clients with whom the volunteers will have considerable contact. Effective screening addresses several different but related goals: to meet organizational needs for extra hands to carry out both ongoing and episodic tasks; to provide satisfying opportunities to match volunteers' motivations for initial involvement as well as promote retention; to make wise use of organizational resources by adding volunteers to the staffing mix, in turn creating a cadre of goodwill ambassadors back to the community; and to build social capital through helping individuals gain firsthand knowledge of the challenges facing society at large.

Whether prospective volunteers are responding to outreach efforts or have made their way to your organization of their own volition, the volunteer manager's task is to make them feel welcome but also to protect the organization and its clients from those whose background suggests they should not be placed in that setting, fortunately a fairly rare occurrence. More often, it is a case of identifying the job that represents the best match between the individual's talents and expectations and organizational needs, and then helping the person see this fit and become enthusiastic about filling the slot. The interview process resembles screening applicants for paid staff positions in many respects, with one big difference: the volunteer candidate may be familiar with the organizational mission yet not have a specific position in mind. Therefore, one of the most important attributes of an effective volunteer manager is the ability to be an active listener, which entails paying attention to both verbal and nonverbal messages to ascertain the person's motives and interests. For those who will be taking on recurring roles, using the psychological contract described earlier in this chapter, the volunteer manager can develop an actual agreement, preferably in writing, that spells out the tasks associated with the position and how these activities reflect what the individual articulated he or she hopes to gain from the experience. Exhibit 16.2 shows what might be included in a contract of this kind.

In the course of the interview, the focus will change from an open-ended presentation about the organization and its various programs to a more structured back-and-forth exchange as the likely assignment emerges. It is crucial at the start to avoid reaching premature conclusions about the most appropriate fit; even though the person's current or former employment is likely to come up, many times individuals want their volunteering to provide what may be lacking in their work. Accordingly, the volunteer manager should be prepared to answer prospects' questions fully and honestly. In addition, volunteers must be informed about organizational requirements applicable to them, such as abiding by confidentiality rules, wearing name badges whenever on the premises, and completing time sheets and any other routine paperwork. A key discussion point is whether the time commitment is flexible. As mentioned above, organizations that are more accommodating of people's busy schedules are likely to be more successful in meeting their volunteer needs.

Exhibit 16.2 An Example of a Psychological Contract

The following agreement has been jointly reached by Theresa Kowalski, volunteer, and Frances Karl, Volunteer Manager for the Multi-Activity Service Center, for the period from January 1, 20__ to December 31, 20__. The agreement may be terminated by either party within thirty days of its initial signing and thereafter by mutual consent. However, the volunteer understands that any serious violation of agency policy may also be cause for immediate termination and that the contract is subject to review at the end of the year.

1. *Assignment.* Based on Mrs. Kowalski's expressed interest in working with older adults and her desire to gain skills that might translate at a later time into a paid position with this population, she is assigned to the Adult Services division in the North Bridge facility, specifically to oversee the Telephone Hotline, a program in which she has volunteered for the past five years.
2. *Supervision.* Her supervisor will be Anita Steinman, director of North Bridge.
3. *Duties.* The volunteer will work Monday through Thursday from 10:00 a.m. to 3:00 p.m. (with a half-hour lunch break). In addition to answering phones and making referrals to community services when MASC itself cannot meet the need, she will assist Ms. Steinman in recruiting and training other volunteers.
4. *Recognition.* In light of the additional responsibilities assumed this year, the volunteer will be invited to attend the advanced training course "Working with Older Adults: Some Further Considerations" from February 2 to 4.

(Signed/dated by Theresa Kowalski)   (Signed/dated by Frances Karl for MASC)

Once the main issues have been resolved, the next steps can vary for traditional and nontraditional volunteers. For the former, depending on the position, before the deal can be finalized, there might be background or reference checks and possibly a second interview that includes the program director or the staff member who will serve as supervisor. Regarding the latter, when a desirable candidate has a narrow window of availability, as Macduff (2006, p. 34) notes, "the coordinator of volunteers must be able . . . to shift gears and learn to live with a looser structure and oversight." Training may also be required before individuals are ready to assume their duties. Finally, prospects should be made aware of the insurance provided to protect them and the organization as well as the procedures in place to serve clients with special needs. Since the decision to go forward is obviously a two-way proposition, the screening process must be designed so that either party can gracefully exit at any point.

Orientation and Training

The orientation held for volunteers is very similar in its basic purpose to the way in which paid staff are introduced to the job. In both cases it is an opportunity for the organization to put its best foot forward and establish the kind of positive relationship that tends to yield the most dedicated performance and long-term commitment, starting with a personal greeting from the top professional of the organization to the newest members of the team. For organizations that have a probationary period for volunteers, often the first thirty days, the orientation may take on even more significance, especially if there was any uncertainty on the volunteers' part in accepting the job or for the agency in making the assignment (McCurley, 1994). Although it is important to strike a professional tone, serving refreshments or perhaps a light meal, if the budget permits, makes a statement that volunteering for this entity is much appreciated. It is also a good idea to give each volunteer a loose-leaf binder to hold the material distributed during the orientation, to which they can add other documents over time.

The content of the orientation can be divided into two broad categories, information on the organization as a whole and information that is job specific, with the volunteer manager providing the former and program staff the latter. Under the first heading, the history and purpose of the agency should be described, and each volunteer should receive a copy of its mission statement. Depending on the composition of the group, explaining how a nonprofit differs from a for-profit may be warranted. Next, there should be some basics about the programs and services provided, with some current demographic and utilization statistics on the consumers and the overall staffing configuration. A useful document is the organization chart, to show the internal structure and reporting relationships and how the volunteer program fits in. A list of the applicable rules and regulations verbally covered during the interview process should be distributed and reviewed. Finally, there ought to be a tour of the facility, allowing the volunteer manager to point out anything specific to the volunteer program, such as where to sign in and out and the room in which in-service training is held.

For the second part of the orientation, the volunteers can be turned over to the person in charge of the area to which they have been assigned. In larger settings that may have several employees acting as volunteer supervisors, the program director should clarify to whom each volunteer will be reporting and make the necessary introductions. This is the time for the staff member to go into detail about the tasks the volunteers will be carrying out and to answer any questions about their role and responsibilities. If not done during the general tour of the facility, the volunteers should be shown where they will actually be working and informed about the equipment and clerical support available to them. The last piece of business is to describe what happens next, which in most instances will include some form of training, and provide an overview of the first few days on the job.

Every volunteer assignment necessitates a certain level of preparation to do the work, but the extent and duration of the training will vary from position to position, and much of it takes place informally in the regular exchanges between supervisor and volunteer. In fact, this informal learning begins with recruitment and continues through the screening process, with the orientation another occasion for imparting a lot of valuable information. For many, however, the availability of some kind of formal training is one of the primary benefits of volunteering, so it is inadvisable to overlook this area even when the budget is rather tight. In most cases, without spending large sums of money, a solid training program can be put together with ingenuity and an understanding of the principles of adult learning, such as offering it online for the short-term volunteer. As Macduff (1994) points out, "Most adults have very immediate needs—and the hows usually take precedence over the whys. It is essential to determine those needs and set about organizing learning to meet them" (p. 592).

In other words, the emphasis should be on the practical skills the volunteers must have to carry out their assignments. Moreover, adults prefer interactive learning, such as role-playing and discussion, rather than lectures, which means showing an agency-made video of a counseling session (with the permission of all participants) followed by a question-and-answer period led by the staff member who counseled the client will have a much greater impact than an outside expert talking in general about fundamental counseling principles. The training provided prior to the start of the assigned tasks will most likely be designed by the organization, but once the volunteers are on the job, they should be included in the planning and evaluation of all subsequent training so that the content and methods used are as relevant as possible. Using experienced volunteers to train newer recruits makes a strong statement and can be a very effective technique.

Supervision

The quality of the supervision provided is an important aspect of the volunteer's satisfaction with the experience. Although many of the concerns about possible friction between employees and volunteers have proven to be unfounded, nevertheless in settings where paid staff show their discomfort with the use of volunteers, even passively, it may be hard to ignore this message despite public statements to the contrary. The development of a positive organizational culture for volunteerism begins with the attitudes and actions of the top leaders. As previously mentioned, involving paid staff from the very start in discussions about the need for and design of the volunteer program will go a long way toward generating a sense of ownership of the new endeavor. An important step is to clarify the roles volunteers will play and to dispel the myths that volunteers and employees often hold about each other, such as that staff work for pay alone but volunteers act out of purely altruistic motives (Netting, Nelson, Borders, & Huber, 2004).

It can be a costly mistake for organizations to assume staff will be able to perform effectively as supervisors of volunteers without specialized training: "Expecting young and/or inexperienced staff members to acquire supervisory skills . . . through a process of 'try it and see' is probably optimistic; expecting volunteers to enjoy the process of experimentation is delusionary" (McCurley, 1994, p. 515). There must also be some sort of reward for staff who take on this responsibility, which does tend to be an add-on to their regular duties, and do it well, both internally when performance reviews are conducted and externally through volunteer recognition events. At the same time, those who demonstrate a weakness in this area should be helped to improve their skills.

Some useful perspectives on management issues emerged from research by Leonard, Onyx, and Hayward-Brown (2004) on the views of women volunteers and volunteer coordinators toward their work. The volunteers valued coordinators who were accessible, good listeners, flexible, and promoted a team approach rather than a hierarchy. Three different management styles emerged from the coordinators' feedback: (1) In the horizontal style, volunteers were treated more like peers, as reflected in open communication and accommodations in scheduling; they had input into decision-making, were respected for their work, and were encouraged to develop new skills and try new roles. (2) The nurturing style is used most frequently, with the coordinators balancing direction with promotion of volunteers' independence; the primary objectives were to establish close personal relationships, to make the volunteers feel their work was valued, and to support the volunteers in taking on new challenges, much like a "good mother." (3) Under the managerial approach, efficiency and effectiveness were stressed, with no real interest in promoting individual volunteer needs; the main concern was to ensure that volunteers followed policies and procedures and did not overstep their marginal helping role. In comparing the two sets of responses, the managerial style was the least compatible with the volunteers' preferences. Even though these findings are especially applicable to the traditional volunteer, they offer some helpful management tips for generating satisfaction across the board.

Performance Reviews and Recognitions

For one-shot, limited-time efforts, other than perhaps keeping track of the dependability of the various individuals, performance reviews are certainly not necessary. However, that is not true for recurring volunteering, especially in settings like hospitals or mental health clinics where volunteers may work with highly vulnerable clients. With the stress today on accountability, these volunteers should receive regular evaluations, to ensure the quality of their work and to identify additional challenges or a more appropriate placement in order to retain their services. Unfortunately, just as many boards express reluctance about evaluating the CEO, volunteer managers often shy away from systematic reviews. In a study of volunteerism in one county in Michigan (Golensky, 1999), only 16 percent of the respondents conducted formal evaluations. One volunteer manager noted her organization had discontinued written evaluations in favor of more informal, verbal reviews, commenting, "Why not get a paid job if you have to go through all that?" Such attitudes beg the question, for good resource management dictates that every undertaking receive some level of assessment to improve the design and implementation before offering the program again.

Another way to view individual evaluations is as a form of recognition of the volunteer's contributions to the organization. Because volunteers do not receive pay, the organization must find different kinds of rewards, combining the psychological with the concrete, to let them know their work is valued. For example, an individual who performs some special service could be the subject of a featured article in the agency newsletter. Given the various types of volunteering now prevalent, the organization may want to consider instituting a system like that used in fund development to acknowledge donors at different giving levels, since neither episodic volunteers nor those who devote countless hours to their assigned work may be comfortable receiving the same rewards. With this approach, short-term volunteers might simply receive a thank-you letter signed by the CEO the first few times they help out. If and when they accumulate some predetermined number of hours, they would be eligible to receive a certificate of appreciation by mail, and with longer, more regular service, an invitation to attend the annual recognition event at the end of the program year.

For recurring volunteers, as a first step, identification cards can be issued at orientation, to acknowledge them as an official part of the program and the agency. If a regular newsletter is published, there should be an article about the volunteers, with pictures, at least once a year. More formal kinds of recognitions, such as an end-of-year dinner, with the executive director and other senior management as well as board members in attendance to present certificates of appreciation, permit the organization to show its gratitude very publicly, but sometimes the best reward is a genuine smile or a heartfelt thank-you from a staff member when casually encountering a volunteer.

Maintaining good records to track every person's history with the organization is a task for the volunteer manager related to both performance reviews and recognitions. For episodic volunteering the files may consist just of dates and times, names, phone numbers, and e-mail addresses. Some typical documents found in a recurring volunteer's file are contact information, a job description for each position held, a list of trainings attended, time sheets, and copies of evaluations. If the agency requires a job application for volunteers and works out individual agreements, these forms would be included as well. The volunteer manager should also keep a list of the staff serving each year as volunteer supervisors. Information derived from these records can be used for reports to the board and funders to demonstrate the program's value, to generate names for fund-raising appeals, and for overall program assessment (Korngold et al., 2006).

FINAL THOUGHTS

Table 16.1 summarizes the steps that must be taken to develop an effective volunteer program, from the organizational perspective. Throughout this chapter, we have also looked

Table 16.1 Developing an effective volunteer program

Element	Pertinent questions
Assessment and planning	What client and organizational needs can volunteers meet?
	What adjustments (re budget, personnel, insurance, etc.) will be required to accommodate the volunteer program?
Recruitment	What are the most likely sources to find volunteers to meet the identified needs?
	Which recruitment method(s) will attract the most suitable individuals?
Screening and placement	What criteria should be used to determine a person's suitability for the program?
	How do we ensure the best match will be made between an assignment and the individual's talents and interests?
Orientation and training	What should be included in the orientation to help new volunteers gain a full sense of the organization and their assignment?
	What kinds of formal and informal mechanisms should be included in the initial and ongoing training for volunteers?
Supervision	What steps should be taken to encourage paid staff to embrace and support the volunteer program?
	How do we appropriately prepare employees to supervise volunteers and reward them for doing a good job?
Performance reviews and recognitions	How can we maximize individual reviews to benefit both the volunteers and the program?
	What types of "rewards" are most effective in showing our appreciation for the volunteers' efforts?

Sources: Adapted from Korngold et al., 2006; McCurley, 1994.

at the process from the volunteer's viewpoint, in terms of motivation, satisfaction, and so forth. Thus, to capture the full flavor of volunteerism in nonprofits, it must be conceived of as an interactive process between the individual and the organization. Although there are costs and benefits on both sides of this exchange, in most cases it seems clear the pluses far outweigh the minuses.

At present, however, as Korngold et al. (2006) observe, the full value of this critical resource is not being realized. They offer three suggestions for enhancing the importance of volunteerism in American society: (1) an increased investment by public and private funders in recruiting, placing, training, and recognizing volunteers through such efforts as AmeriCorps and the Points of Light Institute, created in 2007 through the merger of the Points of Light Foundation and the HandsOn Network; (2) an expansion of community investment through establishing the necessary infrastructure to maximize opportunities for all interested citizens, using local volunteer centers and other similar mechanisms; and (3) a greater investment by businesses and corporations in encouraging and supporting employees who wish to volunteer. Considering the number of people now volunteering on a regular basis, these kinds of investments offer the likelihood of large returns and virtually no risk.

Discussion Questions for Section 4

Chapter 13

1. Is it harder today than in the past for a nonprofit leader to be the ethical, moral compass of the organization? Justify your position.

2. Based on the information provided in the featured case study, it is clear YSN's founder, Trevor Clinton, could not be labeled a servant-leader. Which of his actions seem most at odds with this model and how have they affected the organization over time?

3. If you believe faith-based nonprofits merit special consideration in competing for government support, what expectations of these organizations are justified in return? If you feel special consideration is unwarranted, support your views.

4. What steps should an ethical leader take to protect the organization from risk? Which kind of threat is most detrimental to a nonprofit's good standing in the community and why do you believe this to be true?

Chapter 14

5. Schein (2006) uses the term *career anchors* to refer to individual preferences regarding work. Do you believe "dedication to a cause" is still the primary reason people choose to work in nonprofits? How would you rate the importance of lifestyle balance, autonomy, opportunities for advancement, and entrepreneurial creativity as motivating factors?

6. If you had to choose between a job that provided a great sense of accomplishment but lacked basic social supports versus one valuing teamwork and collegiality but that lacked stimulation in the work itself, which would you prefer and why?

7. In reference to YSN, the nonprofit in the text's featured case study, how would you assess the board's hiring practices, both ethically and practically?

8. Why is it that even the most prominent nonprofits make critical mistakes both in staff recruitment and hiring and in performance evaluation? What can be done to improve these processes?

9. What are the most important steps a nonprofit should take to manage diversity effectively? How would you apply these strategies to women in the workplace? To ethnic and cultural groups?

Chapter 15

10. What does *effectiveness* mean to you when applied to a nonprofit board? Do you believe an effective board leads to an effective organization? If so, how?

11. What are some of the sources of tension between senior staff and the board in a nonprofit? How can these issues be addressed to create a true partnership between the two elements of the leadership core?

12. Do you subscribe to the technocratic view or the democratic view of non-profit boards (see Kramer, 1985)? Support your position.

13. What are some of the ways of educating board members about their roles and responsibilities? Why are both trustees and executives sometimes ambivalent about board education and training?

14. What are the best arguments in favor of boards' conducting a self-assessment on a regular basis? Is there any merit to arguing against this practice? If so, identify the reasons to support this position.

Chapter 16

15. The data in the Corporation for National and Community Service's 2007 report seem to contradict the belief that engagement in American civic life is in a serious decline. What do you believe accounts for these higher rates of volunteerism?

16. There is evidence to support the idea that individuals engaging in volunteering at an early age go on to participate as volunteers later in life. How does your personal experience fit with this idea?

17. How would you compare the effective management of paid staff versus that for volunteers? If you were offered the choice between serving as HR director or volunteer manager for a nonprofit, at an equal salary, which would you pick and why?

18. Why does the belief persist that paid staff and volunteers often have a problematic relationship despite research to the contrary?

19. What are the most effective ways to provide a satisfying volunteer experience, and how do the motivations to volunteer factor into the equation?

SELECTED READINGS FOR SECTION 4

Chapter 13

Cnaan, R. A., Sinha, J. W., & McGrew, C. C. (2004). Congregations as social service providers: Services, capacity, culture, and organizational behavior. *Administration in Social Work, 28*(3/4), 47–68.

Greenlee, J., Fischer, M., Gordon, T., & Keating, E. (2007). An investigation of fraud in nonprofit organizations: Occurrences and deterrents. *Nonprofit and Voluntary Sector Quarterly, 36*, 676–694.

Jeavons, T. H. (1994). Ethics in nonprofit management: Creating a culture of integrity. In R. D. Herman (Ed.), *The Jossey-Bass handbook of nonprofit leadership and management* (pp. 184–207). San Francisco: Jossey-Bass.

Kurzman, P. A. (2006). Managing liability and risk in nonprofit settings. In R. L. Edwards & J. A. Yankey (Eds.), *Effectively managing nonprofit organizations* (Rev. ed., pp. 275–290). Washington, DC: NASW Press.

Manning, S. S. (2003). *Ethical leadership in human services: A multi-dimensional approach.* Boston: Allyn & Bacon.

Reamer, F. G. (2000). The social work ethics audit: A risk-management strategy. *Social Work, 45,* 355–366.

Spears, L. C. (2002). Introduction: Tracing the past, present, and future of servant-leadership. In L. C. Spears & M. Lawrence (Eds.), *Focus on leadership* (pp. 1–16). New York: Wiley & Sons.

Chapter 14

Findler, L., Wind, L. H., & Mor Barak, M. E. (2007). The challenge of workforce management in a global society: Modeling the relationship between diversity, inclusion, organizational culture, and employee well-being, job satisfaction and organizational commitment. *Administration in Social Work, 31*(3), 63–94.

Haley-Lock, A. (2008). Happy doing good? How workers' career orientations and job satisfaction relate in grassroots human services. *Journal of Community Practice, 16*(2), 143–163.

Landsman, M. J. (2008). Pathways to organizational commitment. *Administration in Social Work, 32*(2), 105–132.

Parish, S. L., Ellison, M. J., & Parish, J. K. (2006). Managing diversity. In R. L. Edwards & J. A. Yankey (Eds.), *Effectively managing nonprofit organizations* (Rev. ed., pp. 179–194). Washington, DC: NASW Press.

Pecora, R. J. (1998). Recruiting and selecting effective employees. In R. L. Edwards, J. A. Yankey, & M. A. Altpeter (Eds.), *Skills for effective management of nonprofit organizations* (pp. 155–184). Washington, DC: NASW Press.

Strom-Gottfried, K. (2006). Managing human resources. In R. L. Edwards & J. A. Yankey (Eds.), *Effectively managing nonprofit organizations* (Rev. ed., pp. 141–178). Washington, DC: NASW Press.

Chapter 15

Bradshaw, P. (2002). Reframing board-staff relations: Exploring the governance function using a storytelling metaphor. *Nonprofit Management and Leadership, 12,* 471–484.

Gill, M. D. (2005). *Governing for results: A director's guide to good governance.* Victoria, BC, Canada: Trafford.

Golensky, M. (2000). *Board governance: Perceptions and practices; An exploratory study* (Research Report). Grand Rapids, MI: GVSU School of Social Work.

Kramer, R. M. (1985). Toward a contingency model of board-executive relations. *Administration in Social Work, 9*(3), 15–33.

Tropman, J. E. (2006). Producing high-quality group decisions. In R. L. Edwards & J. A. Yankey (Eds.), *Effectively managing nonprofit organizations* (Rev. ed., pp. 215–238). Washington, DC: NASW Press.

Widmer, C. (1989). Why board members participate. In R. D. Herman & J. Van Til (Eds.), *Nonprofit boards of directors: Analyses and applications* (pp. 8–23). New Brunswick, NJ: Transaction.

Chapter 16

Corporation for National and Community Service. (2007). *Volunteering in America: 2007 state trends and rankings in civic life.* Retrieved February 20, 2009, from http://www.nationalservice.gov/pdf/VIA/VIA_fullreport.pdf

Korngold, A., Voudouris, E. H., & Griffiths, J. (2006). Managing volunteers effectively. In R. L. Edwards & J. A. Yankey (Eds.), *Effectively managing nonprofit organizations* (Rev. ed., pp. 239–251). Washington, DC: NASW Press.

Macduff, N. (2006, Fall). The multi-paradigm model of volunteering. *Volunteer Leadership*, pp. 31–36.

McCurley, S. (1994). Recruiting and retaining volunteers. In R. D. Herman (Ed.), *The Jossey-Bass handbook of nonprofit leadership and management* (pp. 511–534). San Francisco: Jossey-Bass.

Netting, F. E., Nelson, H. W., Jr., Borders, K., & Huber, R. (2004). Volunteer and paid staff relationships: Implications for social work administration. *Administration in Social Work, 28*(3/4), 69–89.

Stukas, A. A., Worth, K. A., Clary, E. G., & Snyder, M. (2009). The matching of motivations to affordances in the volunteer environment. *Nonprofit and Voluntary Sector Quarterly, 38*, 5–28.

Sundeen, R. A., Garcia, C., & Raskoff, S. A. (2008, October 21). Ethnicity, acculturation, and volunteering to organizations: A comparison of African Americans, Asians, Hispanics, and Whites. *Nonprofit and Voluntary Sector Quarterly OnlineFirst.* Retrieved March 2, 2009, from http://nvsq.sagepub.com. (Also in print version of the journal, *38*, 929–955)

Bibliography

The following references include the sources used in each chapter as well as some other books, journal articles, Web sites, and so forth that should be helpful to anyone wishing to delve more deeply into a particular topic. This list is by no means definitive—for some topics, the available references would be sufficient for a small book—but was consciously developed to represent a variety of perspectives, both new and what I call the classics, or works that have stood the test of time.

CHAPTER 1: DEFINITION OF A NONPROFIT ORGANIZATION

Greenfield, J. M. (1999). *Fund raising: Evaluating and managing the fund development process* (2nd ed.). New York: Wiley

Grobman, G. M. (2004). *An introduction to the nonprofit sector: A practical approach for the twenty-first century.* Harrisburg, PA: White Hat Communications.

Hall, P. D. (1992). *Inventing the nonprofit sector and other essays on philanthropy, voluntarism, and nonprofit organizations.* Baltimore: Johns Hopkins University Press.

Internal Revenue Service. (2009). *Tax information for charities and other non-profits.* Retrieved May 6, 2010, from http://www.irs.gov/charities

National Center for Charitable Statistics. (2008). *Statistics and profiles.* Retrieved March 16, 2008, from http://nccsdataweb.urban.org/PubApps/profile1.php?state=US

O'Neill, M. (2002). *Nonprofit nation: A new look at the third America.* San Francisco: Jossey-Bass.

Smucker, B. (1999). *The nonprofit lobbying guide* (2nd ed.). Washington, DC: Independent Sector. (Out of print; can be downloaded from the Web sites of Independent Sector and the Center for Lobbying in the Public Interest.)

Tocqueville, A. de. (1983). Of the use which the Americans make of public associations in civil life [Excerpt from *Democracy in America*]. In B. O'Connell (Ed.), *America's voluntary spirit* (pp. 53–57). New York: Foundation Center.

Wolf, T. (1999). *Managing a nonprofit organization in the twenty-first century* (Rev. ed.). New York: Simon & Schuster.

CHAPTER 2: HISTORICAL DEVELOPMENT OF NONPROFIT ORGANIZATIONS

Arnsberger, P., Ludlum, M., Riley, M., & Stanton, M. (2008, Winter). *A history of the tax-exempt sector: An SOI perspective* (Statistics of Income Bulletin 1136). Washington, DC: Internal Revenue Service.

Boris, E. T. (1999). The nonprofit sector in the 1990s. In C. T. Clotfelter & T. Ehrlich (Eds.), *Philanthropy and the nonprofit sector in a changing America* (pp. 1–33). Bloomington: Indiana University Press.

Bureau of Labor Statistics. (2008, January 23). Volunteering in the United States, 2007. *News*. Washington, DC: U.S. Department of Labor.

Carnegie, A. (1983). The gospel of wealth [Excerpt]. In B. O'Connell (Ed.), *America's voluntary spirit* (pp. 97–108). New York: Foundation Center.

Cass, R. H., & Manser, G. (1983). Roots of voluntarism [Excerpt from *Voluntarism at the crossroads*]. In B. O'Connell (Ed.), *America's voluntary spirit* (pp. 11–22). New York: Foundation Center.

Giving USA 2009. (2009). Glenview, IL: Giving USA Foundation.

Grobman, G. M. (2004). *An introduction to the nonprofit sector: A practical approach for the twenty-first century*. Harrisburg, PA: White Hat Communications.

Gronbjerg, K. A. (2001). The U.S. nonprofit human service sector: A creeping revolution. *Nonprofit and Voluntary Sector Quarterly, 30*, 276–297.

Hall, P. D. (1994). Historical perspectives on nonprofit organizations. In R. D. Herman (Ed.), *The Jossey-Bass handbook of nonprofit leadership and management* (pp. 3–43). San Francisco: Jossey-Bass.

Hammack, D. C. (2001). Introduction: Growth, transformation and quiet revolution in the nonprofit sector over two centuries. *Nonprofit and Voluntary Sector Quarterly, 30*, 157–173.

Jansson, B. S. (2005). *The reluctant welfare state: American social welfare policies; Past, present and future* (5th ed.). Belmont, CA: Brooks/Cole.

Obama announces White House Office of Faith-Based and Neighborhood Partnerships. (2009, February 5). Retrieved December 22, 2009, from www.whitehouse.gov/the_press_office

O'Neill, M. (2002). *Nonprofit nation: A new look at the third America*. San Francisco: Jossey-Bass.

Salamon, L. M. (1999). *America's nonprofit sector: A primer* (2nd ed.). New York: Foundation Center.

Tocqueville, A. de. (1983). Of the use which the Americans make of public associations in civil life [Excerpt from *Democracy in America*]. In B. O'Connell (Ed.), *America's voluntary spirit* (pp. 53–57). New York: Foundation Center.

Volunteering in America research highlights. (2009, July). Retrieved December 22, 2009, from http://www.nationalservice.gov

CHAPTER 3: POLITICAL AND ECONOMIC CONSIDERATIONS

Abzug, R., & Webb, N. J. (1999). Relationships between nonprofit and for-profit organizations: A stakeholder's perspective. *Nonprofit and Voluntary Sector Quarterly, 28*, 416–431.

Bowles, S. (2004). *Microeconomics: Behavior, institutions, and evolution*. New York: Russell Sage Foundation; Princeton, NJ: Princeton University Press.

Brown, L. K., & Troutt, E. (2004). Funding relations between nonprofits and government: A positive example. *Nonprofit and Voluntary Sector Quarterly, 33*, 5–27.

Chambre, S. M., & Fatt, N. (2002). Beyond the liability of newness: Nonprofit organizations in an emerging policy domain. *Nonprofit and Voluntary Sector Quarterly, 31*, 502–524.

Cohen, B. J. (2002). Alternative organizing principles for the design of service delivery systems. *Administration in Social Work, 26*(2), 17–38.

Dart, R. (2004). Being "business-like" in a nonprofit organization: A grounded and inductive typology. *Nonprofit and Voluntary Sector Quarterly, 33*, 290–310.

Edwards, R. L., & Yankey, J. A. (Eds.). (2006). *Effectively managing nonprofit organizations* (Rev. ed.). Washington, DC: NASW Press.

Foster, M. K., & Meinhard, A. G. (2002). A regression model explaining predisposition to collaborate. *Nonprofit and Voluntary Sector Quarterly, 31*, 549–564.

Gibelman, M. (2001–2002). Managed care and ethical social work practice: An oxymoron? *Social Work Forum, 35*, 47–65.

Gibelman, M. (2003). *Navigating human service organizations*. Chicago: Lyceum.

Ginsberg, L. H. (2001). *Social work evaluation: Principles and methods*. Boston: Allyn & Bacon.

Gronbjerg, K. A., & Smith, S. R. (1999). Nonprofit organizations and public policies in the delivery of human services. In C. T. Clotfelter & T. Ehrlich (Eds.), *Philanthropy and the nonprofit sector in a changing America* (pp. 139–171). Bloomington: Indiana University Press.

Herman, R. D., & Heimovics, R. D. (1991). *Executive leadership in nonprofit organizations: New strategies for shaping executive-board dynamics*. San Francisco: Jossey-Bass.

Jaskyte, K. (2004). Transformational leadership, organizational culture, and innovativeness in nonprofit organizations. *Nonprofit Management and Leadership, 15*, 153–168.

Mason, D. E. (1996). *Leading and managing the expressive dimension: Harnessing the hidden power source of the nonprofit sector*. San Francisco: Jossey-Bass.

National Association of Social Workers. (2006). Managed care. In *Social work speaks: National Association of Social Workers Policy Statements, 2006–2009* (7th ed., pp. 260–265). Washington, DC: NASW Press.

Packard, T. (2001). Enhancing staff commitment through organizational values: The case of a homeless shelter. *Administration in Social Work, 25*(3), 35–52.

Perlmutter, F. D., Bailey, D., & Netting, F. E. (2001). *Managing human resources in the human services: Supervisory challenges*. New York: Oxford University Press.

Salamon, L. M. (1995). *Partners in public service*. Baltimore: Johns Hopkins University Press.

Selber, K., & Streeter, C. (2000). A customer-oriented model for managing quality in human services. *Administration in Social Work, 24*(2), 1–14.

Smith, S. R., & Lipsky, M. (1993). *Nonprofits for hire: The welfare state in the age of contracting.* Cambridge, MA: Harvard University Press.

Takahashi, L. M., & Smutny, G. (2002). Collaborative windows and organizational governance: Exploring the formation and demise of social service partnerships. *Nonprofit and Voluntary Sector Quarterly, 31,* 165–185.

Wernet, S. P. (1994). A case study of adaptation in a nonprofit human service organization. *Journal of Community Practice, 1*(3), 93–112.

Wineburg, B. (2007). *Faith-based inefficiency: The follies of Bush's initiatives.* Westport, CT: Praeger.

Young, D. R. (2000). Alternative models of government-nonprofit relations: Theoretical and international perspectives. *Nonprofit and Voluntary Sector Quarterly, 29,* 149–172.

Young, D. R., & Steinberg, R. (1995). *Economics for nonprofit managers.* New York: Foundation Center.

Zald, M. N. (1970). Political economy: A framework for comparative analysis. In M. N. Zald (Ed.), *Power in organizations* (pp. 221–261). Nashville, TN: Vanderbilt University Press.

CHAPTER 4: THE NATURE OF LEADERSHIP
(see also references for chapter 15)

Allison, M. (2002). Into the fire: Boards and executive transitions. *Nonprofit Management and Leadership, 12,* 341–351.

Anderson, C. R. (1984). *Management: Skills, functions, and organization performance.* Dubuque, IA: Wm. C. Brown.

Axelrod, N. R. (1994). Board leadership and board development. In R. D. Herman (Ed.), *The Jossey-Bass handbook of nonprofit leadership and management* (pp. 119–136). San Francisco: Jossey-Bass.

Bacharach, S. B., & Lawler, E. J. (1980). *Power and politics in organizations.* San Francisco: Jossey-Bass.

Block, S. R. (2004). *Why nonprofits fail.* San Francisco: Jossey-Bass.

Brueggemann, W. G. (1996). *The practice of macro social work.* Chicago: Nelson-Hall.

Carver, J. (1990). *Boards that make a difference: A new design for leadership in nonprofit and public organizations.* San Francisco: Jossey-Bass.

Fram, E. H., & Brown, V. (1988). *Policy vs. paper clips.* Milwaukee, WI: Family Services of America.

French, J. R. P., Jr., & Raven, B. (1959). The bases of social power. In D. Cartwright (Ed.), *Studies in social power* (pp. 150–167). Ann Arbor: University of Michigan.

Golensky, M. (1993). The board-executive relationship in nonprofit organizations. *Nonprofit Management and Leadership, 4,* 177–191.

Golensky, M. (1994). *Governance and decision-making in nonprofit organizations: An exploration of the board-executive relationship.* Unpublished doctoral dissertation, City University of New York.

Golensky, M. (2000). *Board governance: Perceptions and practices; An exploratory study* (Research Report). Grand Rapids, MI: GVSU School of Social Work.

Golensky, M. (2005, November). *Applying microeconomic theory to the board-executive relationship in human service organizations.* Paper presented at the 34th annual conference of the Association for Research on Nonprofit Organizations and Voluntary Action, Washington, DC.

Golensky, M. (2008). Choosing a new nonprofit CEO: A longitudinal study. In S. Ramachandran (Ed.), *Good governance in nonprofit organizations* (pp. 207–227). Hyderabad, India: Icfai University Press.

Green, J. C., & Griesinger, D. W. (1996). Board performance and organizational effectiveness in nonprofit social service organizations. *Nonprofit Management and Leadership, 6,* 381–402.

Gummer, B. (1980). Organization theory for social administration. In F. D. Perlmutter & S. Slavin (Eds.), *Leadership in social administration* (pp. 22–49). Philadelphia: Temple University Press.

Harris, M. (1993). Exploring the role of boards using Total Activities Analysis. *Nonprofit Management and Leadership, 3,* 269–281.

Herman, R. D., & Heimovics, R. D. (1991). *Executive leadership in nonprofit organizations: New strategies for shaping executive-board dynamics.* San Francisco: Jossey-Bass.

Hollander, E. P. (1978). *Leadership dynamics.* New York: Free Press.

Houle, C. O. (1989). *Governing boards: Their nature and nurture.* San Francisco: Jossey-Bass.

Howe, F. (1995). *Welcome to the board: Your guide to effective participation.* San Francisco: Jossey-Bass.

Iecovich, E. (2005). Environmental and organizational features and their impact on structural and functional characteristics of boards in nonprofit organizations. *Administration in Social Work, 29*(3), 43–59.

Kirk, W. A. (1986). *Nonprofit organization governance: A challenge in turbulent times.* New York: Carlton Press.

Kramer, R. M. (1985). Toward a contingency model of board-executive relations. *Administration in Social Work, 9*(3), 15–33.

Mathiasen, K., III. (1983, January). *The board of directors is a problem: Exploring the concept of the following and leading board.* (Available from the Management Assistance Group, 1835 K Street, NW, Washington, DC 20006)

Mathiasen, K., III. (1990). *Board passages: Three key stages in a nonprofit board's life cycle.* (Available from BoardSource [formerly National Center for Nonprofit Boards], 1828 L Street, NW, Suite 900, Washington, DC 20036)

Morgan, G. (1986). *Images of organization*. Beverly Hills, CA: Sage.

Nobbie, P. D., & Brudney, J. L. (2003). Testing the implementation, board performance, and organizational effectiveness of the policy governance model in nonprofit boards of directors. *Nonprofit and Voluntary Sector Quarterly, 32*, 571–595.

Nonprofits' Insurance Alliance of California. (2001). *Directors and officers: Key factors about insurance and legal liability*. (Available from NIAC, P.O. Box 8507, Santa Cruz, CA 96061-8507)

Stone, M. M., & Ostrower, F. (2007). Acting in the public interest? Another look at research on nonprofit governance. *Nonprofit and Voluntary Sector Quarterly, 36*, 416–438.

Van Fleet, D. D., & Yukl, G. A. (1989). A century of leadership research. In W. B. Rosenbach & R. L. Taylor (Eds.), *Contemporary issues in leadership* (pp. 65–90). Boulder, CO: Westview.

Wood, M. M. (1989). *The governing board's existential quandary: An empirical analysis of board behavior in the charitable sector* (PONPO Working Paper 143). New Haven, CT: Yale University School of Management.

Wood, M. M. (1992). Is governing board behavior cyclical? *Nonprofit Management and Leadership, 3*, 139–163.

Wood, M. M. (Ed.). (1996). *Nonprofit boards and leadership: Cases on governance, change, and board-staff dynamics*. San Francisco: Jossey-Bass.

CHAPTER 5: THE PRACTICE OF LEADERSHIP

Bass, B. M., & Steidlmeier, P. (1998). *Ethics, character, and authentic transformational leadership*. Binghamton, NY: Binghamton University Center for Leadership Studies, School of Management.

Bennis, W. (1999, Spring). The leadership advantage. *Leader to Leader*, 18–23.

Bolman, L. G., & Deal, T. E. (1991). *Reframing organizations*. San Francisco: Jossey-Bass.

DiPadrova, L. N., & Faerman, S. R. (1998). Managing time. In R. L. Edwards, J. A. Yankey, & M. A. Altpeter (Eds.), *Skills for effective management of nonprofit organizations* (pp. 469–491). Washington, DC: NASW Press.

Edwards, R. L., & Austin, D. M. (2006). Managing effectively in an environment of competing values. In R. L. Edwards & J. A. Yankey (Eds.), *Effectively managing nonprofit organizations* (Rev. ed., pp. 3–25). Washington, DC: NASW Press.

Gardner, J. W. (1990). *On leadership*. New York: Free Press.

Golensky, M., & Walker, M. (2003). Organizational change: Too much, too soon? *Journal of Community Practice, 11*(2), 67–82.

Hofstede, G., & Hofstede, G. J. (2005). *Cultures and organizations: Software of the mind* (2nd ed.). New York: McGraw-Hill.

Hollander, E. P. (1978). *Leadership dynamics*. New York: Free Press.

Hollander, E. P., & Offermann, L. R. (1990). Power and leadership in organizations: Relationships in transition. *American Psychologist, 45*(2), 179–189.

Howell, J. M. (1997). *Organization contexts, charismatic and exchange leadership* (Transformational Leadership Working Papers, Kellogg Leadership Studies Project). College Park, MD: Academy of Leadership Press.

Kuhnert, K. W., & Lewis, P. (1989). Transactional and transformational leadership: A constructive/developmental analysis. In W. B. Rosenbach & R. L. Taylor (Eds.), *Contemporary issues in leadership* (pp 192–205). Boulder, CO: Westview.

Manning, S. S. (2003). *Ethical leadership in human services: A multi-dimensional approach.* Boston: Allyn & Bacon.

Mary, N. L. (2005). Transformational leadership in human service organizations. *Administration in Social Work, 29*(2), 105–118.

Mason, D. E. (1996). *Leading and managing the expressive dimension: Harnessing the hidden power source of the nonprofit sector.* San Francisco: Jossey-Bass.

Morgenstern, J. (2000). *Time management from the inside out.* New York: Henry Holt.

Netting, F. E., Kettner, P. M., & McMurtry, S. L. (2004). *Social work macro practice* (3rd ed.). Boston: Pearson Education/Allyn & Bacon.

Rosenbach, W. E., & Taylor, R. L. (Eds.). (1989). *Contemporary issues in leadership.* (2nd ed.). Boulder, CO: Westview.

Schein, E. H. (1985). *Organizational culture and leadership.* San Francisco: Jossey-Bass.

Schein, E. H. (1990). Organizational culture. *American Psychologist, 45*(2), 109–119.

Schmid, H. (2006). Leadership styles and leadership change in human and community service organizations. *Nonprofit Management and Leadership, 17*, 179–194.

Wallis, J., & Dollery, B. (2003). *Leadership and economic theories of nonprofit organizations* (Working Paper No. 2003-14). Biddeford, ME: University of New England, School of Economics.

Weber, M. (1947). *The theory of social and economic organizations* (T. Parsons, Trans.). New York: Free Press.

Werther, W. B., Jr., Berman, E., & Echols, K. (2005, September–October). The three roles of nonprofit management. *Nonprofit World, 23*(5), 22–23.

CHAPTER 6: DECISION-MAKING

Ben-Arieh, A. (2008). The influence of social indicators data on decision making in regard to children's well-being. *Administration in Social Work, 32*(1), 23–38.

Cohen, M. D., March, J. G., & Olsen, J. P. (1980). A garbage can model of organizational choice. In A. Etzioni & E. W. Lehman (Eds.), *A sociological reader on complex organizations* (3rd ed., pp. 144–159). Austin, TX: Holt, Rinehart, & Wilson.

Cyert, R. M., & March, J. G. (1963). *A behavioral theory of the firm.* Englewood Cliffs, NJ: Prentice Hall.

De Bono, E. (1967). *The use of lateral thinking.* Middlesex, England: Penguin.

De Bono, E. (1969). *The mechanism of mind.* London: Penguin.

De Bono, E. (1994). *Parallel thinking: From Socratic to de Bono thinking.* London: Penguin.

De Bono, E. (1999). *Six thinking hats* (Rev. ed.). Boston: Little, Brown.

Driver, M. J., & Rowe, A. J. (1979). Decision-making styles: A new approach to management decision making. In C. L. Cooper (Ed.), *Behavioral problems in organizations* (pp. 141–179). Englewood Cliffs, NJ: Prentice Hall.

Etzioni, A. (1967). Mixed scanning: A third approach to decision making. *Public Administration Review, 27,* 385–392.

Golensky, M., & DeRuiter, G. L. (1999). Merger as a strategic response to government contracting pressures: A case study. *Nonprofit Management and Leadership, 10,* 137–152.

Hickson, D. J., Butler, R. J., Cray, D., Mallory, G. R., & Wilson, D. C. (1986). *Top decisions.* San Francisco: Jossey-Bass.

Janis, I. L., & Mann, L. (1977). *Decision making.* New York: Free Press.

Kaye, H. (1992). *Decision power.* Englewood Cliffs, NJ: Prentice Hall.

Kettner, P. M., Moroney, R. M., & Martin, L. L. (2008). *Designing and managing programs: An effectiveness-based approach* (3rd ed.). Thousand Oaks, CA: Sage.

Lindblom, C. E. (1959). The science of muddling through. *Public Administration Review, 19,* 79–88.

Lindblom, C. E. (1979). Still muddling, not yet through. *Public Administration Review, 39,* 517–525.

March, J. G., & Simon, H. A. (1958). *Organizations.* New York: Wiley.

Mason, D. E. (1996). *Leading and managing the expressive dimension: Harnessing the hidden power source of the nonprofit sector.* San Francisco: Jossey-Bass.

Nutt, P. C. (1989). *Making tough decisions.* San Francisco: Jossey-Bass.

Skidmore, R. A. (1995). *Social work administration* (3rd ed.). Needham Heights, MA: Allyn & Bacon.

Tropman, J. E. (2006). Producing high-quality group decisions. In R. L. Edwards & J. A. Yankey (Eds.), *Effectively managing nonprofit organizations* (Rev. ed., pp. 215–238). Washington, DC: NASW Press.

Wikipedia. (2008). Consensus decision-making. Retrieved September 27, 2008, from http://en.wikipedia.org/wiki/consensus_decision-making

CHAPTER 7: ORGANIZATIONAL CHANGE

Anderson, C. R. (1984). *Management: Skills, functions, and organization performance.* Dubuque, IA: Wm. C. Brown.

Arsenault, J. (1998). *Forging nonprofit alliances.* San Francisco: Jossey-Bass.

Bailey, D., & Koney, K. M. (2000). *Strategic alliances among health and human services organizations.* Thousand Oaks, CA: Sage.

Bielefeld, W. (1994). What affects nonprofit survival? *Nonprofit Management and Leadership, 5,* 19–36.

Brager, G., & Holloway, S. (1992). Assessing prospects for organizational change: The uses of force field analysis. *Administration in Social Work, 16*(3/4), 15–28.

French, J. R. P., Jr., & Raven, B. (1959). The bases of social power. In D. Cartwright (Ed.), *Studies in social power* (pp. 150–167). Ann Arbor: University of Michigan.

Galaskiewicz, J., & Bielefeld, W. (1998). *Nonprofit organizations in an age of uncertainty.* New York: Aldine de Gruyter.

Gil de Gibaja, M. (2001). An exploratory study of administrative practice in collaboratives. *Administration in Social Work, 25*(2), 39–59.

Golensky, M., & Mulder, C. A. (2006). Coping in a constrained economy: Survival strategies of nonprofit human service organizations. *Administration in Social Work, 30*(3), 5–24.

Golensky, M., & Walker, M. (2003). Organizational change: Too much, too soon? *Journal of Community Practice, 11*(2), 67–82.

Hall, C. S., & Lindzey, G. (1957). *Theories of personality.* New York: Wiley & Sons.

Hocker, J. L., & Wilmot, W. W. (1995). *Interpersonal conflict* (4th ed.). Madison, WI: Wm. C. Brown Communications.

Hofstede, G., & Hofstede, G. J. (2005). *Cultures and organizations: Software of the mind* (2nd ed.). New York: McGraw-Hill.

Hollander, E. P. (1978). *Leadership dynamics.* New York: Free Press.

Jaskyte, K., & Dressler, W. W. (2005). Organizational culture and innovation in nonprofit human service organizations. *Administration in Social Work, 29*(2), 23–41.

Knowles, M. (1990). *The adult learner: A neglected species* (4th ed.). Houston, TX: Gulf.

Kohm, A., & La Piana, D. (2003). *Strategic restructuring for nonprofit organizations.* Westport, CT: Praeger.

Medley, B. C., & Akan, O. H. (2008). Creating positive change in community organizations: A case for rediscovering Lewin. *Nonprofit Management and Leadership, 18*, 485–496.

Miles, R. E., & Snow, C. C. (1978). *Organizational strategy, structure, and process.* New York: McGraw-Hill.

Morris, B. J., & Schunn, C. D. (2004). Rethinking logical reasoning skills from a strategy perspective. In M. J. Roberts & E. J. Newton (Eds.), *Methods of thought: Individual differences in reasoning strategies* (pp. 31–56). New York: Psychology Press.

Perlmutter, F. D., & Gummer, B. (1994). Managing organizational transformations. In R. D. Herman (Ed.), *The Jossey-Bass handbook of nonprofit leadership and management* (pp. 227–246). San Francisco: Jossey-Bass.

Reilly, T. (2001). Collaboration in action: An uncertain process. *Administration in Social Work, 25*(1), 53–74.

Schein, E. H. (1985). *Organizational culture and leadership.* San Francisco: Jossey-Bass.

Schmid, H. (2004). Organization-environment relationships: Theory for management practice in human service organizations. *Administration in Social Work, 28*(1), 97–113.

Schmid, H. (2006). Leadership styles and leadership change in human and community service organizations. *Nonprofit Management and Leadership, 17*, 179–194.

Senge, P. M. (2006). *The fifth discipline* (Rev. ed.). New York: Currency Doubleday.

Sowa, J. E. (2009). The collaboration decision in nonprofit organizations: Views from the front line. *Nonprofit and Voluntary Sector Quarterly, 38*, 1003–1025.

Wernet, S. P. (1994). A case study of adaptation in a nonprofit human service organization. *Journal of Community Practice, 1*(3), 93–112.

Wernet, S. P., & Austin, D. M. (1991). Decision-making style and leadership patterns in nonprofit human service organizations. *Administration in Social Work, 15*(3), 1–17.

Wortman, M. S., Jr. (1981). A radical shift from bureaucracy to strategic management in voluntary organizations. *Journal of Voluntary Action Research, 10*(1), 62–81.

CHAPTER 8: STRATEGIC PLANNING

Anderson, C. R. (1984). *Management: Skills, functions, and organization performance.* Dubuque, IA: Wm. C. Brown.

Bryson, J. M. (1995). *Strategic planning for public and nonprofit organizations: A guide to strengthening and sustaining organizational achievement* (Rev. ed.). San Francisco: Jossey-Bass.

Eadie, D. C. (2006). Planning and managing strategically. In R. L. Edwards & J. A. Yankey (Eds.), *Effectively managing nonprofit organizations* (pp. 375–390). Washington, DC: NASW Press.

Emery, M., & Purser, R. E. (1996). *The search conference.* San Francisco: Jossey-Bass.

Golensky, M., & DeRuiter, G. L. (1999). Merger as a strategic response to government contracting pressures: A case study. *Nonprofit Management and Leadership, 10*, 137–152.

Golensky, M., & Walker, M. (2003). Organizational change: Too much, too soon? *Journal of Community Practice, 11*(2), 67–82.

Grobman, G. M. (2004). *An introduction to the nonprofit sector: A practical approach for the twenty-first century.* Harrisburg, PA: White Hat Communications.

Gross, M. J. (1985). The importance of budgeting. In S. Slavin (Ed.), *Social administration: The management of the social services: Vol. 2. Managing finances, personnel, and information in human services* (2nd ed., pp. 11–25). New York: Haworth.

Hawkins, F., & Gunther, J. (1998). Managing for quality. In R. L. Edwards, J. A. Yankey, & M. A. Altpeter (Eds.), *Skills for effective management of nonprofit organizations* (pp. 525–554). Washington, DC: NASW Press.

Kluger, M. P., Baker, W. A., & Garval, H. S. (1998). *Strategic business planning: Securing a future for the nonprofit organization.* Washington, DC: Child Welfare League of America Press.

Wolf, T. (1999). *Managing a nonprofit organization in the twenty-first century* (Rev. ed.). New York: Simon & Schuster.

CHAPTER 9: PROGRAM DEVELOPMENT

Andrews, A. B., Motes, P. S., Floyd, A. G., Flerx, V. C., & Lopez–De Fede, A. (2005). Building evaluation capacity in community-based organizations: Reflections of an empowerment evaluation team. *Journal of Community Practice, 13*(4), 85–104.

Boehm, A. (2003). Managing the life cycle of a community project: A marketing approach. *Administration in Social Work, 27*(2), 19–37.

Campbell, D. (2002). Outcomes assessment and the paradox of nonprofit accountability. *Nonprofit Management and Leadership, 12*, 243–259.

Chambers, D. E. (2000). *Social policy and social programs: A method for the practical public policy analyst* (3rd ed.). Needham Heights, MA: Allyn & Bacon.

Gardner, F. (2000). Design evaluation: Illuminating social work practice for better outcomes. *Social Work, 45*, 176–182.

Ginsberg, L. H. (2001). *Social work evaluation: Principles and methods.* Boston: Allyn & Bacon.

Kellogg, W. K., Foundation. (1998). *Evaluation handbook.* Battle Creek, MI: Author.

Kellogg, W. K., Foundation. (2004). *Logic model development guide.* Battle Creek, MI: Author.

Kettner, P. M., Moroney, R. M., & Martin, L. L. (2008). *Designing and managing programs An effectiveness-based approach* (3rd ed.). Thousand Oaks, CA: Sage.

Kluger, M. P. (2006). The Program Evaluation Guide: A planning and assessment tool for nonprofit organizations. *Administration in Social Work, 30*(1), 33–44.

Kretzmann, J. P. & McKnight, J. L. (2005). *Discovering community power: A guide to mobilizing local assets and your organization's capacity.* Evanston, IL: Northwestern University, Asset-Based Community Development Institute.

Lackey, J. F. (2006). *Accountability in social services: The culture of the paper program.* New York: Haworth.

Mordock, J. B. (2002). *Managing for outcomes.* Washington, DC: CWLA Press.

Neuman, K. M. (2003). Developing a comprehensive outcomes management program: A ten step process. *Administration in Social Work, 27*(1), 5–23.

Pawlak, E. J., & Vinter, R. D. (2004). *Designing and planning programs for nonprofit and government organizations.* San Francisco: Jossey-Bass.

Savaya, R., & Waysman, M. (2005). The logic model: A tool for incorporating theory in development and evaluation of programs. *Administration in Social Work, 29*(2), 85–103.

Schram, B. (1997). *Creating small scale social programs.* Thousand Oaks, CA: Sage.

Trzcinski, E., & Sobeck, J. (2008). The interrelationship between program development capacity and readiness for change among small to mid-sized nonprofits. *Journal of Community Practice, 16*(1), 11–37.

Unrau, Y. A., & Coleman, H. (2006). Evaluating program outcomes as event histories. *Administration in Social Work, 30*(1), 45–65.

Unrau, Y. A., Gabor, P. A., & Grinnell, R. M., Jr. (2001). *Evaluation in the human services.* Itasca, IL: Peacock.

Zimmermann, J. M., & Stevens, B. W. (2006). The use of performance measurement in South Carolina nonprofits. *Nonprofit Management and Leadership, 16,* 315–327.

CHAPTER 10: RESOURCE GENERATION

Benefield, E. A. S., & Edwards, R. L. (2006). Developing a sustainable fundraising program. In R. L. Edwards & J. A. Yankey (Eds.), *Effectively managing nonprofit organizations* (Rev. ed., pp. 61–82). Washington, DC: NASW Press.

Conway, D. (2003). Practicing stewardship. In H. A. Rosso and associates & E. R. Tempel, (Eds.), *Hank Rosso's achieving excellence in fund raising* (2nd ed., pp. 431–441). San Francisco: Jossey-Bass.

Edwards, R. L., & Austin, D. M. (2006). Managing effectively in an environment of competing values. In R. L. Edwards & J. A. Yankey (Eds.), *Effectively managing nonprofit organizations* (Rev. ed., pp. 3–25). Washington, DC: NASW Press.

Greenfield, J. M. (1999). *Fund-raising: Evaluating and managing the fund development process* (2nd ed.). New York: Wiley.

Gronbjerg, K. A. (1993). *Understanding nonprofit funding.* San Francisco: Jossey-Bass.

Gronbjerg, K. A. (2001). The U.S. nonprofit human service sector: A creeping revolution. *Nonprofit and Voluntary Sector Quarterly, 30,* 276–297.

Guo, B. (2006). Charity for profit? Exploring factors associated with the commercialization of human service nonprofits. *Nonprofit and Voluntary Sector Quarterly, 35,* 123–138.

Hall, M. S., & Howlett, S. (2003). *Getting funded: The complete guide to writing grant proposals* (4th ed.). Portland, OR: Portland State University, External Studies.

Lindahl, W. E. (2008). Three-phase capital campaigns. *Nonprofit Management and Leadership, 18,* 261–273.

Martin, L. L. (2000). Performance contracting in the human services: An analysis of selected state policies. *Administration in Social Work, 24*(2), 29–44.

Martin, L. L. (2001). *Financial management for human service administrators.* Boston: Allyn & Bacon.

Massarsky, C. W. (1994). Enterprise strategies for generating revenue. In R. D. Herman (Ed.), *The Jossey-Bass handbook of nonprofit leadership and management* (pp. 382–402). San Francisco: Jossey-Bass.

Moody, M. (2008). "Building a culture": The construction and evolution of venture philanthropy as a new organizational field. *Nonprofit and Voluntary Sector Quarterly, 37,* 324–352.

Murray, D. J. (1994). *The guaranteed fund-raising system* (2nd ed.). Poughkeepsie, NY: American Institute of Management.

Nobles, M. E. (2006, July 1). Grabbing a cause. *NonProfit Times*, p. 27.

Ostrower, F. (2002). *Trustees of culture: Power, wealth, and status on elite arts boards.* Chicago: University of Chicago Press.

Perry, G. (2003). Foundation fund raising. In H. A. Rosso and associates & E. R. Tempel (Eds.), *Hank Rosso's achieving excellence in fund raising* (2nd ed., pp. 188–199). San Francisco: Jossey-Bass.

Pierpont, R. (2003). Capital campaigns. In H. A. Rosso and associates & E. R. Tempel (Eds.), *Hank Rosso's achieving excellence in fund raising* (2nd ed., pp. 117–138). San Francisco: Jossey-Bass.

Prince, R. A., & File, K. M. (1994). *The seven faces of philanthropy.* San Francisco: Jossey-Bass.

Regenovich, D. (2003). Establishing a planned giving program. In H. A. Rosso and associates & E. R. Tempel (Eds.), *Hank Rosso's achieving excellence in fund raising* (2nd ed., pp. 139–158). San Francisco: Jossey-Bass.

Sargeant, A., Wymer, W., & Hilton, T. (2006). Marketing bequest club membership: An exploratory study of legacy pledgers. *Nonprofit and Voluntary Sector Quarterly, 35,* 384–404.

Schervish, P. G. (2006). The moral biography of wealth: Philosophical reflections on the foundation of philanthropy. *Nonprofit and Voluntary Sector Quarterly, 35,* 477–492.

Seiler, T. L. (2003a). Developing and articulating a case for support. In H. A. Rosso and associates & E. R. Tempel (Eds.), *Hank Rosso's achieving excellence in fund raising* (2nd ed., pp. 49–58). San Francisco: Jossey-Bass.

Seiler, T. L. (2003b). Plan to succeed. In H. A. Rosso and associates & E. R. Temple (Eds.), *Hank Rosso's achieving excellence in fund raising* (2nd ed., pp. 23–29). San Francisco: Jossey-Bass.

Strom, S. (2008a, July 9). Funds misappropriated at 2 nonprofit groups. *New York Times*, p. A16.

Strom, S. (2008b, July 25). Report on Shriners raises questions of wrongdoing. *New York Times*, p. A11.

Strom, S. (2008c, September 10). Lawsuit adds to turmoil for community group. *New York Times*, p. A17.

Warwick, M. (2003). Direct mail. In H. A. Rosso and associates & E. R. Tempel (Eds.), *Hank Rosso's achieving excellence in fund raising* (2nd ed., pp. 245–258). San Francisco: Jossey-Bass.

CHAPTER 11: ORGANIZATIONAL PERFORMANCE INDICATORS

Balser, D., & McClusky, J. (2005). Managing stakeholder relationships and nonprofit organization effectiveness. *Nonprofit Management and Leadership, 15,* 295–315.

Behn, R. D. (1996, March). Cutback management: Six basic tasks. *Governing*, p. 68.

Brueggemann, W. G. (1996). *The practice of macro social work*. Chicago: Nelson-Hall.

Crittenden, W. F. (2000, Supplement). Spinning straw into gold: The tenuous strategy, funding, and financial performance linkage. *Nonprofit and Voluntary Sector Quarterly*, *29*, 164–182.

Golensky, M. (2000). *Board governance: Perceptions and practices; An exploratory study* (Research Report). Grand Rapids, MI: GVSU School of Social Work.

Gormley, W. T., Jr., & Weimer, D. L. (1999). *Organizational report cards*. Cambridge: MA: Harvard University Press.

Greenlee, J. S., & Trussel, J. M. (2000). Predicting the financial vulnerability of charitable organizations. *Nonprofit Management and Leadership*, *11*, 199–210.

Herman, R. D., & Renz, D. O. (2008). Advancing nonprofit organizational effectiveness research and theory: Nine theses. *Nonprofit Management and Leadership, 18*, 399–415.

Jansson, B. S. (2005). *The reluctant welfare state: American social welfare policies; Past, present and future* (5th ed.). Belmont, CA: Brooks/Cole.

Kettner, P. M. (2002). *Achieving excellence in the management of human service organizations*. Boston: Allyn & Bacon.

Kettner, P. M., Moroney, R. M., & Martin, L. L. (2008). *Designing and managing programs: An effectiveness-based approach* (3rd ed.). Thousand Oaks, CA: Sage.

Krug, K., & Weinberg, C. B. (2004). Mission, money, and merit: Strategic decision making by nonprofit managers. *Nonprofit Management and Leadership*, *14*, 325–342.

Lebold, D. A., & Edwards, R. L. (2006). Managing financial uncertainty. In R. L. Edwards & J. A. Yankey (Eds.), *Effectively managing nonprofit organizations* (Rev. ed., pp. 431–456). Washington, DC: NASW Press.

Martin, L. L. (2001). *Financial management for human service administrators*. Boston: Allyn & Bacon.

Moore, S. T. (1995). Efficiency in social work practice and administration. *Social Work, 40*, 602–608.

Mordock, J. B. (2002). *Managing for outcomes*. Washington, DC: CWLA Press.

Packard, T., Patti, R., Daly, D., Tucker-Tatlow, J., & Farrell, C. (2008). Cutback management strategies: Experiences in nine county human service organizations. *Administration in Social Work*, *32*(1), 55–75.

Pokrant, G. C. (2004, Fall). Measuring up. *Nonprofit Advisor*, p. 3. Retrieved November 8, 2008, from www.reznickgroup.com/pdf/NPAdvisor—2004fall.pdf

Richmond, B. J., Mook, L., & Quarter, J. (2003). Social accounting for nonprofits: Two models. *Nonprofit Management and Leadership*, *13*, 308–324.

Ritchie, W. J., & Kolodinsky, R. W. (2003). Nonprofit organization financial performance measurement: An evaluation of new and existing financial performance measures. *Nonprofit Management and Leadership*, *13*, 367–381.

Sowa, J. E., Selden, S. C., & Sandfort, J. R. (2004). No longer unmeasurable? A multidimensional integrated model of nonprofit organizational effectiveness. *Nonprofit and Voluntary Sector Quarterly*, *33*, 711–728.

Speckbacher, G. (2003). The economics of performance management in nonprofit organizations. *Nonprofit Management and Leadership, 13,* 267–281.

Thomas, E. C. (2002). The challenges of cutback management. *Public Policy and Practice, 1*(2), 4–8. Retrieved November 4, 2008, from http://ipspr.sc.edu/ejournal/cutback manage.asp

Thomas, M. S. (2006). Managing the finances of nonprofit organizations. In R. L. Edwards & J. A. Yankey (Eds.), *Effectively managing nonprofit organization* (Rev. ed., pp. 255–274). Washington, DC: NASW Press.

Wolf, T. (1999). *Managing a nonprofit organization in the twenty-first century* (Rev. ed.). New York: Simon & Schuster.

CHAPTER 12: TECHNOLOGY AND COMMUNICATION

Austin, M. J. (2002). Managing out: The community practice dimensions of effective agency management. *Journal of Community Practice, 10*(4), 33–48.

Bhagat, V., Hauf, B., & Donovan, Q. (2007, January). *The Online Marketing (eCRM) Nonprofit Benchmark Index study.* Retrieved November 27, 2008, from http://www.convio .com/files/gd__benchmarkreport.pdf

Brainard, L. A., & Siplon, P. D. (2004). Toward nonprofit organization reform in the voluntary spirit: Lessons from the Internet. *Nonprofit and Voluntary Sector Quarterly, 33,* 435–457.

Brueggemann, W. G. (1996). *The practice of macro social work.* Chicago: Nelson-Hall.

Burt, E., & Taylor, J. A. (2000). Information and communication technologies: Reshaping voluntary organizations? *Nonprofit Management and Leadership, 11,* 131–143.

Carrilio, T. (2005). Management information systems: Why are they underutilized in the social services? *Administration in Social Work, 29*(2), 43–61.

Clerkin, R. M., & Gronbjerg, K. A. (2007). Infrastructure and activities: Relating IT to the work of nonprofit organizations. In M. Cortes & K. M. Rafter (Eds.), *Nonprofits and technology: Emerging research for usable knowledge* (pp. 3–20). Chicago: Lyceum.

Cravens, J. (2006). Involving international online volunteers: Factors for success, organizational benefits, and new views of community. *International Journal of Volunteer Administration, 24*(1), 15–23.

Dhebar, B. B., & Stokes, B. (2008). A nonprofit manager's guide to online volunteering. *Nonprofit Management and Leadership, 18,* 497–506.

Fitch, D. (2007). Designing information systems around decision making. In M. Cortes & K. M. Rafter (Eds.), *Nonprofits and technology: Emerging research for usable knowledge* (pp. 135–147). Chicago: Lyceum.

Grobman, G. M. (2004). *An introduction to the nonprofit sector: A practical approach for the twenty-first century.* Harrisburg, PA: White Hat Communications.

Hart, T. R. (2003). The Internet as a fund raising vehicle. In H. A. Rosso and associates & E. R. Tempel (Eds.), *Hank Rosso's achieving excellence in fund raising* (2nd ed., pp. 259–272). San Francisco: Jossey-Bass.

Kettner, P. M., Moroney, R. M., & Martin, L. L. (2008). *Designing and managing programs: An effectiveness-based approach* (3rd ed.). Thousand Oaks, CA: Sage.

Leavitt, H. J. (1972). *Managerial psychology* (3rd ed.). Chicago: Nelson-Hall.

Manzo, P., & Pitkin, B. (2007). Barriers to information technology usage in the nonprofit sector. In M. Cortes & K. M. Rafter (Eds.), *Nonprofits and technology: Emerging research for usable knowledge* (pp. 51–67). Chicago: Lyceum.

McNutt, J. (2007). Adoption of new-wave electronic advocacy techniques by nonprofit child advocacy organizations. In M. Cortes & K. M. Rafter (Eds.), *Nonprofits and technology: Emerging research for usable knowledge* (pp. 33–48). Chicago: Lyceum.

McNutt, J. G., & Boland, K. M. (1999). Electronic advocacy by nonprofit organizations in social welfare policy. *Nonprofit and Voluntary Sector Quarterly, 28,* 432–451.

Menefee, D., Ahluwalia, U., Pell, D., & Woldu, B. (2000). ABM: An innovative business technology for human service organizations. *Administration in Social Work, 24*(2), 67–84.

Moyer, M. S. (1994). Marketing for nonprofit managers. In R. D. Herman (Ed.), *The Jossey-Bass handbook of nonprofit leadership and management* (pp. 249–278). San Francisco: Jossey-Bass.

O'Looney, J. (2005). Social work and the new semantic information revolution. *Administration in Social Work, 29*(4), 5–34.

Saidel, J. R., & Cour, S. (2003). IT and the voluntary sector workplace. *Nonprofit and Voluntary Sector Quarterly, 32,* 5–24.

Savaya, R., Spiro, S. E., Waysman, M., & Golan, M. (2004). Issues in the development of a computerized clinical information system for a network of juvenile homes. *Administration in Social Work, 28*(2), 63–79.

Schneider, J. A. (2003). Small, minority-based nonprofits in the information age. *Nonprofit Management and Leadership, 13,* 383–399.

Schoech, D., Fitch, D., MacFadden, R., & Schkade, L. L. (2002). From data to intelligence: Introducing the intelligent organization. *Administration in Social Work, 26*(1), 1–21.

Waters, R. D. (2007). Nonprofit organizations' use of the Internet: A content analysis of communication trends on the Internet sites of the Philanthropy 400. *Nonprofit Management and Leadership, 18,* 59–76.

Wolf, T. (1999). *Managing a nonprofit organization in the twenty-first century* (Rev. ed.). New York: Simon & Schuster.

Zimmerman, L. I., & Broughton, A. (2006). Assessing, planning, and managing information technology, In R. L. Edwards & J. A. Yankey (Eds.), *Effectively managing nonprofit organizations* (Rev. ed., pp. 255–274). Washington, DC: NASW Press.

CHAPTER 13: LEADERSHIP BY EXAMPLE

Alliance for Nonprofit Management. (2003–2004). *Frequently asked questions: Risk management.* Retrieved December 19, 2008, from http://www.allianceonline.org/FAQ/risk_management

Bentham, J. (1961). *An introduction to the principles of morals and legislation.* Garden City, NY: Doubleday.

Bolman, L. G., & Deal, T. E. (1991). *Reframing organizations.* San Francisco: Jossey-Bass.

Brueggemann, W. G. (1996). *The practice of macro social work.* Chicago: Nelson-Hall.

Campbell, D. (2002). Beyond charitable choice: The diverse service delivery approaches of local faith-related organizations. *Nonprofit and Voluntary Sector Quarterly, 31,* 207–230.

Cnaan, R. A., Sinha, J. W., & McGrew, C. C. (2004). Congregations as social service providers: Services, capacity, culture, and organizational behavior. *Administration in Social Work, 28*(3/4), 47–68.

Covey, S. R. (1991). *Principle-centered leadership.* New York: Simon & Schuster.

Dewey, J. (1929). *The quest for certainty: A study of the relation of knowledge and action.* New York: Minton, Balch, & Co.

Ebener, D. R., & O'Connell, D. J. (2010). How might servant leadership work? *Nonprofit Management and Leadership, 20,* 315–335.

Gibelman, M. (2003). *Navigating human service organizations.* Chicago: Lyceum.

Gibelman, M., & Gelman, S. R. (2002). Should we have faith in faith-based social services? Rhetoric versus realistic expectations. *Nonprofit Management and Leadership, 13,* 49–65.

Greenlee, J., Fischer, M., Gordon, T., & Keating, E. (2007). An investigation of fraud in nonprofit organizations: Occurrences and deterrents. *Nonprofit and Voluntary Sector Quarterly, 36,* 676–694.

Hollander, E. P., & Offermann, L. R. (1990). Power and leadership in organizations: Relationships in transition. *American Psychologist, 45*(2), 179–189.

Holtfreter, K. (2008). Determinants of fraud losses in nonprofit organizations. *Nonprofit Management and Leadership, 19,* 45–63.

James, W. (1907). *Pragmatism: A new name for some old ways of thinking* (Popular Lectures in Philosophy). New York: Longmans, Green, & Co.

Jeavons, T. H. (1994). Ethics in nonprofit management: Creating a culture of integrity. In R. D. Herman (Ed.), *The Jossey-Bass handbook of nonprofit leadership and management* (pp. 184–207). San Francisco: Jossey-Bass.

Kant, I. (1963). *Lectures on ethics* (L. Infield, Trans.). Indianapolis, IN: Hackett.

Kouzes, J. M., & Posner, B. Z. (1995). *The leadership challenge* (2nd ed.). San Francisco: Jossey-Bass.

Kurzman, P. A. (2006). Managing liability and risk in nonprofit settings. In R. L. Edwards & J. A. Yankey (Eds.), *Effectively managing nonprofit organizations* (Rev. ed., pp. 275–290). Washington, DC: NASW Press.

Kwon, L. (2008, June 7). American Bible Society ousts head. *Christian Post Reporter.* Retrieved December 16, 2008, from http://www.christianpost.com/article/20080607

Lewis, B. M. (2003). Issues and dilemmas in faith-based social service delivery: The case of the Salvation Army of Greater Philadelphia. *Administration in Social Work, 27*(3), 87–106.

Malloy, D. C., & Agarwal, J. (2001). Ethical climate in nonprofit organizations: Propositions and implications. *Nonprofit Management and Leadership, 12,* 39–54.

Manning, S. S. (2003). *Ethical leadership in human services: A multi-dimensional approach.* Boston: Allyn & Bacon.

Mill, J. S. (1998). *Utilitarianism* (R. Crisp, Ed.). New York: Oxford University Press. (Original work published 1861)

National Association of Social Workers. (1999). *Code of ethics.* Washington, DC: Author.

Rawls, J. (1971). *A theory of justice.* Cambridge, MA: Harvard University Press.

Reamer, F. G. (2000). The social work ethics audit: A risk-management strategy. *Social Work, 45,* 355–366.

Ross, W. (1930). *The right and the good.* New York: Oxford University Press.

Rothman, J. C. (Ed.). (2005). *From the front lines: Student cases in social work ethics* (2nd ed.). Boston: Allyn & Bacon.

Rothschild, J., & Milofsky, C. (2006). The centrality of values, passions, and ethics in the nonprofit sector. *Nonprofit Management and Leadership, 17,* 137–143.

Schein, E. H. (1985). *Organizational culture and leadership.* San Francisco: Jossey-Bass.

Schön, D. A. (1983). *The reflective practioner.* San Francisco: Jossey-Bass.

Severson, K. (2010, January 13). For some, "kosher" equals pure. *New York Times,* pp. D1, D5.

Singer, P. (1993). *Practical ethics* (2nd ed.). New York: Cambridge University Press.

Snyder, G. (2005, July/August). Managing the finances of nonprofit organizations. *Nonprofit World, 23*(4), 21–24.

Spears, L. C. (2002). Introduction: Tracing the past, present, and future of servant-leadership. In L. C. Spears & M. Lawrence (Eds.), *Focus on leadership* (pp. 1–16). New York: Wiley & Sons.

Strom, S., & Robbins, J. (2008, April 30). Montana museum board breached duty, court says. *New York Times,* p. A13.

Thomas, M. S. (2006). Managing the finances of nonprofit organizations. In R. L. Edwards & J. A. Yankey (Eds.), *Effectively managing nonprofit organizations* (Rev. ed., pp. 255–274). Washington, DC: NASW Press.

Tremper, C. (1994). Risk management. In R. D. Herman (Ed.), *The Jossey-Bass handbook of nonprofit leadership and management* (pp. 485–508). San Francisco: Jossey-Bass.

Tuskegee University. (n.d.). *Research ethics: The Tuskegee Syphilis Study.* Retrieved December 12, 2008, from http://www.tuskegee.edu/global/story.asp?s= 1207598&ClientType

Vanderwoerd, J. R. (2004). How faith-based social service organizations manage secular pressures associated with government funding. *Nonprofit Management and Leadership, 14,* 239–262.

Young, D. S. (2002). Foresight: The lead that the leader has. In L. C. Spears & M. Lawrence (Eds.), *Focus on leadership* (pp. 245–255). New York: Wiley & Sons.

CHAPTER 14: HUMAN RESOURCES MANAGEMENT

Alliance for Nonprofit Management. (2003–2004). *Frequently asked questions: Risk management.* Retrieved December 19, 2008, from http://www.allianceonline.org/FAQ/risk_management

Allison, M. T. (2001). *Diversity issues and challenges facing youth-related nonprofit agencies.* Tempe: Arizona State University, Center for Nonprofit Leadership and Management, Department of Recreation Management and Tourism.

Bailey, D., & Dunlap, S. K. (2006). Designing and sustaining effective organizational teams. In R. L. Edwards & J. A. Yankey (Eds.), *Effectively managing nonprofit organizations* (Rev. ed., pp. 195–213). Washington, DC: NASW Press.

Brown, W. A., & Yoshioka, C. F. (2003). Mission attachment and satisfaction as factors in employee retention. *Nonprofit Management and Leadership, 14,* 5–18.

Camp Fire USA. (n.d.). *Executive director/CEO recruitment and selection manual.* Kansas City, MO: Author.

Chernesky, R. H. (2003). Examining the glass ceiling: Gender influences on promotion decisions. *Administration in Social Work, 27*(2), 13–18.

Findler, L., Wind, L. H., & Mor Barak, M. E. (2007). The challenge of workforce management in a global society: Modeling the relationship between diversity, inclusion, organizational culture, and employee well-being, job satisfaction and organizational commitment. *Administration in Social Work, 31*(3), 63–94.

Freund, A. (2005). Commitment and job satisfaction as predictors of turnover intentions among welfare workers. *Administration in Social Work, 29*(2), 5–21.

Gibelman, M. (2000). The nonprofit sector and gender discrimination: A preliminary investigation into the glass ceiling. *Nonprofit Management and Leadership, 10,* 251–269.

Giffords, E. D. (2003). An examination of organizational and professional commitment among public, not-for-profit, and proprietary social service employees. *Administration in Social Work, 27*(3), 5–23.

Golensky, M. (1995, March). Smoothing the waters. *NonProfit Times,* pp. 56–57.

Haley-Lock, A. (2007). A workforce or workplace crisis? Applying an organizational perspective to the study of human services employment. *Administration in Social Work, 31*(3), 41–61.

Haley-Lock, A. (2008). Happy doing good? How workers' career orientations and job satisfaction relate in grassroots human services. *Journal of Community Practice, 16*(2), 143–163.

Hoffmann, E. A. (2006). The ironic value of loyalty: Dispute resolution strategies in worker cooperatives and conventional organizations. *Nonprofit Management and Leadership, 17,* 163–177.

Hofstede, G., & Hofstede, G. J. (2005). *Cultures and organizations: Software of the mind* (2nd ed.). New York: McGraw-Hill.

Hostetler, D. W., & Pynes, J. E. (2000). Sexual orientation discrimination and its challenges for nonprofit managers. *Nonprofit Management and Leadership, 11*, 49–63.

Independent Sector. (2004). *Employment in the nonprofit sector*. Retrieved December 30, 2008, from http://www.independentsector.org/media/npemploymentPR

Juby, C., & Scannapieco, M. (2007). Characteristics of workload management in public child welfare agencies. *Administration in Social Work, 31*(3), 95–109.

Kelly, M. J. (2001). Management mentoring in a social service organization. *Administration in Social Work, 25*(1), 17–33.

Kettner, P. M. (2002). *Achieving excellence in the management of human service organizations*. Boston: Allyn & Bacon.

Kunreuther, F. (2003). The changing of the guard: What generational differences tell us about social-change organizations. *Nonprofit and Voluntary Sector Quarterly, 32*, 450–457.

Landsman, M. J. (2008). Pathways to organizational commitment. *Administration in Social Work, 32*(2), 105–132.

Millar, K. I. (1998). Evaluating employee performance. In R. L. Edwards, J. A. Yankey, & M. A. Altpeter (Eds.), *Skills for effective management of nonprofit organizations* (pp. 219–243). Washington, DC: NASW Press.

Mor Barak, M. E. (2000). Beyond affirmative action: Toward a model of diversity and organizational inclusion. *Administration in Social Work, 23*(3/4), 47–68.

Nissly, J. A., Mor Barak, M. E., & Levin, A. (2005). Stress, social support, and workers' intentions to leave their jobs in public child welfare. *Administration in Social Work, 29*(1), 79–100.

Parish, S. L., Ellison, M. J., & Parish, J. K. (2006). Managing diversity. In R. L. Edwards & J. A. Yankey (Eds.), *Effectively managing nonprofit organizations* (Rev. ed., pp. 179–194). Washington, DC: NASW Press.

Pecora, R. J. (1998). Recruiting and selecting effective employees. In R. L. Edwards, J. A. Yankey, & M. A. Altpeter (Eds.), *Skills for effective management of nonprofit organizations* (pp. 155–184). Washington, DC: NASW Press.

Perlmutter, F. D, Bailey, D., & Netting, F. E. (2001). *Managing human resources in the human services: Supervisory challenges*. New York: Oxford University Press.

Privacy Rights Clearinghouse. (2008). *Employment background checks: A jobseeker's guide*. Retrieved January 9, 2009, from http://www.privacyrights.org/fs/fs16-bck.htm

Rivas, R. F. (1998). Dismissing problem employees. In R. L. Edwards, J. A. Yankey, & M. A. Altpeter (Eds.), *Skills for effective management of nonprofit organizations* (pp. 262–278). Washington, DC: NASW Press.

Salamon, L., & Sokolowski, S. W. (2006, December). *Employment in America's charities: A profile* (Nonprofit Employment Bulletin No. 26). Baltimore: Johns Hopkins Center for Civil Society Studies (Available at http://www.JHU.edu/CCSS)

Sampson, S. D., & Moore, L. L. (2008). Is there a glass ceiling for women in development? *Nonprofit Management and Leadership, 18*, 321–339.

Schein, E. (2006). *Career anchors: Self-assessment* (3rd ed.). San Francisco: Jossey-Bass.

Skidmore, R. A. (1995). *Social work administration* (3rd ed.). Needham Heights, MA: Allyn & Bacon.

Strom-Gottfried, K. (2006). Managing human resources. In R. L. Edwards & J. A. Yankey (Eds.), *Effectively managing nonprofit organizations* (Rev. ed., pp. 141–178). Washington, DC: NASW Press.

University of Notre Dame. (2009, January). *Emerging women leaders for nonprofits empowered in Philadelphia* (American Diversity Report). Retrieved January 21, 2009, from http://www.americandiversityreport.com/indexphy?option

University of Washington. (n.d.). *Illegal questions.* Retrieved January 9, 2009, from http://www.stat.washington.edu/jobs/questions

Unser, R. (2008). Retirement plan changes: Don't be a day late and thousands of dollars short. *Nonprofit World, 26*(6), 22–23.

Women running nonprofits earn less than men. (2005, January 18). *Pittsburgh Business Times.* Retrieved January 21, 2009, from http://www.bizjournals.com/pittsburgh/stories/2005/01/07/daily17.html

CHAPTER 15: THE NONPROFIT GOVERNING BOARD

Bradshaw, P. (2002). Reframing board-staff relations: Exploring the governance function using a storytelling metaphor. *Nonprofit Management and Leadership, 12,* 471–484.

Bradshaw, P., Inglis, S., & Purdy, J. (2004, November). *Diversity on nonprofit boards: Examining the emerging fringe.* Paper presented at the 33rd Annual Conference of the Association for Research on Nonprofit Organizations and Voluntary Action, Los Angeles.

Brown, W. A. (2002). Inclusive governance practices in nonprofit organizations and implications for practice. *Nonprofit Management and Leadership, 12,* 369–385.

Brown, W. A. (2007). Board development practices and competent board members: Implications for performance. *Nonprofit Management and Leadership, 17,* 301–317.

Callen, J. L., Klein, A., & Tinkelman, D. (2003). Board composition, committees, and organizational efficiency: The case of nonprofits. *Nonprofit and Voluntary Sector Quarterly, 32,* 493–520.

Carver, J. (1990). *Boards that make a difference: A new design for leadership in nonprofit and public organizations.* San Francisco: Jossey-Bass.

Chait, R. P., Ryan, W. P., & Taylor, B. B. (2005). *Governance as leadership: Reframing the work of nonprofit boards.* Washington, DC: BoardSource; Hoboken, NJ: Wiley & Sons.

Daley, J. M. (2002). An action guide for nonprofit board diversity. *Journal of Community Practice, 10*(1), 33–54.

Gibelman, M. (2004). Reflections on boards and board membership. *Administration in Social Work, 28*(2), 49–62.

Gill, M., Flynn, R. J., & Reissing, E. (2005). The Governance Self-Assessment Checklist: An instrument for assessing board effectiveness. *Nonprofit Management and Leadership, 15,* 271–294.

Gill, M. D. (2005). *Governing for results: A director's guide to good governance.* Victoria, BC, Canada: Trafford.

Golensky, M. (2000). *Board governance: Perceptions and practices; An exploratory study* (Research Report). Grand Rapids, MI: GVSU School of Social Work.

Golensky, M. (2008). Choosing a new nonprofit CEO: A longitudinal study. In S. Ramachandran (Ed.), *Good governance in nonprofit organizations* (pp. 207–227). Hyderabad, India: Icfai University Press.

Green, J. C., Madjidi, F., Dudley, T. J., & Genlen, F. L. (2001). Local unit performance in a national nonprofit organization. *Nonprofit Management and Leadership, 11,* 459–476.

Herman, R. D., & Block, S. R. (1990). The board's crucial role in fund raising. In J. Van Til and associates (Eds.), *Critical issues in American philanthropy* (pp. 222–241). San Francisco: Jossey-Bass.

Herman, R. D., & Renz, D. O. (2008). Advancing nonprofit organizational effectiveness research and theory: Nine theses. *Nonprofit Management and Leadership, 18,* 399–415.

Holland, T. P. (2006). Strengthening board performance. In R. L. Edwards & J. A. Yankey (Eds.), *Effectively managing nonprofit organizations* (Rev. ed., pp. 347–374). Washington, DC: NASW Press.

Hoye, R. (2004). Leader-member exchanges and board performance of voluntary sports organizations. *Nonprofit Management and Leadership, 15,* 55–70.

Iecovich, E., & Bar-Mor, H. (2007). Relationships between chairpersons and CEOs in nonprofit organizations. *Administration in Social Work, 31*(4), 21–40.

Kramer, R. M. (1985). Toward a contingency model of board-executive relations. *Administration in Social Work, 9*(3), 15–33.

Miller-Millesen, J. L. (2003). Understanding the behavior of nonprofit boards of directors: A theory-based approach. *Nonprofit and Voluntary Sector Quarterly, 32,* 521–547.

O'Connell, B. (1993). *The board member's book* (2nd ed.). New York: Foundation Center.

Preston, J. B., & Brown, W. A. (2004). Commitment and performance of nonprofit board members. *Nonprofit Management and Leadership, 15,* 221–238.

Senge, P. M. (2006). *The fifth discipline* (Rev. ed.). New York: Currency Doubleday.

Tropman, J. E. (2006). Producing high-quality group decisions. In R. L. Edwards & J. A. Yankey (Eds.), *Effectively managing nonprofit organizations* (Rev. ed., pp. 215–238). Washington, DC: NASW Press.

Widmer, C. (1989). Why board members participate. In R. D. Herman & J. Van Til (Eds.), *Nonprofit boards of directors: Analyses and applications* (pp. 8–23). New Brunswick, NJ: Transaction.

CHAPTER 16: DIRECT SERVICE VOLUNTEERS

Brudney, J. L., & Gazley, B. (2002). Testing the conventional wisdom regarding volunteer programs: A longitudinal analysis of the Service Corps of Retired Executives and the U.S. Small Business Administration. *Nonprofit and Voluntary Sector Quarterly, 31,* 525–548.

Caputo, R. K. (2009). Religious capital and intergenerational transmission of volunteering as correlates of civic engagement. *Nonprofit and Voluntary Sector Quarterly, 38,* 983–1002.

Corporation for National and Community Service. (2007). *Volunteering in America: 2007 state trends and rankings in civic life.* Retrieved February 20, 2009, from http://www .nationalservice.gov/pdf/VIA/VIA_fullreport.pdf

Ellis, S. J. (1995). *The volunteer management audit* (2nd ed.). Alexandria, VA: United Way of America.

Farmer, S. M., & Fedor, D. B. (1999). Volunteer participation and withdrawal: A psychological contract perspective on the role of expectations and organizational support. *Nonprofit Management and Leadership, 9,* 349–367.

Golensky, M. (1999). *Volunteerism in Kent County, Michigan: A snapshot in time* (Research Report). Grand Rapids, MI: GVSU School of Social Work.

Goss, K. A. (1999). Volunteering and the long civic generation. *Nonprofit and Voluntary Sector Quarterly, 28,* 378–415.

Gronbjerg, K. A., & Never, B. (2004). The role of religious networks and other factors in types of volunteer work. *Nonprofit Management and Leadership, 14,* 263–289.

Handy, F., & Cnaan, R. A. (2007). The role of social anxiety in volunteering. *Nonprofit Management and Leadership, 18,* 41–58.

Handy, F., Mook, L., & Quarter, J. (2008). The interchangeability of paid staff and volunteers in nonprofit organizations. *Nonprofit and Voluntary Sector Quarterly, 37,* 76–92.

Handy, F., & Srinivasan, N. (2004). Valuing volunteers: An economic evaluation of the net benefits of hospital volunteers. *Nonprofit and Voluntary Sector Quarterly, 33,* 28–54.

Hartenian, L. S. (2007). Nonprofit agency dependence on direct service and indirect support volunteers: An empirical investigation. *Nonprofit Management and Leadership, 17,* 319–334.

Hobbs, B. B. (2001). Diversifying the volunteer base: Latinos and volunteerism. *Journal of Extension, 39*(4). Retrieved March 2, 2009, from http://www.joe.org/joe/2001 august/a1.php

Independent Sector. (2004). *Research: America's senior volunteers.* Retrieved February 25, 2009, from http://www.independentsector.org/programs/research/senior_ volunteers _in_america.html

Independent Sector. (2009). *Research: Value of volunteer time.* Retrieved February 22, 2009, from http://www.independentsector.org/programs/research/volunteer_ time.html

Korngold, A., Voudouris, E. H., & Griffiths, J. (2006). Managing volunteers effectively. In R. L. Edwards & J. A. Yankey (Eds.), *Effectively managing nonprofit organizations* (Rev. ed., pp. 239–251). Washington, DC: NASW Press.

Kulik, L. (2007). Explaining responses to volunteering: An ecological model. *Nonprofit and Voluntary Sector Quarterly, 36,* 239–255.

Leonard, R., Onyx, J., & Hayward-Brown, H. (2004). Volunteer and coordinator perspectives on managing women volunteers. *Nonprofit Management and Leadership, 15,* 205–219.

Liao-Troth, M. A. (2001). Attitude differences between paid workers and volunteers. *Nonprofit Management and Leadership, 11*, 423–442.

Macduff, N. (1994). Principles of training for volunteers and employees. In R. D. Herman (Ed.), *The Jossey-Bass handbook of nonprofit leadership and management* (pp. 591–615). San Francisco: Jossey-Bass.

Macduff, N. (2006, Fall). The multi-paradigm model of volunteering. *Volunteer Leadership*, pp. 31–36.

Mayer, B. W., Fraccastoro, K. A., & McNary, L. D. (2007). The relationship among organizational-based self-esteem and various factors motivating volunteers. *Nonprofit and Voluntary Sector Quarterly, 36*, 327–340.

McCurley, S. (1994). Recruiting and retaining volunteers. In R. D. Herman (Ed.), *The Jossey-Bass handbook of nonprofit leadership and management* (pp. 511–534). San Francisco: Jossey-Bass.

Netting, F. E., Nelson, H. W., Jr., Borders, K., & Huber, R. (2004). Volunteer and paid staff relationships: Implications for social work administration. *Administration in Social Work, 28*(3/4), 69–89.

O'Neill, M. (2001). Research on giving and volunteering: Methodological considerations. *Nonprofit and Voluntary Sector Quarterly, 30*, 505–514.

Rotolo, T., & Wilson, J. (2007). The effects of children and employment status on the volunteer work of American women. *Nonprofit and Voluntary Sector Quarterly, 36*, 487–503.

Smith, D. B. (2004). Volunteering in retirement: Perceptions of midlife workers. *Nonprofit and Voluntary Sector Quarterly, 33*, 55–73.

Sundeen, R. A., Garcia, C., & Raskoff, S. A. (2008, October 21). Ethnicity, acculturation, and volunteering to organizations: A comparison of African Americans, Asians, Hispanics, and White. *Nonprofit and Voluntary Sector Quarterly Online First*. Retrieved March 2, 2009, from http://nvsq.sagepub.com (Also in print version of the journal, *38*, 929–955)

Sundeen, R. A., Raskoff, S. A., & Garcia, M. C. (2007). Differences in perceived barriers to volunteering to formal organizations: Lack of time versus lack of interest. *Nonprofit Management and Leadership, 17*, 279–300.

Stukas, A. A., Worth, K. A., Clary, E. G., & Snyder, M. (2009). The matching of motivations to affordances in the volunteer environment. *Nonprofit and Voluntary Sector Quarterly, 38*, 5–28.

Tang, F. (2008). Socioeconomic disparities in voluntary organization involvement among older adults. *Nonprofit and Voluntary Sector Quarterly, 37*, 57–75.

Taniguchi, H. (2006). Men's and women's volunteering: Gender differences in the effects of employment and family characteristics. *Nonprofit and Voluntary Sector Quarterly, 35*, 83–101.

Taylor, T., Mallinson, C., & Bloch, K. (2008). "Looking for a few good women": Volunteerism as an interaction in two organizations. *Nonprofit and Voluntary Sector Quarterly, 37*, 389–410.

Tomkovick, C., Lester, S. W., Flunker, L., & Wells, T. A. (2008). Linking collegiate service-learning to future volunteerism: Implications for nonprofit organizations. *Nonprofit Management and Leadership, 19*, 3–26.

Tschirhart, M., Mesch, D. J., Perry, J. L., Miller, T. K., & Lee, G. (2001). Stipended volunteers: Their goals, experiences, satisfaction, and likelihood of future service. *Nonprofit and Voluntary Sector Quarterly, 30*, 422–443.

Wolf, T. (1999). *Managing a nonprofit organization in the twenty-first century* (Rev. ed.). New York: Simon & Schuster.

Yanay, G. V., & Yanay, N. (2008). The decline of motivation? From commitment to dropping out of volunteering. *Nonprofit Management and Leadership, 19*, 65–78.

Index